# Lecture Notes in Computer Science 9556

Commenced Publication in 1973
Founding and Former Series Editors:
Gerhard Goos, Juris Hartmanis, and Jan van Leeuwen

More information about this series at http://www.springer.com/series/7412

Alessandro Crimi · Bjoern Menze
Oskar Maier · Mauricio Reyes
Heinz Handels (Eds.)

# Brainlesion: Glioma, Multiple Sclerosis, Stroke and Traumatic Brain Injuries

First International Workshop, Brainles 2015
Held in Conjunction with MICCAI 2015
Munich, Germany, October 5, 2015
Revised Selected Papers

 Springer

Editors

Alessandro Crimi
Istituto Italiano di Tecnologia (IIT)
Genova
Italy

Bjoern Menze
TU München, Computer Science
München
Germany

Oskar Maier
Medical Informatics
University of Lübeck
Lübeck
Germany

Mauricio Reyes
Surgical Technology and Biomechanics
Universität Bern
Bern
Switzerland

Heinz Handels
Medical Informatics
University of Lübeck
Lübeck
Germany

ISSN 0302-9743                    ISSN 1611-3349   (electronic)
Lecture Notes in Computer Science
ISBN 978-3-319-30857-9           ISBN 978-3-319-30858-6   (eBook)
DOI 10.1007/978-3-319-30858-6

Library of Congress Control Number: 2016934016

LNCS Sublibrary: SL6 – Image Processing, Computer Vision, Pattern Recognition, and Graphics

Printed on acid-free paper

This Springer imprint is published by Springer Nature
The registered company is Springer International Publishing AG Switzerland

# Preface

This volume contains articles from the Brain Lesion (BrainLes) workshop as well as the Brain Tumor Segmentation (BRATS) and Ischemic Stroke Lesion Segmentation (ISLES) challenges, which were held jointly at the Medical Image Computing for Computer-Assisted Intervention (MICCAI) Conference on October 5, 2015.

The presented works address computer scientific and clinical researchers working on glioma, multiple sclerosis (MS), cerebral stroke, and traumatic brain injuries. This compilation does not claim to provide a comprehensive understanding from all points of view; however, the authors present their latest advances in segmentation, disease prognosis, and other applications to the clinical context.

The volume is divided into three parts: The first part comprises the submissions to the BrainLes workshop, the second contains a selection of papers regarding methods presented at the BRATS challenge, and the third part includes a selection of papers on methods presented at the ISLES challenge.

The aim of the first part is to provide an overview of new advances in medical image analysis in all of the aforementioned brain pathologies. The contributions bring together researchers from the medical image analysis domain, neurologists, and radiologists working on at least one of these diseases. The aim is to consider neuroimaging biomarkers used for one disease applied to the other diseases. This session did not have a specific dataset to be used.

The second part focuses on the papers from the BRATS challenge. In order to gauge the current state of the art in automated brain tumor segmentation and compare different methods, a large dataset of magnetic resonance imagining (MRI) scans of brain tumors was made available. The participants at the challenge compared the results obtained with their methods against manual segmentations.

The third part contains descriptions of the algorithms participating in ISLES, which aimed to provide a fair and direct comparison of methods for ischemic stroke lesion segmentation from multispectral MRI images. A public dataset of diverse ischemic stroke cases and a suitable automatic evaluation procedure were made available for the following two tasks: subacute ischemic stroke lesion segmentation and acute stroke outcome/penumbra estimation.

We heartily hope that this volume will promote further exciting research on brain lesions.

February 2016

Alessandro Crimi
Oskar Maier
Bjoern Menze
Mauricio Reyes
Heinz Handels

# Organization

## Organizing Committee

Alessandro Crimi             Istituto Italiano di Tecnologia, Italia
Heinz Handels                Universität zu Lübeck, Germany
Oskar Maier                  Universität zu Lübeck, Germany
Bjoern Menze                 Technische Universität München, Germany
Mauricio Reyes               Universität Bern, Switzerland
Keyvan Farahani              National Institute of Health, USA
Jayashree Kalpathy-Cramer    Harvard Medical School, USA
Dongjin Kwon                 University of Pennsylvania, USA

## Program Committee

Meritxell Bach Cuadra        University of Lausanne, Switzerland
Guido Gerig                  University of Utah, USA
Ron Kikinis                  Harvard Medical School, USA
Koen Van Leemput             Harvard Medical School, USA
Simon Warfield               Harvard Medical School, USA

## Sponsoring Institutions

Graduate School for Computing in Medicine and Life Sciences, Universität zu Lübeck, Germany

# Contents

**Brain Tumor Image Segmentation**

# Ischemic Stroke Lesion Image Segmentation

## ISLES Introduction

# Brain Lesions, Introduction

Alessandro Crimi(✉)

Istituto Italiano di Tecnologia (IIT), Via Morego, 30, 16163 Genova, Italy
alessandro.crimi@iit.it

**Abstract.** A brain lesion is a brain tissue abnormality which can be seen on a neurological scan, such as magnetic resonance imaging or computerized tomography. Brain tumor, multiple sclerosis, stroke and traumatic brain injuries are different diseases and accidents affecting in different ways the brain. Their unpredictable appearance and shape make them challenging to be segmented in multi-modal brain imaging. Nevertheless, they share similarities in the way they appear in medical images.

## 1 Background

The brain is one of the most studied and important organs of the human body. Despite being protected by the skull, and suspended in cerebrospinal fluid, it is susceptible to a series of damage and disease. Injuries can arise after a trauma with external object or internal complications as stroke. The brain can also be affected by degenerative disorders as Parkinson's [1] and Alzheimer's disease [2], multiple sclerosis (MS) [3], and by tumors [4].

These injuries and damages manifest changes in the brain parenchyma visible on magnetic resonance images (MRIs). The knowledge of the exact location, shape and extent of the pathological tissue is generally vital for precise diagnosis, monitoring, and treatment decisions. For instance in glioma - which is the most common form of malignant brain tumors in adult- the evaluation of treatment mainly relies on the patient survival time and the radiographic response rate or progression-free survival [5]. These radiographic responses are computed on two-dimensional tumor measurements on computed tomography (CT) or MRI [4]. MS is an acquired, inflammatory, demyelinating disease of the central nervous system. It is mostly common in the Northern Hemisphere and it manifests itself very heterogeneously among the patients. Imaging is one of the main investigative tools for MS in both the two phases of the disease (neurodegeneration and inflammation). The early stage is given by focal white matter (WM) inflammation, and then with diffuse lesions of WM, gray-matter (GM) and spinal-cord lesions [3,6]. Consensus has been reached on criteria to identify hyper-intense, contrast-enhanced lesions, and MRI features of cord lesions have also been identified [7].

Most strokes result from a blood clot in relevant blood supply highways for the brain, which can cause damage or destroy nearby brain tissue. Analysis of strokes is further complicated by the fact that damage often crosses into multiple regions of the brain. Stroke is usually diagnosed in the acute phase mostly

© Springer International Publishing Switzerland 2016
A. Crimi et al. (Eds.): BrainLes 2015, LNCS 9556, pp. 1–5, 2016.
DOI: 10.1007/978-3-319-30858-6_1

using CT, and in many cases also using MRI. Since spatial measures of ischemic changes have been shown to correlate with clinical outcome, a metric for damage assessment for CT has been introduced [8]. Moreover, MRI is the main modality for estimating global and regional alterations and its progression in traumatic brain injuries (TBI) [9]. To evaluate the damages, morphological analysis is carried out on T1, T2 and Fluid Attenuated Inversion Recovery (FLAIR). More recently diffusion tensor imaging (DTI) and consequent metrics as Track-Based Spatial Statistics [10] have also been used. Apart from diagnosis and monitoring progression, imaging has been increasingly used in neurosurgery [11] and radio-therapeutic planning [12]. Lastly, most biopsies are guided with contrast-enhanced T1-weighted MR [13].

## 2   Image Analysis

A well-known cumbersome step for the management of all these diseases is the delineation of relevant structures in medical images. This is time-consuming, generally performed manually by an expert physician, and it is sensitive to inter- and intra-operator variability. This led to the introduction of methodologies for automatic segmentation of lesions in brain scans, with the aim of reducing the amount of work for physician and to reduce variability. Despite the progresses, this task is still challenging. The difficulties in automatic tumor and ischemic tissue segmentation arise since active tumors, clots and necrotic tissues vary greatly across patients in their size, location, shape and appearance. Moreover, these lesions often exhibit inhomogeneity in intensity as well as large intensity variations between subjects, especially if they are acquired with different scanners or at different imaging centers. In MS, small lesions can also be mistaken for vessels and other periventricular structures.

Some methods for glioma segmentation rely on spatial prior to derive tumor specific "bio-marker" [14]. However, most methods rely on intensity contrast information from manually annotated images. In this context, voxels depicting tumoral tissue have been modeled as outliers [15], and Markov random fields approaches have been used to encourage similarity among neighboring labels [16]. The same techniques have been used in MS lesion segmentation respectively using outliers detection [17] and texture analysis using conditional random fields [18]. This can be seen as a proof that methods for one disease can be applied to others. Current research on segmentation is also based on deep convolutional neural network [19], and it is expected that in the future a plethora of methods based on this technique will be encountered.

The goodness of the automatic segmentation is generally assessed by comparing the result of the algorithms to the manual segmentation, generally by using the Jaccar or Dice indices [20]. These indices are statistics used for comparing the similarity and diversity of sample sets. The Jaccar index is defined as the size of the intersection of the set of voxels in the manual annotation A and the set of voxels resulting in the automatic annotation B, divided by the size of the union of them. Similarly the Dice index $s$ is given as

$$s = \frac{2|A \cap B|}{|A| + |B|}. \tag{1}$$

These indices yield a single scalar value between 0 and 1, quantifying the goodness of spatial overlap, which can be applied to studies of reproducibility and accuracy in image segmentation. Other ways to measure the segmentation overlap are distance measures as the mean absolute distance and the Hausdorff distance between contours [21], which quantify the distance between manually and automatically segmented surfaces as maximum distance of a set points in one contour to the nearest point in the other contour.

Beyond segmentation itself, image analysis has been employed to extract biomarkers. Some of these are based on shapes, as the VASARI features, which is a comprehensive feature-set to describe the morphology of brain tumors on routine contrast-enhanced MRI [22]; Laplace-Beltrami Eigenvalues [23] and spherical harmonics [24] of the hippocampal shape, to discriminate patients affected by Alzheimer disease from mild cognitive impairment and control; and tensor-like representations to evaluate certain spatio-temporal changes of MS lesions to indicate more severe course of the disease [25].

## 3   Conclusion

Many works have been done to automate clinical practices in neuroimaging for brain-lesions. However, open questions remain. For instance, the use of measures like Dice and Hausdorff scores can be controversial. Despite these are currently the most used tools, it has been informally discussed by the community that reducing the entire process of segmentation to one single value, not necessarily allow a more precise evaluation of the goodness of the segmentation for diagnosis or other clinical purposes. A possible solution could be to use several overlap measures since they may capture different aspects [26], or to allow measures which do not boil down to a single scalar value which yet have to be introduced.

Summarizing, despite there is no general approach of segmentation for all diseases, some methods could be applied to more than one disease interchangeably. It is therefore convenient to exchange ideas between experts of different fields.

## References

1. Jankovic, J.: Parkinsons disease: clinical features and diagnosis. J. Neurol. Neurosurg. Psychiatry **79**(4), 368–376 (2008)
2. Dubois, B., Feldman, H.H., Jacova, C., DeKosky, S.T., Barberger-Gateau, P., Cummings, J., Delacourte, A., Galasko, D., Gauthier, S., Jicha, G., et al.: Research criteria for the diagnosis of Alzheimer's disease: revising the NINCDS-ADRDA criteria. Lancet Neurol. **6**(8), 734–746 (2007)
3. Steinman, L.: Multiple sclerosis: a two-stage disease. Nat. Immunol. **2**(9), 762–764 (2001)

4. Wen, P.Y., Macdonald, D.R., Reardon, D.A., Cloughesy, T.F., Sorensen, A.G., Galanis, E., DeGroot, J., Wick, W., Gilbert, M.R., Lassman, A.B., et al.: Updated response assessment criteria for high-grade gliomas: response assessment in neuro-oncology working group. J. Clin. Oncol. **28**(11), 1963–1972 (2010)
5. van den Bent, M., Wefel, J.S., Schiff, D., Taphoorn, M., Jaeckle, K., Junck, L., Armstrong, T., Choucair, A., Waldman, A., Gorlia, T., et al.: Response assessment in neuro-oncology (a report of the RANO group): assessment of outcome in trials of diffuse low-grade gliomas. Lancet Oncol. **12**(6), 583–593 (2011)
6. Leray, E., Yaouanq, J., Le Page, E., Coustans, M., Laplaud, D., Oger, J., Edan, G.: Evidence for a two-stage disability progression in multiple sclerosis. Brain **133**(7), 1900–1913 (2010)
7. Filippi, M., Rocca, M.A., Arnold, D.L., Bakshi, R., Barkhof, F., De Stefano, N., Fazekas, F., Frohman, E., Wolinsky, J.S.: EFNS guidelines on the use of neuroimaging in the management of multiple sclerosis. Eur. J. Neurol. **13**(4), 313–325 (2006)
8. Pexman, J.W., Barber, P.A., Hill, M.D., Sevick, R.J., Demchuk, A.M., Hudon, M.E., Hu, W.Y., Buchan, A.M.: Use of the Alberta stroke program early CT score (aspects) for assessing CT scans in patients with acute stroke. Am. J. Neuroradiol. **22**(8), 1534–1542 (2001)
9. Kinnunen, K.M., Greenwood, R., Powell, J.H., Leech, R., Hawkins, P.C., Bonnelle, V., Patel, M.C., Counsell, S.J., Sharp, D.J.: White matter damage and cognitive impairment after traumatic brain injury. Brain **134**(pt. 2), 449–463 (2010)
10. Smith, S.M., Jenkinson, M., Johansen-Berg, H., Rueckert, D., Nichols, T.E., Mackay, C.E., Watkins, K.E., Ciccarelli, O., Cader, M.Z., Matthews, P.M., et al.: Tract-based spatial statistics: voxelwise analysis of multi-subject diffusion data. Neuroimage **31**(4), 1487–1505 (2006)
11. Black, P.M., Moriarty, T., Alexander III, E., Stieg, P., Woodard, E.J., Gleason, P.L., Martin, C.H., Kikinis, R., Schwartz, R.B., Jolesz, F.A.: Development and implementation of intraoperative magnetic resonance imaging and its neurosurgical applications. Neurosurgery **41**(4), 831–845 (1997)
12. Brandsma, D., Stalpers, L., Taal, W., Sminia, P., van den Bent, M.J.: Clinical features, mechanisms, and management of pseudoprogression in malignant gliomas. Lancet Oncol. **9**(5), 453–461 (2008)
13. Kelly, P.J., Daumas-Duport, C., Kispert, D.B., Kall, B.A., Scheithauer, B.W., Illig, J.J.: Imaging-based stereotaxic serial biopsies in untreated intracranial glial neoplasms. J. Neurosurg. **66**(6), 865–874 (1987)
14. Prastawa, M., Bullitt, E., Moon, N., Van Leemput, K., Gerig, G.: Automatic brain tumor segmentation by subject specific modification of atlas priors 1. Acad. Radiol. **10**(12), 1341–1348 (2003)
15. Prastawa, M., Bullitt, E., Ho, S., Gerig, G.: A brain tumor segmentation framework based on outlier detection. Med. Image Anal. **8**(3), 275–283 (2004)
16. Lee, C.-H., Wang, S., Murtha, A., Brown, M.R.G., Greiner, R.: Segmenting brain tumors using pseudo–conditional random fields. In: Metaxas, D., Axel, L., Fichtinger, G., Székely, G. (eds.) MICCAI 2008, Part I. LNCS, vol. 5241, pp. 359–366. Springer, Heidelberg (2008)
17. Van Leemput, K., Maes, F., Vandermeulen, D., Colchester, A., Suetens, P.: Automated segmentation of multiple sclerosis lesions by model outlier detection. IEEE Trans. Med. Imaging **20**(8), 677–688 (2001)
18. Karimaghaloo, Z., Rivaz, H., Arnold, D.L., Collins, D.L., Arbel, T.: Adaptive voxel, texture and temporal conditional random fields for detection of gad-enhancing multiple sclerosis lesions in brain MRI. In: Mori, K., Sakuma, I., Sato, Y., Barillot, C.,

Navab, N. (eds.) MICCAI 2013, Part III. LNCS, vol. 8151, pp. 543–550. Springer, Heidelberg (2013)

19. Bengio, Y.: Learning deep architectures for AI. Found. Trends Mach. Learn. **2**(1), 1–127 (2009)

20. Dice, L.R.: Measures of the amount of ecologic association between species. Ecology **26**(3), 297–302 (1945)

21. Gerig, G., Jomier, M., Chakos, M.: Valmet: a new validation tool for assessing and improving 3D object segmentation. In: Niessen, W.J., Viergever, M.A. (eds.) MICCAI 2001. LNCS, vol. 2208, pp. 516–523. Springer, Heidelberg (2001)

22. Gevaert, O., Mitchell, L.A., Achrol, A.S., Xu, J., Echegaray, S., Steinberg, G.K., Cheshier, S.H., Napel, S., Zaharchuk, G., Plevritis, S.K.: Glioblastoma multiforme: exploratory radiogenomic analysis by using quantitative image features. Radiology **273**(1), 168–174 (2014)

23. Reuter, M., Wolter, F.E., Shenton, M., Niethammer, M.: Laplace-Beltrami eigenvalues and topological features of eigenfunctions for statistical shape analysis. Comput. Aided Des. **41**(10), 739–755 (2009)

24. Gerardin, E., Chételat, G., Chupin, M., Cuingnet, R., Desgranges, B., Kim, H.S., Niethammer, M., Dubois, B., Lehéricy, S., Garnero, L., et al.: Multidimensional classification of hippocampal shape features discriminates Alzheimer's disease and mild cognitive impairment from normal aging. Neuroimage **47**(4), 1476–1486 (2009)

25. Crimi, A., Commowick, O., Maarouf, A., Ferré, J.C., Bannier, E., Tourbah, A., Berry, I., Ranjeva, J.P., Edan, G., Barillot, C.: Predictive value of imaging markers at multiple sclerosis disease onset based on gadolinium- and USPIO-enhanced MRI and machine learning. PLoS ONE **9**(4), e93024 (2014)

26. Babalola, K.O., Patenaude, B., Aljabar, P., Schnabel, J., Kennedy, D., Crum, W., Smith, S., Cootes, T., Jenkinson, M., Rueckert, D.: An evaluation of four automatic methods of segmenting the subcortical structures in the brain. Neuroimage **47**(4), 1435–1447 (2009)

# Brain Lesion Image Analysis

# Simultaneous Whole-Brain Segmentation and White Matter Lesion Detection Using Contrast-Adaptive Probabilistic Models

Oula Puonti[1]([⊠]) and Koen Van Leemput[1,2]

[1] Department of Applied Mathematics and Computer Science,
Technical University of Denmark, Kongens Lyngby, Denmark
oupu@dtu.dk
[2] Martinos Center for Biomedical Imaging, MGH,
Harvard Medical School, Boston, USA

**Abstract.** In this paper we propose a new generative model for simultaneous brain parcellation and white matter lesion segmentation from multi-contrast magnetic resonance images. The method combines an existing whole-brain segmentation technique with a novel spatial lesion model based on a convolutional restricted Boltzmann machine. Unlike current state-of-the-art lesion detection techniques based on discriminative modeling, the proposed method is not tuned to one specific scanner or imaging protocol, and simultaneously segments dozens of neuroanatomical structures. Experiments on a public benchmark dataset in multiple sclerosis indicate that the method's lesion segmentation accuracy compares well to that of the current state-of-the-art in the field, while additionally providing robust whole-brain segmentations.

## 1 Introduction

Conditions that affect the integrity of the white matter, including small vessel disease and multiple sclerosis, form a significant health concern. Lesions in the white matter are frequently associated with memory impairment, headaches, depression, muscle weakness, and many other conditions. Because magnetic resonance (MR) imaging can visualize lesion formation with much greater sensitivity than clinical observation, the ability to reliably and efficiently detect white matter lesions from MR scans is of great value to diagnose disease, track progression, and evaluate treatment. Quantifying the independent contribution of white matter lesions to clinical disability is also important for enhancing our understanding of disease mechanisms, and for facilitating efficient testing in clinical trials.

Because of considerable intra- and inter-rater variabilities in manual annotations, and because of the sheer amount of imaging data acquired in clinical trials, there is a strong need for computational tools that can analyze brain images with white matter lesions in a fully automated fashion. Although many partial solutions have been proposed (e.g., [1]), a generally applicable tool that works robustly across disease states and imaging centers remains an open problem [2]. Many of the best performing methods for lesion segmentation currently

© Springer International Publishing Switzerland 2016
A. Crimi et al. (Eds.): BrainLes 2015, LNCS 9556, pp. 9–20, 2016.
DOI: 10.1007/978-3-319-30858-6_2

use extended spatial neighborhoods to provide rich contextual information, using a *discriminative* approach in which the specific intensity characteristics of training images are explicitly used to encode the relationship between image appearance and segmentation labels (e.g., [3–5]). However, because of the dependency of MR intensity contrast on the scanner platform and pulse sequence, and because there exists no standardized clinical MR protocol to study white matter damage, such discriminative methods do not generalize well to cases where the target and training data come from different scanners or centers. Furthermore, these methods do not provide segmentations of the non-lesioned parts of the brain into various cortical and subcortical structures, although regional atrophy patterns convey vital clinical information in diseases such as multiple sclerosis [6].

In this paper, we propose a novel method for jointly segmenting white matter lesions and a large number of cortical and subcortical structures from multi-contrast MR data. The method combines a previously validated method for whole-brain segmentation of healthy brain scans [7] with a novel spatial model for lesion shape and occurrence that is conditioned on surrounding neuroanatomy. In particular we propose to use a restricted Boltzmann machine (RBM) [8] to provide much richer spatial models than the low-order Markov random fields (MRFs) that have traditionally been used in the field for spatial regularization of lesion segmentations [9]. By using a generative rather than a discriminative formulation, the method is able to completely separate models of anatomy (which are learned from manual segmentations of training data) from intensity models (which are estimated on the fly for each individual scan being segmented). Because the *intensities* of training data are never used, the model can be applied to images with new contrast properties without needing new training data.

We test our approach on publicly available data from the MICCAI 2008 MS lesion segmentation challenge [10], demonstrating the feasibility of the method. Compared to related work for simultaneous whole-brain and lesion segmentation [11], the proposed method segments considerably more structures, and learns spatial lesion models automatically from training data rather than relying on a set of hand-crafted rules to remove false positive detections.

## 2   Modeling Framework

We build upon a previously published generative modeling approach [7], in which a forward probabilistic image model is "inverted" to obtain automated segmentations. In the following we first briefly summarize the existing whole-brain segmentation method we build upon; then introduce the proposed RBM lesion model; describe how we integrate it within the model for whole-brain segmentation; and specify how we use the resulting model to obtain automated segmentations.

### 2.1   Existing Whole-Brain Segmentation Method

Let $\mathbf{D} = (\mathbf{d}_1, \ldots, \mathbf{d}_I)$ denote a matrix collecting the (log-transformed) intensities in a multi-contrast brain MR scan with $I$ voxels, where the vector

$\mathbf{d}_i = (d_i^1, \ldots, d_i^N)^T$ contains the intensities in voxel $i$ for each of the available $N$ contrasts. Furthermore, let $\mathbf{l} = (l_1, \ldots, l_I)^T$ be the corresponding segmentation, where $l_i \in \{1, \ldots, K\}$ denotes the one of $K$ possible segmentation labels assigned to voxel $i$. A generative model then consists of a prior segmentation probability distribution $p(\mathbf{l})$ that encodes prior knowledge about human neuroanatomy, and a segmentation-conditional probability distribution $p(\mathbf{D}|\mathbf{l})$ that measures how probable the observed MR intensities are for different segmentations. In [7] the segmentation prior is parametrized by a sparse tetrahedral mesh with node positions $\boldsymbol{\theta}_l$. Assuming conditional independence of the labels between voxels given $\boldsymbol{\theta}_l$, the prior is given by:

$$p(\mathbf{l}) = \int_{\boldsymbol{\theta}_l} p(\mathbf{l}|\boldsymbol{\theta}_l)p(\boldsymbol{\theta}_l)\mathrm{d}\boldsymbol{\theta}_l$$

$$\text{where} \quad p(\mathbf{l}|\boldsymbol{\theta}_l) = \prod_{i=1}^{I} p(l_i|\boldsymbol{\theta}_l),$$

and $p(\boldsymbol{\theta}_l)$ is a topology-preserving deformation prior. The prior model is learned from manual annotations in 39 subjects as described in [7].

For the segmentation-conditional distribution $p(\mathbf{D}|\mathbf{l})$, a Gaussian mixture model (GMM) is associated with each neuroanatomical label to model the relationship between segmentation labels and image intensities. The smoothly varying intensity inhomogeneities ("bias fields") that typically corrupt MR scans are modeled as a linear combination of spatially smooth basis functions that are added to the local voxel intensities. Letting $\boldsymbol{\theta}_d$ denote all bias field and GMM parameters with prior $p(\boldsymbol{\theta}_d) \propto 1$, the resulting segmentation-conditional distribution is given by:

$$p(\mathbf{D}|\mathbf{l}) = \int_{\boldsymbol{\theta}_d} p(\mathbf{D}|\mathbf{l}, \boldsymbol{\theta}_d)p(\boldsymbol{\theta}_d)\mathrm{d}\boldsymbol{\theta}_d,$$

$$\text{where} \quad p(\mathbf{D}|\mathbf{l}, \boldsymbol{\theta}_d) = \prod_{i=1}^{I} p(\mathbf{d}_i|l_i, \boldsymbol{\theta}_d)$$

$$\text{and} \quad p(\mathbf{d}|l, \boldsymbol{\theta}_d) = \sum_{g=1}^{G_l} w_{lg}\mathcal{N}(\mathbf{d} - \mathbf{C}^T\boldsymbol{\phi}^i|\boldsymbol{\mu}_{lg}, \boldsymbol{\Sigma}_{lg}).$$

Here $\mathcal{N}(\cdot)$ denotes a normal distribution; $G_l$ is the number of Gaussian distributions associated with label $l$; and $\boldsymbol{\mu}_{lg}$, $\boldsymbol{\Sigma}_{lg}$, and $w_{lg}$ are the mean, covariance, and weight of component $g$ in the corresponding mixture model. Furthermore, $\boldsymbol{\phi}^i$ evaluates the bias field basis functions at the $i^{\text{th}}$ voxel, and $\mathbf{C} = (\mathbf{c}_1, \ldots, \mathbf{c}_N)$ where $\mathbf{c}_n$ denotes the parameters of the bias field model for the $n^{\text{th}}$ MR contrast.

With this model segmentation proceeds by estimating $\hat{\mathbf{l}} = \arg\max_{\mathbf{l}} p(\mathbf{l}|\mathbf{D})$, using the approximation $p(\mathbf{l}|\mathbf{D}) \simeq p(\mathbf{l}|\mathbf{D}, \hat{\boldsymbol{\theta}}_d, \hat{\boldsymbol{\theta}}_l)$ where $\{\hat{\boldsymbol{\theta}}_d, \hat{\boldsymbol{\theta}}_l\}$ are the parameter values that maximize $p(\boldsymbol{\theta}_d, \boldsymbol{\theta}_l|\mathbf{D})$. These values are estimated using coordinate ascent, where the atlas deformation parameters $\boldsymbol{\theta}_l$ are optimized with a conjugate gradient (CG) algorithm, and the remaining parameters $\boldsymbol{\theta}_d$ with a generalized expectation-maximization (GEM) algorithm [7]. The optimization is done iteratively in an alternating fashion, keeping the deformation parameters fixed while optimizing the intensity model parameters and vice versa until convergence. The GMM parameters are initialized based on the structure probabilities given by the segmentation prior after affine registration to the target scan. We emphasize that the intensity model parameters are learned *given* the target scan and thus automatically adapt to its intensity properties. In [7] the intensity-adaptiveness was demonstrated on several datasets acquired with different sequences, scanners and field strengths.

## 2.2 Spatial Lesion Prior Using a Convolutional RBM

In order to model the spatial configuration of white matter lesions, we employ a restricted Boltzmann machine (RBM) [8], a specific type of MRF in which long-range voxel interactions are encoded through local connections to hidden units, which effectively function as feature detectors. Letting $\mathbf{z} = (z_1, \ldots, z_I)^T$ denote a binary lesion map, where $z_i \in \{0, 1\}$ indicates whether the voxel is part of a lesion, a RBM prior on $\mathbf{z}$ is defined by

$$p(\mathbf{z}) = \sum_{\mathbf{h}} p(\mathbf{z}, \mathbf{h}), \quad \text{with}$$

$$p(\mathbf{z}, \mathbf{h}) \propto \exp\left[ - E_{\mathrm{RBM}}(\mathbf{z}, \mathbf{h}) \right],$$

where $\mathbf{h} = (h_1, \ldots, h_J)^T, h_j \in \{0, 1\}$ denotes a vector of $J$ binary hidden units, and the RBM "energy" is defined as:

$$E_{\mathrm{RBM}}(\mathbf{z}, \mathbf{h}) = -\mathbf{b}^T \mathbf{z} - \mathbf{c}^T \mathbf{h} - \mathbf{h}^T \mathbf{W} \mathbf{z}.$$

The parameters of this model include the vectors $\mathbf{b}$ and $\mathbf{c}$ (which bias individual visible and hidden units to take on certain values), as well as the weight matrix $\mathbf{W}$ (which models the interaction between the hidden and visible units). The attractiveness of this specific MRF model arises from the presence of the hidden units, which increase the expressive power of the model, as well as the property that the values of $\mathbf{z}$ are independent of one another given $\mathbf{h}$ and vice versa, which greatly facilitates inference computations. Specifically, for each hidden unit $h_j$ and lesion $z_i$ the conditional distributions are written as [12]:

$$p(h_j = 1 | \mathbf{z}) = \sigma\left(c_j + \left(\mathbf{W}\mathbf{z}\right)_j\right)$$

$$p(z_i = 1 | \mathbf{h}) = \sigma\left(b_i + \left(\mathbf{h}^T \mathbf{W}\right)_i\right),$$

where $\sigma(x) = (1 + \exp(-x))^{-1}$.

In order to scale this framework to model full-sized images, we use a convolutional approach that imposes a repeated, sparse spatial structure on the parameters [12]. For the sake of clarity of presentation, in the following we describe the case for one-dimensional images, although the technique generalizes readily into three dimensions. In the convolutional RBM a set of $P$ filters $\{\mathbf{f}^p\}_{p=1}^P, \mathbf{f}^p = (f_1^p, \ldots, f_Q^p)^T$ is defined, each of size $Q \ll I$. The parameter matrix $\mathbf{W}$ is then restricted to be of the form

$$\mathbf{W} = \begin{pmatrix} \mathbf{W}^1 \\ \vdots \\ \mathbf{W}^P \end{pmatrix}, \quad \text{where} \quad \mathbf{W}^p = \begin{pmatrix} f_1^p & \ldots & f_Q^p & 0 & \ldots & 0 \\ 0 & f_1^p & \ldots & f_Q^p & \ldots & 0 \\ \vdots & \ddots & \ddots & \ddots & \ddots & \vdots \\ 0 & \ldots & 0 & f_1^p & \ldots & f_Q^p \end{pmatrix},$$

so that each filter detects the same specific feature in different parts of the image, and inference can be done efficiently using convolution. Similarly, in the parameter vector $\mathbf{c}$ each filter output shares the same bias across the image [12]. In our implementation we do not put such a restriction on the visible biases $\mathbf{b}$, as this allows modeling spatially varying prior probabilities of lesion occurrence.

We automatically learn appropriate values for the parameters $\{\mathbf{W}, \mathbf{b}, \mathbf{c}\}$ from manually annotated training data, i.e., binary lesion maps for a number of different subjects. For this purpose, we use the persistent contrastive divergence (PCD) learning algorithm, which performs stochastic gradient ascent on the log-likelihood of the training data using approximate gradients computed with Markov chain Monte Carlo (MCMC) sampling [13].

## 2.3 Joint Model

We incorporate the RBM lesion model into the whole-brain segmentation framework by assuming that a lesion can only occur in a voxel when its underlying neuroanatomical label is white matter ($l = $ wm), effectively changing its status from healthy white matter ($z = 0$) into white matter lesion ($z = 1$). Towards this end, we define a joint segmentation prior on both $\mathbf{l}$ and $\mathbf{z}$:

$$p(\mathbf{l}, \mathbf{z}) = \int_{\boldsymbol{\theta}_l} p(\mathbf{l}, \mathbf{z}|\boldsymbol{\theta}_l)p(\boldsymbol{\theta}_l)\mathrm{d}\boldsymbol{\theta}_l, \quad \text{where}$$

$$p(\mathbf{l}, \mathbf{z}|\boldsymbol{\theta}_l) = \sum_{\mathbf{h}} p(\mathbf{l}, \mathbf{z}, \mathbf{h}|\boldsymbol{\theta}_l) \quad \text{and}$$

$$p(\mathbf{l}, \mathbf{z}, \mathbf{h}|\boldsymbol{\theta}_l) \propto \exp\left[ -E_{\mathrm{RBM}}(\mathbf{z}, \mathbf{h}) + \sum_{i=1}^I \log p(l_i|\boldsymbol{\theta}_l) - \sum_{i=1}^I \phi(l_i, z_i) \right],$$

where in abuse of notation $p(l_i|\boldsymbol{\theta}_l)$ refers to the deformable atlas of the whole-brain segmentation model, and $\phi(l, z)$ evaluates to zero when $l = $ wm or $z = 0$, and infinity otherwise. The role of $\phi(l, z)$ is to restrict lesions to appear only inside white matter – without it the model would devolve into simply

$p(\mathbf{l}, \mathbf{z}) = p(\mathbf{l})p(\mathbf{z})$. In similar vein, we define an intensity model which is conditional on both l and z:

$$p(\mathbf{D}|\mathbf{l}, \mathbf{z}) = \int_{\boldsymbol{\theta}_d} p(\mathbf{D}|\mathbf{l}, \mathbf{z}, \boldsymbol{\theta}_d)p(\boldsymbol{\theta}_d)\mathrm{d}\boldsymbol{\theta}_d,$$

$$\text{where} \quad p(\mathbf{D}|\mathbf{l}, \mathbf{z}, \boldsymbol{\theta}_d) = \prod_{i=1}^{I} p(\mathbf{d}_i|l_i, z_i, \boldsymbol{\theta}_d)$$

$$\text{and} \quad p(\mathbf{d}|l, z, \boldsymbol{\theta}_d) = \sum_{g=1}^{G_l} w_{lg} \mathcal{N}\left(\mathbf{d} - \mathbf{C}^T \boldsymbol{\phi}^i | \boldsymbol{\mu}_{lg}, \gamma^z \boldsymbol{\Sigma}_{lg}\right).$$

This model preserves the original segmentation-conditional GMMs for voxels without lesions ($z = 0$), but widens the variances of the Gaussian components by a user-specified factor $\gamma > 1$ otherwise. Such wide distributions aim to capture the fact that lesions often do not have a clearly defined intensity profile in MR, e.g., ranging from iso-intense to white matter to intensities similar to CSF in T1-weighted contrasts.

## 2.4   Inference

Segmentation with the proposed model can be accomplished by first estimating the parameters $\{\hat{\boldsymbol{\theta}}_d, \hat{\boldsymbol{\theta}}_l\}$ that maximize $p(\boldsymbol{\theta}_d, \boldsymbol{\theta}_l|\mathbf{D})$, and subsequently analyzing $p(\mathbf{l}, \mathbf{z}|\mathbf{D}, \hat{\boldsymbol{\theta}}_d, \hat{\boldsymbol{\theta}}_l)$, as in the whole-brain segmentation method described in Sect. 2.1 [7]. However, optimization of the model parameters is now complicated by the fact that the RBM model introduces non-local dependencies between the voxels through the weighted connections between the lesions and the hidden units. To side-step this difficulty, during the parameter estimation phase – in which we have no interest in accurately segmenting the white matter lesions – we temporarily replace the RBM energy $E_{\mathrm{RBM}}(\mathbf{z}, \mathbf{h})$ with a simple energy of the form:

$$E_{\mathrm{tmp}}(\mathbf{z}, \mathbf{l}) = -\sum_{i=1}^{I} [l_i = \mathrm{wm}] \left(z_i \log(w) + (1 - z_i) \log(1 - w)\right),$$

where $0 \leq w \leq 1$ is a user-specified parameter which essentially defines a uniform spatial prior probability for lesions to occur *within* white matter. This effectively removes the hidden units from the model, and reduces the form of $p(\boldsymbol{\theta}_d, \boldsymbol{\theta}_l|\mathbf{D})$ to the one of the original segmentation method, so that the same optimization strategy can be used. Compared to the original method, the only difference is that each Gaussian distribution $\mathcal{N}(\cdot|\boldsymbol{\mu}_{lg}, \boldsymbol{\Sigma}_{lg})$ associated with the white matter label $l = \mathrm{wm}$ is replaced with a mixture of the form:

$$(1 - w)\mathcal{N}(\cdot|\boldsymbol{\mu}_{lg}, \boldsymbol{\Sigma}_{lg}) + w\mathcal{N}(\cdot|\boldsymbol{\mu}_{lg}, \gamma\boldsymbol{\Sigma}_{lg}), \tag{1}$$

yielding a distribution with the same mean but heavier tails, making parameter estimation more robust to intensity outliers such as white matter lesions.

The adaptation in the GEM algorithm to enforce the parameter sharing between the two mixture components in Eq. (1) is straightforward.

Once the optimal parameter estimates are found, we replace the temporary energy with the original RBM energy and infer the corresponding whole-brain and lesion segmentation by MCMC sampling from $p(\mathbf{l}, \mathbf{z} | \mathbf{D}, \hat{\boldsymbol{\theta}}_d, \hat{\boldsymbol{\theta}}_l)$, exploiting the specific structure of the RBM model. In particular, we generate $S$ triplets $\{\mathbf{l}_s, \mathbf{z}_s, \mathbf{h}_s\}_{s=1}^{S}$ by sampling from the distribution $p(\mathbf{l}, \mathbf{z}, \mathbf{h} | \mathbf{D}, \hat{\boldsymbol{\theta}}_d, \hat{\boldsymbol{\theta}}_l)$ using block-Gibbs sampling. This is straightforward to implement because each of the conditional distributions factorizes over the voxels (for $\mathbf{l}$ and $\mathbf{z}$) or the hidden units (for $\mathbf{h}$). The sampling is performed in two alternating steps: first, we sample the values for the hidden units given the lesions:

$$\mathbf{h}_s \sim \prod_{j=1}^{J} p(h_j = 1 | \mathbf{z}_{s-1}).$$

Then, given the sampled hidden unit values $\mathbf{h}_s$, we jointly sample the labels $\mathbf{l}$ and $\mathbf{z}$ from:

$$\{\mathbf{l}_s, \mathbf{z}_s\} \sim \prod_{i=1}^{I} p(l_i, z_i | \mathbf{d}_i, \mathbf{h}_s, \hat{\boldsymbol{\theta}}_d, \hat{\boldsymbol{\theta}}_l)$$

where

$$p(l_i, z_i | \mathbf{d}_i, \mathbf{h}, \hat{\boldsymbol{\theta}}_d, \hat{\boldsymbol{\theta}}_l) \propto \begin{cases} p(\mathbf{d}_i | l_i, z_i, \hat{\boldsymbol{\theta}}_d) p(l_i | \hat{\boldsymbol{\theta}}_l) p(z_i | \mathbf{h}), & \text{if } l_i = \text{wm or } z_i = 0 \\ 0, & \text{otherwise.} \end{cases}$$

The initial lesion segmentation, i.e., $\mathbf{z}_0$, is obtained as the maximum-a-posteriori estimate using the temporary energy $E_{\text{tmp}}$.

Once we have acquired $S$ triplets, the samples of the hidden units $\{\mathbf{h}_s\}$ are discarded as they are of no interest to us. The "hard" segmentations of $\mathbf{l}$ and $\mathbf{z}$ are obtained by voxel-wise majority voting across $\{\mathbf{l}_s\}$ and $\{\mathbf{z}_s\}$.

## 3   Experiments and Results

### 3.1   Data

We demonstrate the proposed method on the 20 publicly available training cases of the MICCAI 2008 challenge on multiple sclerosis lesion segmentation [10]. This dataset includes 10 subjects scanned at Children's Hospital Boston (CHB) and another 10 scanned at the University of North Carolina (UNC). For each subject the scan set consists of a T1-weighted, a T2-weighted and a FLAIR scan with isotropic resolution of 0.5mm, along with expert segmentations provided by CHB[1]. As a pre-processing step the data was downsampled by a factor of two to a resolution of 1mm isotropic as is customary for this dataset [3,5,14]. No further pre- or post-processing, such as intensity normalization or bias field correction, was applied.

---

[1] Manual segmentations from UNC are now also available, but at the time of the challenge this was not the case [10] so we decided to use only the segmentations provided by CHB.

## 3.2 Implementation

We closely follow the implementation details of the whole-brain segmentation method described in [7]. Because of the small number of manual segmentations available for training the RBM model, we applied two rotations of 10 and $-10$ degrees around the three main axes, producing 6 extra training scans per subject. We trained different RBM models with either $P = 20$ or $P = 40$ filters, with sizes of $(Q \times Q \times Q)$, where $Q$ was either 5, 7 or 9. Each model was trained with 5600 gradient steps of size 0.1 in the PCD algorithm [13]. Based on pilot experiments, we found that using two mixture components for white matter worked well (i.e., $G_{\mathrm{wm}} = 2$), provided that one of the Gaussians is constrained to be a near-uniform distribution that can collect model outliers other than white matter lesions (in practice we use a Gaussian with a fixed scalar covariance matrix $10^6\mathbf{I}$ and weight 0.05). Finally, as the main characteristic of white matter lesions is that they appear hyper-intense compared to normal white matter in FLAIR contrast [2], we decided to only allow voxels to be assigned to lesion in the Gibbs sampling process if their intensity is higher than the estimated white matter mean in FLAIR.

We implemented the algorithm in Matlab, except for the mesh deformation part, which was written in C++, and the RBM convolutions, which were performed on a GPU. In our experiments, estimation of the parameters $\{\hat{\boldsymbol{\theta}}_d, \hat{\boldsymbol{\theta}}_l\}$ was performed on a cluster where each node has two quad-core Xeon 5472 3.0 GHz CPUs and 32 GB of RAM. Only one core was used in the experiments, taking roughly 1.7 h per subject. Gibbs sampling was done on a machine with a GeForce GTX Titan 6 GB GPU. We generated $S = 150$ samples, collected after an initial burn-in of 50 sampling steps, taking approximately 10 min per subject. Thus the full segmentation time for a single target scan is roughly two hours.

## 3.3 Evaluation Set-Up

In order to compare our results against previous methods on the same data, we use the true positive rate $\mathrm{TPR} = \frac{\mathrm{TP}}{\mathrm{TP+FN}}$ and the positive predictive value $\mathrm{PPV} = \frac{\mathrm{TP}}{\mathrm{TP+FP}}$ as performance metrics. Here TP, FP and FN count the true positive, false positive and false negative voxels compared to the expert segmentation. Because our method contains four user-specified parameters $\gamma$, $w$, $Q$ and $P$, which can have a large influence on the obtained results, and because the RBM requires training data to learn its parameters, we perform our evaluation in a cross-validation setting. In particular, we split the available data randomly into five distinct sets, each having 16 training and 4 test subjects. For segmenting each set of 4 test subjects, the remaining 16 are used to train the RBM and to find the best combination $(\gamma, w, Q, P)$, defined as the combination maximizing the product of the mean TPR and PPV over the 16 subjects. Using the product as a measure of fitness promotes parameter combinations that provide both sensitive and specific lesion segmentations.

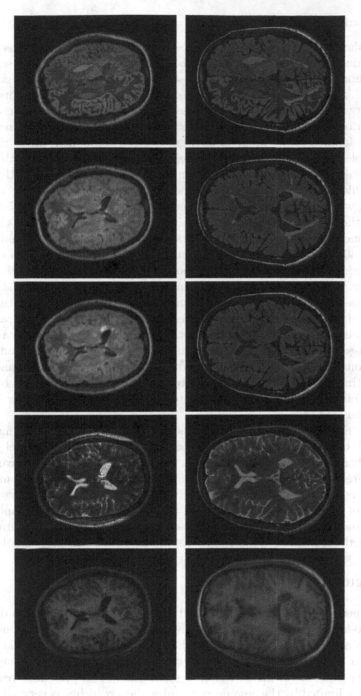

**Fig. 1.** Example segmentations from two subjects: CHB04 (first row) and CHB08 (second row). From left to right: T1-weighted scan, T2-weighted scan, FLAIR scan, manual segmentation overlaid on the FLAIR scan, and the full segmentation obtained using the proposed method. Lesions are denoted in red (Color figure online).

## 3.4   Results

Figure 1 shows two examples of the joint whole-brain and lesion segmentations obtained using the proposed method, along with the manual segmentations. Although our method can segment 41 different neuroanatomical structures in total [7], the MICCAI challenge data only includes manual segmentations of lesions, so validation of the automatic segmentations of these structures could not be performed. However, visual inspection of the 20 cases did not reveal any significant failures in the whole-brain segmentation component of the method.

In Table 1 we compare our lesion segmentation performance with that of two state-of-the-art lesion segmentation tools: a random forest (RF) classifier [3], which is a discriminative method, and a dictionary-learning approach (DL) [14], which is unsupervised and therefore contrast-adaptive (as is the proposed method). Compared to the winning method [15] of the MICCAI 2008 lesion segmentation challenge, which obtained a mean TPR of 0.21 and a mean PPV of 0.30, all the methods show greatly improved segmentation results. On average the proposed method achieves better results than both the DL and RF approaches, although the improvement over the RF approach is very slight. We note that neither of the two benchmark methods segments other structures than lesions, and that the RF classifier is specifically trained on the contrast properties of this particular data set, and is therefore less generally applicable than the proposed and DL methods. Note that the results of the DL method are not entirely comparable, as the authors used a different set of manual annotations for validating the UNC subjects. This explains the quite large difference in performance of the DL method compared to the two other methods for subjects UNC01 and UNC06.

In very recently published work [5], the authors present a lesion segmentation framework based on deep convolutional encoder networks. This model is somewhat similar to the proposed method in the sense that both use convolutional architectures for learning suitable features for lesion detection automatically. The authors also report results on the MICCAI 2008 dataset, obtaining an average TPR of 0.40 and an average PPV of 0.41 which ties the performance of the proposed method. However, their approach suffers from the same limitations as the RF method, i.e., it is a discriminative method that only segments lesions.

## 4   Discussion

In this paper we have proposed a method for joint white matter lesion detection and whole-brain segmentation using a novel spatial lesion model. Due to the generative modeling approach, the method is not tied to one specific scanner platform or imaging protocol, and shows good performance when compared to the current state-of-the-art in lesion segmentation. The presented results are significantly limited by the amount of training data, which was very small given the number of parameters and potential expressive power of the RBM model. Future work will involve further experimentation with different RBM training algorithms and sampling strategies, and an extensive performance validation on

**Table 1.** Quantitative comparison with two state-of-the-art methods.

| | DL [14] | | RF [3] | | Proposed | | | DL [14] | | RF [3] | | Proposed | |
|---|---|---|---|---|---|---|---|---|---|---|---|---|---|
| Patient | TPR | PPV | TPR | PPV | TPR | PPV | Patient | TPR | PPV | TPR | PPV | TPR | PPV |
| CHB01 | 0.60 | 0.58 | 0.49 | **0.64** | **0.75** | 0.57 | UNC01 | **0.33** | **0.29** | 0.02 | 0.01 | 0.02 | 0.01 |
| CHB02 | 0.27 | 0.45 | 0.44 | **0.63** | **0.57** | 0.48 | UNC02 | 0.54 | **0.51** | 0.48 | 0.36 | **0.75** | 0.29 |
| CHB03 | 0.24 | 0.56 | 0.22 | 0.57 | **0.30** | **0.69** | UNC03 | **0.64** | 0.27 | 0.24 | **0.35** | 0.28 | 0.19 |
| CHB04 | 0.27 | 0.66 | 0.31 | **0.78** | **0.59** | 0.49 | UNC04 | 0.40 | **0.51** | 0.54 | 0.38 | **0.62** | 0.40 |
| CHB05 | 0.29 | 0.33 | 0.40 | **0.52** | **0.45** | 0.39 | UNC05 | 0.25 | 0.10 | **0.56** | **0.19** | 0.50 | 0.18 |
| CHB06 | 0.10 | 0.36 | **0.32** | **0.52** | 0.19 | 0.50 | UNC06 | 0.13 | **0.55** | 0.15 | 0.08 | **0.17** | 0.10 |
| CHB07 | 0.14 | 0.48 | **0.40** | 0.54 | 0.34 | **0.65** | UNC07 | 0.44 | 0.23 | **0.76** | 0.16 | 0.60 | **0.26** |
| CHB08 | 0.21 | **0.73** | **0.46** | 0.65 | 0.37 | 0.70 | UNC08 | 0.43 | 0.13 | **0.52** | **0.32** | 0.27 | 0.21 |
| CHB09 | 0.05 | 0.22 | **0.23** | 0.28 | 0.04 | **0.55** | UNC09 | **0.69** | 0.06 | 0.67 | **0.36** | 0.67 | 0.21 |
| CHB10 | 0.15 | 0.12 | **0.23** | 0.39 | 0.19 | **0.69** | UNC10 | 0.43 | 0.23 | **0.53** | 0.34 | 0.47 | **0.48** |

| | DL [14] | | RF [3] | | Proposed | |
|---|---|---|---|---|---|---|
| Mean | TPR=0.33 | PPV=0.37 | TPR=0.40 | PPV=**0.40** | TPR=**0.41** | PPV=**0.40** |

larger data sets of white matter lesions. We further plan to also evaluate the obtained healthy structure segmentations by quantifying local atrophy patterns in large collections of brain images of MS patients.

**Acknowledgements.** This research was supported by NIH NCRR (P41-RR14075), NIBIB (R01EB013565), the Lundbeck Foundation (R141-2013-13117), and financial contributions from the Technical University of Denmark.

# References

1. Tomas-Fernandez, X., Warfield, S.: A model of population and subject (MOPS) intensities with application to multiple sclerosis lesion segmentation. IEEE Trans. Med. Imaging **34**(6), 1349–1361 (2015)
2. García-Lorenzo, D., Francis, S., Narayanan, S., Arnold, D.L., Collins, D.L.: Review of automatic segmentation methods of multiple sclerosis white matter lesions on conventional magnetic resonance imaging. Med. Image Anal. **17**(1), 1–18 (2013)
3. Geremia, E., Menze, B.H., Clatz, O., Konukoglu, E., Criminisi, A., Ayache, N.: Spatial Decision Forests for MS Lesion Segmentation in Multi-Channel MR Images. In: Jiang, T., Navab, N., Pluim, J.P.W., Viergever, M.A. (eds.) MICCAI 2010, Part I. LNCS, vol. 6361, pp. 111–118. Springer, Heidelberg (2010)
4. Karimaghaloo, Z., Rivaz, H., Arnold, D.L., Collins, D.L., Arbel, T.: Adaptive voxel, texture and temporal conditional random fields for detection of Gad-Enhancing multiple sclerosis lesions in brain MRI. In: Mori, K., Sakuma, I., Sato, Y., Barillot, C., Navab, N. (eds.) MICCAI 2013, Part III. LNCS, vol. 8151, pp. 543–550. Springer, Heidelberg (2013)
5. Brosch, T., Yoo, Y., Tang, L.Y.W., Li, D.K.B., Traboulsee, A., Tam, R.: Deep Convolutional Encoder Networks for Multiple Sclerosis Lesion Segmentation. In: Navab, N., Hornegger, J., Wells, W.M., Frangi, A.F. (eds.) MICCAI 2015, Part II. LNCS, vol. 9351, pp. 3–11. Springer, Heidelberg (2015)

6. Filippi, M., Rocca, M.A., Arnold, D.L., Bakshi, R., Barkhof, F., De Stefano, N., Fazekas, F., Frohman, E., Wolinsky, J.S.: EFNS guidelines on the use of neuroimaging in the management of multiple sclerosis. Eur. J. Neurol. **13**(4), 313–325 (2006)
7. Puonti, O., Iglesias, J.E., Van Leemput, K.: Fast, sequence adaptive parcellation of brain MR using parametric models. In: Mori, K., Sakuma, I., Sato, Y., Barillot, C., Navab, N. (eds.) MICCAI 2013, Part I. LNCS, vol. 8149, pp. 727–734. Springer, Heidelberg (2013)
8. Smolensky, P.: Parallel Distributed Processing: Explorations in the Microstructure of Cognition, vol. 1, pp. 194–281. MIT Press, Cambridge (1986)
9. Van Leemput, K., Maes, F., Vandermeulen, D., Colchester, A., Suetens, P.: Automated segmentation of multiple sclerosis lesions by model outlier detection. IEEE Trans. Med. Imaging **20**(8), 677–688 (2001)
10. Styner, M., Lee, J., Chin, B., Chin, M., Commowick, O., Tran, H., Markovic-Plese, S., Jewells, V., Warfield, S.: 3D segmentation in the clinic: a grand challenge II: MS lesion segmentation. MIDAS J., 1–5 (2008)
11. Shiee, N., Bazin, P.L., Ozturk, A., Reich, D.S., Calabresi, P.A., Pham, D.L.: A topology-preserving approach to the segmentation of brain images with multiple sclerosis lesions. NeuroImage **49**(2), 1524–1535 (2010)
12. Lee, H., Grosse, R., Ranganath, R., Ng, A.Y.: Convolutional deep belief networks for scalable unsupervised learning of hierarchical representations. In: Proceedings of the 26th Annual International Conference on Machine Learning, ICML 2009, pp. 609–616. ACM, New York (2009)
13. Tieleman, T.: Training restricted Boltzmann machines using approximations to the likelihood gradient. In: Proceedings of the 25th International Conference on Machine Learning, ICML 2008, pp. 1064–1071. ACM, New York (2008)
14. Weiss, N., Rueckert, D., Rao, A.: Multiple sclerosis lesion segmentation using dictionary learning and sparse coding. In: Mori, K., Sakuma, I., Sato, Y., Barillot, C., Navab, N. (eds.) MICCAI 2013, Part I. LNCS, vol. 8149, pp. 735–742. Springer, Heidelberg (2013)
15. Souplet, J., Lebrun, C., Ayache, N., Malandain, G.: An automatic segmentation of T2-FLAIR multiple sclerosis lesions. In: The MIDAS Journal - MS Lesion Segmentation (MICCAI 2008 Workshop) (2008)

# Stroke Lesion Segmentation
# Using a Probabilistic Atlas
# of Cerebral Vascular Territories

Alexandra Derntl[1]([⊠]), Claudia Plant[1], Philipp Gruber[2], Susanne Wegener[2], Jan S. Bauer[3], and Bjoern H. Menze[4]

[1] Helmholtz Zentrum München, TU München, Munich, Germany
alexandra.derntl@tum.de
[2] Department of Neurology, University Hospital, Zürich, Switzerland
[3] Department of Neuroradiology, Klinikum Rechts der Isar, TU München,
Munich, Germany
[4] Institute for Advanced Study and Department of Computer Science, TU München,
Munich, Germany

**Abstract.** The accurate segmentation of lesions in magnetic resonance images of stroke patients is important, for example, for comparing the location of the lesion with functional areas and for determining the optimal strategy for patient treatment. Manual labeling of each lesion turns out to be time-intensive and costly, making an automated method desirable. Standard approaches for brain parcellation make use of spatial atlases that represent prior information about the spatial distribution of different tissue types and of anatomical structures of interest. Different from healthy tissue, however, the spatial distribution of a stroke lesion varies considerably, limiting the use of such brain image segmentation approaches for stroke lesion analysis, and for integrating brain parcellation with stroke lesion segmentation. We propose to amend the standard atlas-based generative image segmentation model by a spatial atlas of stroke lesion occurrence by making use of information about the vascular territories. As the territories of the major arterial trees often coincide with the location and extensions of large stroke lesions, we use 3D maps of the vascular territories to form patient-specific atlases combined with outlier information from an initial run, following an iterative procedure. We find our approach to perform comparable to (or better than) standard approaches that amend the tissue atlas with a flat lesion prior or that treat lesion as outliers, and to outperform both for large heterogeneous lesions.

**Keywords:** Stroke lesion segmentation · Atlas construction · Prior knowledge · Cerebral vascular territories · Outlier-inlier

## 1 Introduction

The accurate segmentation of anatomical structures and of lesions that are visible in magnetic resonance image (MRI) of stroke patients has been a somewhat

© Springer International Publishing Switzerland 2016
A. Crimi et al. (Eds.): BrainLes 2015, LNCS 9556, pp. 21–32, 2016.
DOI: 10.1007/978-3-319-30858-6_3

neglected topic in the development of automated brain image segmentation algorithms until very recently [1]. Most algorithms for segmenting structures of the brain in MRI use prior knowledge on the location and the appearance of white matter, gray matter, etc. On the one hand, there are discriminative approaches using, for example, random forests together with local image features [2,3], that often have a high accuracy, but that can only be applied to images acquired with the exact same MR imaging sequences as the training data. Generative models, on the other hand, describe the intensity distribution in a more informative and flexible fashion: Seghier et al. [4] proposed a method that constructs a lesion atlas using fuzzy clustering. However, in the clinical workflow often other modalities have to be taken into account. Dalca et al. [5] proposed a method based on the intensity distribution which differentiates between stroke pathologies and leukoaraiosis lesions. However, the stroke segmentation bases only on the intensity model and ignores spatial information according to the cerebral vascular territories [6]. [7] already considered an atlas of vascular territories as a post-processing step in order to give the physician an idea in which territory the lesion might have occurred but so far did not use this information as prior knowledge in a probabilistic inference process. Some approaches consider lesions as clearly distinct outliers of a Gaussian Mixture Model (GMM) whose parameters $\mu$ and $\Sigma$ are optimized by an Expectation-Maximization (EM) algorithm. An early attempt for automated model outlier detection using a GMM was proposed by Leemput et al. [8] for multiple sclerosis lesions which are in most cases rather small and therefore more likely to be homogeneous in their intensity. Probabilistic atlases of healthy tissue classes provide a mapping from location to intensity. However, in particular for extensive stroke lesions this is not the case: lesion and healthy tissue intensities might overlap, leading to an improper separation of those classes.

We propose a fully automated method for stroke lesion segmentation in MR images that is using GMMs as a generative model by taking into account both cerebral vascular territories (CVT) [6] and model outlier information [8]. Similar efforts have been undertaken by [9] for brain tumor segmentation which used pre/post T1-weighted contrast images to calculate a patient-specific lesion prior. By contrast, our method does not require such specific modalities, making it more flexible to available data. Further, [10,11] proposed a latent atlas which is inferred from the given data through an alternating optimization procedure.

In the following we describe the overall model and the resulting iterative approach (Sect. 2), we present experiments (Sect. 3), and offer conclusions (Sect. 4). More specifically, our paper provides as contributions the usage of cerebral vascular territories as additional prior spatial information (Sect. 2.3) for iterative lesion atlas construction (Sect. 2.4).

## 2 Methods

Our overall approach relies on a two-steps procedure: First, the algorithm setting tries to fit a *robust* GMM of the intensity distribution using healthy tissue atlases. It first identifies lesion candidates according to [8]. Then, these *outliers* provide spatial hints used as a separate lesion atlas which makes them *inliers* in a second EM run where they are an additional component of the GMM in a *standard* non-robust EM segmenter. We therefore consider the method an *outlier-inlier* approach. The calculated outlier-atlases are further enhanced by incorporating contextual knowledge using the information of CVT. Territories are weighted proportionally to the number of lesion candidates found in their spatial region. In each EM iteration, this lesion atlas gets optimized until the best model parameters with respect to the likelihood of the data are found. Further postprocessing is applied in the form of Conditional Random Fields and morphological operators to eliminate false positives resulting from the intensity-based estimation. In this paper, we will mainly analyze ischemic stroke lesions since they occur most often in practice, accounting for up to 87 % of all strokes [12]. Those steps are reflected in Fig. 1 where we start with pre-processing as co-registration, bias field correction and skull stripping. Then we perform the model outlier detection followed by a lesion atlas construction. We initialize a standard EM segmentation algorithm with the previously obtained lesion atlas and iterate until the best model parameters are found. In order to further eliminate false positives, we either perform morphological operations or apply conditional random fields (CRF).

## 2.1   Generative Model for Stroke Lesion Segmentation

We first revisit important concepts from [8,13] upon which our method is based. Images are given by maps from a finite $D$-dimensional coordinate space to the intensity space which may be one-dimensional for gray-scale images. We denote MR images as flattened, i.e., 1-dimensional vectors $v = \{v_1, v_2, \ldots, v_N\}$ where $I = \{1, \ldots, N\}$ is the index set of all voxels and $v_i$ is the intensity (as grayvalue) of voxel $i$. The segmentation is described by labels $c = \{c_1, c_2, \ldots, c_N\}$ mapping a voxel to a tissue class, possibly including stroke lesion. For a voxel $i$, $c_i$ indicates to which tissue type it belongs. $C$ is a finite set of tissue classes, e.g., $\{WM, GM, CSF\}$ or $\{WM, GM, CSF, LES\}$. The latent segmentation $l$ has to be inferred from the observed intensities $v$. We optimize the model parameters $\Theta = (\mu_c, \Sigma_c)_{c \in C}$ to find the $\Theta^*$ that yields the maximal likelihood with respect to the data set $v$ using, e.g. the EM algorithm. Recall that the probability density function (PDF) of a GMM with respect to $C$ is given by:

$$p(x) = \sum_{c \in C} \alpha_c \cdot \frac{1}{(\sqrt{2\pi})^D \sqrt{|\Sigma_c|}} \exp(-\tfrac{1}{2}(x - \mu_c)^T \Sigma_c^{-1} (x - \mu_c)) \qquad (1)$$

where $\sum_{c \in C} \alpha_c = 1, \forall c \in C, \alpha_c \geq 0$. The individual Gaussian PDFs corresponding to $c \in C$ are also referred to as *components* or *classes*. Each component $c$ consists of a centroid (or mean) $\mu_c$, a covariance $\Sigma_c$ and a given weight $\alpha_c$. In healthy tissue, we relate each Gaussian component to one major tissue type (WM, GM, CSF) to quantify those compartments in each modality for the multimodal case. The assumption that one Gaussian component models the intensities of one tissue type turns out to work well in practice [14,15]. In our approach, lesions are eventually modeled as an additional component in the GMM.

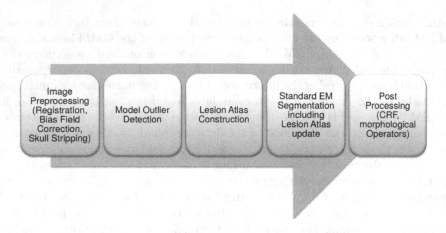

**Fig. 1.** Overview of the segmentation pipeline.

## 2.2 Robust Model Outlier Detection

Standard GMM model parameter optimization assumes that each data point is indeed generated by at least one class. Outliers in the data set are therefore hard to explain by only considering a GMM, in particular, if a point does not seem to fit *any* of the classes. To illustrate this, recall that in GMMs, our goal is to maximize the log-likelihood of the observed data.

$$Q(\Theta) = \sum_{i \in I} \log \left( \sum_{c \in C} p(c) f_c(v_i \mid \Theta) \right), \tag{2}$$

where $p(c)$ denotes the prior probability of component $c$ and $f_c$ refers to the PDF of the component $c$ of the GMM spanned by $\Theta$.

Maximizing (2) with respect to $\Theta$ (for a fixed number of components) is however not robust to outliers as those occurring in lesions [8]. In particular, consider a voxel $i$ with intensity $v_i$ that does not fit well to *any* class $c \in C$. Since a probability distribution $p(c \mid v_i)$ has to normalize to 1, the voxel cannot show small probability for *all* classes at the same time. Consequently, the algorithm has to consider very high covariances to include outliers which severely affects the results. Additionally, outliers having small probabilities strongly negatively influence the likelihood of the model in (2). This can be seen since $\log f_c(x \mid \Theta) \to -\infty$ as $f_c(x \mid \Theta) \to 0$.

This problem is alleviated by means of robust statistics [13]. Instead of fitting standard Gaussian PDFs, a *contaminated* variant is proposed where each data point is either generated by a Gaussian $\mathcal{N}(\mu, \Sigma)$ with probability $1 - \varepsilon$ or by a unknown uniform outlier distribution $\delta$ with probability $\varepsilon$. The density function converges to a standard Gaussian density by setting $\varepsilon = 0$. The question upon seeing $v_i$ is whether it stems from $\mathcal{N}(\mu, \Sigma)$ or from $\delta$. A perfect classification separates data points $v_i$ into a set $G$ of "good" samples drawn from $\mathcal{N}(\mu, \Sigma)$ (*inliers*) and a set $B$ of "bad" samples (*outliers*) originating from $\delta$.

$$G = \{v_i \text{ generated by } \mathcal{N}(\mu, \Sigma) \mid i \in I\} \tag{3}$$

$$B = \{v_j \text{ not generated by } \mathcal{N}(\mu, \Sigma) \mid j \in I\} \tag{4}$$

Since $G$ and $B$ cannot be perfectly restored from the observed data, a practical classification method is needed. Therefore, we want to classify a data point as outlier if it exceeds a certain distance threshold $\kappa$ to the distributions spanned by our model. The distance between a data point $v_i$ and the calculated mean $\mu_c$ of one class $c$ is estimated by the Mahalanobis-Distance

$$d_c^2(x_i) = (x_i - \mu_c)\Sigma_c^{(-1)}(x_i - \mu_c) \tag{5}$$

We classify a voxel as outlier if and only if $d_c(x_i) > \kappa$, leading to the sets $G_\kappa$ and $B_\kappa$; the smaller $\kappa$ the more lesion candidates are detected. Letting $\kappa \to \infty$ results in a standard (outlier-free) EM segmenter [8]:

$$G_\kappa = \{i : \exists c \in C : d_c(v_i) \leq \kappa \mid i \in \{1, \ldots, N\}\} \tag{6}$$

$$B_\kappa = \{j : \forall c \in C : d_c(v_j) > \kappa \mid j \in \{1, \ldots, N\}\} \tag{7}$$

The best values for $\kappa$ are determined experimentally as done in Sect. 3.

## 2.3 Cerebral Vascular Territories

In spite of spatial information given by an atlas, we search for adequate replacements in stroke lesions. It turns out that radiologists use common patterns about cerebral vascular territories (CVT) that specify the area which is covered by one of the main vessel trees to diagnose strokes since the extensions of large stroke lesions often follow the outlines of the territory the blocked artery is feeding [16].

Figure 2 shows the spatial appearance of the three territories which are covered by one of the three main vessel trees. Following [16], we particularly manually label anterior cerebral artery (ACA), posterior cerebral artery (PCA) and middle cerebral artery (MCA) territories for our evaluation. A recent study on 2213 patients [17] has shown that the majority of stroke lesions appear in the MCA territory. Incidentally, large and heterogeneous lesions tend to occur in this particular territory.

## 2.4 Construction of the Personalized Lesion Atlas

Based on estimated model outliers and the 3D CVT atlas we construct a new patient-specific lesion prior (see Fig. 2c). We assume the set of outliers $B_\kappa$ to be determined by the first EM run using only healthy tissue classes. Suppose $I = \{1, \ldots, N\}$ let $v : I \to [0, 1]$ be an image mapping voxel indices to MR intensity values (we write $v_i$ for the intensity at voxel $i$) and $\mathcal{V}$ be the set of all images. The lesion atlas is a particular image $l \in \mathcal{V}$ where $l_i$ can be interpreted as proportional to the probability of $i$ being part of a lesion. We write $t \in T = \{ACA, MCA, \ldots\}$ for a vascular *territory*. Each vascular territory is characterized by its included voxels $I_t \subseteq I$ (see Fig. 2a).

For each vascular territory $t$, we estimate an atlas by setting voxels in $I_t \cap B_\kappa$ to 1 and smoothing this image. Formally, we first obtain images $v^{(t)} : I \to [0, 1]$

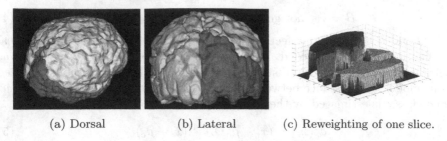

(a) Dorsal          (b) Lateral          (c) Reweighting of one slice.

**Fig. 2.** Cerebral vascular territories drawn in 3D with ITKSNAP from a 2D template depicted by [6]. Yellow denotes MCA, turquoise ACA and violet PCA for the right hemisphere. The left hemisphere was labeled equivalently (Color figure online).

by setting $v^{(t)}(i) = 1$ if $i \in I_t \cap B_\kappa$ and 0 otherwise. We smooth this image using a Gaussian filter in 3D. We denote the smoothed image as $\tilde{v}^{(t)} = smooth(v^{(t)})$. Then, we estimate a normalized *voting* coefficient proportional to the probability of the lesion occurring in $t$ by

$$vCoeff_t = \frac{\sum_{i \in I_t} \tilde{v}^{(t)}(i)}{|B_\kappa|} \qquad (8)$$

Finally, we obtain the *voted* territory by

$$v^{(t)}(i) = v^{(t)}(i) \cdot vCoeff_t \qquad (9)$$

Each territory consequently gets reweighted as can be seen in Fig. 2c. The overall lesion atlas used for the second EM-run is finally obtained by the image $\hat{l}(i) \in \mathcal{V}$, defined by

$$\hat{l}(i) = \prod_{t \in T} \hat{v}^{(t)}(i) \qquad (10)$$

to achieve a multiplicative, smoothing effect in bordering regions. Care has to be taken if for a voxel $i$, either of $\hat{v}^{(t)}(i)$ is 0, effectively erasing all other values. We avoid this problem by substituting 0 by 1 in $\hat{l}(i)$ temporarily and replacing these artificially inserted ones by zeros later on. Figure 2c shows the main approach we used to construct the lesion prior out of the cerebral vascular territory atlas. An important detail is to label left and right hemispheres individually, according to their perfusion pattern. Otherwise, e.g., the large MCA region (including weak false positives) is weighted disproportionally high.

## 3   Results

We applied our stroke lesion segmentation framework onto 13 different patient datasets with 152 manually annotated ground truth slices (axial, coronal and sagittal) including a variety of stroke types and shapes. Stroke lesions are characterized as T1 hypo-, T1gad hyper-, T2 hyper-, and FLAIR hyper-intense.

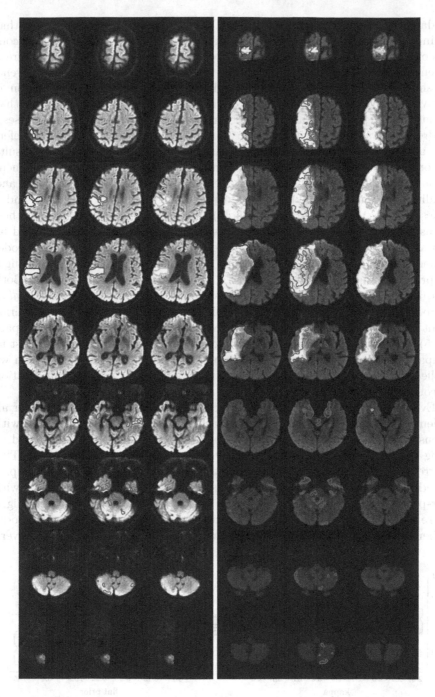

**Fig. 3.** Qualitative Comparison of the manual ground truth segmentation (blue line), Model Outlier Detection (red line) and our proposed method (green line) presented for FLAIR MRI of patient 1 (left) and 13 (right) using morphological operators as post-processing (Color figure online).

All datasets where co-registered onto a T1-weighted reference image such that the input images are aligned with the tissue atlases. Each patient dataset consists of T1-weighted, T1-Gadolinium, T2-weighted, and FLAIR MRI scans from patients in the sub-acute phase, acquired about one or two day after the event. We show FLAIR in the qualitative analysis because in FLAIR the lesion is best visible. We drew the CVT atlas with ITK-SNAP [18]. To make sure that the atlas is aligned with all the other images (i.e., MRI images and atlases), we drew the vascular territories onto the above-mentioned T1-weighted reference image. We first did a quantitative assessment of the segmentation results by computing the dice score [19] (also known as F1-score for binary segmentation) with different post-processing techniques (morphological operator and Conditional Random Fields) and parameter settings (different flat priors and $\kappa$ values($= kappa$) for the outlier threshold). We decided to evaluate our method against other approaches on the same patient datasets since the dice should be seen as a relative rather than an absolute measure. Figure 4 depicts the model outlier detection with different $\kappa$ settings. It performs clearly better than using a flat prior for a dedicated lesion class in Fig. 5 after morphological operators. Both Figs. 6 and 7 illustrate the performance of different $\kappa$ settings on the *outlier-inlier* approach. It became clear that simply adding an additional class with a flat prior is not competitive to Model Outlier Detection or CVT-Outlier-Inlier (compare Fig. 5). Furthermore, with the best setting we applied a paired student t-test to compare those methods statistically. In order to obtain a valid comparison we applied all the methods on the same datasets and used the best configuration we could obtain from them.

Even though the Model Outlier Detection works better *on average* over all patients, we could show that our approach performs better on patients with extensive lesions at a significance level of $\alpha = 0.005$ since it is considered as being very significant, i.e., very unlikely to be a result of a random effect. This subgroup of patients was selected prior to the evaluation. All results are presented in Table 1 the first row without post-processing, and the other rows with post-processing. Qualitative results from patient 1 and 13 are shown in Fig. 3 where we can observe that with CVTs we get less outliers compared to model outlier detection. Admittedly, the CVT-based approach has difficulties with very

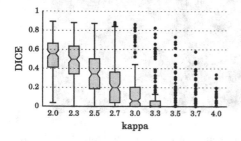

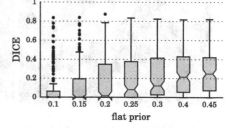

**Fig. 4.** Model outlier detection with morphological operators as post-processing.

**Fig. 5.** Lesion class with flat prior with morphological operators as post-processing.

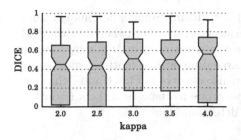

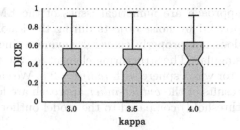

**Fig. 6.** CVT Outlier-inlier with morphological operators.

**Fig. 7.** CVT Outlier-inlier with CRF as post-processing.

small lesions (e.g., patient 5, 8, or 11) where model outlier detection is more robust but it provides much more confidence with large lesions (e.g., patient 13 or 7). When nearly the whole area of one main tissue compartments is covered by stroke, it can happen that the lesion intensities are explained by a (larger) healthy tissue compartment and not identified as lesion. This happens since the EM algorithm is agnostic about symmetric assignments of classes to intensities after initialization with given tissue atlas. Intuitively, class, say, 5 (initially representing outlier intensities) may "swap" positions with class 4 that represented white matter. The reason for the high variance of the dice in the *outlier-inlier*

**Table 1.** Patient dice scores for different segmentation algorithms with different post-processing approaches. Bold-faced numbers indicate cases with the best score for each patient.

| Pat. id | CVT no post | MO morph. | CVT morph. | MO CRF | CVT CRF |
|---|---|---|---|---|---|
| Patient 1 | 0.57 | 0.54 | **0.61** | 0.55 | 0.51 |
| Patient 2 | 0.21 | 0.62 | 0.67 | **0.72** | 0.64 |
| Patient 3 | 0.26 | **0.41** | 0.37 | 0.19 | 0.34 |
| Patient 4 | 0.36 | 0.47 | **0.5** | 0.35 | 0.42 |
| Patient 5 | 0.05 | **0.39** | 0.01 | 0.3 | 0.0 |
| Patient 6 | 0.28 | 0.61 | 0.62 | **0.65** | 0.4 |
| Patient 7 | 0.4 | 0.51 | **0.72** | 0.46 | 0.62 |
| Patient 8 | 0.23 | **0.51** | 0.0 | 0.1 | 0.0 |
| Patient 9 | 0.32 | 0.53 | **0.56** | 0.08 | 0.42 |
| Patient 10 | 0.0 | **0.19** | 0.06 | 0.13 | 0.01 |
| Patient 11 | 0.03 | **0.57** | 0.01 | 0.43 | 0.0 |
| Patient 12 | 0.31 | **0.6** | 0.5 | 0.4 | 0.44 |
| Patient 13 | **0.87** | 0.62 | 0.81 | 0.42 | 0.77 |
| Average | 0.3 | 0.51 | 0.42 | 0.37 | 0.35 |
| Stdev | 0.23 | 0.12 | 0.29 | 0.2 | 0.26 |

approach are numerical issues of the EM algorithm. Smaller lesions get suppressed by noise objects during the lesion atlas update and therefore the EM does not properly converge anymore since the covariance matrix may become singular. The structuring element for the three-dimensional morphological operator was a sphere with *radius* = 2.5. We can also observe in Figs. 6 and 7 that the results of the *outlier-inlier* approach are less prone to changes of the $\kappa$ (=outlier threshold) compared to the model outlier detection alone.

## 4   Conclusion

We investigated an automated method for stroke lesion segmentation that could prove to be useful, e.g., in the analysis of images acquired in clinical studies. Our method extends previous work in model outlier detection for lesions, first applied to multiple sclerosis patients using a GMM. Using robust statistics, outliers can be detected and classified as lesion. However, for large and heterogeneous lesions this is not enough, as a lesion spans a spectrum of intensity values which can better be captured by a dedicated Gaussian component in the mixture model. Drawing inspiration from the way radiologists perform stroke detection, we incorporated knowledge about cerebral vascular territories that is combined with outlier information to form a lesion atlas. This lesion atlas is then reweighted proportionally to the incurred outliers of each territory in each iteration until maximum likelihood model parameters are found. Several approaches to construct this atlas were examined and compared to a flat prior as a baseline.

Our evaluation showed that the outlier-inlier approach on average performs comparable to the model outlier detection for an overall set of 13 patients and significantly better than a uniform prior for a lesion class. The performance was enhanced by the postprocessing methods: conditional random fields and morphological operators. Considering large stroke lesion patients alone, our method dominates the other approaches evaluated in this paper.

In future work, we consider additional features and disease patterns to improve segmentation. One way would to substitute the EM-Algorithm optimizing a GMM by maximum likelihood estimation with an approximate Bayesian inference framework. For instance, we could employ the expectation propagation and the clutter problem by [20] or enhance the re-weighting scheme for patient-specific lesion atlas in a more advanced manner in order to improve the segmentation results. Another possible improvement would be to model each tissue compartment with more than one Gaussian.

## References

1. Rekik, I., Allassonnire, S., Carpenter, T.K., Wardlaw, J.M.: Medical image analysis methods in MR/CT-imaged acute-subacute ischemic stroke lesion: segmentation, prediction and insights into dynamic evolution simulation models a critical appraisal. NeuroImage Clin. **1**(1), 164–178 (2012)

2. Maier, O., Wilms, M., von der Gablentz, J., Krmer, U.M., Mnte, T.F.: Extra tree forests for sub-acute ischemic stroke lesion segmentation in MRI sequences. J. Neurosci. Methods **240**, 89–100 (2015)
3. Mitra, J., Bourgeat, P., Fripp, J., Ghose, S., Rose, S., Salvado, O., Connelly, A., Campbell, B., Palmer, S., Sharma, G., Christensen, S., Carey, L.: Lesion segmentation from multimodal mri using random forest following ischemic stroke. NeuroImage **98**, 324–335 (2014)
4. Seghier, M.L., Ramlackhansingh, A., Crinion, J., Leff, A.P., Price, C.J.: Lesion identification using unified segmentation-normalisation models and fuzzy clustering. NeuroImage **41**, 1253–1266 (2008)
5. Dalca, A., Sridharan, R., Cloonan, L., Fitzpatrick, K., Kanakis, A., Furie, K., Rosand, J., Wu, O., Sabuncu, M., Rost, N., Golland, P.: Segmentation of cerebrovascular pathologies in stroke patients with spatial and shape priors. Med. Image Comput. Comput. Assist Interv. **17**, 773–780 (2014)
6. Savoiardo, M.: The vascular territories of the carotid and vertebrobasilar systems. Diagrams based on CT studies of infarcts. Ital. J. Neurol. Sci. **7**, 405–409 (1986)
7. Kabir, Y., Dojat, M., Scherrer, B., Garbay, C., Forbes, F.: Multimodal MRI segmentation of ischemic stroke lesions. In: 29th Annual International Conference of the IEEE Engineering in Medicine and Biology Society (EMBS 2007), pp. 1595–1598. IEEE (2007)
8. Leemput, K.V., Maes, F., Vandermeulen, D., Colchester, A.C.F., Suetens, P.: Automated segmentation of multiple sclerosis lesions by model outlier detection. IEEE Trans. Med. Imaging **20**, 677–688 (2001)
9. Moon, N., Bullitt, E., Van Leemput, K., Gerig, G.: Automatic brain and tumor segmentation. In: Dohi, T., Kikinis, R. (eds.) MICCAI 2002, Part I. LNCS, vol. 2488, pp. 372–379. Springer, Heidelberg (2002)
10. Riklin-Raviv, T., Van Leemput, K., Menze, B.H., Wells, W.M., Golland, P.: Segmentation of image ensembles via latent atlases. Med. Image Anal. **14**, 654–665 (2010)
11. Menze, B.H., van Leemput, K., Lashkari, D., Weber, M.-A., Ayache, N., Golland, P.: A generative model for brain tumor segmentation in multi-modal images. In: Jiang, T., Navab, N., Pluim, J.P.W., Viergever, M.A. (eds.) MICCAI 2010, Part II. LNCS, vol. 6362, pp. 151–159. Springer, Heidelberg (2010)
12. American Stroke Association: Ischemic strokes (clots) (2015). http://www.strokeassociation.org/STROKEORG/AboutStroke/TypesofStroke/IschemicClots/Ischemic-Strokes-Clots_UCM_310939_Article.jsp. Accessed 28 March 2015
13. Zhuang, S., Huang, Y., Palaniappan, K., Zhao, Y.: Gaussian mixture density modeling, decomposition, and applications. IEEE Trans. Image Process. **5**, 1293–1302 (1996)
14. Greenspan, H., Ruf, A., Goldberger, J.: Constrained gaussian mixture model framework for automatic segmentation of MR brain images. IEEE Trans. Image Process. **25**, 1233–1245 (2006)
15. Van Leemput, K., Maes, F., Vandermeulen, D., Suetens, P.: Automated model-based tissue classification of MR images of the brain. IEEE Trans. Image Process. **18**, 897–908 (1999)
16. Damasio, H.: A computed tomographic guide to the identification of cerebral vascular territories. Arch. Neurol. **40**, 138–142 (1983)
17. Ng, Y.S., Stein, J., Ning, M., Black-Schaffer, R.M.: Comparison of clinical characteristics and functional outcomes of ischemic stroke in different vascular territories. Stroke **38**, 2309–2314 (2007)

18. Yushkevich, P.A., Piven, J., Hazlett, H.C., Smith, R.G., Ho, S., Gee, J.C., Gerig, G.: User-guided 3D active contour segmentation of anatomical structures: significantly improved efficiency and reliability. Neuroimage **31**, 1116–1128 (2006)
19. Sørensen, T.: A method of establishing groups of equal amplitude in plant sociology based on similarity of species and its application to analyses of the vegetation on danish commons. Biol. Skr. **5**, 1–34 (1948)
20. Minka, T.P.: Expectation propagation for approximate bayesian inference. In: Proceedings of the Seventeenth Conference on Uncertainty in Artificial Intelligence, pp. 362–369. Morgan Kaufmann Publishers Inc. (2001)

# Fiber Tracking in Traumatic Brain Injury: Comparison of 9 Tractography Algorithms

Emily L. Dennis[1](✉), Gautam Prasad[1], Madelaine Daianu[1],
Liang Zhan[1], Talin Babikian[2], Claudia Kernan[2], Richard Mink[3],
Christopher Babbitt[4], Jeffrey Johnson[5], Christopher C. Giza[6],
Robert F. Asarnow[2,7], and Paul M. Thompson[1,2,8]

[1] Imaging Genetics Center, Keck USC School of Medicine,
Marina del Rey, CA, USA
emily.dennis@ini.usc.edu
[2] Department of Psychiatry and Biobehavioral Sciences, Semel Institute for
Neuroscience and Human Behavior, UCLA, Los Angeles, CA, USA
[3] Department of Pediatrics, Harbor-UCLA Medical Center and Los Angeles
BioMedical Research Institute, Torrance, CA, USA
[4] Miller Children's Hospital, Long Beach, CA, USA
[5] Department of Pediatrics, LAC+USC Medical Center, Los Angeles, CA, USA
[6] UCLA Brain Injury Research Center, Department of Neurosurgery and
Division of Pediatric Neurology, Mattel Children's Hospital,
Los Angeles, CA, USA
[7] Department of Psychology, UCLA, Los Angeles, CA, USA
[8] Departments of Neurology, Pediatrics, Psychiatry, Radiology, Engineering,
and Ophthalmology, USC, Los Angeles, USA

**Abstract.** Traumatic brain injury (TBI) can cause widespread and long-lasting damage to white matter. Diffusion weighted imaging methods are uniquely sensitive to this disruption. Even so, traumatic injury often disrupts brain morphology as well, complicating the analysis of brain integrity and connectivity, which are typically evaluated with tractography methods optimized for analyzing normal healthy brains. To understand which fiber tracking methods show promise for analysis of TBI, we tested 9 different tractography algorithms for their classification accuracy and their ability to identify vulnerable areas as candidates for longitudinal follow-up in pediatric TBI participants and matched controls. Deterministic tractography models yielded the highest classification accuracies, but their limitations in areas of extensive fiber crossing suggested that they generated poor candidates for longitudinal follow-up. Probabilistic methods, including a method based on the Hough transform, yielded slightly lower accuracy, but generated follow-up candidate connections more coherent with the known neuropathology of TBI.

## 1 Introduction

Traumatic brain injury (TBI) can cause extensive white matter (WM) damage that can be long-lasting and far reaching in its associated impairments. Diffuse axonal injury (DAI) is partly responsible, and is frequently detected in the corpus callosum, brain

© Springer International Publishing Switzerland 2016
A. Crimi et al. (Eds.): BrainLes 2015, LNCS 9556, pp. 33–44, 2016.
DOI: 10.1007/978-3-319-30858-6_4

stem, gray-white matter junctions, and the parasagittal white matter. DAI can only be definitively diagnosed *post mortem*, but diffusion-weighted imaging (DWI) shows considerable potential in detecting these disruptions in the living brain. While histology and tract tracing certainly offer more accurate information in studying brain injury, MRI (magnetic resonance imaging) sequences offer non-invasive methods for assessing brain injury in humans.

Disruptions in WM integrity associated with TBI are typically observable on DTI as decreased FA (fractional anisotropy) and increased MD (mean diffusivity), suggesting myelin disruption [1]. We previously examined this dataset using tract-based measures of WM integrity extracted with autoMATE (automated multi-atlas tract extraction) [2, 3], finding widespread differences in MD and RD [4]. We recently found that combining HARDI measures with measures of interhemispheric transfer time from EEG resulted in improved prediction of cognitive function [5]. Additionally, we have experimented with other processing parameters, examining fiber turning angle. We found trends towards more significant group differences detected when more stringent turning angles were used in tractography [6]. These FA "dropouts" can make advanced analyses such as tractography difficult, as tract-propagation methods may stop in regions where the fractional anisotropy is abnormally low; some methods even use a threshold on FA to limit fiber propagation. As tractography algorithms vary in the equations and models they use reconstruct tracts, they may also vary in their success in tracking fibers through disrupted regions. Such limitations are vital to understand, as fibers that appear to differ in a TBI patient may either be overtly lost, or just not detected due to interactions between the algorithm used and diffusion signal changes associated with TBI. To investigate how different fiber tracking methods perform on scans from children with TBI, we tested 9 different tractography algorithms to see how sensitive the resulting connectivity matrices were in differentiating between our groups. These 9 algorithms were selected as they have previously been evaluated by our group, so we have other results to compare ours to in the event that one algorithm consistently demonstrates superior performance [7, 8].

In the developing brain, TBI is especially disruptive. In animal studies, TBI during development can decrease experience-dependent plasticity - a key process for brain maturation and development [9]. Given the long course of WM development and maturation, TBI during development can delay or alter the maturation of WM tracts. Even today, little is known about how TBI affects developing brains, what course recovery may follow, and what interventions may assist in the process. Some children experience a full, speedy recovery, while others continue to be affected by the injury years later. Injury severity accounts for a large portion of this variance in outcome, but a considerable amount is still unexplained. We expect that neuroimaging biomarkers hold the key to explaining more of the variance and improving outcome predictions. Developing the most sensitive biomarkers to cover the range of disruption is a challenge. In this paper we focus on tractography algorithms that most successfully distinguish between TBI and control children more than a year post-injury.

# 2 Methods

## 2.1 Subjects and Image Acquisition

TBI participants were recruited from 4 Pediatric Intensive Care Units (PICUs) at Level 1 Trauma Centers in Los Angeles County. Healthy controls, matched for age, sex, and educational level, were recruited from the community through flyers, magazines, and school postings. Participants were studied in the chronic phase (13–19 months post-injury). We included 17 TBI participants (3 female) and 17 controls, in a "yoked" control design (individually matched for age and sex). *Inclusion criteria*: non penetrating moderate-severe TBI (intake or post-resuscitation GCS score between 3 and 12), 8–19 years old, right handed, normal vision, English proficiency. *Exclusion criteria*: history of neurological illness or injury, motor deficits or metal implant preventing safe MRI scanning, history of psychosis, ADHD, Tourette's, learning disability, mental retardation, autism, or substance abuse. Participants with large space-occupying lesions were not included in analyses.

Participants were scanned with 3T MRI (Siemens Trio) with whole-brain anatomical and 72-gradient diffusion imaging. Diffusion-weighted images (DWI) were acquired with these acquisition parameters: GRAPPA mode; acceleration factor PE = 2; TR/TE = 9500/87 ms; FOV = 256 × 256 mm; isotropic voxel size = 2 mm. 72 images were collected per subject: 8 $b_0$ and 64 diffusion-weighted images ($b$ = 1000 s/mm$^2$).

## 2.2 Data Preprocessing and Cortical Extraction

Non-brain regions were automatically removed from a b0 image from the DWI volume using the *bet* function in the FSL toolbox (http://fsl.fmrib.ox.ac.uk). Brainsuite was used for the T1-weighted images (http://brainsuite.org); these brain extractions were refined by a neuroanatomical expert. All T1-weighted scans were linearly aligned to a common template using 9 DOF registration. DWI volumes were corrected for eddy current distortion using FSL's *eddy correct* function. Averaged $b_0$ maps were elastically registered to the structural scan using a mutual information cost function to compensate for EPI-induced susceptibility artifacts. The transformation matrix from the linear alignment of the mean $b_0$ to the T1-weighted volume was applied to each of the 64 gradient directions to reorient them. Based on the eddy-corrected DWIs, whole brain tractography was conducted using 9 different deterministic and probabilistic tracking algorithms. Elastic deformations obtained from the EPI distortion correction were applied to the tracts' 3D coordinates for accurate alignment. Very short fibers (<10 mm) and duplicate fibers were filtered out.

34 cortical labels per hemisphere [10] were automatically extracted from aligned T1-weighted structural MRI scans using FreeSurfer version 5 (http://surfer.nmr.mgh. harvard.edu/), aligned to the T1-weighted images, and downsampled using nearest neighbor interpolation to the space of the DWIs. To ensure tracts would intersect cortical label boundaries, labels were dilated with an isotropic box kernel of width 5 voxels. We created nine 68 × 68 connectivity matrices for each subject using each separate tractography method (listed below). Each element of the matrix described the

number of fibers that intersected each pair of cortical labels or regions of interest (ROIs). We also created a separate set of connectivity matrices normalized by the total number of fibers reconstructed, and matrices that were both count-normalized and normalized by the ROI volume (the sum of the volumes of the two terminal ROIs). Of course, other normalization methods are possible, but these were selected as among the most commonly used.

## 2.3 Tractography

We tested nine different tractography methods, including four tensor-based deterministic algorithms: FACT [11], 2nd order Runge-Kutta (RK) [12], streamline (SL) [13], and tensorline (TL) [14], and two deterministic tractography algorithms based on the 4th-order spherical harmonic derived orientation distribution functions (ODFs)–FACT and RK. We also tested the Hough voting method [15], which is based on ODFs represented by 4th order spherical harmonics, and the Probabilistic Index of Connectivity (PICo) [16], based on ODFs represented by 6th order spherical harmonics. For the Hough method, tract reconstruction was constrained to 10,000 fibers.

The six deterministic methods were run with Diffusion Toolkit (http://trackvis.org/ dtk/). Fiber tracking was restricted to regions with fractional anisotropy (FA) $\geq 0.2$ to avoid gray matter and cerebrospinal fluid; fiber paths were stopped if the fiber direction encountered a sharp turn (with a critical angle threshold $\geq 30°$). Recent reports suggest that fiber angles as sharp as 90° may be biologically plausible [17], but such a large threshold can also allow for large numbers of false positive fibers.

The Hough method was performed as described previously [15]. Voxels with an FA $\geq 0.2$ were probabilistically seeded, and 10,000 fibers were reconstructed. PICo was conducted with Camino (http://cmic.cs.ucl.ac.uk/camino/). For PICo, voxels with FA $\geq 0.2$ were seeded, and ODFs were estimated using 6th-order spherical harmonics and a maximum of 3 non-redundant local ODF maxima were detected. The fiber turning angle threshold was set to 30°/voxel, and tracing was stopped at any voxels with an FA $< 0.2$. *Probtrackx* was performed after *Bedpostx* [18]. Up to 3 fibers were modeled per voxel. *Probtrackx* was run on all voxels with FA $> 0.2$. *Probtrackx* repeatedly samples from the voxel-wise principal diffusion direction calculated in *Bedpostx*, creating a new streamline at each iteration, building a distribution on the likely tract location and path. 1000 iterations were chosen to ensure convergence of the Markov chains, from which the posterior distributions of the local estimate of the fiber orientation distribution were sampled.

## 2.4 Support Vector Machine (SVM) Classifier

SVMs [19] are one popular form of supervised learning model that we used to classify our connectivity features, to differentiate connectivity patterns in TBI and normal development. Clearly other machine learning models are possible, but here we chose SVMs as their properties are well-understood. SVMs classify 2-class data by training a model, or classification function, to find the optimal hyperplane between the 2 classes in the data. Let $x_i \in \mathbb{R}^d$ represent the connectivity feature vectors, where $d$ is the dimension of the feature set of interest and $Y_i = \pm$ be their label with $-1$ and $1$ representing TBI and control. Our target hyperplane is:

$$\langle w, x \rangle + b = 0,$$

where $w \in \mathbb{R}^d$ should separate as many data points as possible. We find this hyperplane by solving the L2-norm problem:

$$\arg\min_{w,b,v} \left( \frac{1}{2} \langle w, w \rangle + D \sum_i v_i^2 \right),$$

such that

$$y_i(\langle w, x_i \rangle + b) \geq 1 - v_i, \qquad v_i \geq 0$$

where $v_i$ are slack variables and $D$ is a penalty parameter. In many instances, a hyperplane cannot be found that completely separates the 2 classes of data, and slack variables are added to create soft margins to separate most of the points.

Our classification design was to test the information provided by the connectivity features with repeated stratified 10-fold cross-validation [20]. We repeated the cross-validation 10 times. Each repeat represents a different random grouping of dataset for 10-fold cross-validation. For cross-validation, our performance metric was accuracy (number of correctly identified subjects divided by the total number of subjects).

For each classifier, we also ranked the features by their relationship to the hyperplane [21]. The ranking was computed by sorting in decreasing order the $|w|$ values from the hyperplane. Features with high values contribute the most to the decision boundary between the classes. In our experiments, we fit the SVM model to the entire dataset to compute the rankings. These rankings indicate which network measure or what element of a connectivity matrix is most important to the classifier in the context of all others in a feature set.

We used the linear SVM implementation in scikit-learn 0.16.1 with the default parameters. These have been suggested to work well in a wide array of problems, but it may have been possible to boost the accuracies we computed in this work by optimizing these parameters using a nested cross-validation on the training data to improve the performance of the classifier. Because the connectivity matrices are symmetric, we converted the lower triangular part of each matrix (including the diagonal as it provides useful information about each ROI) to a feature vector in the classifier to avoid including redundant data.

## 3 Results

### 3.1 Comparing Tractography Algorithm Outputs

We first compared the outputs of the different tractography algorithms, in terms of the average and maximum tract length reconstructed across the TBI and control groups.

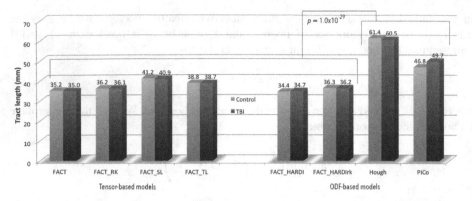

**Fig. 1.** The average (in mm) reconstructed across tractography algorithms for the TBI and control groups. This information was not available for *Probtrackx*. There was significant difference between average tract lengths of the probabilistic and deterministic methods ($p = 1.0 \times 10^{-29}$).

This was done to understand effects attributable to any bias in the ability to track fibers in the TBI group versus controls. Any method displaying a significant group difference in ability to track might be useful in classification analyses, although the meaning of the group difference would unclear, as it would be confounded by an interaction between tracking accuracy and diagnosis. We evaluated tract length (rather than tract numbers) as FA drop out is a known problem in TBI, which could presumably lead to shorter tracts in TBI if the tracking was disrupted. Results of these evaluations are shown in Fig. 1. This information was not available for *Probtrackx*, because it outputs voxels rather than points along a curve. Interestingly, there was no detectable difference between groups in the average or maximum tract lengths across any of the tractography algorithms. As expected, the probabilistic models were more successful in reconstructing long fibers, as evidenced by significantly longer average tract lengths in both groups for the Hough and PICo models, which are both probabilistic ($p = 1.0 \times 10^{-29}$). Hough outputs will have a longer average, as it is limited to 10,000 fibers.

### 3.2 SVM Accuracy of Connectivity Matrices

To rank the tractography algorithms, we compared the accuracies of the SVM associated with the matrices. Results are shown in Fig. 2. These chart the average accuracy and standard deviation across the 10 repeats of the 10 fold cross-validation. The connectivity matrices that had been normalized for total fiber count and for ROI volume had significantly higher classification accuracy ($p = 0.033$). Among the tensor-based models, FACT-SL and FACT-TL had the highest classification accuracy. Among the ODF-based models, FACT-HARDI and FACT-HARDIrk had the highest accuracy.

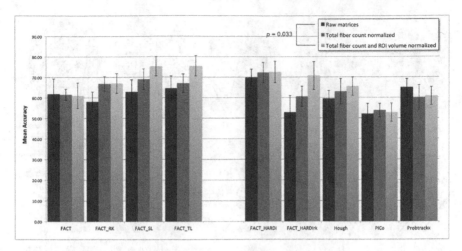

**Fig. 2.** SVM classification accuracy across the 4 tensor-based models, 4 ODF-based models, and 1 ball-and-stick model. Accuracy of the raw matrices, fiber count norm. Matrices, and count and ROI-volume norm. Matrices are shown. Accuracy (above columns) is the mean accuracy across 10-fold cross validation, repeated 10 times. One-way ANOVA found significant differences between raw matrix accuracy and count- and volume-normalized matrix accuracy (Color figure online).

### 3.3   Most Robust Elements in Connectivity Matrix

After determining the accuracy of the different tractography algorithms, we further investigated which connections contributed most to the classification. Figure 3 displays the connections that ranked in the top 1 % of classification weights (of the non-zero matrix elements) across all 9 tractography models. These results reveal an important pattern in our results. While many of the FACT algorithms ranked well in accuracy, the connections contributing most to this differentiation do not necessarily fit with prior knowledge on the expected neuropathology of TBI. The connections with the highest classification weight for the Hough method, PICo, and *Probtrackx*, on the other hand, include long anterior-posterior connections, and those that involve the corpus callosum. These are the pathways that are most consistently implicated in post mortem ultra-structural evidence of DAI in TBI.

### 3.4   Group Differences

As classification weights can be noisy, we examined our data in several other ways. We ran linear regressions comparing TBI and control, including age and sex as covariates. We corrected for multiple comparisons using FDR ($q < 0.05$). We did not find any significant group differences in matrix elements across any of the algorithms tested. With only 34 participants, we believe this is a power issue. Heterogeneity is a issue in TBI, which means that group differences need to outweigh the considerable within group variance for significant differences to arise.

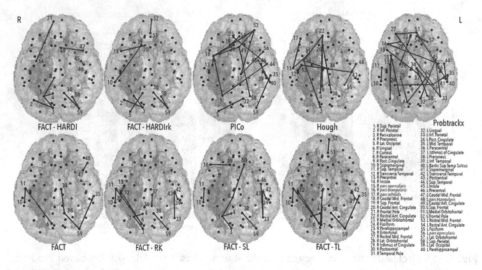

**Fig. 3.** Connections with highest classification weight across 9 tractography algorithms. The top 1 % of connections (of non-zero matrix elements) are shown in *blue*, with all ROIs indicated by black spheres. Left in the image is right in brain. Count- and vol.-norm. matrices were used (Color figure online).

### 3.5    Reliability Between Algorithms

We also examined the reliability between algorithms, focusing on cross-hemispheric connections as the corpus callosum is so vulnerable in TBI. Specifically we wanted to see whether the FACT algorithms failed to detect differences in cross-hemispheric connections, or failed to reconstruct them altogether. Focusing on connections that appeared in at least 95 % of subjects, the vast majority of interhemispheric connections we examined were only found by one method. Only 4 interhemispheric connections were detected by all methods. Probtrackx reconstructed the most interhemispheric connections, followed by Camino and Hough.

## 4    Discussion

TBI causes widespread damage to WM integrity, but there has been little comparison of fiber tracking methods that may be used to examine this damage. Here we compared 9 tractography algorithms, testing which methods best separated TBI patients from controls. Several of the deterministic tractography algorithms performed very well in terms of classification accuracy, but the neuropathology of TBI needs to be considered when selecting candidate tracts as targets for longitudinal analysis. There is considerable heterogeneity in outcome following TBI, much of it unexplained. Tracking the integrity of these vulnerable areas may help clinicians identify those individuals who would benefit from additional intervention.

Unlike degenerative brain disorders such as Alzheimer's disease and its prodromal state MCI (mild cognitive impairment), where classification aids greatly in understanding the gradual progression of disease, there is little uncertainty as to whether an individual has suffered a moderate or severe TBI. The primary usefulness of this work with TBI is instead identifying reliable methods to detect areas of disruption to follow longitudinally. The corpus callosum (CC) is the most commonly reported area of disruption [22], but deterministic methods often give poor reconstructions in areas of crossing fibers. Such fiber crossing is extensive where the projections of the CC body intersect with the corticospinal tract, cingulum, and inferior fronto-occipital fasciculus. Visual inspection of the tracts revealed that tract dropoff was indeed a significant problem in the CC across all 6 deterministic models, for both TBI and controls. Prior studies show some disruption in tract projections in the parietal and occipital lobes, which is perhaps what the deterministic methods are detecting. Even so, disruption in the CC tends to be more pronounced [4–6], found using autoMATE (automated multi-atlas tract extraction) [2–6]. Hough tractography should be more robust to lesions than eigenvector propagation methods as it minimizes a curvilinear integral through the data, so it should traverse lesions rather than stop. All tractography methods have weaknesses, and some are more problematic in TBI than others. From a purely classification point of view, those that fail more in TBI might have better classification accuracy but would prove less useful in developing biomarkers. Classification in itself is not the point, finding biologically meaningful, statistically reliably biomarkers is.

Long anterior-posterior tracts such as the cingulum, superior longitudinal fasciculus, and inferior fronto-occipital fasciculus also tend to be disrupted in TBI. The deterministic methods we evaluated scored higher in classification accuracy, but probabilistic methods, such as Hough, identified regions that are already consistently implicated in the TBI literature, perhaps making them better targets for longitudinal study. The highest classification weights for the Hough method are shown in Fig. 4. This figure displays the connections with the top classification weights, terminal ROIs, and underlying fibers. We also must acknowledge that there are varied outcomes in TBI, and heterogeneity in injury severity, type, location, and a range of other mitigating factors. This heterogeneity undoubtedly affected our results. Through our inclusion/exclusion criteria, and only including patients in a circumscribed post-injury window (13–19 months), we have minimized some sources of heterogeneity, but others persist and cannot be controlled for in a study of this size.

Our classifier was based on the fiber density of these connections (meaning the number of detected fibers that intersect each pair of regions), normalized by the total fiber count and the total ROI volume. Prior studies report long-lasting differences in FA and MD [23], so weighting the connectivity matrices using these diffusivity measures as well, may increase classification accuracy. Also, we used a linear SVM classifier. Non-linear SVM methods would likely lead to higher accuracy. A larger sample size would also almost certainly improve our results. As this is an on-going study, this is a question we will continue to investigate.

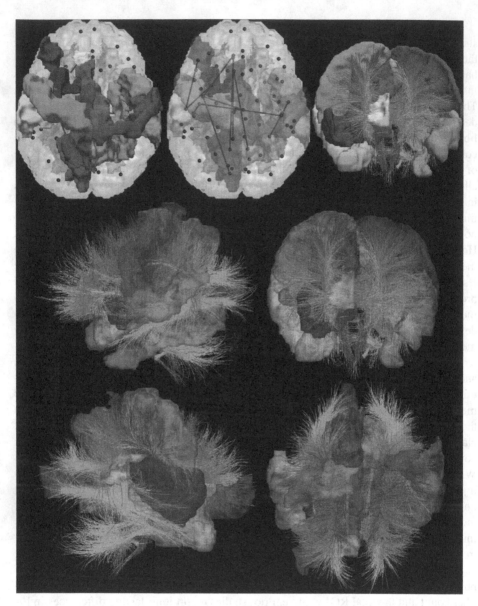

**Fig. 4.** *Top left* – Highest classification-weighted connections from Hough tractography algorithm, with corresponding region labels overlaid. *Top right and bottom two rows* – Hough tractography with region labels overlaid. Only those regions that were endpoints for high classification weight connections for the Hough method are shown.

# 5  Conclusion

We compared 9 tractography algorithms, first for their ability to distinguish pediatric TBI patients from matched controls but secondly, and more importantly, to identify connections that show group differences, to study longitudinally. The deterministic methods we tested yielded higher classification accuracies generally, but suffered from a limited ability to track the projections of the corpus callosum, a prime area of disturbance in TBI. The Hough transform probabilistic method had slightly lower classification accuracy, but for the classification it relied most strongly on connections that are consistent with our understanding of the neuropathology of TBI – which consistently implicates cross-hemispheric and long anterior-posterior connections. The success of the probabilistic models in identifying several known areas of disruption indicate that probabilistic tractography may be beneficial in analyses of TBI.

**Acknowledgements.** This study was supported by the NICHDS (R01 HD061504). ELD, YJ, and PT are also supported by NIH grants to PT: U54 EB020403, R01 EB008432, R01 AG040060, and R01 NS080655. CCG is supported by the UCLA BIRC, NS027544, NS05489, Child Neurology Foundation, and the Jonathan Drown Foundation. Scanning was supported by the Staglin IMHRO Center for Cognitive Neuroscience. We gratefully acknowledge the contributions of Alma Martinez and Alma Ramirez in assisting with participant recruitment and study coordination. Finally, the authors thank the participants and their families for contributing their time to this study.

# References

1. Xu, J., Rasmussen, I.-A., Lagopoulos, J., Håberg, A.: Diffuse axonal injury in severe traumatic brain injury visualized using high-resolution diffusion tensor imaging. J. Neurotrauma **24**, 753–765 (2007)
2. Jin, Y., Shi, Y., Zhan, L., Gutman, B., de Zubicaray, G.I., McMahon, K.L., Wright, M.J., Toga, A.W., Thompson, P.M.: Automatic clustering of white matter fibers in brain diffusion MRI with an application to genetics. NeuroImage **100**, 75–90 (2014)
3. Jin, Y., Shi, Y., Zhan, L., de Zubicaray, G.I., McMahon, K.L., Martin, N.G., Wright, M.J., Thompson, P.M.: Labeling white matter tracts in HARDI by fusing multiple tract atlases with applications to genetics. In: 10th Proceedings of the IEEE International Symposium Biomed Imaging, pp. 512–515 (2013)
4. Dennis, E.L., Jin, Y., Villalon-Reina, J., Zhan, L., Kernan, C., Babikian, T., Mink, R., Babbitt, C., Johnson, J., Giza, C.C.: White matter disruption in moderate/severe pediatric traumatic brain injury: advanced tract-based analyses. NeuroImage: Clinical **7**, 493–505 (2015)
5. Dennis, E.L., Ellis, M.U., Marion, S.D., Jin, Y., Kernan, C., Babikian, T., Mink, R., Babbitt, C., Johnson, J., Giza, C.C., Thompson, P.M., Asarnow, R.F.: Callosal function in pediatric traumatic brain injury linked to disrupted white matter integrity. J. Neurosci. **35**, 10202–10211 (2015)
6. Dennis, E.L., Jin, Y., Kernan, C.L., Babikian, T., Mink, R., Babbitt, C., Johnson, J., Giza, C.C., Asarnow, R.F., Thompson, P.M.: White matter integrity in traumatic brain injury: effects of permissible fiber turning angle. In: 12th Proceedings IEEE International Symposium Biomed Imaging, pp. 930–933 (2015)

7. Zhan, L., Zhou, J., Wang, Y., Jin, Y., Jahanshad, N., Prasad, G., Nir, T.M., Leonardo, C.D., Ye, J., Thompson, P.M., for The Alzheimer's Disease Neuroimaging, I.: Comparison of nine tractography algorithms for detecting abnormal structural brain networks in Alzheimer's disease. Front. Aging Neurosci. **7**, 48 (2015)

8. Zhan, L., Jahanshad, N., Jin, Y., Toga, A.W., McMahon, K.L., de Zubicaray, G., Martin, N. G., Wright, M.J., Thompson, P.M.: Brain network efficiency and topology depend on the fiber tracking method: 11 tractography algorithms compared in 536 subjects. In: 10th Proceedings of the IEEE International Symposium Biomed Imaging, pp. 1134–1137 (2013)

9. Giza, C.C., Maria, N.S., Hovda, D.A.: N-methyl-D-aspartate receptor subunit changes after traumatic injury to the developing brain. J. Neurotrauma **23**, 950–961 (2006)

10. Desikan, R.S., Ségonne, F., Fischl, B., Quinn, B.T., Dickerson, B.C., Blacker, D., Buckner, R.L., Dale, A.M., Maguire, R.P., Hyman, B.T., Albert, M.S., Killiany, R.J.: An automated labeling system for subdividing the human cerebral cortex on MRI scans into gyral based regions of interest. NeuroImage **31**, 968–980 (2006)

11. Mori, S., Crain, B.J., Chacko, V.P., van Zijl, P.C.M.: Three-dimensional tracking of axonal projections in the brain by magnetic resonance imaging. Ann. Neurol. **5**, 1–23 (1999)

12. Basser, P.J., Mattiello, J., LeBihan, D.: MR diffusion tensor spectroscopy and imaging. Biophys. J. **66**, 259–267 (1994)

13. Conturo, T.E., Lori, N.F., Cull, T.S., Akbudak, E., Snyder, A.Z., Shimony, J.S., McKinstry, R.C., Burton, H., Raichle, M.E.: Tracking neuronal fiber pathways in the living human brain. Proc. Nat. Acad. Sci. U.S.A. **96**, 10422–10427 (1999)

14. Lazar, M., Weinstein, D.M., Tsuruda, J.S., Hasan, K.M., Arfanakis, K., Meyerand, M.E., Badie, B., Rowley, H.A., Haughton, V., Field, A.: White matter tractography using diffusion tensor deflection. Hum. Brain Mapp. **18**, 306–321 (2003)

15. Aganj, I., Lenglet, C., Jahanshad, N., Yacoub, E., Harel, N., Thompson, P.M., Sapiro, G.: A Hough transform global probabilistic approach to multiple-subject diffusion MRI tractography. Med. Image Anal. **15**, 414–425 (2011)

16. Parker, G.J., Haroon, H.A., Wheeler-Kingshott, C.A.: A framework for a streamline-based probabilistic index of connectivity (PICo) using a structural interpretation of MRI diffusion measurements. J. Magn. Reson. Imaging **18**, 242–254 (2003)

17. Wedeen, V.J., Rosene, D.L., Wang, R., Dai, G., Mortazavi, F., Hagmann, P., Kaas, J.H., Tseng, W.Y.: The geometric structure of the brain fiber pathways. Science **335**, 1628–1634 (2012)

18. Basser, P.J., Pajevic, S., Pierpaoli, C., Duda, J., Aldroubi, A.: In vivo fiber tractography using DT-MRI data. Magn. Reson. Med. **44**, 625–632 (2000)

19. Cortes, C., Vapnik, V.: Support-vector networks. Mach. Learn. **20**, 273–297 (1995)

20. Kohavi, R.: A study of cross-validation and bootstrap for accuracy estimation and model selection. IJCAI **14**, 1137–1145 (1995)

21. De Martino, F., Valente, G., Staeren, N., Ashburner, J., Goebel, R., Formisano, E.: Combining multivariate voxel selection and support vector machines for mapping and classification of fMRI spatial patterns. NeuroImage **43**, 44–58 (2008)

22. Hulkower, M.B., Poliak, D.B., Rosenbaum, S.B., Zimmerman, M.E., Lipton, M.L.: A decade of DTI in traumatic brain injury: 10 years and 100 articles later. AJNR **34**, 2064–2074 (2013)

23. Wilde, E.A., Ayoub, K.W., Bigler, E.D., Chu, Z.D., Hunter, J.V., Wu, T.C., McCauley, S. R., Levin, H.S.: Diffusion tensor imaging in moderate-to-severe pediatric traumatic brain injury: changes within an 18 month post-injury interval. Brain Imaging Behav. **6**, 404–416 (2012)

# Combining Unsupervised and Supervised Methods for Lesion Segmentation

Tim Jerman(✉), Alfiia Galimzianova, Franjo Pernuš,
Boštjan Likar, and Žiga Špiclin

Laboratory of Imaging Technologies, Faculty of Electrical Engineering,
University of Ljubljana, Tržaška 25, 1000 Ljubljana, Slovenia
tim.jerman@fe.uni-lj.si

**Abstract.** White-matter lesions are associated to several diseases, which can be characterized by neuroimaging biomarkers through lesion segmentation in MR images. We present a novel automated lesion segmentation method consisting of an unsupervised mixture model based extraction of candidate lesion voxels, which are subsequently classified by a random decision forest (RDF) using simple visual features like multi-sequence MR intensities sourced from connected voxel neighborhoods. The candidate lesion extraction prior to RDF training and classification balanced the number of non-lesion and lesion voxels and the number of non-lesion classes versus a lesion class. Thereby, the RDF established highly discriminating decision rules based on such simple visual features, which have the benefit of no computational overhead and easy extraction from the MR images. On MR images of 18 patients with multiple sclerosis the proposed method achieved the median Dice similarity of 0.73, sensitivity of 0.90 and positive predictive value of 0.61, which indicate accurate segmentation of white-matter lesions.

**Keywords:** White-matter lesion · Random decision forest · Segmentation

## 1 Introduction

Neuroimaging biomarkers are early and thus important surrogates of clinical signs in a number of neurological and cerebrovascular diseases, and mental disorders. To reduce a high socio-economic impact of these diseases, development of the biomarkers is very important as it enables early disease characterization, monitoring and prompt treatment optimization. However, extraction of the biomarkers requires accurate and reliable *in vivo* quantification of normal and pathological brain structures, usually from magnetic resonance (MR) images. In multiple sclerosis (MS) patients, for instance, inflammatory lesions in brain parenchyma are visible in T2-weighted and FLAIR MR sequences. To obtain MS biomarkers such as lesion volume, count and location, accurate segmentation of these lesions in brain MR images is required.

© Springer International Publishing Switzerland 2016
A. Crimi et al. (Eds.): BrainLes 2015, LNCS 9556, pp. 45–56, 2016.
DOI: 10.1007/978-3-319-30858-6_5

Segmentation of MS lesions can be performed manually, however, this task is time-consuming and subjective and, thus, the obtained segmentations are generally not reliable enough for biomarker extraction. On the other hand, automated segmentation of brain MR images is challenging because of MR acquisition imperfections (MR bias field and image noise), patient-to-patient variations of rather complex brain anatomy and varying manifestation of pathology. For these reasons none of the current methods can yet be considered a standard method [3], and the development of accurate, reliable and efficient automated lesion segmentation remains an open challenge [14].

In a recent review [3] the methods for lesion segmentation in brain MR images were classified into unsupervised and supervised. Most unsupervised methods are based on the estimation of a generative model of multi-sequence MR (msMR) intensity distributions (e.g. of T1w, T2w and FLAIR), but may also use combined intensity-space distributions [4]. The generative model is designed to capture the intensity distribution of the normal brain structures, while the voxels with msMR intensities that deviate far from the estimated model are considered as lesions. While using a simple generative model like Gaussian mixture with one component per major normal brain structure may not sufficiently capture typical variations of the msMR intensity distributions, more complex generative models are very difficult to accurately estimate [16]. An atlas based unsupervised method was developed by Shiee et al. [10] that first performs a rigid registration of topological and statistical brain atlases to the msMR images. The atlases are employed in an interleaved fuzzy segmentation and fast marching based extraction of topologically consistent normal brain regions and lesions. The method jointly identifies the white-matter (WM) and lesions. Lesions are further distinguished from the WM based on their fuzzy class membership and intensity centroid and a rather complex structure relationship model, which was introduced to reduce false positives at the boundary of gray-matter (GM) and WM tissues and between WM and the ventricles. While the unsupervised methods are somewhat effective at accounting for heterogeneity of normal structures, their main limitation is the lack of capacity to account for the large heterogeneity of the visual appearance and location of lesions.

Supervised methods aim to directly account for the heterogeneity of lesion appearance and location by learning a set of optimal visual features and discriminative classifiers based on training msMR images with manual lesion segmentations. Most supervised methods compute a rich set of visual features on the training images and then prune the set in the process of learning the discriminative classifiers like $k$ nearest neighbors [11], random decision forest (RDF) [5], logistic regression model [12], etc. Interestingly, simple low-level visual features such as raw msMR intensities have so far been rarely used as the only features for training the discriminative classifiers, possibly due to rather large intensity variations within and across brain structures and lesions and across different MR image datasets. Supervised methods often employ high-level visual features like labels or priors of co-registered brain atlas [15], morphologic properties of candidate lesion regions and sagittal brain symmetry [5], aggregative intensity, shape and location [1], etc. Aside from the atlas based features, however, most high-level features are computed from low-level features like the msMR intensities. The selection and means of computing the high-level features is based on the understanding of the lesion classification, which is subjective. Hence, besides the added computational overhead of computing the high-level features, these may discard important information contained in the low-level features that is needed for accurate discrimination of lesions from the other structures.

In this paper, we propose a combined unsupervised and supervised method for WM lesion segmentation. Unsupervised method was based on a generative model of major brain structures and model-outlier driven extraction of candidate lesion voxels, in which the number of non-lesion and lesion voxels and the number of non-lesion classes versus a lesion class are more balanced compared to considering all voxels. This was important for a subsequently applied supervised method based on RDF, which employed simple visual features in the form of low-level msMR intensities sourced from connected voxel neighborhoods of the candidate lesion voxels. Retrospective analysis of the trained RDF showed that the balancing of the number of voxels and classes by the unsupervised method enabled the RDF to establish highly discriminating decision rules based on such simple visual features. On msMR images of 18 patients with MS, the proposed method achieved the median Dice similarity of 0.73, sensitivity of 0.90 and positive predictive value of 0.61, which indicate accurate segmentation of WM lesions.

## 2   Methods

Lesion segmentation is obtained by consecutively executing an unsupervised and supervised method on preprocessed msMR images, which comprise T1-weighted (T1w), T2-weighted (T2w), and fluid attenuated inversion recovery (FLAIR) sequences. Preprocessing that was performed on each dataset consisted of brain mask extraction on T1w image [6], intra-subject affine registration of the three MR sequences [7], and followed by N4 intensity inhomogeneity correction on masked MR sequences [13] and per sequence intensity normalization by matching the quartile positions of intensity histogram of a masked MR sequence to the mean quartile positions obtained across multiple MR datasets [9]. Prior to segmentation, the MR images were resampled to $1\,mm^3$ isotropic resolution.

In overview, the proposed lesion segmentation approach first applies the unsupervised method based on three-component Gaussian mixture modeling and FAST-TLE [8], which extract the candidate lesion voxels $S_{CL}$ from the msMR images. Next, an RDF based supervised method, trained on $S_{CL}$ of training image datasets and employing low-level msMR intensities in connected voxel neighborhoods, further distinguishes the $S_{CL}$ of a test image into true and false positive lesion voxels. In the following, the unsupervised step for the extraction of candidate lesion voxels, computation of visual features and the supervised RDF based step are described in more detail.

## 2.1  Unsupervised Extraction of Candidate Lesion Voxels

For each voxel $\mathbf{x} \in \mathbb{R}^3$ in registered T1w, T2w, and FLAIR MR images 3-vectors $I(\mathbf{x}) = \{I_{T1w}(\mathbf{x}), I_{T2w}(\mathbf{x}), I_{FLAIR}(\mathbf{x})\}$ was formed. The distribution of $I(\mathbf{x}) : \mathbf{x} \in \mathcal{S}$, where $\mathcal{S}$ is a brain mask [6], was modeled by a three-component Gaussian mixture, which represented three major normal-appearing brain structures, i.e. cerebrospinal fluid (CSF), GM and WM. By registering the MNI atlas to T1w image, the atlas priors of CSF, GM and WM structures were used to initialize the corresponding weights, means and covariances of the Gaussian mixture components. The final mixture parameters were obtained using the FAST-TLE [8] with an outlier trimming fraction set to 0.1. Then, a set of candidate lesion voxels $\mathcal{S}_{CL}$ was formed from voxels, which had the FLAIR intensity higher than the mean GM intensity, estimated on the FLAIR sequence. In this way, the number of voxels $|\mathcal{S}_{CL}|$ for further classification was reduced approximately by a factor of five compared to $|\mathcal{S}|$ with a small trade-off in overall sensitivity to actual lesion voxels (cf. Fig. 1b, c).

## 2.2  Visual Features for RDF

For each candidate lesion voxel $\mathbf{x}_c \in \mathcal{S}_{CL}$ an ensemble of visual features $\phi(\mathbf{x}_c)$ was extracted from $I(\mathbf{x})$ in a 3D neighborhood $\mathcal{N}(\mathbf{x}_c, N)$, in which the central voxel $\mathbf{x}_c$ was enclosed by $(2N+1) \times (2N+1) \times (2N+1)$ cubic neighborhood (Fig. 1d). Ensemble of visual features for point $\mathbf{x}_c$ was obtained as:

$$\phi(\mathbf{x}_c, N) = \{I_i(\mathbf{x}) : \mathbf{x} \in \mathcal{N}(\mathbf{x}_c, N); i = \text{T1w}, \text{T2w}, \text{FLAIR}\}, \tag{1}$$

which comprises all the msMR intensity values contained in $\mathcal{N}(\mathbf{x}_c, N)$. For later analysis of feature influence the neighborhood $\mathcal{N}(\mathbf{x}_c, N)$ was decomposed into non-overlapping layers $\mathcal{L}(\mathbf{x}_c, L)$; $L = 0, \ldots, N$ (Fig. 1e). For instance, $\mathcal{N}(\mathbf{x}_c, 2)$ was decomposed into three non-overlapping layers $\mathcal{L}(\mathbf{x}_c, 0)$, $\mathcal{L}(\mathbf{x}_c, 1)$ and $\mathcal{L}(\mathbf{x}_c, 2)$. Analogously to (1), the ensemble of visual features in a layer $L$ was obtained as $\phi_L(\mathbf{x}_c, L) = \{I_i(\mathbf{x}) : \mathbf{x} \in \mathcal{L}(\mathbf{x}_c, L); i = \text{T1w}, \text{T2w}, \text{FLAIR}\}$.

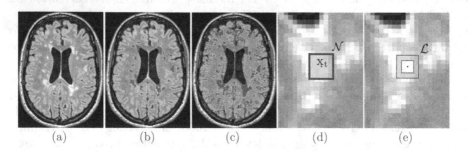

$$\begin{array}{ccccc} \text{(a)} & \text{(b)} & \text{(c)} & \text{(d)} & \text{(e)} \end{array}$$

**Fig. 1.** (a) FLAIR image with (b) reference segmentation $\mathcal{S}_{REF}$ (*red*) and (c) the estimated volume of interest $\mathcal{S}_{CL}$ (*blue*). (d) A $5 \times 5 \times 5$ neighborhood $\mathcal{N}(\mathbf{x}_c, 2)$ around the voxel $\mathbf{x}_c \in \mathcal{S}_{CL}$. (e) The second layer of $\mathcal{N}(\mathbf{x}_c, 2$ denoted as $\mathcal{L}(\mathbf{x}_c, 2)$.

## 2.3  RDF Based Lesion Classification

The RDF used for classification was trained on $M$ msMR images $I_m(\mathbf{x})$; $m = 1,$ $\ldots, M$, for which reference lesion segmentation $\mathcal{S}_{REF}$ was available (Fig. 1b). A set of true positives (TP) $\mathcal{S}_{TP}$ and a set of false positive (FP) $\mathcal{S}_{FP}$ lesion voxels were created for training the RDF. The set $\mathcal{S}_{TP}$ contained those points $\mathbf{x}_c \in \mathcal{S}_{CL}$, which were also part of $\mathcal{S}_{REF}$ (Fig. 1b). The set of FPs was selected such that $\mathcal{S}_{FP} = \{\mathbf{x} : \mathbf{x} \notin \mathcal{S}_{TP} \wedge \mathbf{x} \in \mathcal{S}_{CL}\}$. To balance the cardinality $|\cdot|$ of the two point sets, the points in smaller of the two sets $\mathcal{S}_{TP}$ and $\mathcal{S}_{FP}$ were randomly multiplicated such that $|\mathcal{S}_{TP}| \approx |\mathcal{S}_{FP}|$.

The visual features for training the RDF were computed as $\phi(\mathbf{x}_c)$. Corresponding class indicator variable $c(\mathbf{x}_c) \in \{\text{TP}, \text{FP}\}$ was set according to the reference segmentation $\mathcal{S}_{REF}$. The RDF had $T$ independent decision trees $\Psi_t$; $t = 1, \ldots, T$ of depth $D$ and, to determine optimal node splits for each tree, was trained by maximizing information gain [2]. The number of points in the training sets $\mathcal{S}_{TP}$ and $\mathcal{S}_{FP}$ that reach a certain leaf were used to compute the posterior probabilities $p_t(c(\mathbf{x}_c)|\phi(\mathbf{x}_c))$ at each leaf in the $t$-th tree.

A trained RDF was used to classify candidate lesion voxels in $\mathcal{S}_{CL}$ as extracted by the unsupervised method. For each $\mathbf{x}_c \in \mathcal{S}_{CL}$ the ensemble of visual features $\phi(\mathbf{x}_j)$ was computed, then the posterior probabilities over $T$ trained trees were evaluated by the RDF and, finally, averaged so as to obtain the final posterior probability map $\mathcal{P}(\mathbf{x}_c)$:

$$\mathcal{P}(\mathbf{x}_c) = \frac{1}{T} \sum_{t=1}^{T} p_t(c(\mathbf{x}_c) = \text{TP}|\phi(\mathbf{x}_c)), \tag{2}$$

Classification into non-lesion or lesion was obtained by thresholding $\mathcal{P}(\mathbf{x}_c)$ by $\tau_L \in [0, 1]$. The set of voxels classified as lesion was $\mathcal{S}_L = \{\mathbf{x} : \mathcal{P}(\mathbf{x}) > \tau_L \wedge \mathbf{x} \in \mathcal{S}_{CL}\}$.

# 3  Experiments and Results

## 3.1  MR Datasets and Ground Truth

For the purpose of evaluating the lesion segmentation method a cohort of 18 patients with MS were imaged on a 3T Siemens Magnetom Trio MR system at the University Medical Centre Ljubljana (UMCL). All 18 subjects have given written informed consent at the time of enrollment for imaging. The authors have obtained approval from the UMCL to use the data. The authors confirm that the data was analyzed anonymously.

Each patient dataset consisted of brain MR images with multi-slice axial T1w and T2w (3 mm slice thickness), and a 3D FLAIR sequence (1 mm$^3$ isotropic). Reference lesion segmentations were created manually by two neuroradiologists, who could observe in side-by-side view the T1w, T2w and FLAIR registered in the 1 mm$^3$ isotropic space of the FLAIR images. The neuroradiologists then merged and jointly revised the merged segmentations to obtain final consensus reference segmentations, which were used to evaluate the lesion segmentation methods. The range of lesion volume computed from the reference segmentations varied from 4.1 to 55.9 ml across all datasets.

## 3.2  Experiments

The supervised RDF method was evaluated using three-fold cross-validation: 18 datasets were randomly split into three groups of six images, the RDF train-test process was repeated three times, each time using two different groups of total 12 datasets for training and the remaining group of 6 datasets for testing. The RDF was trained using $T = 20$ trees with a depth of $D = 10$ with the T1w, T2w and FLAIR intensities, which were sourced from connected voxel neighborhoods. To analyze the impact of different voxel neighborhoods of size $N$ on lesion segmentation, the neighborhood sizes $N = 0, 1, 2$ were tested. Further, for neighborhood size $N = 1$, we performed three additional experiments to test the impact of using only the intensities of FLAIR or the intensities of a pair of sequences ({T1w, FLAIR} and {T2w, FLAIR}) compared to using all three sequences ({T1w, T2w, FLAIR}).

Performance of the proposed lesion segmentation was evaluated on all 18 datasets by computing Dice similarity coefficient (DSC), sensitivity as true positive rate (TPR) and positive predictive value (PPV) between the reference and lesion segmentations, obtained by thresholding the average posterior probability maps $\mathcal{P}(\mathbf{x}_j)$ with $\tau_L = 0.5$. For comparison we also evaluated on all 18 datasets the state-of-the-art unsupervised topology-preserving anatomical segmentation method (LTOADS) [10].

The impact of particular feature on the RDF based lesion classification was analyzed across layers $\mathcal{L}(\mathbf{x}_c, L); L = 0, \ldots, N$ and across MR sequences by observing the frequency of feature $\phi_L(\mathbf{x}_c, L); L = 0, \ldots, N$ selection across tree nodes in the RDF. The obtained frequency was normalized according to the highest frequency across layers or sequences.

## 3.3  Results

Results of evaluation of the lesion segmentation methods are given in Table 1. Figure 2 shows box-whisker plots of the DSC values computed for the visual features in connected voxel neighborhoods of sizes $N = 0, 1, 2$. Using voxel intensities ($N = 0$) gives similar DSC values compared to the unsupervised LTOADS method. Compared to $N = 0$, the use of msMR intensities of the $3 \times 3 \times 3$ connected voxel neighborhood ($N = 1$) as visual features significantly increased the DSC. Further increasing $N$ to 2 only slightly increased the DSC value.

The proposed method had a very low DSC in one case, in which lesion load was the lowest. This case contained a number of small regions of high FLAIR intensity in the GM that were erroneously classified as lesions by the proposed method. Consequently, a high number of false positive lesion voxels and the low number of true positive lesion voxels resulted in a low DSC value.

**Table 1.** Median values of DSC, TPR and PPV computed across 18 test datasets. FLAIR was abbreviated as F.

| Metric | Unsupervised | | Supervised, {T1w,T2w,F} | | | Supervised, $N = 1$ | | |
|---|---|---|---|---|---|---|---|---|
| | LTOADS | $\mathcal{S}_{CL}$ | $N = 0$ | $N = 1$ | $N = 2$ | {F} | {T1w,F} | {T2w,F} |
| DSC | 0.63 | 0.15 | 0.57 | 0.71 | 0.73 | 0.68 | 0.70 | 0.69 |
| TPR | 0.48 | 0.92 | 0.85 | 0.91 | 0.90 | 0.89 | 0.90 | 0.90 |
| PPV | 0.88 | 0.08 | 0.44 | 0.59 | 0.61 | 0.57 | 0.58 | 0.58 |

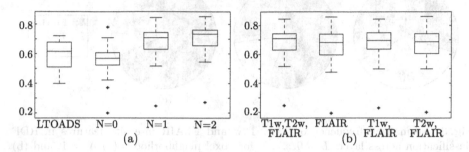

**Fig. 2.** Box-whisker plots of DSC values for (a) LTOADS method [10] and the proposed method tested with three connected voxel neighborhood sizes ($N = 0, 1, 2$), and (b) the proposed method ($N = 1$) based on intensity features of different MR sequences.

Figure 2b shows box-whisker plots of the DSC values computed using features sourced from various sets of MR sequences and a $3 \times 3 \times 3$ connected voxel neighborhood ($N = 1$). Compared to Fig. 2a the selection of the neighborhood size has a greater impact on the DSC values compared to the selection of MR sequences. Using less than all the three sequences only slightly decreased the DSC values, but increased the variability of DSC values observed across the 18 datasets. Though not shown here, the DSC values obtained without the use of FLAIR sequence were significantly worse. This was expected, since the intensities of FLAIR were generally the most frequent visual feature employed in RDF classification in any of the tested sequence sets containing FLAIR, but also because the lesions are most clearly depicted in FLAIR and thus neuroradiologists mainly relied on FLAIR to create the reference segmentations.

Figure 3 shows the normalized frequency of visual features $\phi(\mathbf{x}_c)$ in RDF for each of the two or three layers $\mathcal{L}$ (Fig. 3a and b, respectively) and per sequence, from which the intensities were sourced (Fig. 3c–e). Features from the zeroth layer $L = 0$ (i.e. central voxel) were most frequently used in RDF classification, while features in the second layer $L = 2$ did not contribute much to classification. Increasing the connected voxel neighborhood $N$ from 0 to 2 (cf. Fig. 3c, e) noticeably changed the balance between the normalized feature selection frequencies across sequences. While all sequences equally contributed to the lesion classification with $N = 0$, the normalized frequency of FLAIR features generally increased with larger $N$.

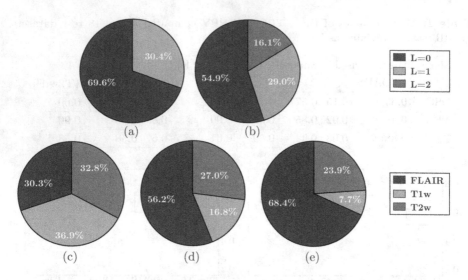

**Fig. 3.** Normalized frequency of T1w, T2w and FLAIR intensity features in RDF classification across layers $L = 0, \ldots, N$ for voxel neighborhoods (a) $N = 1$, and (b) $N = 2$ and sequences for voxel neighborhoods (c) $N = 0$, (d) $N = 1$, and (e) $N = 2$.

Figure 4 shows the contribution of each visual feature $\phi(\mathbf{x}_c)$ in the $5 \times 5 \times 5$ ($N = 2$) connected voxel neighborhood to the classification of lesion candidates $\mathcal{S}_{CL}$. As features are propagated through the RDF during classification, the number of tree nodes that selected a particular feature type (e.g. intensity of T1w, T2w, FLAIR from $L = 0, 1, 2$) was accumulated across all trees for each voxel in the brain mask. As observed in Fig. 3, FLAIR features were used more frequently than the T1w and T2w features. In the zeroth layer $L = 0$, the FLAIR and T2w features were mainly used to detect the lesions (TPs), while FLAIR was also frequently used to distinguish FPs at WM-GM tissue interface. The T1w intensity in $L = 0$ was rarely used, however, interestingly, the intensity from the first layer $L = 1$ of T1w was frequently used to eliminate FPs at WM-GM tissue interface. In all the layers $L = 0, 1, 2$ the T1w sequence was sometimes used to resolve FPs due to dirty appearing WM, as observed between the two lesions posterior to the left ventricle (Fig. 4).

Figure 5 shows the obtained lesion segmentations for LTOADS and the proposed method based on RDF features sourced from three different connected voxel neighborhood sizes ($N = 0, 1, 2$), with the reference segmentation superimposed onto the FLAIR sequence. Using $N = 0$ resulted in more FPs compared to using a larger $N$, while there was little or no visual difference between lesion segmentations obtained with $N = 1$ and $N = 2$. This is also reflected in minor changes of evaluation metrics between $N = 1$ and $N = 2$ in Table 1. Compared to the proposed method, LTOADS segmentations have less false detections, however, they have quite a substantial amount of non detected lesions.

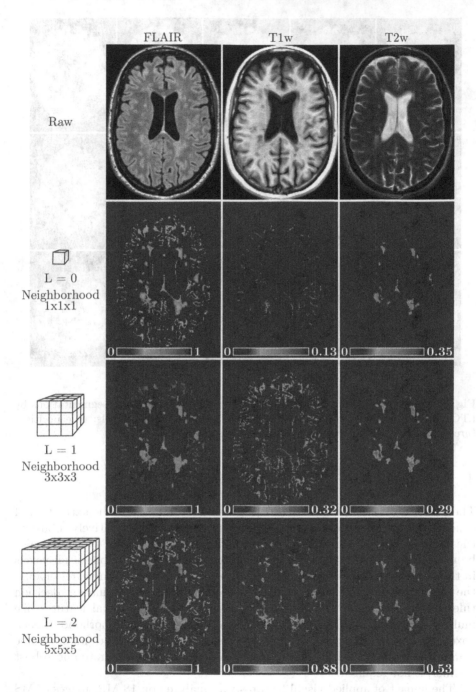

**Fig. 4.** Normalized frequency of visual features across sequences (T1w, T2w, FLAIR) and connected voxel neighborhood layers ($L = 0, 1, 2$) with respect to the voxel location. Reference lesion segmentation is superimposed (*red*) onto the FLAIR image.

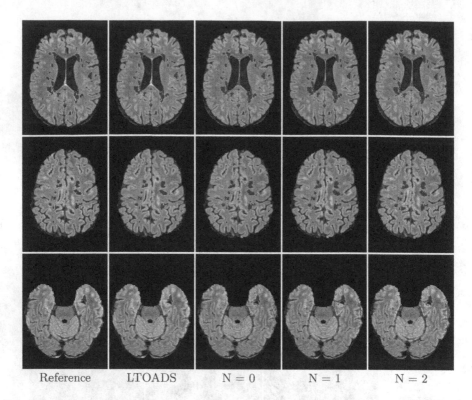

Reference     LTOADS      $N = 0$      $N = 1$      $N = 2$

**Fig. 5.** Axial cross-sections of the reference and the obtained lesion segmentations by LTOADS [10] and the proposed method for $N = 0, 1, 2$. Color labels: true positives (*green*), false positives (*red*), and false negatives (*blue*).

## 4   Discussion

The advantage of the proposed lesion segmentation method is the extraction of candidate lesion voxels using an unsupervised step, which is relatively robust to the heterogeneity of MR intensity of normal brain structures and which may also be used to compensate these variations. Compared to the number of all voxels in the image, the obtained relatively small set of candidate lesion voxels enables the supervised method based on RDF to learn highly discriminating decision rules during the training phase based on simple low-level visual features like multi-sequence MR intensities sourced from a connected neighborhood of each voxel. Hence, the extraction of high-level features, which, besides adding some computational overhead, is often difficult to perform in an accurate and robust manner, is not required.

The impact of applied visual features was analyzed on 18 MR images of MS patients, which contained lesions in the WM, so as to determine the optimal size of the connected voxel neighborhood as a trade-off between the discriminative power of added features and their number used in RDF training and execution.

Namely, a high number of features might not be feasible in view of increased computational and storage complexity. Performance of lesion segmentation for differently sized connected voxel neighborhoods was evaluated using three quantitative metrics: DSC, TPR, and PPV. The median values of all three metrics (Fig. 2, Table 1) increased significantly by using the $3 \times 3 \times 3$ connected neighborhood ($N = 1$), as compared to using central voxel only ($N = 0$), in the ensemble of visual features. Furthermore, increasing $N$ to 2 only slightly increased the median values of metrics, however, the gain was rather small compared to the added number of features. A similar comparison between different sets of MR sequences showed only a marginal change in metrics if, compared to FLAIR, either the T1w or T2w or both were used for classification. As long as FLAIR is used for lesion classification in the RDF, the choice of the set of MR sequences has a much lower impact on the final lesion segmentation performance than the size of connected voxel neighborhood.

A detailed analysis of the contribution of each feature to classification performance of the RDF (Figs. 3 and 4) showed a high influence of FLAIR intensity features irrespective of the neighborhood size, layer or voxel location. Conversely, T2w intensity features were used only to classify voxels belonging to the lesions in reference segmentation, and T1w was used to classify lesion borders and to resolve FPs at major tissue interfaces like WM-GM. An analogy can be drawn to the manual segmentations, where a neurologist mainly relied on the FLAIR sequence to perform lesion segmentation.

A combination of unsupervised and supervised methods can improve segmentation of white-matter lesions, wherein the former reduces the training set of visual features used later in the latter and thus improves its discriminative power for lesion classification. Further, simple visual features from connected voxel neighborhoods present no computational overhead and are easy to extract from the MR images.

**Acknowledgments.** This research was supported by the Slovenian Research Agency under grants J2-5473, L2-5472, and J7-6781. The authors would also like to acknowledge Aleš Koren and Matej Lukin from the University Medical Centre Ljubljana for creating the reference segmentations.

# References

1. Akselrod-Ballin, A., Galun, M., Gomori, J.M., Filippi, M., Valsasina, P., Basri, R., Brandt, A.: Automatic segmentation and classification of multiple sclerosis in multichannel MRI. IEEE Trans. Biomed. Eng. **56**(10), 2461–2469 (2009)
2. Criminisi, A., Shotton, J. (eds.): Decision Forests for Computer Vision and Medical Image Analysis. Springer, London (2013)
3. García-Lorenzo, D., Francis, S., Narayanan, S., Arnold, D.L., Collins, D.L.: Review of automatic segmentation methods of multiple sclerosis white matter lesions on conventional magnetic resonance imaging. Med. Image Anal. **17**(1), 1–18 (2013)

4. García-Lorenzo, D., Prima, S., Collins, L., Arnold, D.L., Morrissey, S.P., Barillot, C.: Combining robust expectation maximization and mean shift algorithms for multiple sclerosis brain segmentation. In: Proceedings of MICCAI Workshop on Medical Image Analysis on Multiple Sclerosis (MIAMS 2008), pp. 82–91 (2008)
5. Geremia, E., Clatz, O., Menze, B.H., Konukoglu, E., Criminisi, A., Ayache, N.: Spatial decision forests for MS lesion segmentation in multi-channel magnetic resonance images. NeuroImage 57(2), 378–390 (2011)
6. Iglesias, J., Liu, C.Y., Thompson, P., Tu, Z.: Robust brain extraction across datasets and comparison with publicly available methods. IEEE Trans. Med. Imaging 30(9), 1617–1634 (2011)
7. Klein, S., Staring, M., Murphy, K., Viergever, M.A., Pluim, J.P.W.: elastix: a toolbox for intensity-based medical image registration. IEEE Trans. Med. Imaging 29(1), 196–205 (2010)
8. Neykov, N., Filzmoser, P., Dimova, R., Neytchev, P.: Robust fitting of mixtures using the trimmed likelihood estimator. Comput. Stat. Data Anal. 52(1), 299–308 (2007)
9. Shah, M., Xiao, Y., Subbanna, N., Francis, S., Arnold, D.L., Collins, D.L., Arbel, T.: Evaluating intensity normalization on MRIs of human brain with multiple sclerosis. Med. Image Anal. 15(2), 267–282 (2011)
10. Shiee, N., Bazin, P.L., Ozturk, A., Reich, D.S., Calabresi, P.A., Pham, D.L.: A topology-preserving approach to the segmentation of brain images with multiple sclerosis lesions. NeuroImage 49(2), 1524–1535 (2010)
11. Steenwijk, M.D., Pouwels, P.J.W., Daams, M., van Dalen, J.W., Caan, M.W.A., Richard, E., Barkhof, F., Vrenken, H.: Accurate white matter lesion segmentation by k nearest neighbor classification with tissue type priors (kNN-TTPs). NeuroImage Clin. 3, 462–469 (2013)
12. Sweeney, E.M., Shinohara, R.T., Shiee, N., Mateen, F.J., Chudgar, A.A., Cuzzocreo, J.L., Calabresi, P.A., Pham, D.L., Reich, D.S., Crainiceanu, C.M.: OASIS is automated statistical inference for segmentation, with applications to multiple sclerosis lesion segmentation in MRI. NeuroImage Clin. 2, 402–413 (2013)
13. Tustison, N.J., Avants, B.B., Cook, P.A., Zheng, Y., Egan, A., Yushkevich, P.A., Gee, J.C.: N4ITK: improved N3 bias correction. IEEE Trans. Med. Imaging 29(6), 1310–1320 (2010)
14. Vrenken, H., Jenkinson, M., Horsfield, M.A., Battaglini, M., Schijndel, R.A., Rostrup, E., Geurts, J.J.G., Fisher, E., Zijdenbos, A., Ashburner, J., Miller, D.H., Filippi, M., Fazekas, F., Rovaris, M., Rovira, A., Barkhof, F., de Stefano, N., Group, M.S.: Recommendations to improve imaging and analysis of brain lesion load and atrophy in longitudinal studies of multiple sclerosis. J. Neurol. 260(10), 2458–2471 (2013)
15. Warfield, S.K., Kaus, M., Jolesz, F.A., Kikinis, R.: Adaptive, template moderated, spatially varying statistical classification. Med. Image Anal. 4(1), 43–55 (2000)
16. Xiao, Y., Shah, M., Francis, S., Arnold, D.L., Arbel, T., Collins, D.L.: Optimal Gaussian mixture models of tissue intensities in brain MRI of patients with multiple-sclerosis. In: Wang, F., Yan, P., Suzuki, K., Shen, D. (eds.) MLMI 2010. LNCS, vol. 6357, pp. 165–173. Springer, Heidelberg (2010)

# Assessment of Tissue Injury in Severe Brain Trauma

Christophe Maggia[1,2], Senan Doyle[3], Florence Forbes[4], Olivier Heck[5],
Irène Troprès[1,5,6,7], Corentin Berthet[5], Yann Teyssier[5], Lionel Velly[8],
Jean-François Payen[1,2,5], and Michel Dojat[1,2]([✉])

[1] Grenoble Institut des Neurosciences, GIN, Univ. Grenoble Alpes, 38000 Grenoble,
France
[2] INSERM, U1216, 38000 Grenoble, France
Michel.Dojat@univ-grenoble-alpes.fr
[3] Pixyl, 38000 Grenoble, France
[4] INRIA Grenoble, LJK, Grenoble, France
[5] CHU de Grenoble, 38000 Grenoble, France
[6] CNRS, UMR 3552, 38000 Grenoble, France
[7] INSERM, US 017, 38000 Grenoble, France
[8] Hôpital de la Timone, 13000 Marseille, France

**Abstract.** We report our methodological developments to investigate,
in a multi-center study using mean diffusivity, the tissue damage caused
by a severe traumatic brain injury (GSC < 9) in the 10 days post-
event. To assess the diffuse aspect of the injury, we fuse several atlases to
parcel cortical, subcortical and WM structures into well identified regions
where MD values are computed and compared to normative values. We
used P-LOCUS to provide brain tissue segmentation and exclude voxels
labeled as CSF, ventricles and hemorrhagic lesion and then automatically
detect the lesion load. Preliminary results demonstrate that our method
is coherent with expert opinion in the identification of lesions. We outline
the challenges posed in automatic analysis for TBI.

## 1 Introduction

Traumatic brain injury (TBI) remains a leading cause of death and disability among young people worldwide and current methods to predict long-term
outcome are not strong. TBI initiates a cascade of events that can lead to
secondary brain damage or exacerbate the primary injury, and these develop
hours to days after the initial accident. The concept of secondary brain damage
is the focus of modern TBI management in Intensive Care Units. The imbalance between oxygen supply to the brain tissue and utilization, i.e. brain tissue hypoxia, is considered the major cause for the development of secondary
brain damage, and hence poor neurological outcome Monitoring brain tissue
oxygenation after TBI using brain tissue $O_2$ pressure (Pbt$O_2$) probes surgically
inserted into the parenchyma, may help clinicians to initiate adequate actions
when episodes of brain ischemia/hypoxia are identified. The aggressive treatment of low Pbt$O_2$ values (< 15 mmHg for more than 30 min) was associated

© Springer International Publishing Switzerland 2016
A. Crimi et al. (Eds.): BrainLes 2015, LNCS 9556, pp. 57–68, 2016.
DOI: 10.1007/978-3-319-30858-6_6

with better outcome compared to standard therapy in some cohort studies of severe head-injury patients [1]. However, another study was unable to find similar benefits to patient outcome [2]. We are in the process of starting a randomized controlled multi-center trial (23 centers, 400 patients) in order to assess the impact of such therapeutic strategies (standard vs $PbtO_2$-based).

MRI is an excellent modality for estimating global and regional alterations in TBI and for following their longitudinal evolution [3]. To assess the complexity of TBI, several morphological sequences are required: FLAIR (Fluid Attenuated Inversion Recovery) and T2-weighted images for visualizing respectively non hemorrhagic lesions and hemorrhagic lesions, and 3D T1-weighted image (such as MPRAGE) for assessing volume loss. Moreover, diffusion tensor imaging (DTI) offers the most sensitive modality for the detection of changes in the acute phase of TBI [4,5] and increases the accuracy of long-term outcome prediction compared to the available clinical/radiographic pronostic score [6]. Mean Diffusivity (MD) or Apparent Diffusion Coefficient (ADC) have been widely used to determine the volume of ischemic tissue, and assess intra- and extracellular conditions. A reduction of MD is related to cytotoxic edema (intracellular) while an increase of MD indicates a vasogenic edema (extracellular). Changes of MD are expected with severe TBI. The volume of lesions on DTI shows a strong correlation with neurological outcome at patient discharge [6]. We consider a clinically relevant criterion to be the volume of vulnerable brain lesions after TBI, as previously suggested [7]. In consequence, we need an automatic segmentation method to assess the tissue damage in severe trauma (GSC < 9), acute phase i.e. before 10 days after the event.

There are only a few studies that investigated alterations in TBI, mainly on moderate or mild TBI (Glasgow score > 12) (see [8] for a review) and very few on severe TBI, in chronic stage i.e. more than several months post-injury [9–13] or acute phase, less than 10 days post-injury [6,14]. Clearly, current proposed methods lack sufficient robustness to capture TBI-related changes without excessive user input [15]. Skull deformation, the presence of blood in the acute phase, the high variability of brain damage that excludes the use of anatomical *a priori* information and the diffuse aspect of brain injury affecting potentially all brain structures render TBI segmentation particularly demanding. To assess the diffuse aspect of the injury, the brain is firstly divided into ROIs using an atlas [6,9,16] or multiple atlases [17]. Then, a selection of the structures frequently implicated in TBI such as thalamus, putamen, brainstem and occipital cortices is considered [13,17]. The methods proposed in the literature are mainly concerned with volumetric changes following TBI and scarcely report lesion load.

In this paper, we report about our methodological developments to assess lesion load in severe brain trauma in the entire brain. We use P-LOCUS [18] to provide brain tissue segmentation and exclude voxels labeled as CSF, ventricles and hemorrhagic lesion. We propose a fusion of several atlases to parcel cortical, subcortical and white matter (WM) structures into well identified regions where MD values can be expected to be homogenous. Abnormal voxels are detected in these regions by comparing MD values with normative values computed from healthy volunteers. The preliminary results, evaluated in a single center, are a first step in defining a robust methodology intended to be used for in multi-center studies.

## 2 Materials and Methods

### 2.1 Patients

The patients ($n = 5$) had a GCS < 9 with a diagnosis of severe trauma. The control group ($n = 2$) had no evidence of a past or present brain trauma. The study was approved by the Institutional Review Board at the Hospital of Marseille and informed consents were obtained prior to participation directly from the participants (controls) or next of kin (patients). Compared to the standard CT scan, MR imaging allows to detect more brain lesions. For this reason, the participation to this trial may offer benefits to each individual that largely outweighs the risks.

### 2.2 Data Acquisition

Images were acquired on a Siemens Verio 3 T system whole body scanner (CHU Marseille-Timone). The following morphological sequences were acquired: axial FLAIR (TR/TE/TI:7840/96/2500 ms, 27 contiguous slices, $0.7 \times 0.7 \times 5$ mm$^3$), and T2 Susceptibility Weighted-Imaging (TR/TE: 35/20 ms, $0.8 \times 0.8 \times 1.6$ mm$^3$), 3D sagittal T1-weighted sequence (MPRAGE,TR/TE/TI: 2300/2.98/ 900 ms, $1 \times 1 \times 1$ mm3). In addition, DTI was acquired in an axial plane perpendicular to the main field B0. The DTI parameters used were: field of view of 300 mm, matrix size 96 96, and slice thickness 2 mm (resulting in nearly isotropic voxels). Magnetic field gradients were applied in 63 directions with a value of 1000 mT/m.

### 2.3 Image Processing

**Preprocessing.** All MRI scans were reviewed to check for motion and other artifacts. T1-weighted and FLAIR images were processed using P-LOCUS, a Bayesian HMRF approach for tissue and lesion segmentation [18] and resampled at a resolution of $2 \times 2 \times 2$ mm$^3$. DTI images were first denoised [19] and preprocessed using the FSL software[1]. The images were corrected for geometric distortions caused by Eddy currents and intensity inhomogeneity. The diffusion tensor was estimated, and the local diffusion parameter MD was calculated for the entire brain in each patient and control. These parameters were computed from the three estimated eigenvalues that quantify the parameters of water diffusion in three orthogonal directions. Brain extraction, coregistration and resampling were successfully realized using P-LOCUS even in cases exhibiting large skull deformations.

---

[1] http://www.fmrib.ox.ac.uk/fsl/.

**Segmentation Model Specification.** We consider a finite set $V$ of $N$ voxels on a regular 3D grid. We denote by $\mathbf{y} = \{\mathbf{y}_1, \ldots, \mathbf{y}_N\}$ the intensity values observed respectively at each voxel. Each $\mathbf{y}_i = \{y_{i1}, \ldots, y_{iM}\}$ is itself a vector of $M = 2$ intensity values corresponding to T1-weighted and FLAIR sequences. The segmentation task is to assign each voxel $i$ to one of $K$ classes considering the observed features data $\mathbf{y}$. This assignment is considered latent data and is denoted by $\mathbf{z} = \{\mathbf{z}_1, \ldots, \mathbf{z}_N\}$. Typically, the $\mathbf{z}_i$'s corresponding to class memberships, take their values in $\{e_1, \ldots, e_K\}$ where $e_k$ is a K-dimensional binary vector whose $k^{th}$ component is 1, all other components being 0. We will denote by $\mathcal{Z} = \{e_1, \ldots, e_K\}^N$ the set in which $\mathbf{z}$ takes its values. We considered 5 classes, 4 for tissues: WM, grey matter (GM), and cephalo spinal fluid (CSF) divided in two classes (ventricles and extra-ventricular), plus an additional lesion class. The set of voxels $V$ is associated to a neighborhood system. Spatial dependencies between voxels are modeled by assuming a Markov Random Field (MRF) prior. Denoting $\psi = \{\eta, \phi\}$ additional parameters, we assume that the joint distribution $p(\mathbf{y}, \mathbf{z}; \psi)$ is a MRF with the following energy function:

$$H(\mathbf{y}, \mathbf{z}; \psi) = H_{\mathbf{Z}}(\mathbf{z}; \eta) + \sum_{i \in V} \log g(\mathbf{y}_i|\mathbf{z}_i; \phi), \tag{1}$$

where the $g(\mathbf{y}_i|\mathbf{z}_i; \phi)$'s are probability density functions of $\mathbf{y}_i$.

The energy decomposes into a data term and missing data term further specified below. For brain data, the data term $\sum_{i \in V} \log g(\mathbf{y}_i|\mathbf{z}_i; \phi)$ in (1) corresponds to the modelling of tissue dependent intensity distributions. For our multi-dimensional observations, we consider M-dimensional Gaussian distributions with diagonal covariance matrices. For each class $k$, $(\mu_{k1}, \ldots, \mu_{kM})$ is the mean vector and $\{s_{k1}, \ldots, s_{kM}\}$ the covariance matrix components. We will use the notation $\mu_m = {}^t(\mu_{km}, k = 1 \ldots K)$ and $s_m = {}^t(s_{km}, k = 1 \ldots K)$. When $\mathbf{z}_i = e_k$ then $\mathcal{G}(y_{im}; \langle \mathbf{z}_i, \phi_m \rangle)$ and $\mathcal{G}(y_{im}; \langle \mathbf{z}_i, \mu_m \rangle, \langle \mathbf{z}_i, s_m \rangle)$ both represent the Gaussian distribution with mean $\mu_{km}$ and variance $s_{km}$. The entire set of Gaussian parameters is denoted by $\phi = \{\phi_{km}, k = 1, \ldots K, m = 1, \ldots, M\}$. Our data term is then defined by setting $g(\mathbf{y}_i|\mathbf{z}_i; \phi) \propto \prod_{m=1}^{M} \mathcal{G}(y_{im}; \langle \mathbf{z}_i, \phi_m \rangle)$.

The missing data term $H_{\mathbf{Z}}(\mathbf{z}; \beta)$ involving $\mathbf{z}$ in (1) is set as follows. The dependencies between neighboring $Z_i$'s are modeled by further assuming that the joint distribution of $\{Z_1, \ldots, Z_N\}$ is a discrete MRF on the voxels grid :

$$P(\mathbf{z}; \beta) = W(\eta)^{-1} \exp\left(-H_{\mathbf{Z}}(\mathbf{z}; \eta)\right) \tag{2}$$

where $\eta$ is a set of parameters, $W(\eta)$ is a normalizing constant and $H_{\mathbf{Z}}$ is a function restricted to pair-wise interactions,

$$H_{\mathbf{Z}}(\mathbf{z}; \eta) = -\sum_{i \in S} z_i^t \gamma - \sum_{\substack{i,j \\ i \sim j}} z_i^t \mathbb{B} z_j,$$

where we write $z_i^t$ for the transpose of vector $z_i$ and $i \sim j$ when voxels $i$ and $j$ are neighbors. The set of parameters $\eta$ consists of two sets $\eta = (\gamma, \mathbb{B})$. Parameter $\gamma$ is a $K-$dimensional vector which acts as weights for the different values of $z_i$.

When $\gamma$ is zero, no tissue is favored, *i.e.* for a given voxel $i$, if no information on the neighboring voxels is available, then all tissues have the same probability. Then, $\mathbb{B}$ is a $K \times K$ matrix that encodes interactions between the different classes. If in addition to a null $\gamma$, $\mathbb{B} = b \times I_K$ where $b$ is a real scalar and $I_K$ is the $K \times K$ identity matrix, parameters $\eta$ reduce to a single scalar interaction parameter $b$ and we get the Potts model traditionally used for image segmentation.

Note that the standard Potts model is often appropriate for classification since it tends to favor neighbors that are in the same class. However, this model penalizes pairs that have different classes with the same penalty, regardless of the tissues they represent. In practice, it may be more appropriate, to encode higher penalties when the tissues are known to be unlikely neighbors. For example, the penalty for a white matter and CSF pair is expected to be greater than that of a grey matter and CSF pair, as these two classes are more likely to form neighborhoods.

In practice, these parameters can be tuned according to experts, *a priori* knowledge, or they can be estimated from the data. More generally, when prior knowledge indicates that, for example, two given classes are likely to be next to each other, this can be encoded in the matrix with a higher entry for this pair. Conversely, when there is enough information in the data, a full free $\mathbb{B}$ matrix can be estimated and will reflect the class structure (*i.e.* which class is next to which as indicated by the data) and will then mainly serve as a regularizing term to encode additional spatial information.

For the distribution of the observed variables $\mathbf{y}$ given the classification $\mathbf{z}$, the usual conditional independence assumption is made. It follows that the conditional probability of the hidden field $\mathbf{z}$ given the observed field $\mathbf{y}$ is

$$P(\mathbf{z}|\mathbf{y}; \psi, \eta) = W(\eta)^{-1} \exp\left(-H_\mathbf{z}(\mathbf{z}; \eta) + \sum_{i \in S} \log g(y_i|z_i, \phi)\right).$$

Parameters are estimated using the variational EM algorithm which provides a tractable solution for non trivial Markov models [20].

**Atlas-Based Approach.** Given the variability in the spatial extent and the magnitude of the injury in case of severe TBI, the use of values averaged from large regions of WM would not allow the accurate detection of 'abnormal' values. Indeed, if the lesions are focal, the detection power is hampered by the averaging with healthy tissues values. The standard way is to use an atlas-based approach where MD at each voxel is compared with normative values computed from homogeneous regions of interest (ROIs) of a healthy volunteer's brain acting as a reference. We expect MD values to be homogenous inside well identified brain regions defining local normative values. In order to be as exhaustive as possible, we combined two atlases found in the literature. First, the Neuromorphomet-rics atlas[2], as provided with SPM12[3] for academic use, was used to demarcate

---

[2] http://www.neuromorphometrics.com/.
[3] http://www.fil.ion.ucl.ac.uk/spm/software/spm12/.

cortical and sub-cortical regions (mainly GM). For WM regions, we used the ICBM DTI81 atlas, largely used in tractography studies to demarcate the principal fiber tracts. In the case of overlapping labels, the ICBM DTI81 label was selected. However these tracts represent only a small part of the WM volume. To our knowledge there is no atlas dividing the entire volume of WM volume into anatomically meaningful subregions. Consequently, we automatically divided the remaining volume into cubes of $20 \, mm^3$. This size allows to obtain sufficiently local information while maintaining WM regions large enough to compute reliable normative values. Our combined atlas defines 238 ROIs.

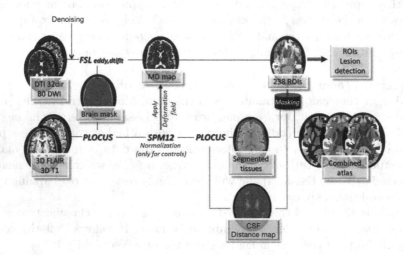

**Fig. 1.** Overview of the processing pipeline. After denoising, we used PLOCUS for brain extraction and tissue segmentation, FSL for mean diffusion (MD) map creation and SMP12 for realignment to a template (normalization). The atlas and the brain tissue maps were combined to define 238 ROIs where detection of lesion was performed.

Our final combined atlas was then realigned (non-linear deformation using P-LOCUS) to our control subject's images and MD values were computed for each ROI. Figure 1 shows the different processing steps. In the literature, for lesion detection, authors usually transform DTI scalar maps (mostly FA) into z-score maps to detect extreme values [3]. Given that MD value distribution is not normal, the z-score would give a biased measure of extreme values. To avoid this effect we chose to use two different thresholds: percentile-based and size-based. By fixing percentile thresholds $\alpha 1$ for minimal and $\alpha 2$ for maximal values, we identified clusters of extreme values. The skewness of the distribution is directed toward high values of MD and knowing these values are a marker of cell death and vasogenic edema, which are very frequent in severe TBI, we used a more lenient threshold for $\alpha 2$. Figure 2 indicates the form of the MD distribution for our two control subjects.

We considered lesions as clusters with a size higher than a given threshold $\beta$. P-LOCUS [18] uses T1-weighted and FLAIR images conjointly to perform brain seg-

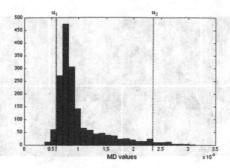

**Fig. 2.** Histogram of MD values for control subjects. Percentile thresholds α1 for minimal and α2 for maximal values.

mentation in five classes WM, GM, Lesion and CSF (ventricles extra-ventricular). Voxels labeled as CSF and hemorrhagic lesion were automatically excluded. The three thresholds were empirically set on control data to keep the lesion volume under 1% of the brain volume. α1 was fixed at the 2nd percentile, α2 at the 97.5th percentile (i.e. 2.5% for the highest values) and β at 21 contiguous voxels (i.e. 168 ml). These thresholds were the used for lesion detection on patient data.

**Manual Approach.** To quantify the volume of lesions, three neuroradiologists (OH, CB and YT) with extensive experience in lesion assessment manually segmented the lesion area using the MRIcron software[4]. They underwent a specific intensive training to visually detect focal lesions in MD images. Focal lesions included any focal regions of abnormal signal in the MD map. The task was time-consuming: for each subject (n = 5) and each rater (n = 3), fifty slices were examined to detect high values and low values of MD. The raters were unsatisfied with their results: they were not familiar with such precise manual delineation and despite training the task remained particularly difficult because of low contrast and low spatial resolution in the MD images compared to FLAIR and T1-weighted images. To obtain a reference from these segmentations we used the STAPLE algorithm [21]. The algorithm considers our collection of segmentations and computes a probabilistic estimate of the true segmentation and a measure of the performance level represented by each segmentation. To assess the inter-rater variability we also computed three STAPLE segmentation references using manual results in a leave-one-out strategy. We used four evaluation measures to evaluate the quality of the automatic segmentation compared to the reference ground-truth: The Dice coefficient (DC) denotes the volume overlap (DC value of 0 indicates no overlap, a value of 1 perfect similarity), the average symmetric surface distance (ASSD) the surface fit (the lower the better), the Hausdorff distance (HD) the maximum error (the lower the better) and precision & recall (see details in evaluation measures computation in http://www.isles-challenge.org/).

---

[4] http://www.mccauslandcenter.sc.edu/mricro/mricron/.

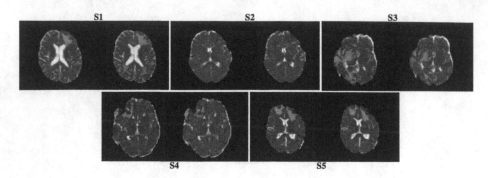

**Fig. 3.** Automatic and manual lesion delineation for five subjects (S1 to S5). For each subject: left: automatic delineation, right: manual delineation. Green: abnormal low MD values, Red: abnormal high MD values (Color figure online).

## 3  Results

Figure 3 shows for our five patients, on transverse views, the reference segmentation computed using STAPLE from three rater segmentations and the corresponding automatic segmentation. The normative values were computed from two controls in each of the 238 ROIs to keep lesion below 1% for controls.

Figure 4 indicates the volumetric comparison between manual vs automatic delineation for high MD and low MD values respectively for our five patients. Using STAPLE, for each subject, we computed three references from the manual segmentation provided by two raters among three. This allows to highlight the important inter-rater variability (for instance see for S2). Volume agreements between manual and automatic results are not perfect. Clearly, the automatic delineation minimizes high MD values (Fig. 4, left). This is confirmed by the low precision values with high recall values for high MD (see Table 1). Table 1 reports the values for our different evaluation measures for our five subjects. To our knowledge no such values are available in the literature for a comparison.

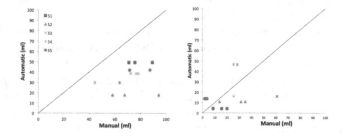

**Fig. 4.** Left: Automatic vs manual high MD values in voxels. Right: Automatic vs manual low MD values in voxels. Using a leave-one-out strategy we obtained three values for each subject. Black line correlation slope.

**Table 1.** Measures to evaluate the quality of the automatic segmentation compared to the reference ground-truth. DC: the Dice coefficient, ASSD: the average symmetric surface distance, HD: the Hausdorff distance

| Evaluation measure | S1 | | S2 | | S3 | | S4 | | S5 | |
|---|---|---|---|---|---|---|---|---|---|---|
| | Low | High | Low | High | Low | High | Low | High | Low | High |
| DC | 0.05 | 0.34 | 0.36 | 0.36 | 0.26 | 0.39 | 0.21 | 0.42 | 0.15 | 0.58 |
| ASSD (in mm) | 21.48 | 6.71 | 5.24 | 4.14 | 7.99 | 4.28 | 6.85 | 6.74 | 10.37 | 3.06 |
| HD (in mm) | 83.76 | 35.78 | 46.39 | 45.61 | 50.99 | 39.45 | 44.36 | 44.77 | 48.17 | 56.67 |
| Precision | 0.03 | 0.29 | 0.33 | 0.23 | 0.20 | 0.28 | 0.28 | 0.31 | 0.37 | 0.45 |
| Recall | 0.10 | 0.42 | 0.42 | 0.85 | 0.37 | 0.63 | 0.17 | 0.65 | 0.10 | 0.82 |

# 4 Discussion

In our study, vulnerable brain lesions were defined based on morphological images and by abnormal values of MD using DTI to distinguish between cytotoxic and vasogenic edema. We used specific analysis of each individual case because the spatial distribution of brain trauma lesion is highly heterogeneous and can not be revealed by a group study. We compared lesion volume delineation using a multi-modal atlas-based automatic method to that of manual delineation by three neuroradiologists. Our results show that the proposed method allows identification of some lesions in severe TBI in coherence with that defined by our experts. Several measures that assess the quality of the automatic segmentation compared to the reference ground-truth (see Table 1) reveal that some discrepancies exist between manual and automatic methods. Clearly, these results should be improved. To our knowledge no such measures have been published yet for automatic lesion detection in severe TBI. These values may serve as a starting point for comparison with alternative techniques. Our trained experts reported that there were not totally confident with their final rating. We observed that lesions were particularly difficult to segment manually due to low contrast and low spatial resolution in diffusion images compared to FLAIR or T1-weighted images; these latter being more familiar to the experts. This was reflected by the high inter-rater variations across the experts (see Fig. 4). We used STA-PLE to compute a probabilistic estimate of the true segmentation. However, the low number of raters involved (n = 3) and high inter-rater variability limit the validity of such a "ground truth". This could explain in part the observed discrepancies between manual vs automatic approaches. The manual task required a specific training and was time-consuming. Consequently, it was difficult to involve more trained experts to define an "expert consensus" and limit bias. In this study we considered mean diffusivity (MD), a physiological parameter extracted from DTI scans, to distinguish between vasogenic and cytotoxic edema. While MD is sensitive to sparse small lesions with low MD values (corresponding to high-level intensity spots in FLAIR) and allows physical quantification of the lesion in terms of water molecule diffusivity alteration, high-level contrast in FLAIR images allows an easy delineation of large damaged regions with high MD values. Further work should be done to improve brain injury characterisation in exploiting such complementary information with our automatic method.

The methodological difficulties in performing MRI in the acute phase of severe TBI explain the rarity of studies for this period. Only two studies [6,14] address the problem of severe trauma (Glasgow score $< 9$) in acute phase i.e. less than 10 days post-injury. The former, a multi-center study, aimed to define a long-term outcome prediction from quantitative parameters extracted from DTI in specific ROIs in white matter. The latter was concerned with the evolution of ADC values in the traumatic lesions. No quantitative measurement of the lesion volume was reported for these two studies. Compared to Tumor, Stroke or Multiple Sclerosis, a few papers addressed automatic lesion segmentation in TBI[5]. The majority of TBI studies report volume changes computed in specific ROIs. Few approaches report the lesion load [15,22]. Because the spatial distribution of the lesion cannot be anticipated, our approach considered the entire brain without any *a priori* spatial hypothesis. We used two atlases to parcel the entire brain. MD was then computed in each ROI. An MD-driven alternative will be to search for homogenous MD territories clustering directly from the set of control DTI. Strangman et al. [13] reported inadequate skull stripping and poor subcortical structure segmentation with the most common method, FreeSurfer. Using non-linear deformation of *a priori* tissue probability maps on individual T1-weighted and FLAIR images we successfully used P-LOCUS to provide brain tissue segmentation and exclude voxels labeled as CSF in ventricules and hemorrhagic lesions. To detect outlier/abnormal MD values, we defined normative values on normal controls. Such normative values are highly scanner and sequence dependent and, as in our multi-center study, should be defined for each center involved. Because the influence of age on MD values, the range of normal control age should be matched with TBI patients. The influence of the size of the normal control population on the norm definition should be evaluated. Recently, [23] proposed a method to harmonize diffusion MRI data across multiple scanners. Several rotation-invariant features are computed from spherical harmonic basis functions and used to estimate a region-based linear mapping between signal from different scanners. Such a method might be used to define normative values in pooling normal controls from different sites. A poor estimation of the normative mean in each ROI of the control group biases the detection of aberrant values [22]. Instead of an atlas-based approach, a voxel-based approach to segment abnormal values directly from individual diffusion-weighted images could be introduced avoiding the definition of normative values. However, such an approach remains difficult due to the low contrast present in these images.

In conclusion, this paper reports the image processing steps and the difficulties encountered of the first program aiming to assess the impact of a therapeutic strategy based on PbtO$_2$ in monitoring the volume of severe post-trauma

---

[5] Between 2004–2014, more than 500 papers were published on lesion segmentation for each of these pathologies and only 53 for TBI. Source WebOfScience with keywords: Brain and MRI and (Segmentation or Classification) and 'Pathology'.

cerebral lesions and on neurological outcome in a randomized controlled trial. We hypothesise that early monitoring of brain oxygenation with $PbtO_2$ can reduce the volume of vulnerable brain lesions and, possibly, improve neurological outcome in TBI patients from an unfavorable to a favorable neurological outcome. These preliminary results obtained on a small number of subjects in one center are encouraging and a larger evaluation including more controls and patients is undergoing.

**Acknowledgments.** Grenoble MRI facility IRMaGe was partly funded by the French program Investissement d' avenir run by the Agence Nationale pour la Recherche; grant Infrastructure d' avenir en Biologie Santé - ANR-11-INBS-0006. Research funded by French ministry of research and education under the Projet Hospitalier de Recherche Clinique grant OXY-TC to JFP.

# References

1. Spiotta, A.M., Stiefel, M.F., Gracias, V.H., et al.: Brain tissue oxygen-directed management and outcome in patients with severe traumatic brain injury. J. Neurosurg. **113**(3), 571–580 (2010)
2. Green, J.A., Pellegrini, D.C., Vanderkolk, W.E., et al.: Goal directed brain tissue oxygen monitoring versus conventional management in traumatic brain injury: an analysis of in hospital recovery. Neurocrit. Care **18**(1), 20–25 (2013)
3. Davenport, N.D., Lim, K.O., Armstrong, M.T., Sponheim, S.R.: Diffuse and spatially variable white matter disruptions are associated with blast-related mild traumatic brain injury. Neuroimage **59**(3), 2017–2024 (2012)
4. Narayana, P.A., Yu, X., Hasan, K.M., et al.: Multi-modal mri of mild traumatic brain injury. Neuroimage Clin. **7**, 87–97 (2015)
5. Yuh, E.L., Mukherjee, P., Lingsma, H.F., et al.: Magnetic resonance imaging improves 3-month outcome prediction in mild traumatic brain injury. Ann. Neurol. **73**(2), 224–235 (2013)
6. Galanaud, D., Perlbarg, V., Gupta, R., et al.: Assessment of white matter injury and outcome in severe brain trauma: a prospective multicenter cohort. Anesthesiology **117**(6), 1300–1310 (2012)
7. Cunningham, A.S., Salvador, R., Coles, J.P., et al.: Physiological thresholds for irreversible tissue damage in contusional regions following traumatic brain injury. Brain **128**(Pt 8), 1931–1942 (2005)
8. Shenton, M.E., Hamoda, H.M., Schneiderman, J.S., et al.: A review of magnetic resonance imaging and diffusion tensor imaging findings in mild traumatic brain injury. Brain Imaging Behav. **6**(2), 137–192 (2012)
9. Bigler, E.D., Wilde, E.A.: Quantitative neuroimaging and the prediction of rehabilitation outcome following traumatic brain injury. Front. Hum. Neurosci. **4**, 228 (2010)
10. Kasahara, K., Hashimoto, K., Abo, M., Senoo, A.: Voxel- and atlas-based analysis of diffusion tensor imaging may reveal focal axonal injuries in mild traumatic brain injury - comparison with diffuse axonal injury. Magn. Reson. Imaging **30**(4), 496–505 (2012)
11. Newcombe, V.F., Correia, M.M., Ledig, C., et al.: Dynamic changes in white matter abnormalities correlate with late improvement and deterioration following tbi: a diffusion tensor imaging study. Neurorehabil. Neural Repair **30**(1), 49–62 (2016)

12. Sidaros, A., Skimminge, A., Liptrot, M.G., et al.: Long-term global and regional brain volume changes following severe traumatic brain injury: a longitudinal study with clinical correlates. Neuroimage **44**(1), 1–8 (2009)

13. Strangman, G.E., O'Neil-Pirozzi, T.M., Supelana, C., et al.: Regional brain morphometry predicts memory rehabilitation outcome after traumatic brain injury. Front. Hum. Neurosci. **4**, 182 (2010)

14. Pasco, A., Ter Minassian, A., Chapon, C., et al.: Dynamics of cerebral edema and the apparent diffusion coefficient of water changes in patients with severe traumatic brain injury. a prospective mri study. Eur. Radiol. **16**(7), 1501–1508 (2006)

15. Irimia, A., Chambers, M.C., Alger, J.R., et al.: Comparison of acute and chronic traumatic brain injury using semi-automatic multimodal segmentation of mr volumes. J. Neurotrauma **28**(11), 2287–2306 (2011)

16. Hasan, K.M., Wilde, E.A., Miller, E.R., et al.: Serial atlas-based diffusion tensor imaging study of uncomplicated mild traumatic brain injury in adults. J. Neurotrauma **31**(5), 466–475 (2014)

17. Ledig, C., Heckemann, R.A., Hammers, A., et al.: Robust whole-brain segmentation: application to traumatic brain injury. Med. Image Anal. **21**(1), 40–58 (2015)

18. Doyle, S., Forbes, F., Dojat, M.: P-locus, a complete suite for brain scan segmentation. In: 9h IEEE International Symposium on Biomedical Imaging (ISBI) (2012)

19. Manjon, J.V., Coupe, P., Concha, L., Buades, A., Collins, D.L., Robles, M.: Diffusion weighted image denoising using overcomplete local pca. PLOS One **8**(9), e73021 (2013)

20. Forbes, F., Doyle, S., Garcia-Lorenzo, D., Barillot, C., Dojat, M.: A weighted Multi-sequence Markov model for brain lesion segmentation. In: The Thirteenth International Conference on Artificial Intelligence and Statistics (AISTATS), pp. 225–232 (2010)

21. Warfield, S.K., Zou, K.H., Wells, W.M.: Validation of image segmentation by estimating rater bias and variance. Philos. Trans. A Math. Phys. Eng. Sci. **366**(1874), 2361–2375 (2008)

22. Kim, N., Branch, C.A., Kim, M., Lipton, M.L.: Whole brain approaches for identification of microstructural abnormalities in individual patients: comparison of techniques applied to mild traumatic brain injury. PLoS One **8**(3), e59382 (2013)

23. Mirzaalian, H., de Pierrefeu, A., Savadjiev, P., Pasternak, S., Bouix, S., Kubicki, M., Westin, C., Shenton, M., Rathi, Y.: Harmonizing diffusion mri data across multiple sites and scanners. Med. Image Comput. Comput. Assist. Interv. **18**(Pt 2), 12–19 (2015)

# A Nonparametric Growth Model for Brain Tumor Segmentation in Longitudinal MR Sequences

Esther Alberts[1,2,6]([✉]), Guillaume Charpiat[3], Yuliya Tarabalka[4],
Thomas Huber[1], Marc-André Weber[5], Jan Bauer[1], Claus Zimmer[1],
and Bjoern H. Menze[2,6]

[1] Neuroradiology, Klinikum Rechts der Isar, TU München, Munich, Germany
esther.alberts@tum.de
[2] Department of Computer Science, TU München, Munich, Germany
[3] TAO Research Project, Inria Saclay, Palaiseau, France
[4] Titane Research Project, Inria Sophia-Antipolis, Valbonne, France
[5] Diagnostic and Interventional Radiology, University of Heidelberg,
Heidelberg, Germany
[6] Institute for Advanced Study, TU München, Munich, Germany

**Abstract.** Brain tumor segmentation and brain tumor growth assessment are inter-dependent and benefit from a joint evaluation. Starting from a generative model for multimodal brain tumor segmentation, we make use of a nonparametric growth model that is implemented as a conditional random field (CRF) including directed links with infinite weight in order to incorporate growth and inclusion constraints, reflecting our prior belief on tumor occurrence in the different image modalities. In this study, we validate this model to obtain brain tumor segmentations and volumetry in longitudinal image data. Moreover, we use the model to develop a probabilistic framework for estimating the likelihood of disease progression, i.e. tumor regrowth, after therapy. We present experiments for longitudinal image sequences with T1, T1c, T2 and FLAIR images, acquired for ten patients with low and high grade gliomas.

## 1 Introduction

The assessment of disease progression after brain tumor treatment is very important in clinical practice for disease surveillance and treatment planning, but also in drug trials and clinical studies for evaluating drug or treatment efficacy.

Automatic tumor segmentation is well-suited for tumor volumetry. In contrast to expensive manual segmentations, they obtain fast, reproducible and objective results. Over the past years, several automatic tumor segmentation methods have been developed [1]. Among these, longitudinal methods have been implemented to explicitly use time information. For example in [2], 4-dimensional (4D) spatio-temporal cliques are included in a CRF, enforcing regularisation over time. However, this temporal regularisation tends to smooth sudden growth events and the empirical temporal smoothness parameters are not easy to learn.

© Springer International Publishing Switzerland 2016
A. Crimi et al. (Eds.): BrainLes 2015, LNCS 9556, pp. 69–79, 2016.
DOI: 10.1007/978-3-319-30858-6_7

The authors of [3] present a model based on a 4D CRF using infinite link functions that effectively constrain voxel classifications depending on predefined conditions, which allow to constrain tumor segmentations to grow or shrink for every time transition. This model can handle abrupt changes in tumor growth and only includes one parameter for spatial regularisation.

In literature, tumor growth is often modelled by means of parametric models based on cell kinetics and reaction-diffusion processes, as reported in [4]. These models often aim to *predict* tumor growth (rather than study it in retrospect) and do not calculate tumor segmentations in itself (prior tumor segmentations are included for initialisation purposes). The authors of [5] were the first to use a parametric growth model to assist in brain tumor segmentation. However, parametric models are computationally expensive, make assumptions about tumor growth regularity and cannot easily handle post-operative tumor structures with resection cavities.

We believe tumor growth modelling and segmentation are inter-dependent, and aim to exploit this property by jointly optimising both in the same framework. We adopt the longitudinal segmentation model developed in [3] and implement it as a nonparametric tumor growth segmentation model. We further develop the model to include a fast and robust estimation of the spatial regularisation parameter and extend this model to detect tumor regrowth in longitudinal sequences. We consider the clinical scenario where a tumor shrinks after therapy and automatically detect the time point at which tumor regrowth begins.

## 2    Methods

An overview of the model is depicted in Fig. 1. We start from a set of 3D MR intensity images, consisting of $M$ modalities (T1, T1c, T2 and FLAIR), each available for $T$ time points: $\boldsymbol{I} = \{\boldsymbol{I}_{st}\}_{s\in(1,...,M),t\in(1,...,T)}$, where $s$ is a modality index and $t$ a time index. Furthermore, we use prior tumor probability maps as an input to our model: $\boldsymbol{X} = \{\boldsymbol{X}_{st}\}_{s\in(1,...,M),t\in(1,...,T)}$. These can for example be calculated by means of generative models lacking spatial, temporal and inter-modality coherence.

The growth model is specified through growth and inclusion constraints. The growth constraints specify whether the tumor is expected to grow or shrink for each time transition. They can either be specified in the model as to incorporate prior information (as in Experiment 1, Sect. 3.2) or they can be learned in a probabilistic framework (as in Experiment 2, Sect. 3.3). They are represented by a binary array indexed over all time transitions, $\boldsymbol{g} = [g_1, g_2, \ldots, g_{T-1}], \boldsymbol{g} \in \{0,1\}^{T-1}$, where each element $g_i$ imposes growth (1) or shrinkage (0) in between time points $i$ and $i+1$.

The inclusion constraints are represented by a set of pairs of modality indices, $(s', s'') \in S_{incl}$, such that all tumor voxels in the first modality, $s'$, are a subset of the tumor voxels in the second modality, $s''$. The inclusion constraints allow us

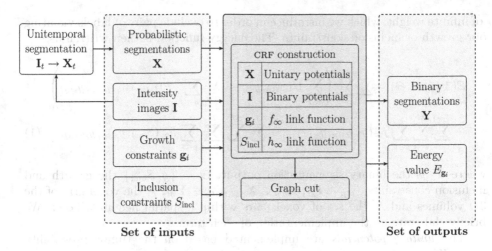

**Fig. 1.** Overview of the proposed method. The inputs are listed and incorporated in certain terms of the energy function of the CRF. Inference is calculated by means of graph cut and outputs a binary segmentation. In this work we also use the energy value as an output of the CRF, in order to evaluate the likelihood of the growth constraints.

to incorporate our prior knowledge of tumor occurrence across different modalities: the tumor voxels in T1 and T1c are to be a subset of the tumor voxels in T2 and the tumor voxels in T2 are to be a subset of the tumor voxels in FLAIR.

## 2.1 A 4D CRF as a Nonparametric Growth Model (NPGM)

**Graph Construction.** The CRF is implemented as a graph consisting of *nodes* $\mathcal{V}$, which are represented by the voxel grid and the tumor/non-tumor labels, and *edges* $\mathcal{E}$, which are quantified by edge weights and represent the affinity between nodes: $\mathcal{G} = \langle \mathcal{V}, \mathcal{E} \rangle$. The edge weights define an energy function $E$ as a function of the output segmentation $\boldsymbol{Y} = \{\boldsymbol{Y}_{st}\}_{s \in (1,...,M), t \in (1,...,T)}$. The energy function quantifies how well the output segmentation $\boldsymbol{Y}$ reflects the affinity between nodes as specified by the edge weights.

**Implementation of the Energy Function.** The energy function $E$ is implemented as in [3]. It is modelled such that favourable states of $\boldsymbol{Y}$ yield low energies. Minimisation of the energy function $E$ solves for the optimal output segmentation $\boldsymbol{Y}$.

In general, the energy function consists of unitary potentials $U$ and pairwise potentials $P$, weighted by a spatial regularisation parameter $\lambda$. The unitary potentials describe individual label preferences and the pairwise potentials describe voxel interactions encouraging spatial coherency. In this study, we extended the energy function by two functions, $f_\infty$ and $h_\infty$, to account for edges of infinite weight, which we introduce in order to exclude pairs of labels violating our growth or inclusion constraints. The energy function is then written as:

$$E(\boldsymbol{Y}|\boldsymbol{I},\boldsymbol{X},\boldsymbol{\Theta}) = \sum_{t=1}^{T}\sum_{s=1}^{M} \left( \sum_{p\in\mathcal{P}} U(x_{stp}, y_{stp}) + \lambda \sum_{(p,q)\in\mathcal{N}} P(i_{stp}, i_{stq}, y_{stp}, y_{stq}) \right)$$
$$+ \sum_{t=1}^{T-1}\sum_{s=1}^{M}\sum_{p\in\mathcal{P}} f_\infty(g_t, y_{stp}, y_{s(t+1)p}) + \sum_{t=1}^{T}\sum_{s'=1}^{M}\sum_{s''=1}^{M}\sum_{p\in\mathcal{P}} h_\infty(S_{\text{incl}}, y_{s'tp}, y_{s''tp}), \quad (1)$$

where $\boldsymbol{Y}$ is the binary segmentation output, $\boldsymbol{\Theta} = \{g, S_{\text{incl}}\}$ the growth and inclusion constraints, $i_{stp} \in \boldsymbol{I}_{st}$, $x_{stp} \in \boldsymbol{X}_{st}$, $y_{stp} \in \boldsymbol{Y}_{st}$, $\mathcal{P}$ the voxel grid of the 3D volumes and $\mathcal{N}$ the set of voxel pairs within a spatial neighbourhood. We briefly elaborate on the implementation of each term.

The *unitary potentials* are implemented based on the tumor probability maps $\boldsymbol{X}$:

$$U(x_{stp}, y_{stp}) = y_{stp}(1 - x_{stp}) + (1 - y_{stp})(x_{stp}). \quad (2)$$

The spatial *pairwise potentials* are implemented within the 3D volumes. They are quantified by a Gaussian, modelling the MR intensity difference between each voxel pair within a 3D neighbourhood matrix $\mathcal{N}_{26}$:

$$P(i_{stp}, i_{stq}, y_{stp}, y_{stq}) = \begin{cases} d(p,q)^{-1}\exp{-\dfrac{(i_{stp} - i_{stq})^2}{2\sigma^2}} & \text{if } y_{stp} \neq y_{stq}, \\ 0 & \text{else}, \end{cases} \quad (3)$$

where $d(p,q)$ is proportional to the voxel spacing and $\sigma^2$ is set to the variance of image intensities present in the 3D volume.

The *growth constraints* are imposed on voxel pairs belonging to the same modality, having the same index within the 3D volumes, and being strictly consecutive in time. An infinite penalty is imposed if ($a$) growth is imposed but the voxels switch from tumor, $y_{stp} = 1$, to non-tumor, $y_{s(t+1)p} = 0$, or ($b$) shrinkage is imposed but the voxels switch from non-tumor, $y_{stp} = 0$, to tumor, $y_{s(t+1)p} = 1$:

$$f_\infty(g_t, y_{stp}, y_{s(t+1)p}) = \begin{cases} \infty & \text{if } (g_t = 1) \wedge (y_{stp} > y_{s(t+1)p}), \\ \infty & \text{if } (g_t = 0) \wedge (y_{stp} < y_{s(t+1)p}), \\ 0 & \text{else}. \end{cases} \quad (4)$$

The *inclusion constraints* are imposed on voxel pairs of the same time point and having the same index within the 3D volumes. An infinite penalty is imposed if the voxels belong to two modalities in between which the inclusion constraint holds, $(s', s'') \in S_{\text{incl}}$, and if the voxel in $s'$ is tumor and the voxel in $s''$ is not:

$$h_\infty(y_{s'tp}, y_{s''tp}) = \begin{cases} \infty & \text{if } ((s', s'') \in S_{\text{incl}}) \wedge (y_{s'tp} > y_{s''tp}), \\ 0 & \text{else}. \end{cases} \quad (5)$$

Once the edge weights have been assigned based on this energy function, the CRF is solved by graph cut, as described in [6].

**Spatial Regularisation Parameter $\lambda$.** The regularisation parameter, $\lambda$, is an important system parameter: an overly high value leads to under-segmentation and an overly low value leads to poor spatial regularisation. Moreover, a good value for $\lambda$ differs from one case to another. There are several methods to learn this parameter. A fairly easy, fast and robust method is adopted in [7], where the parameter is made spatially adaptable. That is, $\lambda$ is set to lower values for voxels close to the edges of the images:

$$\lambda_{stp} = (1 - L_{stp})\lambda_{\max}, \tag{6}$$

where $L_{stp}$ is the edge probability of a single voxel and $\lambda_{\max}$ is empirically set to 3. We calculate the edge probability map $L$ based on the tumor probability maps $X$, by applying an edge detector and subsequent Gaussian smoothing.

## 2.2 Switching from Tumor Shrinkage to Tumor Regrowth

Once the CRF is solved by graph cut, we obtain an energy value. In [8] these energy values are used to calculate the confidence in spatial voxel classifications. More precisely, the confidence in a single voxel classification in [8] is based on the energies acquired from graph cuts with and without a voxel classification constraint, which is imposed by an infinite link.

As our growth constraints are enforced by the same infinite link functions, we can transfer this spatial uncertainty measure to the temporal domain and quantify uncertainties – or confidences – in specific tumor growth constraints.

First, consider a growth constraint for a single time transition from $t$ to $t + 1$: $g_t = a$. We define the min-marginal energy for this growth constraint $\psi_{t,a}$ ($t$ being the time index, $a \in \{0, 1\}$ the shrinkage/growth constraint), as the minimal energy within the family of energies obtained from graph cuts for all growth constraint patterns where $g_t$ is kept equal to $a$:

$$\psi_{t,a} = C^{-1} \min_{g,Y} E(Y|X,g) , \quad \forall g \in \{\{0,1\}^{T-1}|g_t = a\}, \tag{7}$$

with C as the number of voxels constrained with an infinite temporal link. Note that the calculation of $\psi_{t,a}$ requires $2^{T-2}$ graph cuts. The confidence in the growth constraint for this single time transition, $\sigma_{t,a}$, can then be calculated as a function of the min-marginal energies $\psi_{t,a}$, similar to [8]:

$$\sigma_{t,a} = \frac{\exp{(-\psi_{t,a})}}{\exp{(-\psi_{t,a})} + \exp{(-\psi_{t,1-a})}}, \quad a \in \{0, 1\}. \tag{8}$$

This calculation requires $2^{T-1}$ graph cuts. Note that this set of graph cuts covers all possible patterns of growth constraints. The energies of these graph cut solutions can be re-used to calculate $\sigma_{t',a'}$ for all other time points $t'$.

The confidence in the entire pattern of growth constraints, $\sigma_g$, is then calculated as the product of confidences over all time transitions: $\sigma_g = \prod_{i=1}^{T-1} \sigma_{i,g_i}$.

## 3  Experiments

### 3.1  Data Specifications

We used ten patient-specific datasets acquired at the German Cancer Research Center (DKFZ), yielding a total of 248 images. Each patient-specific dataset contains four multimodal sequences (T1, T1c, T2 and FLAIR) for three to nine time points, with time intervals of $\pm$ 90 days. Patients initially suffered from low grade gliomas, but some developed high grade gliomas in the course of the study.

All images within the same dataset are skull-stripped and affinely co-registered. For each image, manual ground truth segmentation is available in three orthogonal slices intersecting at the tumor centre. The manual segmentations were acquired by a clinical expert who took images of several time points into account at once.

We calculated tumor probability maps with a generative model based on an Expectation-Maximisation (EM) segmenter, as in [9]. Modalities belonging to the same time point are processed together, but time points are processed independently. The segmentation maps are concatenated over all time points, to obtain a valid input for the NPGM.

### 3.2  Experiment 1: Segmentation Accuracy

In this experiment we compare (*a*) EM segmentations (i.e. acquired from generative model), (*b*) NPGM segmentations (i.e. acquired from the nonparametric growth model) where no growth constraints are included, (*c*) NPGM segmentations where the tumor is constrained to grow over all time transitions and (*d*) NPGM segmentations where the spatial regularisation parameter is voxel-adaptive as in (6).

Table 1 reports the FLAIR Dice scores for all ten datasets, for each of these segmentations. Dice scores of T2 and T1 are comparable and not all datasets are suitable for T1c segmentations. The Dice scores are highest for the segmentation where the tumor is constrained to grow along time and where the spatial regularisation parameter is voxel-adaptive.

Figure 2 shows tumor volumetry for three datasets along time. This figure illustrates that the use of growth constraints does not only attain higher Dice scores, but also results in a more realistic progress in tumor volume. T2 and FLAIR segmentations are shown for three patients in Fig. 3 and segmentations for all modalities are shown for one patient in Fig. 4. These figures illustrate a clear improvement from EM to NPGM segmentations.

In terms of computation time, a NPGM segmentation of a dataset of eight time points and four modalities takes $\pm$10 s on a Intel® Xeon® Processor E3-1225 v3.

### 3.3  Experiment 2: Detection of Tumor Regrowth

We adopt the probabilistic formulation for different patterns of growth constraints (Sect. 2.2) to detect at which point tumor regrowth begins. We shorten

**Table 1.** FLAIR Dice scores for all ten datasets segmented by the EM segmenter and by the nonparametric growth model (NPGM) with different parameter settings concerning growth constraints and spatial regularisation parameter.

| EM segmentation: [79 % ± 8 %] | | | | | | | | | |
|---|---|---|---|---|---|---|---|---|---|
| 63 % | 79 % | 89 % | 77 % | 67 % | 84 % | 80 % | 79 % | 84 % | 86 % |
| **NPGM - no growth constraints, adaptive $\lambda$: [81 % ± 5 %]** | | | | | | | | | |
| 78 % | 80 % | 90 % | 82 % | 71 % | 84 % | 80 % | 80 % | 82 % | 87 % |
| **NPGM - constrained to grow, fixed $\lambda$: [82 % ± 5 %]** | | | | | | | | | |
| 74 % | 78 % | 91 % | 81 % | 80 % | 85 % | 81 % | 82 % | 83 % | 86 % |
| **NPGM - constrained to grow, adaptive $\lambda$: [83 % ± 4 %]** | | | | | | | | | |
| 81 % | 78 % | 93 % | 82 % | 81 % | 84 % | 83 % | 82 % | 83 % | 87 % |

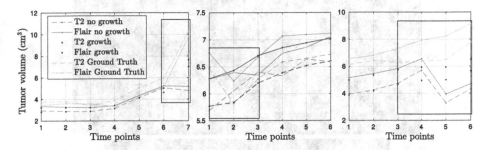

**Fig. 2.** Tumor volumetry of T2 (*dashed lines*) and FLAIR (*solid lines*) showing a clear advantage in the application of growth constraints (*red*) rather than leaving them out (*green*) when comparing with ground truth (*blue*) (Color figure online).

the datasets to include three time points. Based on the ground truth volumes, we rearranged the order of the three time points in order to get 84 sequences with:

1. tumor shrinking for both time increments, that is: $g_0 = [0, 0]$,
2. tumor shrinking for the first time increment and growing for the second time increment, that is: $g_1 = [0, 1]$.

Using the probabilistic growth framework explained in Sect. 2.2, we now calculate the probabilities of $g_0$ or $g_1$ for each sequence. This experiment is of clinical relevance: tumors tend to shrink temporarily after therapy and tumor regrowth needs to be detected as soon as possible. For each sequence, the algorithm will estimate confidence measures in $g_0$ and $g_1$. We obtain probabilities for both tumor growth patterns by normalising these confidence measures:

$$[p_{g_0}, p_{g_1}] = [\sigma_{g_0}, \sigma_{g_1}]/(\sigma_{g_0} + \sigma_{g_1}). \tag{9}$$

Figure 5 illustrates the amount of correctly classified tumor growth patterns. Of 168 datasets, 128 datasets were correctly classified, 35 datasets were falsely

Tumor segmentations constrained to grow, $\mathbf{g} = [1, 1, \ldots, 1]$

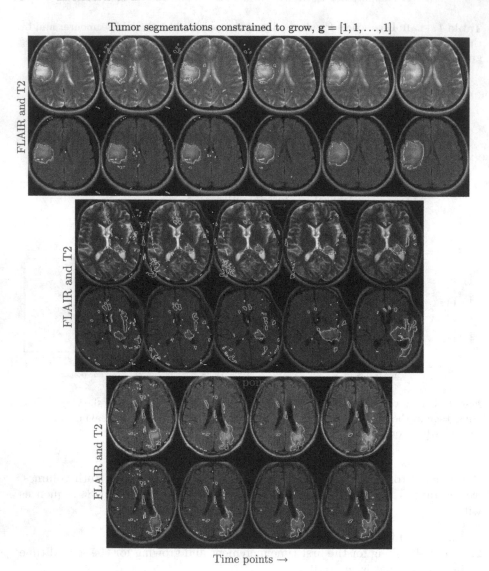

Time points $\rightarrow$

**Fig. 3.** FLAIR and T2 images for three patients with 6, 5 and 4 time points, annotated with EM segmentations (*yellow*), NPGM segmentations with a strict growth constraint along time (*red*) and ground truth (*blue*) (Color figure online).

estimated to grow after the second time point (false positives) and only 5 datasets were falsely estimated to keep shrinking after the second time point (false negatives). To the right in Fig. 5, one can see that the accuracy of tumor regrowth detection is highly related to the relative increase in tumor volume between the last time points. As expected, the difference in the tumor growth pattern probabilities ($|p_{g_1} - p_{g_0}|$) tends to be lower for misclassified tumor growth patterns.

Tumor segmentations constrained to grow, $\mathbf{g} = [1, 1, \ldots, 1]$

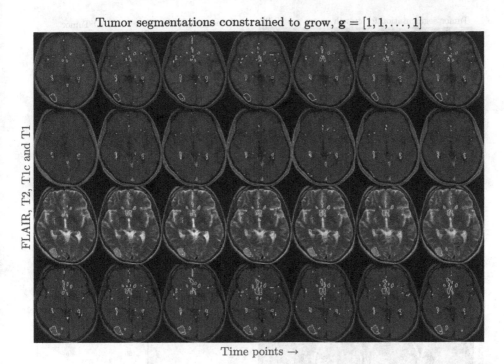

Time points →

**Fig. 4.** FLAIR, T2, T1c and T1 images for one patient with 7 time points, annotated with EM segmentations (*yellow*), NPGM segmentations with a strict growth constraint along time (*red*) and ground truth (*blue*). Ground truth for T1 and T1c is not shown. These segmentations illustrate the spatial regularisation of the CRF (Color figure online).

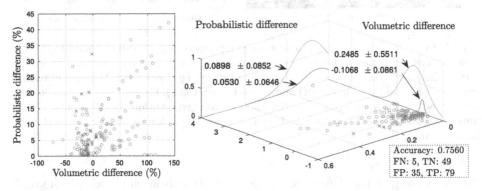

**Fig. 5.** Distribution of correctly (○) and incorrectly (×) classified tumor growth patterns as a function of the difference in the growth pattern probabilities ($|p_{g_1} - p_{g_0}|$) and as a function of the relative increase in tumor volumes between the last time points.

Note that our classification detects either shrinkage or growth. In other words, it does not account for cases of 'stable disease', where the tumor is neither

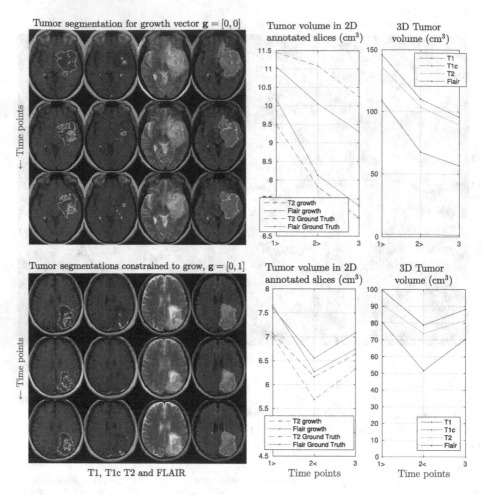

**Fig. 6.** *Upper row*: dataset depicting tumor shrinkage over both time transitions, *lower row*: dataset depicting tumor regrowth occurring at the second time point. The brain image slices are annotated with EM segmentations (*yellow*), NPGM segmentations with $g = [0,0]$ and $g = [0,1]$ (*red*) and ground truth (*blue*). Ground truth for T1 is not shown and tumor is not present in T1c. Volumes are given within the 2D ground truth annotated slices (*in the middle*) and for the entire 3D volumes (*to the right*) (Color figure online).

shrinking nor growing. This injects noise in our classification model, which gives rise to misclassifications.

Figure 6 illustrates segmentations of two rearranged datasets – one dataset with a tumor shrinking over two time increments and one with a tumor shrinking for the first time increment, but growing for the second time increment – together with tumor volumetry of T1, T1c, T2 and FLAIR.

# 4   Conclusion

In this study, we present a nonparametric model to segment brain tumors and to estimate the occurrence of tumor growth and/or shrinkage along time. We show the advantage of including longitudinal information in order to acquire more accurate tumor segmentations and volumetry. Furthermore, we adopt a fast and practical solution for the estimation of the spatial regularisation parameter in the CRF energy function. Our model was extended to include probabilistic formulations for tumor regrowth after therapy, and it was shown to succeed in accurately estimating the occurrence of tumor regrowth.

# References

1. Menze, B.H., Jakab, A., Bauer, S., et al.: The multimodal brain tumor image segmentation benchmark (BRATS). IEEE Trans. Med. Imag. **34**(10), 1993–2024 (2015)
2. Bauer, S., Tessier, J., Krieter, O., Nolte, L.P., Reyes, M.: Integrated spatio-temporal segmentation of longitudinal brain tumor imaging studies. In: Menze, B., Langs, G., Montillo, A., Kelm, M., Müller, H., Tu, Z. (eds.) MCV 2013. LNCS, vol. 8331, pp. 74–83. Springer, Switzerland (2013)
3. Tarabalka, Y., et al.: Spatio-temporal video segmentation with shape growth or shrinkage constraint. IEEE Trans. Image Process. **23**(9), 3829–3840 (2014)
4. Angelini, E.D., Clatz, O., Mandonnet, E., et al.: Glioma dynamics and computational models: a review. Curr. Med. Imaging Rev. **3**, 262–276 (2007)
5. Gooya, A., Pohl, K.M., Bilello, M., Biros, G., Davatzikos, C.: Joint segmentation and deformable registration of brain scans guided by a tumor growth model. In: Fichtinger, G., Martel, A., Peters, T. (eds.) MICCAI 2011, Part II. LNCS, vol. 6892, pp. 532–540. Springer, Heidelberg (2011)
6. Boykov, Y., Kolmogorov, V.: An experimental comparison of min-cut/max-flow algorithms for energy minimisation in vision. IEEE Trans. Pattern Anal. Mach. Intell. **26**(9), 1124–1137 (2004)
7. Candemir, S., Akgül, Y.S.: Adaptive regularization parameter for graph cut segmentation. In: Campilho, A., Kamel, M. (eds.) ICIAR 2010. LNCS, vol. 6111, pp. 117–126. Springer, Heidelberg (2010)
8. Kohli, P., Torr, P.H.S.: Measuring uncertainty in graph cut solutions. Comput. Vis. Image Underst. **112**, 30–38 (2008)
9. Menze, B.H., van Leemput, K., Lashkari, D., Weber, M.-A., Ayache, N., Golland, P.: A generative model for brain tumor segmentation in multi-modal images. In: Jiang, T., Navab, N., Pluim, J.P.W., Viergever, M.A. (eds.) MICCAI 2010, Part II. LNCS, vol. 6362, pp. 151–159. Springer, Heidelberg (2010)

# A Semi-automatic Method for Segmentation of Multiple Sclerosis Lesions on Dual-Echo Magnetic Resonance Images

Loredana Storelli[1], Elisabetta Pagani[1], Maria Assunta Rocca[1],
Mark A. Horsfield[2], and Massimo Filippi[1(✉)]

[1] Division of Neuroscience, Neuroimaging Research Unit, Institute of Experimental
Neurology, San Raffaele Scientific Institute,
Vita-Salute San Raffaele University, Milan, Italy
`filippi.massimo@hsr.it`
[2] Xinapse Systems, Colchester CO6 3BW, UK

**Abstract.** The identification and segmentation of focal hyperintense lesions on magnetic resonance images (MRI) are essential steps in the assessment of disease burden in multiple sclerosis (MS) patients. Manual lesion segmentation is considered to be the gold standard, although it is time-consuming and has poor intra- and inter-operator reproducibility. Here, we present a segmentation method based on dual-echo MR images initialized by manual identification of lesions and *a priori* information. The classification technique is based on a region growing approach with a final segmentation refinement step. The results have revealed high similarity between the segmentation performed with this method and that performed manually by an expert operator, as well as a low misclassification of lesions. Moreover, the time required for segmentation is drastically reduced.

## 1 Introduction

The analysis of disease burden on magnetic resonance images (MRI) from patients with multiple sclerosis (MS), both for research and clinical trials, requires the quantification of the volume of hyperintense lesions on a T2-weighted MRI sequence [1].

While many automatic methods for MS lesion segmentation have been proposed in the last 15 years, manual segmentation is still considered the gold standard although it is time-consuming and introduces inter and intra-observer variability [2].

The situation on available automatic methods for lesion segmentation is somewhat confused and fragmentary, complicating the difficult task of selecting one of the methods. Methods for fully-automated MS lesion segmentation are usually validated on a restricted dataset of cases and without a common framework, using different evaluation metrics, making the results difficult to compare.

A. Crimi et al. (Eds.): BrainLes 2015, LNCS 9556, pp. 80–90, 2016.
DOI: 10.1007/978-3-319-30858-6_8

Moreover, those methods are usually not trained or validated using dual-echo (DE) PD/T2-weighted MRI scans that have historically been used for the quantification of hyperintense MS lesions. The FLAIR sequence is now more commonly used because of the better contrast between focal lesions and the surrounding tissue [3,7]; however, large dual-echo datasets are in existence, and these represent a great resource for research, so there is a need to implement new methods to speed up lesion segmentation on those datasets.

The correct segmentation of all lesions is an important issue of the fully-automatic methods, since they often identify false positives and false negatives [9].

With these considerations in mind, we chose to implement a new method, based on DE MR images, that could guarantee the correct identification of all lesions by having an expert physician manually perform this task, but then automating the lesion segmentation phase which is the most time-consuming part, contributes most to variability.

This paper presents a semi-automatic method for MS lesion segmentation based on manual identification of lesions on DE MR images, using *a priori* information. It gave high similarity with the ground truth and it also provides a considerable reduction in the time required for whole task of lesion segmentation.

## 2    Materials and Methods

### 2.1    Patients

The dataset consisted of 10 MS patients used for training the algorithm, and 20 MS patients with a range of lesion loads [0.3 – 9 ml] used for the validation. For each patient, a brain DE turbo spin-echo MRI sequence was obtained using a 3.0 T scanner (Achieva Philips Medical Systems, Best, The Netherlands), (TR/TE = 2910/16,80 ms, ETL=6; flip angle=90°, matrix size=256 × 256, FOV= 240 × 240 mm$^2$, 50 axial 3 mm-thick slices).

Manual identification of lesions by an expert physician was used to initialize the algorithm, whereas manual segmentation, performed by the same expert, was used for validation purposes. Both steps were performed using software for medical image analysis (Jim Version 6, Xinapse Systems, Colchester, UK).

Approval was received from the ethical standards committee on human experimentation of San Raffaele Scientific Institute. Written informed consent was obtained from all subjects prior to study enrollment.

### 2.2    Methods

The following are the operational phases of the method.

**Image Standardization.** One difficulty with non-quantitative MRI techniques is that image intensities are arbitrary, even within the same protocol, for the same scanner and the same subject. This is a problem if a threshold value is to be used for a region growing approach, as described in the next section. Thus, proton density weighted (PD-w) image intensity values were standardized to correct for the arbitrary intensity scaling for different acquisitions [5]. The method used requires a training step, to be performed only once for a given MRI protocol on a cohort of patients, in which three intensity parameters are estimated from each histogram: the brightest peak position ($\mu$) that corresponds to the grey matter (GM) peak, and the first and last percentiles ($p_1$ and $p_2$ respectively) set at 1 % and 98 %.

The intensity range of values [$s_1, s_2$] for the standard histogram in which to project the first and last percentiles intensity values of each input image, is selected according to a theorem, stated in [6], that guarantees in its formulation that each intensity value of the original image corresponds unequivocally a new intensity value on the standard image, so that no image compression is performed during the transformation. Thus, if standardization is done respecting these conditions, then there is no loss of information and the original image can be obtained by inverting the standardized image. The $s_1$ value is fixed to 1, while $s_2$ is extracted as follows, according to the cited theorem, where the index $i$ identified each volume $V$ of the training set:

$$s_1 = 1; \tag{1}$$

$$s_2 - s_1 \geq (max_{V_i} |(\mu_i - p_{1i})| + max_{V_i} |(p_{2i} - \mu_i)|) * F \tag{2}$$

$$F = \max(\frac{max_{V_i} |(\mu_i - p_{1i})|}{min_{V_i} |(\mu_i - p_{1i})|}; \frac{max_{V_i} |(p_{2i} - \mu_i)|}{min_{V_i} |(p_{2i} - \mu_i)|}) \tag{3}$$

$$s_2 \geq (s_2 - s_1) - s_1 \tag{4}$$

The intensity value for the standard GM peak is calculated as the mean of the GM peak intensities of the training dataset.

During the transformation phase, the intensity value of the GM peak (brightest peak) of each input volume was fixed to the standard GM peak intensity value, and a linear intensity transformation that passes through this point and minimizes the distance from the two percentiles to the standard intensity range was applied. In this way the intensity histogram of each given image is rescaled into the standard one.

Figure 1 shows three PD-w MRI histograms after the standardization process.

**Region Growing Algorithm.** The core of the algorithm is the pixel-based region growing segmentation method. This approach to segmentation examines neighbouring pixels of initial "seed points" and determines whether the pixel neighbours should be added to the region according to similarity constraints [4]. The process is iterated as a clustering algorithm and stops when the similarity condition is violated.

The main constraint used for the growth of the segmented region is the intensity similarity, based on a threshold that varies according to a relationship determined by a training process described below.

**Training.** The region growing segmentation approach is applied to the training dataset where lesions were manually identified using a marker point and outlined by an expert physician. Region growing starts in each lesion from the markers,

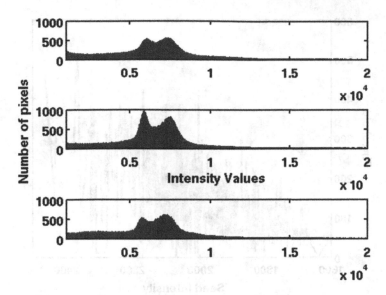

**Fig. 1.** An example of three PD-w MRI histograms after the standardization process. The highest intensity mode and the intensity scales are comparable.

and lesion outlines are used as reference results to find the optimal threshold that pushes/stops the growth of the segmented region as close as possible to the manual segmentation. In this way, the optimal values of the threshold associated with each seed point are extracted and collected, as shown in Fig. 2. The threshold values extracted represent the difference between the seed point intensity value and the minimum intensity value inside the segmented region which stop the segmentation of the lesion. Due to the heterogeneity of MS lesions, threshold values are very noisy, as shown in Fig. 2. A straight line is fitted to those data to obtain a function for the validation dataset that unequivocally associates a threshold with each marker point on the PD-w image.

**Segmentation.** Lesions are first manually identified by an expert physician who places markers on the PD-w images while also having the T2-w image visible as a reference.

Starting from each marker (seed point), expansion of the segmented region continues to the adjacent pixels constrained according to a threshold value. This value ($T_i$) is different for each lesion and it is extracted by the threshold function computed during the training phase:

$$T_i = m_f * (seed_i) + q_f \tag{5}$$

where $m_f$ and $q_f$ are respectively the slope and the intercept of the threshold function; $seed_i$ is the intensity value of the $i - th$ lesion marker point.

To avoid the segmentation going outside lesions, the region growing approach is combined with edge detection of lesions. For this purpose a half-way contrast image is obtained by averaging the non-standardized PD-w and T2-w images.

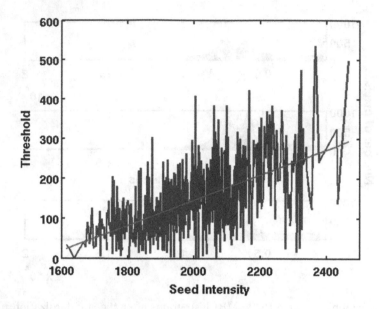

**Fig. 2.** Threshold values extracted after the training process on the manual segmented lesions. The red line is the fitted line used to select the threshold function for the region growing approach. Lesion load ranging from 0.8 to 3.8 (Color figure online).

The PD-w image has better contrast between white matter (WM) and cerebrospinal fluid (CSF) than the T2-w image, while the latter shows better contrast between WM and GM than the PD-w image. The "mean" image is created to take advantage of both images tissue contrasts, as shown in Fig. 3.

This image is filtered using a high-pass unsharp filter to create an image in which the high-frequency components (edges) are amplified [8]. The edge-enhanced image is subtracted from the original image, to obtain an image in which lesion edges are zero-crossing points between negative and positive values, representing respectively the internal and the external side of the lesion.

A new image $S$ is obtained, as shown in Fig. 4:

$$S = I - filt(I);\qquad(6)$$

where $I$ is the original image and $filt(I)$ is the filtered image.

This result is finally employed to restrict the growth of lesion segmentation when a lesion edge is reached.

Since the two constraints did not perform satisfactorily if used alone, because of noise or artefacts on the images, the intensity threshold is combined with the detection of lesion edges to obtain the stop condition of the region growing algorithm:

$$StopCondition = (\|I_s - I_{pi}\| > T) \cap (S_{pi} > 0);\qquad(7)$$

where $I_s$ is the intensity of the seed point, $I_{pi}$ is the intensity of the $i - th$ adjacent pixel to classify in the standardized PD-w image and $T$ is the threshold

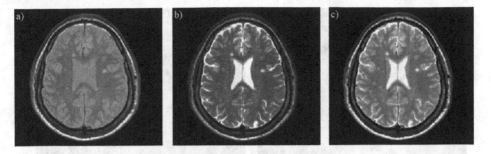

**Fig. 3.** An example half-way contrast image (c) obtained by averaging the PD-w image (a) and the T2-w image (b).

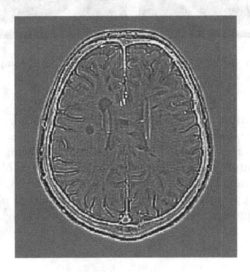

**Fig. 4.** An example of edge enhanced subtraction image.

value previously extracted, just once for each lesion before the start of the region growing algorithm.

To stop the growth of the segmented region both conditions need to be satisfied.

**Threshold Refinement Step.** The threshold curve is used only to initialize the growth of the segmented region, and after an initial segmentation a more robust intensity threshold is estimated. For each segmented lesion, the distribution of intensity values is extracted after the first step of segmentation and the refined threshold of this distribution is used as a new intensity threshold to restart the region growing.

The refined threshold is selected according to the dimensions of the lesion: if a lesion is small (less than 10 pixels) the intensity distribution extracted is unreliable due to the low number of samples, so that the twentieth percentile of the distribution is selected as the refined threshold to avoid the inclusion of outliers. On the other hand, if a lesion is large (more than 10 pixels), the fifth

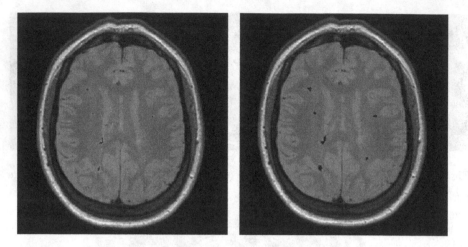

**Fig. 5.** An example of initial segmentation on the left figure, compared to the lesion segmentation after the refinement step, on the right.

percentile of the distribution is selected as the new threshold, since the intensity distribution is more reliable.

According to the new threshold values, the region growing is restarted from the previous segmentation. A final refined segmentation is obtained using the same stopping condition but with a new threshold $T$ (Fig. 5).

The method is implemented in MatLab® and the output of the algorithm is the mask of the segmented lesions and the lesion load in $mm^3$.

## 3    Validation

Manual segmentation by an expert operator was used as the gold standard.
The metrics used for the validation are computed considering each lesion separately and then overall lesions.

1. Dice Similarity Coefficient (DSC), to assess the similarity between the segmentation performed manually and that performed with the proposed method for each lesion:

$$DSC = \frac{2|A_v \cap M_v|}{|A_v| + |M_v|};\qquad(8)$$

where $|A_v \cap M_v|$ is the number of voxels classified as lesion by both this method and the expert operator. $|A_v|$ is the number of voxels classified as lesion by this method and $|M_v|$ is the number of voxels classified as lesion by the expert operator.

2. Root Mean Square Error of lesion load (RMSE) in ml:

$$RMSE = \sqrt{\frac{1}{n}\sum_{i=1}^{n}(M_i - A_i)^2}\qquad(9)$$

where $n$ is the number of lesions; $M_i$ is the $i-th$ manually detected lesion load and $A_i$ is the $i-th$ automatically detected lesion load.

3. True Positive Fraction (TPF); False Positive Fraction (FPF); False Negative Fraction (FNF):

$$TPF = \frac{|A_v \cap M_v|}{|M_v|}; \tag{10}$$

$$FPF = \frac{|A_v \cap \neg M_v|}{|M_v|}; \tag{11}$$

$$FNF = \frac{|\neg A_v \cap M_v|}{|M_v|}; \tag{12}$$

where $|A_v \cap \neg M_v|$ is the number of voxels classified as lesion only by the new method and not by the expert operator, while $|\neg A_v \cap M_v|$ is the number of voxels classified as lesions only by the expert operator and not by this method.

## 4    Results

Fig. 6 shows example lesion segmentations. The manually segmented lesion mask can be visually compared to the output lesion mask of the new method. The validation metrics were extracted for each lesion load of each patient. Lesions are labelled in 3-D to compute these metrics.

In Fig. 7, the metrics evaluated over all lesions for each patient are graphically reported. Averaging the metrics over all patients the following values were obtained: DSC = 0.78; RMSE = 0.17 ml; TPF = 0.81; FPF = 0.14; FNF = 0.20.

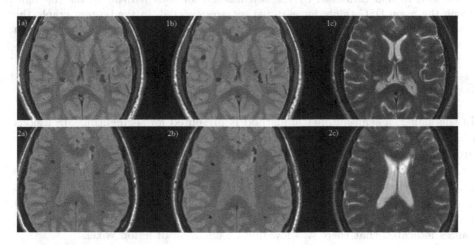

**Fig. 6.** Examples of lesion segmentation for two different patients performed by an expert operator (1a and 2a) compared to the performance of the new method (1b and 2b). The corresponding T2-w images are shown in 1c and 2c.

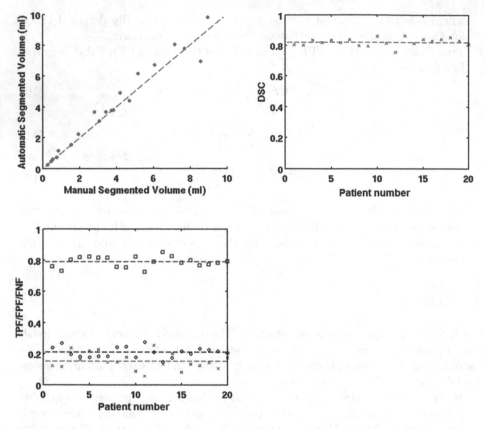

**Fig. 7.** In the top left graph a scatter plot is shown to compare manually estimated lesion load to that estimated by the new method for each patient. In the top right graph the mean DSC values for each patient are reported. In the bottom graph, the mean TPF (blue squares), FPF (red crosses) and FNF (black circles) values for each patient are shown (Color figure online).

## 5   Discussion

In this paper, a semi-automatic method is presented for segmenting MS lesions on DE MRI, based on the manual identification of lesions and a trained region-growing algorithm with prior intensity standardization.

Lesion segmentation obtained using the new method was very similar to the ground truth, with a high degree of overlap (DSC = 0.78 and TPF = 0.81). The lesion load obtained with this segmentation method is comparable with that obtained with the manual segmentation (RMSE = 0.17 ml). FPF and FNF values indicated that there was low misclassification of lesion voxels.

Moreover, the operator time required to process the images was drastically reduced: for the images evaluated here, the average time for manual lesion segmentation was about 40 min, while for the method proposed the average time was about 50 s, regardless manually marking the seed points.

The comparison of this method with other proposed automatic or semi-automatic MS lesion segmentation methods is very challenging. The difficulty would be to find an available method that can be used with our own data (PD/T2-w scans). On the other hand, the full re-implementation of a published, but not freely-accessible method might introduce some small differences or errors in the code which could mean that the method performs badly. We therefore chose to compare the method with expert manual segmentation, which is still considered to be the gold standard. Moreover, it was difficult to find a MS lesion challenge with a shared PD-T2w MRI dataset for an easy comparison of the results with other lesion segmentation methods.

Due to the heterogeneous nature of MS lesions, the method sometimes encountered difficulties in segmenting those lesions with blurred and poorly-defined borders, which are also difficult for a human observer to delineate. Those lesions have poor contrast on PD/T2-w scans, thus confounding the constraints for the region growing approach, and the segmentation exceeded the external borders of the lesion. This might be improved by introducing further information about the spatial location of lesions, perhaps using co-registered T1-w images.

The method has been validated on data from a single center, and from a single type of MRI scanner. Further validation is required by testing the method on a multi-center dataset with different scanners and scanner operators. Another additional validation would be to test the sensitivity of the method with respect to the location of the seed points.

While accuracy is certainly important, it is essential that we assess the reproducibility in future. If a technique is inaccurate or has a bias, as long as this bias is consistent it should still be possible to measure changes over time. However, if the reproducibility is poor, real changes in longitudinal studies can be masked by random variations due to poor measurement.

In future, it may be also possible to fully automate the method, by removing the need to manually identify lesions by employing FLAIR or double inversion recovery (DIR) sequences.

# References

1. Filippi, M., Rocca, M.A., De Stefano, N., Enzinger, C., Fisher, E., Horsfield, M.A., Inglese, M., Pelletier, D., Comi, G.: Magnetic resonance techniques in multiple sclerosis: the present and the future. Arch. Neurol. **68**(12), 1514–1520 (2011). doi:10.1001/archneurol.2011.914.Review
2. Garcia-Lorenzo, D., Francis, S., Narayanan, S., Arnold, D.L., Collins, D.L.: Review of automatic segmentation methods of multiple sclerosis white matter lesions on conventional magnetic resonance imaging. Med. Image Anal. **17**, 1–18 (2013)
3. Garcia-Lorenzo, D., Prima, S., Arnold, D.L., Collins, D.L., Barillot, C.: Trimmed-likelihood estimation for focal lesions and tissue segmentation in multisequence MRI for multiple sclerosis. IEEE Trans. Med. Imaging **30**, 1455–1467 (2011)
4. Kamdi, S., Krishna, R.K.: Image segmentation and region growing algorithm. Int. J. Comput. Technol. Electron. Eng. **2**, 103–107 (2012)

5. Nyul, L.G., Udupa, J.K.: On standardizing the MR image intensity scale. Magn. Reson. Med. **42**, 1072–1081 (1999)
6. Nyul, L.G. and Udupa, J.K.: On standardizing the MR image intensity scale. Technical Report MIPG.250, Medical Image Processing Group, Department of Radiology, University of Pennsylvania (1999)
7. Schmidt, P., Gaser, C., Arsic, M., Buck, D., Forschler, A., Erthele, A., Hoshi, M., Ilg, R., Schmid, V.J., Zimmer, C., Hemmer, B., Muhlau, M.: An automated tool for detection of FLAIR-hyperintense white-matter lesions in multiple sclerosis. Neuroimage **59**, 3774–3783 (2012)
8. Luft, T., Colditz, C., Deussen, O.: Image enhancement by unsharp masking the depth buffer. Association for Computing Machinery (2006)
9. Van Leemput, K., Maes, F., Vandermeulen, D., Colchester, A., Suetens, P.: Automated segmentation of multiple sclerosis lesions by model outlier detection. IEEE Trans. Med. Imaging **20**(8), 677–688 (2001)

# Bayesian Stroke Lesion Estimation for Automatic Registration of DTI Images

Félix Renard[1(✉)], Matthieu Urvoy[2], and Assia Jaillard[1,2,3,4]

[1] EA AGEIS, Univ. J. Fourier, Grenoble, France
felixrenard@gmail.com
[2] SFR RMN Biomédicale Et Neurosciences, Univ. J. Fourier, Grenoble, France
[3] Pôle Recherche, CHU de Grenoble, Grenoble, France
[4] Unité IRM 3T - Recherche, CHU de Grenoble, Grenoble, France

**Abstract.** Diffusion Tensor Imaging (DTI), the Fractional Anisotropy (FA) is used to measure the integrity of the white matter (WM); it is considered as a biomarker for stroke recovery. This measure is highly sensitive to applied pre-processing steps; in particular, the presence of a lesion may result into severe misregistration. In this paper, it is proposed to quantitatively assess the impact of large stroke lesions onto the registration process. To reduce this impact, a new registration algorithm, that localizes the lesion via Bayesian estimation, is proposed.

**Keywords:** Lesion · DTI · Registration · Segmentation

## 1 Introduction

Diffusion Tensor Imaging (DTI) is increasingly used to examine structural connectivity in the brain in various conditions, including stroke. Studies have suggested that recovery after stroke is related to the structural remodeling of white matter (WM) tracts in both ipsilesional and contralesional hemispheres [10]. The Fractional Anisotropy (FA), a metric derived from DTI, is currently the most commonly used metric to measure the microstructural status of white matter. Regional FA values are decreased in the corticospinal tract of the lesioned hemisphere and correlated with motor impairment score [10,11]. Indeed, FA appears to be a promising neuroimaging biomarker for stroke recovery [6].

In the context of brain lesions, the registration and normalization of diffusion images from the subject to the common reference space is crucial for group comparison [3]. This notably involves a non-rigid registration step that is not robust to images featuring stroke lesions, therefore resulting into distorted and skewed images [7].

The underlying problem resides in the fact that current registration algorithms generally assume that both the image to be registered and its template present the same but distorted information. Existing solutions target either small deformations [5] or large deformations [2], with diffeomorphic (metric) mapping.

A. Crimi et al. (Eds.): BrainLes 2015, LNCS 9556, pp. 91–103, 2016.
DOI: 10.1007/978-3-319-30858-6_9

In stroke brain imaging, however, the lesioned areas have no match in the normal template. As a consequence, incorrect registration may (for instance) artificially shrink the lesion to fit the originate template. A very limited number of studies have been focusing on this problem. In [4], it is proposed to estimate the lesion contents by inpainting from neighbouring brain areas, therefore assuming that the brain is normal. However, this method cannot be applied to large lesions. As an alternative, it is proposed in [1] to mask the lesion by zeroing the contribution of its voxels in the registration cost function. However, lesioned areas did not match anymore. It should be noted that the lesions were segmented by manual delineation of T1-weighted images. Their findings suggest that the use of masked normalization based on non-linear registration (using DARTEL) was required to provide accurate results, even though manually segmented masks were rather coarse.

In DTI, the issue of registration errors induced by stroke lesions of different sizes remains almost unexplored. Therefore, the aim of this study is twofold: (i) to quantitatively assess registration errors in both contra and ipsilesional hemispheres; (ii) to evaluate a new registration algorithm that automatically segments and masks lesions in order to refine the initial registration step.

To this end, we simulated different sizes of spherical lesions to demonstrate the effect of non-linear registration on the FA images. Moreover, both ipsi and contra-lesional hemispheres are investigated, which has not been studied yet. While registration errors are likely to be larger in the ipsilesional hemisphere, one may also expect that mis-realignments spread to the contralesional hemisphere.

In existing software, a mask can be fed to the registration process, yet automatic methods capable of segmenting the lesions are still under development[1]. In this paper, we estimate the lesion mask with a Bayesian approach, and integrate it into a two-stage registration algorithm, whose accuracy outperforms state-of-the-art methods, notably within the contralesional hemisphere. We evaluate our algorithm in 26 clinical stroke brain lesions, provided by the ISIS-HERMES stroke study (PHRC 2010 site web). Diffusion magnetic resonance imaging, consisting of High Angular Resolution Diffusion Imaging (HARDI) with 60 non collinear directions of gradients, was performed on a Philips 3T Magnet at the University Hospital of Grenoble (France). Parameters acquisition were: FOV $= 240 \times 240 \times 140 mm$; 70 slices; voxels size $= 1.6 \times 1.6 \times 2 \ mm^3$; b-value $= 1000 \ s/mm^2$.

## 2  Quantitative Assessment of Registration Errors

To the best of our knowledge, no study has been quantifying the registration errors induced by the use of a lesion, in both contra and ipsilesional hemispheres. In this section, we assess the effect of lesions on linear and non-linear registration methods, with and without taking into account the corresponding lesion mask. First we consider lesions of radius $k = 20 \, mm$, then we analyse the impact of different sizes of lesions.

---

[1] See  BRATS  (http://braintumorsegmentation.org)  and  ISLES  (http://www.isles-challenge.org): 2015' medical imaging challenges on lesion segmentation.

## 2.1  Methods

**Generation of Simulated Stroke Images.** FA images $I_P^{(p)}$, $0 < p < N_P$ were obtained in $N_P = 10$ healthy people. These images were registered to the standard template provided by FSL. Then the inverse transformations to align the image in the patient space were estimated. For each of these images, an impaired twin $I_S^{(p,k)}$ was generated by simulating a spherical lesion of radius $k$ mm in the template space, then transformed back into the patient space. This way, all the lesions were localised at the same position. The radius $k$ varies from 5 mm to 20 mm. The volume of the resulting lesions respectively varies from $0.523\,\mathrm{cm}^3$ to $33.49\,\mathrm{cm}^3$ , which is below the mean volume of lesions in stroke patients ($100\,\mathrm{cm}^3$) that were considered in this study. The different sizes of the lesions are illustrated in Fig. 1.

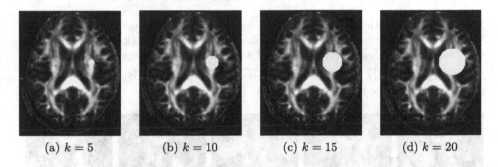

(a) $k = 5$          (b) $k = 10$          (c) $k = 15$          (d) $k = 20$

**Fig. 1.** Different sizes of lesions displayed in the template space.

**Registration of Original and Impaired Images.** Registration was performed with FSL [5]. Linear and non-linear transforms were applied. The registration cost function was chosen to be the correlation coefficient between the initial and the registered image. The target image $I_T$ corresponded to the standard template provided by FSL. $\mathcal{R}$ denotes the registration operator; associated superscripts $w/$ and $w/o$ respectively indicate that the registration is performed with or without taking into account the lesion mask, while subscripts $Lin$ and $N$-$Lin$ respectively indicate that a linear or a non-linear transform has been chosen. A flow chart in Fig. 2 summarizes the procedure of generation of simulated lesions and the comparison of different registrations.

## 2.2  Qualitative Assessment of Registered Images for Lesions of Radius $k = 20$ mm

Figure 3 shows a simulated image $I_S$, and its registered twins for lesions of radius $k = 20$ mm. The linear transform provides visually similar images, with and without lesion mask. This stands in contrast with non-linear registration: without mask, the lesion is shrunk to fit the template, thus providing erroneous results. Still, the contra-lesional hemisphere seems – **visually** – to be correctly registered in all scenarios.

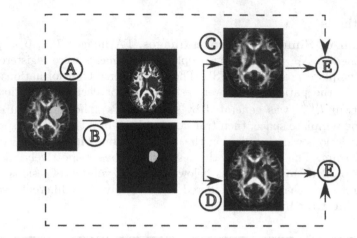

**Fig. 2.** (A) Generation of the simulated lesion in the template space. (B) Transformation of this lesion in the patient space to obtain the mask of the lesion and the image $I_S^{(p,k)}$. (C) and (D) correspond respectively to the registration procedure with $(\mathcal{R}_{\text{N-Lin}}^{\text{w/}}\left(I_S^{(p,k)}\right))$ and without mask $(\mathcal{R}_{\text{N-Lin}}^{\text{w/o}}\left(I_S^{(p,k)}\right))$ The step (E) compares the ground truth and the two obtained images.

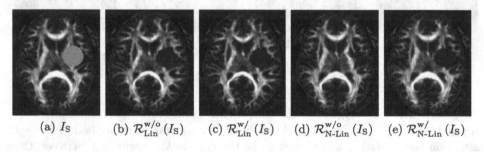

     (a) $I_S$      (b) $\mathcal{R}_{\text{Lin}}^{\text{w/o}}(I_S)$      (c) $\mathcal{R}_{\text{Lin}}^{\text{w/}}(I_S)$      (d) $\mathcal{R}_{\text{N-Lin}}^{\text{w/o}}(I_S)$      (e) $\mathcal{R}_{\text{N-Lin}}^{\text{w/}}(I_S)$

**Fig. 3.** Effect of the transform and the lesion mask on the registration of a simulated image $I_S$ for a lesion of radius $k = 20$ mm. (a). Linear (resp. non-linear) registration is performed in (b) and (c) (resp. (c) and (e)). Masks are taken into account in (c) and (e) only.

**Table 1.** Linear registration (for a lesion of radius $k = 20$ mm): RMSD (average and standard deviation) in three scenarios: influence of ($a$) the lesion, ($b$) the lesion mask, and ($c$) the cost function.

| Scenario | ($a$) $\mathcal{R}_{\text{Lin}}^{\text{w/o}}(I_P)$ vs $\mathcal{R}_{\text{Lin}}^{\text{w/}}(I_S)$ | ($b$) $\mathcal{R}_{\text{Lin}}^{\text{w/o}}(I_S)$ vs $\mathcal{R}_{\text{Lin}}^{\text{w/}}(I_S)$ | ($c$) $\mathcal{R}_{\text{Lin}}^{\text{w/}}(I_S)$ vs $\mathcal{R}_{\text{Lin}}^{\text{w/}}(I_S)$ |
|---|---|---|---|
| RMSD (mm) | $0.28 \pm 0.07$ | $0.36 \pm 0.18$ | $4.88 \pm 1.20$ |

## 2.3 Quantitative Error Analysis in Linear Registration for Lesions of Radius $k = 20\,\mathrm{mm}$

Visual inspection of registered images tends to show that the linear registration is robust to large lesions. We quantified the corresponding registration errors in terms of Root Mean Square Deviation (RMSD). Mean RMSD (and standard deviation) (in mm) were compared for linear registrations of: (a) original images $I_\mathrm{P}^{(p)}$ versus impaired images $I_\mathrm{S}^{(p)}$, (b) the impaired images $I_\mathrm{S}^{(p)}$ with versus without a lesion mask, and (c) the same images with the correlation versus the mutual information as cost functions for the registration.

Table 1 displays the resulting RMSDs; our results show a discete effect of the lesion (scenario a), as the obtained RMSD is way below the RMSD associated with a change in the cost function (scenario c). Similarly, whether the lesion mask is accounted for or not does not make any difference (scenario b).

## 2.4 Quantitative Error Analysis in Non-linear Registration for Lesions of Radius $k = 20\,\mathrm{mm}$

In order to fully appreciate the effect of a lesion on the estimated non-linear registration transforms, we quantified – for each pair $(I_\mathrm{P}^{(p)}, I_\mathrm{S}^{(p)})$, $0 < p < N_\mathrm{P}$, of original and simulated FA images – the registration differences in terms of: (i) transform Jacobians, and (ii) resulting FA intensities. Only the differences located in the template's skeleton ($I_\mathrm{T} > 0.2$) [9] of the White Matter (WM) are considered. Contra and ipsi-lesional hemispheres are investigated separately.

Figure 4 plots the histograms of Jacobians differences $\Delta_\mathrm{J}^{(p)}$ and FA intensity differences $\Delta_\mathrm{FA}^{(p)}$ that were observed within each pair $\left\{ \mathcal{R}_\mathrm{N\text{-}Lin}^{\mathrm{w/o}} \left( I_\mathrm{P}^{(p)} \right), \mathcal{R}_\mathrm{N\text{-}Lin}^{\mathrm{w/}} \left( I_\mathrm{S}^{(p)} \right) \right\}$. As can be seen, both ipsi and contra-lesional hemispheres are affected by the introduction of the simulated lesion, which, in the latter case, was hardly detectable visually. In terms of FA intensities, this results in registration errors as high as 0.2 (resp. 0.1) in the ispilesional(resp. contra-lesional) hemisphere. Finally, Fig. 4 also shows that the integration of lesion mask, in either linear or non-linear registration methods, led to reducing misregistration.

## 2.5 Quantitative Error Analysis in Non-linear Registration for Different Sizes of Lesions

The registration procedures with and without the knowledge of the mask were achieved for different sizes of lesion (radius $k = [5, 10, 15, 20]\,\mathrm{mm}$). The obtained results $\mathcal{R}_\mathrm{N\text{-}Lin}^{\mathrm{w/o}} (I_\mathrm{S})$ and $\mathcal{R}_\mathrm{N\text{-}Lin}^{\mathrm{w/}} (I_\mathrm{S})$ can be observed respectively in Fig. 5.

We tested the difference of measures $\Delta_\mathrm{FA}^{(p,k)}$ of FA values for different sizes of lesion to determine whether $\Delta_\mathrm{FA}^{(p,k)}$ is identical for the procedures with and without the mask. Because the $\Delta_\mathrm{FA}^{(p,k)}$ in the ten subjects and both hemispheres, did not show normal distribution, the non parametric Wilcoxon matched-pair

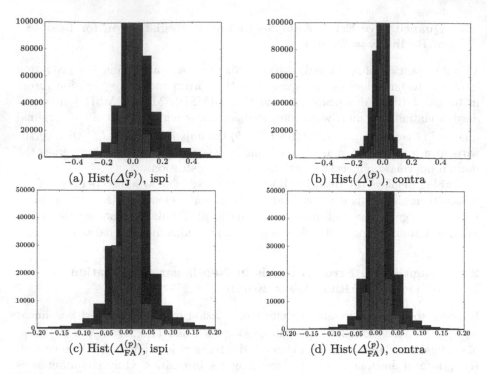

**Fig. 4.** Registration errors: histograms of Jacobian differences (top row) and FA differences (bottom row). Differences in the ipsilesional hemisphere are plotted on the left, while those in contralesional hemispheres are plotted on the right. The first (resp. second) column corresponds to the ipsilesional (resp. contra-lateral) hemisphere. Finally, blue (resp. green) histograms correspond to registrations with mask (resp. without mask) (Color figure online).

signed-rank test was used. It tests the null hypothesis that two related paired samples come from the same distribution. The results showed significant differences between the two related paired samples. In addition, the corresponding z-statistics of the Wilcoxon test are reported.

In Fig. 6, the obtained z-statistics for ipsi and contra hemispheres are displayed for several values of radius $k$. The z-statistics of $\Delta_{FA}^{(p,k)}$ are lower in the ipsilesional than the contralesional hemisphere for each values of $k$, suggesting that the differences of FA measures between the two methods (with and without a mask) are even more important in the contralesional hemisphere.

It should be noted that the differences of FA measures increase with the size of the lesion, showing the necessity of using a mask for registration of images with lesions, especially in the case of large lesions.

In the second step of this paper, we analyse the deformation induced by the lesion during the registration procedure, in the stroke brain lesions, with and without mask, and in the simulated lesion (the ground truth). For that purpose, we analysed the Dice Coefficient (DC) and the False Negative Errors (FNE).

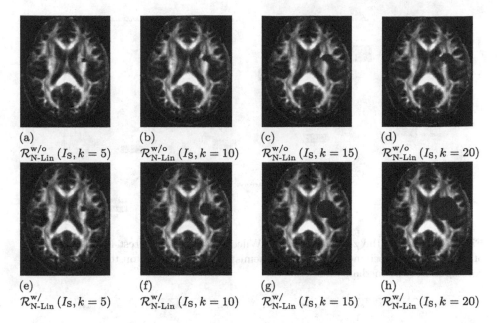

(a) $\mathcal{R}_{\text{N-Lin}}^{\text{w/o}}\left(I_{\text{S}}, k=5\right)$    (b) $\mathcal{R}_{\text{N-Lin}}^{\text{w/o}}\left(I_{\text{S}}, k=10\right)$    (c) $\mathcal{R}_{\text{N-Lin}}^{\text{w/o}}\left(I_{\text{S}}, k=15\right)$    (d) $\mathcal{R}_{\text{N-Lin}}^{\text{w/o}}\left(I_{\text{S}}, k=20\right)$

(e) $\mathcal{R}_{\text{N-Lin}}^{\text{w/}}\left(I_{\text{S}}, k=5\right)$    (f) $\mathcal{R}_{\text{N-Lin}}^{\text{w/}}\left(I_{\text{S}}, k=10\right)$    (g) $\mathcal{R}_{\text{N-Lin}}^{\text{w/}}\left(I_{\text{S}}, k=15\right)$    (h) $\mathcal{R}_{\text{N-Lin}}^{\text{w/}}\left(I_{\text{S}}, k=20\right)$

**Fig. 5.** (a–d)$\mathcal{R}_{\text{N-Lin}}^{\text{w/o}}\left(I_{\text{S}}\right)$ and (e–h)$\mathcal{R}_{\text{N-Lin}}^{\text{w/}}\left(I_{\text{S}}\right)$ for different radius $k$. We can observe that the shape of the lesions is well preserved when the mask of the lesion is considered.

The DC permits to focus on the similarity of two sets (here the simulated lesion and one lesion of the two registration procedures, while the FNE highlights the error to fit the simulated lesion. The DC and FNE results are displayed in Figs. 7 and 8 respectively.

Our findings underline the importance of the masking registration procedure. The FNE show that the lesions are shrunk during no apriori registration. In addition, the effect of the lesion is increased with the size of the lesions.

## 3 Proposed Unsupervised Registration Algorithm

In the previous section, we showed that the presence of lesions introduces significant registration artifacts when using a non-linear transform. Conversely, linear registration showed to be quite robust to lesions with similar registered images with or without applying a lesion mask. Building up on these features, we propose registration algorithm that splits the registration process into two steps: (i) a coarse estimation of the registration parameters for which the output is used to estimate the lesion mask, (ii) a refined estimation step that accounts for the obtained masks.

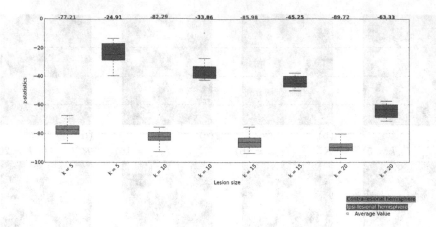

**Fig. 6.** Boxplot of the z-statistics of the Wilcoxon signed rank test for different sizes of lesions and for ipsi and contralesional hemisphere. The values on top of the boxplot correspond to the median values.

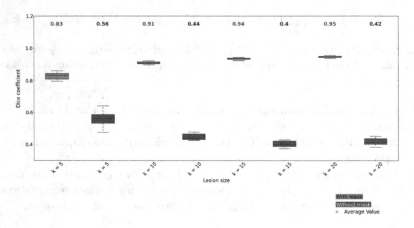

**Fig. 7.** Dice coefficient between the simulated lesions and the lesions obtained after registration with and without mask, for different sizes of lesions and for ipsi and contralesional hemisphere. The values on top of the boxplot correspond to the median values.

### 3.1 Bayesian Estimation of the Lesion Mask

Let $I_{\mathrm{T}}$ denote the FA registration template image, as provided by the FSL software [5]. Let $I_{\mathrm{P}}$ be a patient's image and $\mathcal{R}_{\mathrm{Lin}}^{\mathrm{w/o}}(I_{\mathrm{P}})$ its coarsely registered twin, where $\mathcal{R}_{\mathrm{Lin}}^{\mathrm{w/o}}$ is the linear registration operator, without mask.

**Gold Standard Segmentation Masks.** $N_{\mathrm{P}} = 26$ patient images $I_{\mathrm{P}}^{(p)}$, $0 < p < N_{\mathrm{P}}$, were linearly registered into the template space. Lesions were manually delineated by an expert neuroradiologist. When occuring in the left hemisphere

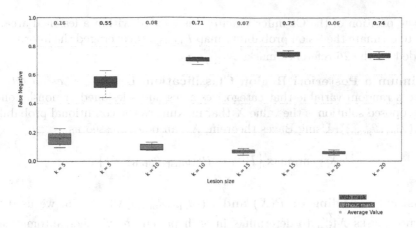

**Fig. 8.** False Negative errors between the simulated lesions and the lesions obtained after registration with and without mask, for different sizes of lesions and for ipsi and contralesional hemisphere. The values on top of the boxplot correspond to the median values.

(the contalesional hemisphere in this study), images were mirrored (w.r.t. the mid-saggital plane) so that they are now all located in the right hemisphere (ipsi-lateral). Obtained masks $\mathcal{M}_{\text{Ref}}^{(p)}$ serve as reference segmentation maps in this study.

**Initial Localization of WM Alterations.** Within the template space, the difference $I_\Delta = I_T - \mathcal{R}_{\text{Lin}}^{\text{w/o}}(I_P)$, between the template image and the coarsely registered image, is used to estimate an initial lesion mask $\mathcal{M}_\tau$. Typically, the values of FA voxels inside a lesion are very low (around 0.1). Also, it is commonly admitted that WM voxel intensities are greater than 0.2. For these reasons, the initial mask $\mathcal{M}_\tau$ includes voxels for which the difference $I_\Delta$ exceeds a certain threshold $\tau$ (in this study, $\tau$ was empirically set to 0.3). Region labeling is used to extract set of segmented regions $\{\mathcal{A}^{(r)}, 1 < r < N_R\}$ from the computed mask.

**Characterization of Segmented Lesions.** Besides WM lesion areas, the initial mask may include other regions: (i) registration errors due to the linear transform, and (ii) possible atrophy related to leukoaraiosis (close to the cerebral ventricules for example). Of course, such areas should be excluded from the mask. We propose to model two lesion characteristics to distinguish actual lesions from false positive lesioned areas.

While lesions present with a rather spherical shape, registration errors are likely to result into elongated or sinuous shapes. Let $\nu^{(r)} \in \mathcal{A}^{(r)}$ be the voxel whose distance to the edge of $\mathcal{A}^{(r)}$ is maximal; this distance $\theta_{\text{dist}}(r)$ is known as the Chamfer distance. We used $\theta_{\text{dist}}(r)$ to characterize the shape of a region $\mathcal{A}^{(r)}$: those with large Chamfer distances are likely to be lesions.

However, some regions with atrophy may be shaped similarly to lesions. Therefore, a second feature $\theta_{\text{prob}}(r) = \mathcal{P}_{\text{Lesion}}(\nu^{(r)})$ is proposed: the probability that the position of the Chamfer voxel $\nu^{(r)}$ is located within a lesioned area. In order to estimate the lesion probability map $\mathcal{P}_{\text{Lesion}}$, we averaged the information provided by the 26 reference masks $\mathcal{M}_{\text{Ref}}^{(p)}$.

**Maximum a Posteriori Region Classification.** Let $X \in \{Lesion, Other\}$ denote a random variable that categorizes a region as lesioned or non-lesioned. The proposed solution is the value $\widehat{X}$ that maximizes the conditional probability $P(X|(\theta_{\text{dist}}, \theta_{\text{prob}}))$. Using Bayes theorem, $\widehat{X}$ can be expressed as

$$\widehat{X} = \underset{X}{\text{argmax}} \left\{ P(X) \cdot P((\theta_{\text{dist}}, \theta_{\text{prob}})|X) \right\}. \tag{1}$$

**Statistical modeling of $P(X)$ and $P((\theta_{\text{dist}}, \theta_{\text{prob}})|X)$.** Again, we used the reference masks $\mathcal{M}_{\text{Ref}}^{(p)}$ to determine, in each patient $p$, whether automatically segmented regions $\mathcal{A}^{(p,r)}$ truly corresponded to lesioned areas or not. Segmented regions were then split into two groups: the lesioned regions $\mathcal{A}_{\text{Lesion}}^{(p,l)}$ and other regions $\mathcal{A}_{\text{Other}}^{(p,o)}$, $0 < p < N_{\text{P}}$, $0 < l < N_{\text{L}}(p)$, $0 < o < N_{\text{O}}(p)$.

$P(X)$ is modeled by a Bernoulli distribution; its probability of success is given by the ratio of the number of lesioned regions to the total number of regions:

$$P(X = Lesion) = \frac{1}{N_{\text{P}}} \sum_{p=0}^{N_{\text{P}}-1} \frac{N_{\text{L}}(p)}{N_{\text{L}}(p) + N_{\text{O}}(p)}, \tag{2}$$

$P((\theta_{\text{dist}}, \theta_{\text{prob}})|X)$ was estimated via kernel density estimation (with Gaussian kernels and automatic bandwith selection) [8] It is estimated for the two alternatives $X = \{Lesion, Other\}$; Fig. 9a and b plot the obtained 2D probability maps for scenarios.

As shown in Fig. 9, the feature pair $\Theta = \{\theta_{\text{dist}}, \theta_{\text{prob}}\}$ successfully discriminates between lesions and other kinds of WM alterations, while the sole use of either one or the other doest not.

**Lesion Mask Post-processing.** Sole regions classifed as lesioned are kept into the computed mask $\mathcal{M}_{\tau}$. Finally, morphological closing is applied to the refined mask: this fills remaining holes, and also recovers lesioned gray matter located in-between detected lesioned WM.

### 3.2 General Overview of the Proposed Registration Algorithm

The proposed registration algorithm operates iteratively. Initially, the mask $\mathcal{M}_{\tau}^{(0)}$ is set to zero ($X = Other$) in all voxels. Each iteration $i$ includes two steps:

1. $I_{Reg}^{(i)} = \mathcal{R}_{\text{Lin}}^{\text{w/}} \left( I_{\text{P}}, \mathcal{M}_{\tau}^{(i-1)} \right)$: linear registration of the patient image $I_{\text{P}}$ into the template space, using the mask $\mathcal{M}_{\tau}^{(i-1)}$ estimated at previous iteration;
2. update of the lesion mask $\mathcal{M}_{\tau}^{(i)}$ using the procedure described in Sect. 3.1, with image difference $I_{\Delta}^{(i)} = I_{\text{T}} - I_{Reg}^{(i)}$ as input.

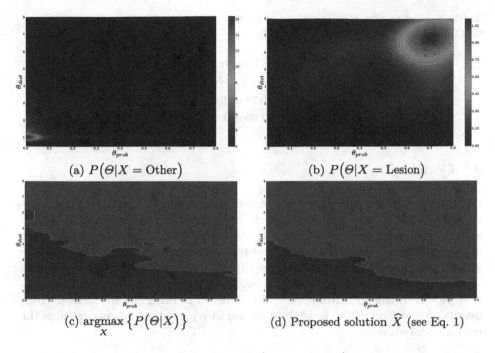

(a) $P(\Theta|X = \text{Other})$    (b) $P(\Theta|X = \text{Lesion})$

(c) $\underset{X}{\mathrm{argmax}}\left\{P(\Theta|X)\right\}$    (d) Proposed solution $\widehat{X}$ (see Eq. 1)

**Fig. 9. Top:** color map of the probability $P((\theta_{\text{dist}}, \theta_{\text{prob}})|X)$ for $X = Lesion$ (right) and $X = Other$ (left). **Bottom:** decision maps in the feature plane; red (resp. blue) areas correspond to $X = $ Other (resp. $X = $ Lesion). Superimposed green dots (resp. red crosses) correspond to lesioned (resp. other) regions obtained in $\mathcal{M}_{\text{Ref}}^{(p)}$. **Bottom-left:** erroneous decisions due to the missing term $P(X)$. **Bottom-right:** the proposed solution provides correct decision (Color figure online).

The algorithm iterates until the Sum of Absolute Differences (SAD) between two consecutive estimations of the mask drops below a certain threshold $\tau_{\mathcal{R}}$. Finally, the estimated linear transform and the final lesion mask are used to initiate a non-linear registration step ($\mathcal{R}_{\text{N-Lin}}^{\text{w/}}$), which further refines the registered image.

### 3.3    Evaluation of the Proposed Registration Algorithm

We evaluated the proposed registration algorithm with a Leave-One-Out (LOO) strategy in 26 stroke patient real images $I_{\text{P*}}^{(p)}$, $0 < p < 26$, for which manually delineated lesion masks were available. For the LOO strategy, one image was tested and the rest of the set, equals to 25 images, was used to tune the Bayesian model. Then we analysed another untested image, and so on, until all the images of the set are tested. Table 2 shows that the proposed registration $\mathcal{R}_{\text{N-Lin}}^{\text{proposed}}$ outperforms the classical non-linear registration (without knowledge of the lesion mask) in both ipsi and contra lateral hemispheres.

**Table 2.** Registration RMSD estimated for the LOO procedure for different registration process onto the skeleton of WM [9].

| Ground truth $\mathcal{R}_{\text{N-Lin}}^{\text{w/}}(I_{\text{P*}})$ | versus | Compared registered images | |
|---|---|---|---|
| | | $\mathcal{R}_{\text{N-Lin}}^{\text{w/o}}(I_{\text{P*}})$ | $\mathcal{R}_{\text{N-Lin}}^{\text{proposed}}(I_{\text{P*}})$ |
| | contra | $0.78 \pm 0.46$ | $\mathbf{0.37 \pm 0.25}$ |
| | ipsi | $1.09 \pm 0.46$ | $\mathbf{1.01 \pm 0.55}$ |

## 4  Conclusion

Our findings evidenced that the use of non masking procedure during the registration of brain with large lesions induced erroneous FA measures in both the ipsi and contralesional hemisphere. These features are mainly due to misrealignement in the registration procedure, as it has been showed with simulated lesions. The algorithm we developed could minimize the effect of the lesion in the registration step. In agreement with [1], a rough mask is sufficient for an accurate registration. However, this algorithm has to be validated in other datasets. Meanwhile, manual delineation of the lesion and its use in registration process remains the referent procedure.

**Acknowledgments.** This study was partially supported by PHRC-HERMES, and by French ANR projects e-SwallHome (ANR-13-TECS-0011) and ERATRANIRMA (ANR-12-EMMA-0056).

## References

1. Andersen, S.M., Rapcsak, S.Z., Beeson, P.M.: Cost function masking during normalization of brains with focal lesions: still a necessity? NeuroImage **53**(1), 78–84 (2010)
2. Beg, M., Miller, M., Trouvé, A., Younes, L.: Computing large deformation metric mappings via geodesic flows of diffeomorphisms. Int. J. Comput. Vis. **61**(2), 139–157 (2005)
3. Brett, M., Leff, A.P., Rorden, C., Ashburner, J.: Spatial normalization of brain images with focal lesions using cost function masking. Neuroimage **14**(2), 486–500 (2001)
4. Ceccarelli, A., Jackson, J., Tauhid, S., Arora, A., Gorky, J., Dell'Oglio, E., Bakshi, A., Chitnis, T., Khoury, S., Weiner, H., Guttmann, C., Bakshi, R., Neema, M.: The impact of lesion in-painting and registration methods on voxel-based morphometry in detecting regional cerebral gray matter atrophy in multiple sclerosis. Am. J. Neuroradiol. **33**(8), 1579–1585 (2012)
5. Jenkinson, M., Beckmann, C.F., Behrens, T.E., Woolrich, M.W., Smith, S.M.: FSL. NeuroImage **62**(2), 782–790 (2012)
6. Lindenberg, R., Renga, V., Zhu, L.L., Betzler, F., Alsop, D., Schlaug, G.: Structural integrity of corticospinal motor fibers predicts motor impairment in chronic stroke. Neurology **74**(4), 280–287 (2010)

7. Ripolles, P., Marco-Pallares, J., de Diego-Balaguer, R., Miro, J., Falip, M., Juncadella, M., Rubio, F., Rodriguez-Fornells, A.: Analysis of automated methods for spatial normalization of lesioned brains. Neuroimage **60**(2), 1296–1306 (2012)

8. Scott, D.W.: Multivariate density estimation and visualization. Handbook of Computational Statistics, pp. 549–569. Springer, Heidelberg (2012)

9. Smith, S.M., Jenkinson, M., Johansen-Berg, H., Rueckert, D., Nichols, T.E., Mackay, C.E., Watkins, K.E., Ciccarelli, O., Cader, M.Z., Matthews, P.M., Behrens, T.E.: Tract-based spatial statistics: voxelwise analysis of multi-subject diffusion data. NeuroImage **31**(4), 1487–1505 (2006)

10. Song, J., Young, B.M., Nigogosyan, Z., Walton, L.M., Nair, V.A., Grogan, S.W., Tyler, M.E., Farrar-Edwards, D., Caldera, K.E., Sattin, J.A., Williams, J.C., Prabhakaran, V.: Characterizing relationships of DTI, fMRI, and motor recovery in stroke rehabilitation utilizing brain-computer interface technology. Frontiers in Neuroengineering **7**, 31 (2014)

11. Vargas, P., Gaudron, M., Valabrgue, R., Bertasi, E., Humbert, F., Lehricy, S., Samson, Y., Rosso, C.: Assessment of corticospinal tract (CST) damage in acute stroke patients: comparison of tract-specific analysis versus segmentation of a CST template. J. Magn. Reson. Imaging **37**(4), 836–845 (2013)

# A Quantitative Approach to Characterize MR Contrasts with Histology

Yaël Balbastre[1,2], Michel E. Vandenberghe[1],
Anne-Sophie Hérard[1], Pauline Gipchtein[1], Caroline Jan[1],
Anselme L. Perrier[3,4], Philippe Hantraye[1], Romina Aron-Badin[1],
Jean-François Mangin[2], and Thierry Delzescaux[1(✉)]

[1] UMR9199, CEA-MIRCen-CNRS, Université Paris-Saclay,
Fontenay-aux-Roses, France
thierry.delzescaux@cea.fr
[2] UNATI, CEA-NeuroSpin, Université Paris-Saclay, Gif-sur-Yvette, France
[3] Inserm U861, Evry, France
[4] UEVE U861, I-STEM, AFM, Evry, France

**Abstract.** Immunohistochemistry is widely used as a gold standard to inspect tissues, characterize their structure and detect pathological alterations. As such, the joint analysis of histological images and other imaging modalities (MRI, PET) is of major interest to interpret these physical signals and establish their correspondence with the biological constitution of the tissues. However, it is challenging to provide a meaningful characterization of the signal specificity. In this paper, we propose an integrated method to quantitatively evaluate the discriminative power of imaging modalities. This method was validated using a macaque brain dataset containing: 3 immunohistochemically stained and 1 histochemically stained series, 1 photographic volume and 1 *in vivo* T2 weighted MRI. First, biological regions of interest (ROIs) were automatically delineated from histological sections stained for markers of interest and mapped on the target non-specific modalities through co-registration. These non-overlapping ROIs were considered ground truth for later classification. Voxels were evenly split in training and testing sets for a logistic regression model. The statistical significance of resulting accuracy scores was evaluated through *null* distribution simulations. Such an approach could be of major interest to assess relevant biological characteristics from various imaging modalities.

## 1 Introduction

In order to study physiopathological phenomena, a large range of imaging modalities can be considered, either *in vivo* or *ex vivo*. On the one hand, *in vivo* techniques such as magnetic resonance imaging (MRI) or positron emission tomography (PET) are useful to apprehend anatomical and functional aspects of organs longitudinally with a millimetric resolution. On the other hand, histology is regarded as a gold standard to characterize the structure of the tissue, which sections can be imaged at a microscopic resolution.

In this domain, there are two basic manners to analyze tissue features: histochemistry and immunohistochemistry. Hematoxylin & Eosin (H&E) is one of the most

A. Crimi et al. (Eds.): BrainLes 2015, LNCS 9556, pp. 104–115, 2016.
DOI: 10.1007/978-3-319-30858-6_10

common histochemical stains used in anatomopathology. This kind of staining relies on the physicochemical properties of the dye and the tissue. It requires the expertise of a pathologist to accurately recognize various biological structures as well as their healthy or pathological state. Besides, immunohistochemistry (IHC) relies on the high specificity of antibodies raised against identified proteins, and that will bind to the antigen expressed in the tissue. In this case, a positive staining accounts directly for the presence of the target.

Histology sections can be imaged with various methods, depending on the resolution needed and the dye characteristics: flatbed scanners, whole slide microscopy imaging, two-photon imaging, *etc*. Because of high resolution and specificity, images arising from histology are of great value to characterize *in vivo* imaging and validate the specificity of MR contrast agents or PET radioligands [1–3].

In the current practice, it is common to perform comparisons of histological and MRI sections visually selected by the operator. Indeed, due to their intrinsically different dimensions the joint use of 3D *in vivo* volumes and 2D *ex vivo* images raises challenges. Yet, the lack of accounting for differences in incidence can result in erroneous associations.

It has been twenty years since the question of automatically matching brain histology sections with MR or PET images arose [1, 4]. A range of existing methods consists in reconstructing histology volumes, ensuring their anatomical consistency either by propagative registration [5], blockface photographs guidance [6] or MRI guidance [7]. These techniques carry high costs in terms of tissue and image processing. As a matter of fact, they have been successfully used in various group studies in mice [8, 9] and their application in non-human primates (NHP) and humans remains prototypal to this day [10].

Let us mention that recently intact tissue imaging techniques such as knife-edge microscopy [11], serial two-photon tomography [12] and tissue clearing coupled with light-sheet microscopy [13–16] have been proposed. Deformations induces by cutting can thus be avoided; however, these methods require whole brain immunolabelling, are limited to fluorescence microscopy and generate huge amounts of data. As such they have only effectively been used in small animals and are not yet suited for primate brain imaging.

Despite the advances in histology reconstruction and in multimodal registration, few quantitative analyses of MR and PET images supervised by histology have been carried out. In a survey we conducted, between 1999 and today, only 6 articles out of 40 dealing with MRI and histology registration achieved a quantitative analysis of the MR signal based on histochemistry [17–19] or immunohistochemistry [20–22].

Stem cell-based therapies are promising to cure neurological diseases marked by a neuronal loss such as stroke, multiple sclerosis (MS), Huntington's or Parkinson's diseases [23, 24]. In the case of Huntington's disease (HD), a genetic neurodegenerative disorder that leads to a progressive loss of neurons in the striatum, and ultimately in various cerebral regions, several studies have shown the ability of fetal and pluripotent stem cell grafts to reverse cognitive deficits in various animal models [25, 26], as well as in patients [27]. The longitudinal follow-up of such grafts is of major importance, and several ways to label the injected cells have been developed [28–30]. Taking advantage of both histology and MRI is particularly pertinent to thoroughly validate MR contrast in stem cell grafts, an essential issue addressed in this work. It could represent a valuable manner to acquire relevant information, to tune the protocol, to supervise the entire study and thus validate the use of MR modality to perform *in vivo* follow up during animal model creation or therapy assessment.

Data used in this article originated from a study we carried out on the therapeutic potential and safety of induced pluripotent stem cell (iPSC) transplantation in a non-human primate model of HD. A phenotypical HD model was obtained through injections of quinolinic acid (QA), a neurotoxin that induces severe cerebral lesions. iPSC were subsequentely implanted in the brain. A question that arose in a translational context was the characterization of T2 MR signal in and around the graft in order to enable *in vivo* longitudinal follow-up of the transplanted cells and of the inflammatory response.

Consequently, we proposed a generic method to quantitatively assess differences in an imaging modality signal between different biological regions of interest (ROI) automatically delineated from immunolabelled histological sections. This method uses classification scores to measure the discriminative power of the modality. Their significance can then be assessed by inferring null distributions from random simulations. To further illustrate the genericity of our method, we also investigated two supplementary modalities available in our study: unstained blockface photographs and hematoxylin & eosin (H&E) stained histological sections, both of which present weakly specific contacts.

## 2  Materials and Methods

### 2.1  Data Acquisition

An adult *macaca fascicularis* received injections of QA bilaterally in the caudate nucleus and unilaterally in the sensorimotor putamen. Two weeks later, the macaque was grafted with GFP (Green Fluorescent Protein) positive iPSC-striatal derivatives [31] around the injured regions. One anatomical T2-weighted MRI sequence was obtained on a Varian 7T scanner ($0.48 \times 0.48 \times 1$ mm, $240 \times 240 \times 70$ matrix, coronal acquisition) at 6 month after transplantation. Two weeks later, the macaque was euthanized and the brain was embedded with a colored medium and sectioned in the coronal plane on a freezing microtome (40-$\mu$m-thick sections). Every fourth section, before cutting, a blockface photograph (BFP) was taken. Four series of ten regularly spaced sections (one every 32 section, inter-section distance: 1280 $\mu$m) located in the striatum area were respectively stained with anti-GFAP (Glial Fibrillary Acidic Protein), anti-GFP, anti-DARPP-32 (Dopamine- and cAMP-Regulated neuronal PhosphoProtein) antibodies and H&E. Slides were then digitized at a resolution of 0.44 $\mu$m/pixel with a Zeiss Axio ScanZ.1.

GFAP is an intermediate filament protein expressed in astrocytes, a multifunctional cell type of the central nervous system (blood-brain barrier constituency among other). GFAP is particularly expressed when astrocytes respond to damaged neurons. It was thus a marker of the inflammatory response of the nervous system.

GFP is a naturally fluorescent protein commonly used as a reporter of gene expression. Grafted stem cells were engineered to express it and were thus labelled by the anti-GFP antibodies.

DARPP-32 is a protein expressed in the dopaminergic pathway and was used as a marker for striatal neurons.

Examination of the tissues revealed first a large loss of striatal neurons (marked by DARPP-32) due to the QA injection, second that the grafted cells (marked by GFP) were surrounded by a strong glial scar (reactive astrocytes, marked by GFAP). The following analyses aimed at rating the discriminative power of 3 modalities – T2 MRI, blockface photographs, H&E sections – regarding 3 tissue types: striatum, graft and glial scar. All modalities are visible in Fig. 1.

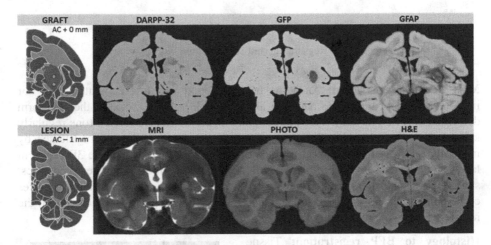

**Fig. 1.** Reference (first row) and investigated (second row) modalities One of the putamen lesion and graft sites are also depicted on sections issued from [38]

## 2.2   Registration and Segmentation

First, MR intensity bias was corrected using BrainVISA's bias correction tool (www. brainvisa.info).

All modalities were then resampled with a combination of median subsampling and cubic resampling at the same 160-µm-isotropic resolution. Histological sections at a mesoscopic scale were sufficient to detect the markers of interest while image size was greatly reduced. In contrast, the MRI volume resolution increased, especially in the anteroposterior direction. Consequently, MRI and histological coronal sections had a closer aspect, facilitating their comparison.

In the following steps of the procedure, the chosen reference space will always be the BFP. While its anatomy differs slightly from that of the brain *in vivo*, it is closely related to both the MRI (in 3D) and the histological sections (in 2D) and constitutes the optimal intermediate. The general registration and segmentation workflow is depicted in Fig. 2, and the registration procedure follows that of Dauguet *et al.* [32], except that the MRI is warped to meet the BFP geometry.

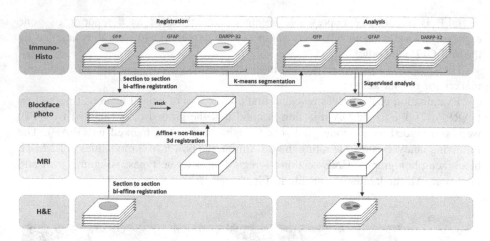

**Fig. 2.** Registration and segmentation workflow

**MRI to BFP registration:** An affine transformation was first computed with our implementation of the block-matching algorithm [33]. Then, we used the free-form deformation (FFD) model [34, 35] to compute an elastic transformation (one regularly spaced $10 \times 10 \times 10$ grid of control points). Registration quality was evaluated by manually selecting 13 anatomical landmarks on both volumes. To ensure 3D coherent landmarks, we chose recognizable extreme points of known 3D structures (ventricles, sulci, corpus callosum, anterior and posterior commissures, etc.). Ten coronal slices corresponding to the stained histological series were subsequently extracted from the registered MR volume and from the BFP volume.

**Histology to BFP registration:** Tissue masks were computed from histological images based on pixel color ($k$-means algorithm, $k = 2$). Hemispheres were manually separated and linearly registered to the corresponding photograph with the block-matching algorithm. Registration quality was validated by manually selecting 15 to 22 anatomical landmarks per section. Roughly half of those were located in the cortex and half in the basal ganglia, the latter being the structure of interest in this study. Landmarks were either extreme points from recognizable 2D structures (sulci, ventricles) or apparent lesions, as depicted Fig. 3.

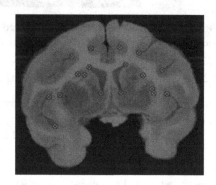

**Fig. 3.** 2D landmarks on a selected BFP section.

**Staining segmentation:** Three biological ROIs were extracted from the histological sections stained for DARPP-32 (striatal neurons), GFP (graft) and GFAP (reactive astrocytes). We automatically segmented positive staining from the masked color images with $k$-means algorithm ($k = 2$). ROIs were refined by filtering out small connected components (GFP and DARPP-32: 50 pixels, GFAP: 25 pixels). GFAP filtering was less stringent because of the less compact nature of the glial scar.

### 2.3   Signal Analysis and Machine Learning

Voxels belonging to the three mapped ROIs (GFP, GFAP, DARPP-32) were extracted from MRI, BFP and H&E images. MR values were of dimension one, whereas BFP and H&E values were of dimension 3 (red, green and blue intensities). Mapped ROIs are depicted Fig. 4 and the corresponding intensity histograms are represented Fig. 5. The observations in each class were numerous, correlated and not necessarily normal, which violate the assumptions of a parametric analysis such as the $t$-test.

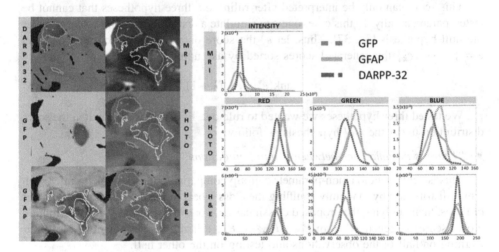

Fig. 4.  Segmented ROIs.          Fig. 5.  Intensity histograms for each class

Classification approaches, such as clustering or machine learning, offer a much more flexible framework. First, classification scores directly account for the discriminative power of the modality. Second, the large range of classification procedures allows one to test different separability hypotheses.

To quantify the effect size, we used a supervised classification approach. The following protocol was applied separately to the three studied modalities. First, the data set was evenly split at the voxel level into training and testing sets. Then, for each possible pair of classes, training observations were fed to a binary logistic regression model. The choice of this classifier was led by its renowned good results on ill-separated data as well as its simplicity. The later minimizes the possibility of over-fitting, especially with spatially correlated data. We used the $l1$ penalty and weighted the observations inversely to their class frequencies. This formulation is equivalent to minimizing the following function, with $n$ observations, $f$ features, $c \in R$ the intercept, $b \in R^f$ the coefficients, $X \in R^{n \times f}$ the observations, $Y \in \{-1, 1\}^n$ the targets, $w_1$ and $w_2$ the weights for each class:

$$F(c,b) = \|b\|_1 + \sum_{i=1}^{n} w_{Y_i} \log\left(1 + \exp\left(-Y_i\left(X_i^T b + c\right)\right)\right) \qquad (1)$$

The models were then used to classify the testing observations. To measure the quality of the resulting classification and to equally take into account the two unbalanced classes, we used a weighted accuracy score with each observation weighted by the inverse of its class frequency, which we write $a$. Let $Y \in \{1, 2\}^n$ the ground truth classes for the testing set, $P \in \{1, 2\}^n$ the associated predicted classes, $I = (Y_j = P_j)_{1 \leq j \leq n}$ an indicator vector, $w \in R^n$ the weights for each observation:

$$a = w^T I / \left(\sum_{i=1}^{n} w_i\right) \qquad (2)$$

This score can only be interpreted after ruling out three hypotheses that cannot be tested parametrically. In this case, one can simulate a distribution of the $a$ scores under the null hypothesis [36, 37]. Thus, let $e^*$ the score obtained on the original data, let $e = \{e_1, \cdots, e_k\}$ the generated scores sorted by ascending value, then:

$$p = \text{rank}(e^* \text{in } e) / (k+1) \qquad (3)$$

We tested three hypotheses we wanted to rule out. For each, we computed the score distribution under the *null* hypothesis as follow:

- *"There is no difference between group populations"*

This is equivalent to a non-parametric group comparison. It is possible to infer such a null distribution by randomly shuffling the class labels in the data set a great number of times, then applying the proposed classification workflow. Formally, the distribution $e$ of $a$ scores is generated from $P = \{P_1, \cdots, P_k\}$ a family of permutations of $Y$ after learning on half of the observations and testing on the other half.

- *"The classification is as good as that of a random classifier"*

By testing this hypothesis, we compared the regression results against that of a dummy classification. This allows us to discard a purely lucky result. In this case, the null distribution was inferred by performing $k$ random classifications. Each observation was randomly assigned to a class with a probability equal to that of its frequency.

- *"The classification is as good as that of a random logistic regression classifier"*

Here we checked that the classification score is not solely due to the strategy of the clustering model, but that the learning step also matters. A family of $k$ random logistic regression models was generated from $k$ permutations of the training set labels. The original testing set was classified by each of these models.

In each case, we used 1000 permutations which was the minimum number of permutations necessary to detect a significant result, when correcting for multiple comparisons.

## 3 Results

Registration yielded good results as shown by manual validation. Average distances between landmarks from photographic and MR volumes are 360 ± 218 μm in the anteroposterior direction, 267 ± 189 μm in the dorsoventral direction and 227 ± 280 μm in the lateral direction. The anteroposterior error is largely inferior to the inter-slice distance (1280 μm), which shows the validity of comparing histological and MRI sections.

Regarding histology/BFP registration, mean distances respectively for DARPP-32, GFP, GFAP and H&E are 456 ± 309 μm (cortex: 536 ± 331 μm, striatum: 373 ± 261 μm), 498 ± 440 μm (cortex: 548 ± 318 μm, striatum: 446 ± 533 μm), 534 ± 330 μm (cortex: 579 ± 377 μm, striatum: 489 ± 269 μm) and 346 ± 232 μm (cortex: 385 ± 267 μm, striatum: 308 ± 187 μm). Errors are especially low in the striatum, which is the anatomical region of interest in this study.

Table 1. Logistic regression's weighted accuracy scores and *p-values* for tested hypotheses.

| | H&E | Photo | MRI |
|---|---|---|---|
| **Weighted accuracy** | | | |
| **DARPP-32 GFAP** | 0.74 | 0.83 | 0.48 |
| **DARPP-32 GFP** | 0.60 | 0.84 | 0.67 |
| **GFAP GFP** | 0.63 | 0.51 | 0.62 |
| *p* against random groups | | | |
| **DARPP-32 GFAP** | *0.001* | *0.001* | 1.0 |
| **DARPP-32 GFP** | *0.001* | *0.001* | *0.001* |
| **GFAP GFP** | *0.001* | 0.044 | *0.001* |
| *p* against random classifier | | | |
| **DARPP-32 GFAP** | *0.001* | *0.001* | 1.0 |
| **DARPP-32 GFP** | *0.001* | *0.001* | *0.001* |
| **GFAP GFP** | *0.001* | 0.17 | *0.001* |
| *p* against random LogReg classifier | | | |
| **DARPP-32 GFAP** | 0.021 | *0.001* | 0.50 |
| **DARPP-32 GFP** | 0.023 | *0.001* | *0.001* |
| **GFAP GFP** | 0.022 | 0.39 | 0.16 |

Table 1 shows the weighted accuracy scores for each group comparison, as well as the *p-values* obtained for each statistical test. *P-values* printed in bold are those significant at a 0.002 threshold (Bonferroni correction) while the italic ones reached the minimal level for 1000 simulations. Weighted accuracy varied from 0.48 to 0.84, and given that the expected weighted accuracy for a random classifier is 0.5, it was hard to rate at first sight the significance of these scores. Obtained *p-values* reported that the effect of chance could not be discarded for GFP/GFAP comparisons in MRI and photo, and DARPP-32/GFAP comparisons in MRI. Once the statistical significance was asserted, accuracy score conveyed information about the size effect and represented the confidence one could have in the classification result.

Our multimodal dataset enabled scoring of various types of images. Especially, with a significant accuracy score of 0.67, *in vivo* T2-weighted MRI showed its ability to discriminate among grafted stem-cells and striatal parenchyma.

# 4  Discussion and Conclusion

Based on a pilot study, we were able to characterize the T2 MR contrasts created by different brain tissue types in a macaque grafted with stem cells. In a first phase, we associated the graft with a hyper signal in the MR image thanks to co-registration between MRI and IHC images. We rated the difference in signal between the graft and the surrounding endogenous tissue with an extremely simple supervised classifier, and concluded that this modality was suitable for *in vivo* graft follow up. Interestingly, those results are coherent with an ongoing spin off study conducted in our lab in which macaques showed a hyper intense T2 signal in their surviving grafts.

Let us note that, because we were working with a sole animal, we were forced to perform cross-validation at the voxel level, whereas in a group study a leave-one-image-out strategy would avoid learning and testing on correlated values. A way to diminish the correlation between the training and the testing sets could be to split values at a block level, which would force neighbor voxels to belong to the same fold. We argue however that in this case, because of the extreme simplicity of the classification strategy, the risk of over-fitting the data was limited, and thus that spatial correlation did not fundamentally impact the classification results. Nonetheless, this issue should be considered when dealing with highly flexible models such as random forests or neural networks.

Additionally, the proposed framework is extremely flexible: the existing range of machine learning models can help answer different questions, based on the characteristics of the studied signal. It is for instance possible to compute spatial features from the signal to take into account its texture. Moreover, several modalities can be investigated: an exciting application would be the validation of PET radiotracers or of innovative MR contrast agents.

Besides, because of the high specificity of IHC, positive staining is easy to segment, making the whole procedure free of any manual intervention. This both prevents operator bias and favors its use in large scale studies.

Perspectives include investigating the histology sections at the cellular level to extract more pertinent information and expanding the set of antibodies used to wholly represent the structure of the tissue. Furthermore, we could use regression rather than classification to more thoroughly characterize the *in vivo* physical signal.

**Acknowledgements.** This study was partially supported by the French National Agency for Research (ANR-2010-RFCS-003 "HD-SCT") and by the Laboratoire d'Excellence Revive (Investissement d'Avenir; ANR-10-LABX-73). We thank Martine Guillermier, Susannah Williams, Aurore Bugi and Nicolas Souedet for their contribution to this work.

# References

1. Mega, M.S., Chen, S.S., Thompson, P.M., Woods, R.P., Karaca, T.J., Tiwari, A., Vinters, H.V., Small, G.W., Toga, A.W.: Mapping histology to metabolism: coregistration of stained whole-brain sections to premortem PET in Alzheimer's disease. Neuroimage **5**, 147–153 (1997)
2. Piert, M., Park, H., Khan, A., Siddiqui, J., Hussain, H., Chenevert, T., Wood, D., Johnson, T., Shah, R.B., Meyer, C.: Detection of aggressive primary prostate cancer with 11C-choline PET/CT using multimodality fusion techniques. J. Nucl. Med. **50**, 1585–1593 (2009)
3. Lavisse, S., Guillermier, M., Hérard, A.-S., Petit, F., Delahaye, M., Van Camp, N., Ben Haim, L., Lebon, V., Remy, P., Dollé, F., Delzescaux, T., Bonvento, G., Hantraye, P., Escartin, C.: Reactive astrocytes overexpress TSPO and are detected by TSPO positron emission tomography imaging. J. Neurosci. **32**, 10809–10818 (2012)
4. Bürgel, U., Schormann, T., Schleicher, A., Zilles, K.: Mapping of histologically identified long fiber tracts in human cerebral hemispheres to the MRI volume of a reference brain: position and spatial variability of the optic radiation. Neuroimage **10**, 489–499 (1999)
5. Ourselin, S., Roche, A., Subsol, G., Pennec, X., Ayache, N.: Reconstructing a 3D structure from serial histological sections. Image Vis. Comput. **19**, 25–31 (2001)
6. Bardinet, E., Ourselin, S., Dormont, D., Malandain, G., Tandé, D., Parain, K., Ayache, N., Yelnik, J.: Co-registration of histological, optical and MR data of the human brain. In: Dohi, T., Kikinis, R. (eds.) MICCAI 2002, Part I. LNCS, vol. 2488, pp. 548–555. Springer, Heidelberg (2002)
7. Malandain, G., Bardinet, E., Nelissen, K., Vanduffel, W.: Fusion of autoradiographs with an MR volume using 2-D and 3-D linear transformations. Neuroimage **23**, 111–127 (2004)
8. Lebenberg, J., Hérard, A., Dubois, A., Dhenain, M., Hantraye, P., Delzescaux, T.: A combination of atlas-based and voxel-wise approaches to analyze metabolic changes in autoradiographic data from Alzheimer's mice. Neuroimage **57**, 1447–1457 (2011)
9. Oh, S.W., Harris, J.A., Ng, L., Winslow, B., Cain, N., Mihalas, S., Wang, Q., Lau, C., Kuan, L., Henry, A.M., Mortrud, M.T., Ouellette, B., Nguyen, T.N., Sorensen, S.A., Slaughterbeck, C.R., Wakeman, W., Li, Y., Feng, D., Ho, A., Nicholas, E., Hirokawa, K.E., Bohn, P., Joines, K.M., Peng, H., Hawrylycz, M.J., Phillips, J.W., Hohmann, J.G., Wohnoutka, P., Gerfen, C.R., Koch, C., Bernard, A., Dang, C., Jones, A.R., Zeng, H.: A mesoscale connectome of the mouse brain. Nature **508**, 207–214 (2014)
10. Amunts, K., Lepage, C., Borgeat, L., Mohlberg, H., Dickscheid, T., Rousseau, M.-É., Bludau, S., Bazin, P.-L., Lewis, L.B., Oros-Peusquens, A.-M., Shah, N.J., Lippert, T., Zilles, K., Evans, A.C.: BigBrain: an ultrahigh-resolution 3D human brain model. Science **340**, 1472–1475 (2013)
11. Mayerich, D., Abbott, L., McCormick, B.: Knife-edge scanning microscopy for imaging and reconstruction of three-dimensional anatomical structures of the mouse brain. J. Microsc. **231**, 134–143 (2008)
12. Ragan, T., Kadiri, L.R., Venkataraju, K.U., Bahlmann, K., Sutin, J., Taranda, J., Arganda-Carreras, I., Kim, Y., Seung, H.S., Osten, P.: Serial two-photon tomography for automated ex vivo mouse brain imaging. Nat. Methods **9**, 255–258 (2012)
13. Ertürk, A., Becker, K., Jährling, N., Mauch, C.P., Hojer, C.D., Egen, J.G., Hellal, F., Bradke, F., Sheng, M., Dodt, H.-U.: Three-dimensional imaging of solvent-cleared organs using 3DISCO. Nat. Protoc. **7**, 1983–1995 (2012)
14. Chung, K., Wallace, J., Kim, S.-Y., Kalyanasundaram, S., Andalman, A.S., Davidson, T.J., Mirzabekov, J.J., Zalocusky, K.A., Mattis, J., Denisin, A.K., Pak, S., Bernstein, H., Ramakrishnan, C., Grosenick, L., Gradinaru, V., Deisseroth, K.: Structural and molecular interrogation of intact biological systems. Nature **497**, 332–337 (2013)

15. Renier, N., Wu, Z., Simon, D.J., Yang, J., Ariel, P., Tessier-Lavigne, M.: iDISCO: a simple, rapid method to immunolabel large tissue samples for volume imaging. Cell **159**, 896–910 (2014)
16. Susaki, E.A., Tainaka, K., Perrin, D., Kishino, F., Tawara, T., Watanabe, T.M., Yokoyama, C., Onoe, H., Eguchi, M., Yamaguchi, S., Abe, T., Kiyonari, H., Shimizu, Y., Miyawaki, A., Yokota, H., Ueda, H.R.: Whole-brain imaging with single-cell resolution using chemical cocktails and computational analysis. Cell **157**, 726–739 (2014)
17. Osechinskiy, S., Kruggel, F.: Quantitative comparison of high-resolution MRI and myelin-stained histology of the human cerebral cortex. In: 31st Annual International Conference of the IEEE Engineering in Medicine and Biology Society, pp. 85–89 (2009)
18. Bol, K., Haeck, J.C., Alic, L., Niessen, W.J., de Jong, M., Bernsen, M., Veenland, J.F.: Quantification of DCE-MRI: a validation of three techniques with 3D-histology. In: 2012 9th IEEE International Symposium on Biomedical Imaging (ISBI), pp. 1044–1047. IEEE (2012)
19. van Engelen, A., Niessen, W.J., Klein, S., Groen, H.C., Verhagen, H.J.M., Wentzel, J.J., van der Lugt, A., de Bruijne, M.: Supervised in-vivo plaque characterization incorporating class label uncertainty. In: 2012 9th IEEE International Symposium on Biomedical Imaging (ISBI), pp. 246–249. IEEE (2012)
20. Stille, M., Smith, E.J., Crum, W.R., Modo, M.: 3D reconstruction of 2D fluorescence histology images and registration with in vivo MR images: application in a rodent stroke model. J. Neurosci. Methods **219**, 27–40 (2013)
21. Coquery, N., Francois, O., Lemasson, B., Debacker, C., Farion, R., Rémy, C., Barbier, E.L.: Microvascular MRI and unsupervised clustering yields histology-resembling images in two rat models of glioma. J. Cereb. Blood Flow Metab. **34**, 1354–1362 (2014)
22. Goubran, M., Hammond, R.R., de Ribaupierre, S., Burneo, J.G., Mirsattari, S., Steven, D.A., Parrent, A.G., Peters, T.M., Khan, A.R.: Magnetic resonance imaging and histology correlation in the neocortex in temporal lobe epilepsy. Ann. Neurol. **77**, 237–250 (2015)
23. Lindvall, O., Kokaia, Z.: Stem cells for the treatment of neurological disorders. Nature **441**, 1094–1096 (2006)
24. Ross, C.A., Akimov, S.S.: Human-induced pluripotent stem cells: potential for neurodegenerative diseases. Hum. Mol. Genet. **23**, R17–R26 (2014)
25. Palfi, S., Condé, F., Riche, D., Brouillet, E., Dautry, C., Mittoux, V., Chibois, A., Peschanski, M., Hantraye, P.: Fetal striatal allografts reverse cognitive deficits in a primate model of Huntington disease. Nat. Med. **4**, 963–966 (1998)
26. Mu, S., Wang, J., Zhou, G., Peng, W., He, Z., Zhao, Z., Mo, C., Qu, J., Zhang, J.: Transplantation of induced pluripotent stem cells improves functional recovery in Huntington's disease rat model. PLoS ONE **9**, e101185 (2014)
27. Bachoud-Lévi, A.-C., Rémy, P., Nguyen, J.-P., Brugières, P., Lefaucheur, J.-P., Bourdet, C., Baudic, S., Gaura, V., Maison, P., Haddad, B., Boissé, M.-F., Grandmougin, T., Jény, R., Bartolomeo, P., Barba, G.D., Degos, J.-D., Lisovoski, F., Ergis, A.-M., Pailhous, E., Cesaro, P., Hantraye, P., Peschanski, M.: Motor and cognitive improvements in patients with Huntington's disease after neural transplantation. Lancet **356**, 1975–1979 (2000)
28. Modo, M., Mellodew, K., Cash, D., Fraser, S.E., Meade, T.J., Price, J., Williams, S.C.: Mapping transplanted stem cell migration after a stroke: a serial, in vivo magnetic resonance imaging study. Neuroimage **21**, 311–317 (2004)
29. Guzman, R., Uchida, N., Bliss, T.M., He, D., Christopherson, K.K., Stellwagen, D., Capela, A., Greve, J., Malenka, R.C., Moseley, M.E., Palmer, T.D., Steinberg, G.K.: Long-term monitoring of transplanted human neural stem cells in developmental and pathological contexts with MRI. Proc. Natl. Acad. Sci. U.S.A. **104**, 10211–10216 (2007)

30. Kraitchman, D.L., Gilson, W.D., Lorenz, C.H.: Stem cell therapy: MRI guidance and monitoring. J. Magn. Reson. Imaging **27**, 299–310 (2008)
31. Nicoleau, C., Varela, C., Bonnefond, C., Maury, Y., Bugi, A., Aubry, L., Viegas, P., Bourgois-Rocha, F., Peschanski, M., Perrier, A.L.: Embryonic stem cells neural differentiation qualifies the role of Wnt/β-Catenin signals in human telencephalic specification and regionalization. Stem Cells **31**, 1763–1774 (2013)
32. Dauguet, J., Delzescaux, T., Condé, F., Mangin, J.-F., Ayache, N., Hantraye, P., Frouin, V.: Three-dimensional reconstruction of stained histological slices and 3D non-linear registration with in-vivo MRI for whole baboon brain. J. Neurosci. Methods **164**, 191–204 (2007)
33. Ourselin, S., Roche, A., Prima, S., Ayache, N.: Block matching: a general framework to improve robustness of rigid registration of medical images. In: Delp, S.L., DiGoia, A.M., Jaramaz, B. (eds.) MICCAI 2000. LNCS, vol. 1935, pp. 557–566. Springer, Heidelberg (2000)
34. Rueckert, D., Sonoda, L.I., Hayes, C., Hill, D.L., Leach, M.O., Hawkes, D.J.: Nonrigid registration using free-form deformations: application to breast MR images. IEEE Trans. Med. Imaging **18**, 712–721 (1999)
35. Mattes, D., Haynor, D.R., Vesselle, H., Lewellen, T.K., Eubank, W.: PET-CT image registration in the chest using free-form deformations. IEEE Trans. Med. Imaging **22**, 120–128 (2003)
36. Golland, P., Fischl, B.: Permutation tests for classification: towards statistical significance in image-based studies. Inf. Process. Med. Imaging. **18**, 330–341 (2003)
37. Ojala, M., Garriga, G.C.: Permutation tests for studying classifier performance. In: 2009 Ninth IEEE International Conference on Data Mining, pp. 908–913. IEEE (2009)
38. Bakker, R., Tiesinga, P., Kötter, R.: The scalable brain atlas: instant web-based access to public brain atlases and related content, pp. 353–366 (2013). arXiv Preprint: arXiv1312.6310

# Brain Tumor Image Segmentation

# Image Features for Brain Lesion Segmentation Using Random Forests

Oskar Maier[1,2(✉)], Matthias Wilms[1], and Heinz Handels[1]

[1] Institute of Medical Informatics, Universität zu Lübeck, Lübeck, Germany
maier@imi.uni-luebeck.de
[2] Graduate School for Computing in Medicine and Life Sciences,
Universität zu Lübeck, Lübeck, Germany

**Abstract.** From clinical practice as well as research methods arises the need for accurate, reproducible and reliable segmentation of pathological areas from brain MR scans. This paper describes a set of hand-selected, voxel-based image features highly suitable for the tissue discrimination task. Embedded in a random decision forest framework, the proposed method was applied to sub-acute ischemic stroke (ISLES 2015 - SISS), acute ischemic stroke (ISLES 2015 - SPES) and glioma (BRATS 2015) segmentation with only minor adaptation. For all of these three challenges, our generic approach received high ranks, among them a second place. The outcome underlines the robustness of our features for segmentation in brain MR, while simultaneously stressing the necessity for highly specialized solution to achieve state-of-the-art performance.

**Keywords:** Ischemic stroke · Lesion segmentation · Magnetic resonance imaging · Brain MR · MRI · Random forest · RDF · Acute · Sub-acute · Glioma · Tumor · ISLES 2015 · BRATS 2015 · SISS · SPES

## 1 Introduction

Many diseases and injuries manifest as pathological changes to the brain and magnetic resonance (MR) scans are often acquired for diagnosis and assessment, as this modality exhibits a high soft tissue contrast and is highly customizable. Examples of such brain lesion causing afflictions are cerebral stroke, multiple sclerosis, brain tumors and traumatic brain injury.

Knowledge about the exact location, shape and extent of the pathological tissue is often crucial for precise diagnosis [23], monitoring [4], informed treatment decisions [10], surgical or radiotherapeutic planning [9], biomarker discovery [8], drug efficacy or effectiveness studies [12,13] and neuroscientific insight [11]. Put simply, all of these domains would benefit from automatic segmentation of lesions in brain MR scans.

This demand has reached the medical image processing community and many groups have approached the problem with a wide range of methods. Sub-acute ischemic stroke lesions are highly variable in appearance, as they still undergo

© Springer International Publishing Switzerland 2016
A. Crimi et al. (Eds.): BrainLes 2015, LNCS 9556, pp. 119–130, 2016.
DOI: 10.1007/978-3-319-30858-6_11

development on a molecular level. A good overview by Rekik et al. [24] summarizes the early years of the field and an increasing number of new propositions have been made since then [6,7,16,19,25,26]. Acute stroke poses quite a different challenge, where the main goal is the estimation of the penumbra area, i.e. the potentially salvageable tissue [1]. The set of MR sequences most suitable is distinct from the sub-acute case [18] and while the acute stroke lesions are less variable in their gray-level appearance, a hard time constraint of a few minutes is imposed on all practical applications. Common clinical practice is a simple thresholding and mismatch approach, although more complex methods are known to perform better [5]. A multi-class problem is the segmentation of glioma, which has been recently summarized in an extensive comparison work [17]. Here, an exact delineation of the complete tumor as well as a breakdown into its sub components (e.g. core, enhancing) is beneficial for surgical and radiotherapeutic planning.

The published methods are usually highly adapted to the task at hand and cannot be readily transferred to similar problems. In this paper, we therefore introduce a set of hand-selected, voxel-based image features for differentiating between pathological and healthy brain tissue, which are modeled after human experts discrimination criteria. To detect the non-linear decision boundaries for each application task, we employ the machine learning method of random forests.

Automatic feature detection approaches, such as convolutional neural networks [2] or random scanning of large feature spaces [27], are explicitly left out to assess the selected features robustness and suitability for a range of brain lesion segmentation tasks.

For a fair and direct evaluation under medically realistic conditions, we participated in three medical image segmentation challenges (ISLES 2015 - SISS, ISLES 2015 - SPES, BRATS 2015) with only minor adaptation to our method.

## 2    Method

In this section, we describe the general random forest framework in which the features are embedded. Then, we introduce the features as well as the motivation behind them. Finally, we present the three segmentation tasks, their image data, evaluation metrics and specific adaptations to our approach.

### 2.1    Random Decision Forest Framework

Our approach is centered around a standard random forest classifier, preceded by a number of pre-processing steps for the MR scans and followed by a few crude morphological post-processing operations (see Fig. 1). An adaptive training set sub-sampling scheme additionally reduces the training effort at minimal costs of accuracy. These elements are common to all three segmentations tasks, possible deviations are described in Sect. 2.3.

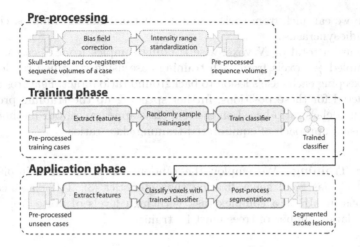

**Fig. 1.** Pipeline schema.

**Pre-processing.** Training as well as testing images are assumed to be of a common voxel resolution, already co-registered and skull-stripped.

Bias field is a low-frequency, smooth signal that corrupts MR scans in an additive and/or multiplicative manner and thus causes homogeneous tissue types to be represented by different intensity values, rendering their classification more difficult. We employ the MR Intensity Bias Field Correction tool [14] from the Computational Morphometry Toolkit (CMTK) to first estimate and then remove the bias field effect, increasing the intensity homogeneity over the tissue types.

As opposed to computed tomography (CT), the intensity values of most MR sequences do not directly reflect physical properties of the depicted tissue following a known relationship. Instead, intensity values of a single tissue type as well as differences between tissue types can differ greatly not only between the same sequences acquired with different scanners, but even between repeated acquisitions on the same machine. With a learning based intensity standardization method implemented in MedPy [15] and based on [20] we harmonize each sequences intensity profile. This method has the advantage of not requiring a fixed template image and it signals a warning when presented with outliers. A side effect is a strong spreading of the images' histograms, which does not affect our approach.

**Training Set Sub-sampling.** Since we employ voxel-wise classification for segmentation, the available training samples can easily surpass the ten million, leading to long training times. We have shown previously [16], that a carefully selected, representative subset can considerably reduce the training time with only a minimal loss in accuracy.

As usual in machine learning applications, we first require a sufficient number of cases as base training set, which represent the whole domain of the segmentation task. Then we can pick from each case a number of training samples, chosen to reflect its idiosyncrasies.

To acquire a total of $N$ voxel-wise training samples from $C$ cases, we randomly sampled $\frac{N}{C}$ voxels from each training case using stratified random sampling, i.e. keeping each case's lesion to background ratio intact. Features are then only extracted for these positions, further speeding up the training procedure. By choosing a class ratio based on the real class appearance, our method differs from the usual approach of equilibrated training class ratios.

**Classifier Training.** We employ the random forest classifier implemented in [22], which has good generalization characteristics [3]. The classification of brain lesions in MR is a complex task with high levels of noise [16], hence a sufficiently large number of trees must be trained.

**Post-processing.** The output of the forest classifier is an a-posteriori lesion probability map with a value between 0 and 1 for each voxel and class. In the multi-class case, the class with the highest probability is assigned to each voxel. For the binary case, a threshold value $t$ can be defined to counter over- or under-segmentation effects. Finally, the crisp segmentation results can be furthermore processed with morphological operations, e.g. to close holes in the segmentation or reduce the dominance of certain labels.

### 2.2    Features for Brain Lesion Segmentations

Brain lesions differ strongly in shape, location, homogeneity and intensities and even for a single pathology, the lesion appearance can vary greatly [16]. It is therefore often difficult to develop task specific features.

We present a set of features chosen to model a human observers discriminative criteria and, instead of trying to capture the characteristics of a single pathology, concentrate on enabling a general distinction between healthy and pathological tissue. In other words, we concentrate on the least common denominators: the fact that we look at a brain, even if in a, to different extents, degenerated state.

Figures 2, 3 and 4 show examples of a range of brain lesions for which automatic segmentation would be desirable. Visible differences are largely based on intensity attributes and most brain lesions show up either hyper- or hypo-intense. But where the human observer easily assesses the symmetry of the brain and hence identifies the lesion as outlier, the computer would have a hard time comparing the right areas and making the necessary simplifications at different levels of the process. Instead, the classifier has to be directly provided with the necessary information.

Others tasks the human brain is especially good at is clustering, generalizing and edge detection. Some of above examples barely exhibit an edge when observed at close range, but an observer would still be able to outline the lesion roughly, based on vague criteria such as 'togetherness', 'shape' and 'consistency', despite the obvious fact that the lesions can hardly be called homogeneous, of consistent shape or strongly connected.

Keeping these observations in mind, we selected the following features. Many of them are kept imprecise on purpose to avoid the danger of overfitting and to model the human observers simplification abilities. The decision on which of these have the highest discriminative ability for a given task is left to the classifier during training.

*Intensity.* First feature is the voxel's intensity value. After conducting the pre-processing steps, this should contain some information about the tissue type represented by the voxel.

*Gaussian.* Due to the often low signal-to-noise ratio in MR scans and intensity inhomogeneities of the tissue types, we furthermore regard each voxel's value after a smoothing of the volume with a 3D Gaussian kernel at three sizes: $\sigma = 3, 5, 7$ mm. This feature allows for a more robust estimation of the underlying tissue type than the voxel's intensity value alone. Furthermore, by using both of these features, the magnitude of difference to the neighboring voxels can be used in the decision finding process. The three scales have been selected to allow for a fine tuning and hence a multi-resolution similar approach where necessary.

*Hemispheric Difference.* While many brain lesions can affect both hemispheres, most do not display symmetric properties. Therefore, we extract the hemispheric difference (in intensities) after a Gaussian smoothing of $\sigma = 1, 3, 5$ mm to account for noise, which supplies a rough measure of deviation from hemispheric symmetry, a strong criteria of human observers. Using three scales, the rough as well as the finer details are considered. The computation of the hemispheric difference feature requires the detection of the sagittal midline, which, while relatively easy for a human, is no trivial task to a computer. In this work, the central slice of the sagittal view is taken as a sufficiently close approximation of the sagittal midline. Note that a direct application to medical data might require a rough alignment of the cases, i.e. through rigid registration to a template.

*Local Histogram.* Many brain lesions are largely inhomogeneous in appearance and incorporate a wide range of intensities that often overlap with healthy tissue types. As previously proposed in [16], we model the intensity distribution in a cubical area through a normalized histogram under the assumption, that the local distribution of intensity values differs between lesioned and healthy brain tissue. The histogram range is set to the whole image's intensity range. The number of bins should be selected large enough to be able to model a large number of possible distributions while being small enough to not inflate the feature vector and at least one neighborhood patch size should be selected to fit smoothly inside the smallest lesions. The neighborhoods considered in this work were $R = 5^3, 10^3, 15^3$ mm, the histogram was fixed to 11 bins.

*Center Distance.* Exploiting the rough symmetry of the brain for another feature, we extract the 2D euclidean distance to the image center (assumed here to coincide roughly with the brain's center of mass) in mm in each dimension.

Note that this feature is not intensity based, but rather discloses each voxel's rough location inside the brain. Thus, skull-near can be treated differently to periventricular regions, where e.g. hyper-intense bone residues from an imperfect skull-stripping are unlikely to occur. This feature is deliberately chosen to represent the location only roughly, as (a) an exact localization would require a costly and error-prone inter-subject registration and (b) holds the danger of learning the explicit location of the training lesions, resulting in poor generalization.

## 2.3    Segmentation Tasks

To evaluate our features, the method participated in three recent medical image segmentation challenges concerning brain lesions. For each, the organizers provided a training dataset with associated ground truth expert segmentations and a task representative testing dataset. The ground truth of the second is not revealed and the organizers evaluated all participating methods in a fair and direct comparison of methods. In this section, the three tasks, their image data and evaluation metrics are described.

**ISLES 2015 - SISS.** The Sub-acute Ischemic Stroke lesion Segmentation (SISS) is a sub-task of the overarching Ischemic Stroke LEsion Segmentation (ISLES) challenge[1] concerned with the delineation of stroke lesions in the sub-acute (here defined as >12 h and <2 weeks) development phase from multi-spectral MR scans. A summary of the set-up is given in Table 1.

Table 1. Summary of the three evaluation tasks.

|  | SISS | SPES | BRATS |
|---|---|---|---|
| #cases training | 28 | 30 | 274 |
| #cases testing | 36 | 20 |  |
| #raters training | 1 | 1 | 1-4 (consent), partially automatic |
| #raters testing | 2 | 1 | 4 (consent) |
| #centers training | 1 | 1 | Multiple |
| #centers testing | 2 | 1 | Multiple |
| MR sequences | FLAIR, T2, T1, DWI | T1c, T2, DWI, CBF, CBV, TTP, Tmax | FLAIR, T2, T1, T1c |

Employed evaluation metrics are the Dice's coefficient (DC), which denotes the volume overlap, the average symmetric surface distance (ASSD), denoting the volume surface distance, and the Hausdorff distance (HD), revealing outliers. For a detailed definition of these metrics, please refer to the challenge's web page.

---

[1] http://isles-challenge.org.

**ISLES 2015 - SPES.** The Stroke Penumbra EStimation (SPES) is another sub-task of the ISLES challenge. Its goal is the estimation of the penumbra from multi-spectral MR scans acquired at the acute ($<6$ h) development phase. Table 1 also provides a summary of this task.

The employed metrics are the same as for SISS, only the HD has been left out, as the ground truth segmentations contain voxel-sizes holes.

**BRATS 2015.** The multimodal BRAin Tumor Segmentation (BRATS) challenge[2] approaches the task of segmenting high- as well as low-grade glioma. The ground truth consists of four different classes: the edema, the non-enhancing solid core, the necrotic/cystic core and the enhancing core. In its configuration, the 2015 version of the challenge was equal to the previous years [17]. The details of this years set-up are shown in Table 1.

For BRATS, three structures are evaluated: the whole tumor (all 4 labels), the tumor core (non-enhancing solid core, necrotic/cystic core, enhancing core) and the active tumor (enhancing core). Employed evaluation metrics were DC, the positive prediction values (PPV), the sensitivity (SE) and the kappa value. The exact definitions of these metrics have not been provided by the organizers.

# 3 Results

This section describes the experimental settings for each task and presents the results obtained on the testing as well as training sets.

## 3.1 Results for ISLES 2015 SISS.

*Parameter Settings.* For the SISS task, $N = 1,000,000$ voxel-wise samples are extracted from the training cases. The random forest consists of $T = 50$ trees trained without limits and Gini impurity is employed as split criteria. At each node, a subset of $\sqrt{F}$ of the $F$ total features are regarded.

*Post-processing.* The a-posteriori class probabilities produced by the forest are thresholded at a value of $t = 0.4$, to counter a slight under-segmentation. Further post-processing has been the filling of holes in the segmentation, a morphological closing operation of size 1 and a removal of all unconnected components smaller than 1000 ml as presumed outliers.

*Evaluation.* On the day of a challenge, we achieved a respectable sixth place among the fourteen participants. The results obtained on the testing dataset are summarized in Table 2 and a visual example is given in Fig. 2.

---

[2] http://braintumorsegmentation.org.

**Table 2.** SISS account. Some of our segmentation masks were empty or failed completely to intersect with the ground truth and hence were not taken into acount for the average values of the ASSD and HD. But the DC has been computed over all 36 cases.

| Cases | DC [0,1] | ASSD (mm) | HD (mm) |
|---|---|---|---|
| 31/36 | $0.42 \pm 0.33$ | $10.21 \pm 9.44$ | $49.17 \pm 29.6$ |

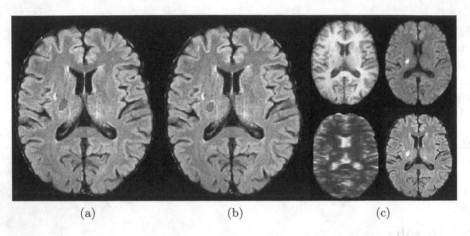

(a)          (b)          (c)

**Fig. 2.** Exemplary SISS result (training set, case 23): (a) Ground truth on Flair (b) Segmentation on Flair (c) sequences, from top-left clockwise: T1, T1c, Flair, T2

## 3.2 Results for ISLES 2015 SPES

*Deviation from the Default Approach.* The SPES data are of high quality with a, if at all, then only barely perceptible bias field. We therefore refrained from applying the bias field correction step in the pre-processing. Preliminary experiments revealed no benefits. Furthermore, we did not apply the intensity range standardization to the perfusion maps, as these are considered to directly reflect physical quantities derived from the cerebral blood flow. Finally, we chose to cap the Tmax sequence at an upper value of 100, as larger values are known to be of no significance [21].

*Parameter Settings.* The training settings for SPES are the same as for SISS above.

*Post-processing.* The a-posteriori class probabilities produced by the forest are thresholded at a value of 0.35, to counter a slight under-segmentation. As further post-processing, all but the largest connected binary component was removed.

*Evaluation.* In the SPES challenge, we reached the second place of seven participants. The results obtained on the testing dataset are summarized in Table 3. A visual example is displayed in Fig. 3.

**Table 3.** SPES testing dataset results. ASSD as well as DC has been computed over all testing cases.

| Cases | DC [0,1] | ASSD (mm) |
|---|---|---|
| 20/20 | 0.81 ± 0.09 | 1.65 ± 1.40 |

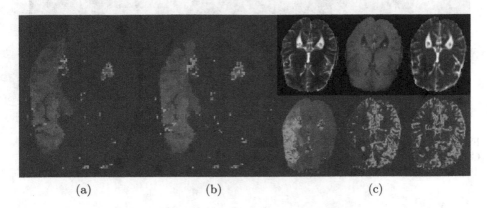

|   |   |   |
|---|---|---|
| (a) | (b) | (c) |

**Fig. 3.** Exemplary SPES result (training set, case 16): (a) Ground truth (b) Segmentation (c) sequences, from top-left clockwise: T2, T1c, DWI, TTP, CBF, CBF

## 3.3   Results for BRATS 2015

*Parameter Settings.* The training settings for BRATS are the same as for SISS above, except that we took care to extract a minimum of 500 samples for each class per case. This had become necessary due to the multi-class problem posed by BRATS. Note that still an overall number of approximately $1,000,000$ training samples is sampled.

*Post-processing.* For post-processing, the edema was allowed to grow morphological with a size of 1 into the background and then the inner non-enhancing solid core to perform similar, but only at the expense of the edema label. This corresponds roughly to a slight inflation of the non-enhancing solid core and a subsequent adaptation of the surrounding edema.

*Evaluation.* Table 4 details the results obtained on the BRATS training dataset, as the results on the testing dataset have not been made public, yet.

**Table 4.** BRATS training dataset results. Some of our segmentation masks were empty and hence did not count into the average values presented here.

| Cases | DC | | | PPV | | | SE | | | Kappa |
|---|---|---|---|---|---|---|---|---|---|---|
| | comp | core | enha | comp | core | enha | comp | core | enha | |
| 252/274 | 0.75 | 0.60 | 0.56 | 0.71 | 0.56 | 0.59 | 0.88 | 0.81 | 0.64 | 0.98 |

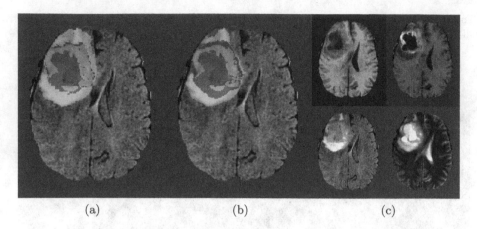

(a)                          (b)                          (c)

**Fig. 4.** Exemplary BRATS result (training set, case brats_tcia_pat374_0001): (a) Ground truth on Flair (b) Segmentation on Flair (c) sequences, from top-left clockwise: T1, T1c, Flair, T2

At the day of the challenge, our methods made the fifth place overall and the fourth of the completely automatic methods on the testing dataset. A visual example is displayed in Fig. 4.

## 4    Discussion and Conclusion

We have introduced a set of image features tailored towards lesion segmentation in MR brain scans. An evaluation on three public datasets with favorable ranking in all of them underlines their suitability for a range of tasks. All are implemented for direct use in the MedPy library [15].

Especially for the SPES task, state-of-the-art results are obtained. For SISS, the method failed mainly to adapt to the second center cases not represented in the training dataset. The BRATS results show, that the features are not only suited to distinguish between healthy and other brain areas, but also different pathological tissues.

We can conclude that, for seemingly easier tasks like the SPES challenge, the feature selection is sufficient. But for more complex segmentation problems, such as posed by BRATS and SISS, more specialized features and/or a combination with other methods is required to achieve state-of-the-art results. Another option would be to employ random feature detection methods [27], which work by generating large amounts of random feature instances under the assumption that a few might be informative. Nevertheless, we have shown that the presented feature set constitutes a good base for a wider range of brain lesion segmentation tasks.

For each application, we determined a different a-posteriori probability map threshold using the training set. For the testing data they were kept constant. The differences in ideal thresholds could arise (1) from the unbalanced class ratios in the training data and/or (2) from classifier intrinsic tendencies to over- or undersegment.

For the stroke case, we investigated the information content of the different sequences in a previous work [16] and found FLAIR to be the most informative sequence by large. But we furthermore found the decision forests to behave very robust against uninformative features or sequences, hence we did not investigate the issue further in this work.

It remains to demonstrate the basic fitness of the features for further tasks, such as e.g. MS and TBI lesion segmentation.

# References

1. Astrup, J., Siesjö, B.K., Symon, L.: Thresholds in cerebral ischemia-the ischemic penumbra. Stroke **12**(6), 723–725 (1981)
2. Cireşan, D.C., Giusti, A., Gambardella, L.M., Schmidhuber, J.: Mitosis detection in breast cancer histology images with deep neural networks. In: Mori, K., Sakuma, I., Sato, Y., Barillot, C., Navab, Nassir (eds.) MICCAI 2013, Part II. LNCS, vol. 8150, pp. 411–418. Springer, Heidelberg (2013)
3. Criminisi, A., Shotton, J., Konukoglu, E.: Decision forests: a unified framework for classification, regression, density estimation, manifold learning and semi-supervised learning. Found. Trends® Comput. Graph. **7**(2–3), 81–227 (2012)
4. Filippi, M., Rocca, M.A.: MR imaging of multiple sclerosis. Radiology **259**(3), 659–681 (2011). http://www.ncbi.nlm.nih.gov/pubmed/21602503
5. Ghosh, N., Yuan, X., Turenius, C.I., et al.: Automated core-penumbra quantification in neonatal ischemic brain injury. J. Cereb. Blood Flow Metab. **32**(12), 2161–2170 (2012)
6. de Haan, B., Clas, P., Juenger, H., Wilke, M., Karnath, H.O.: Fast semi-automated lesion demarcation in stroke. NeuroImage Clin. **9**, 69–74 (2015). http://www.sciencedirect.com/science/article/pii/S2213158215001199
7. Hevia-Montiel, N., Jimenez-Alaniz, J., Medina-Banuelos, V., et al.: Robust non-parametric segmentation of infarct lesion from diffusion-weighted MR images. IEEE EMBS **2007**, 2102–2105 (2007)
8. Joy, J.E., Johnston, R.B.: Multiple Sclerosis: Current Status and Strategies for the Future. National Academies Press, Washington (2001). http://www.ncbi.nlm.nih.gov/books/NBK222399/
9. Kaus, M.R., Warfield, S.K., Nabavi, A., et al.: Automated segmentation of MR images of brain tumors. Radiology **218**(2), 586–591 (2001)
10. Kemmling, A., Flottmann, F., Forkert, N.D., et al.: Multivariate dynamic prediction of ischemic infarction and tissue salvage as a function of time and degree of recanalization. J. Cereb. Blood Flow Metab. **35**(9), 1397–1405 (2015)
11. Krämer, U.M., Solbakk, A.K., Funderud, I., et al.: The role of the lateral prefrontal cortex in inhibitory motor control. Cortex **49**(3), 837–849 (2013)
12. La Mantia, L., Di Pietrantonj, C., Rovaris, M., et al.: Interferons-beta versus glatiramer acetate for relapsing-remitting multiple sclerosis. Cochrane Database Syst. Rev. **7**, CD009333 (2014). http://www.ncbi.nlm.nih.gov/pubmed/25062935
13. Lansberg, M.G., Straka, M., Kemp, S., et al.: MRI profile and response to endovascular reperfusion after stroke (DEFUSE 2): a prospective cohort study. Lancet. Neurol. **11**(10), 860–867 (2012). http://www.thelancet.com/article/S147444221270203X/fulltext

14. Likar, B., Viergever, M.A., Pernus, F.: Retrospective correction of MR intensity inhomogeneity by information minimization. IEEE Trans. Med. Imag. **20**(12), 1398–1410 (2001)
15. Maier, O.: MedPy. https://pypi.python.org/pypi/MedPy. Accessed 29 March 2015
16. Maier, O., Wilms, M., et al.: Extra tree forests for sub-acute ischemic stroke lesion segmentation in MR sequences. J. Neurosci. Methods **240**, 89–100 (2015)
17. Menze, B., Jakab, A., Bauer, S., et al.: The multimodal brain tumor image segmentation benchmark (BRATS). IEEE Trans. Med. Imaging **34**(10), 1993–2024 (2015)
18. Mishra, N.K., Albers, G.W., Christensen, S., et al.: Comparison of magnetic resonance imaging mismatch criteria to select patients for endovascular stroke therapy. Stroke **45**(5), 1369–1374 (2014). http://stroke.ahajournals.org/content/45/5/1369.full
19. Mitra, J., Bourgeat, P., Fripp, J., et al.: Lesion segmentation from multimodal MRI using random forest following ischemic stroke. Neuroimage **98**, 324–335 (2014)
20. Nyul, L., Udupa, J., Zhang, X.: New variants of a method of MRI scale standardization. IEEE Trans. Med. Imaging **19**(2), 143–150 (2000)
21. Olivot, J.M., Mlynash, M., Thijs, V.N., et al.: Optimal Tmax threshold for predicting penumbral tissue in acute stroke. Stroke **40**(2), 469–475 (2009). http://stroke.ahajournals.org/content/40/2/469.abstract
22. Pedregosa, F., Varoquaux, G., et al.: Scikit-learn: machine learning in Python. J. Mach. Learn. Res. **12**, 2825–2830 (2011)
23. Polman, C.H., Reingold, S.C., Banwell, B., et al.: Diagnostic criteria for multiple sclerosis: 2010 revisions to the McDonald criteria. Ann. Neurol. **69**(2), 292–302 (2011). http://www.pubmedcentral.nih.gov/articlerender.fcgi?artid=3084507&tool=pmcentrez&rendertype=abstract
24. Rekik, I., Allassonniere, S., Carpenter, T.K., Wardlaw, J.M.: Medical image analysis methods in MR/CT-imaged acute-subacute ischemic stroke lesion: segmentation, prediction and insights into dynamic evolution simulation models. A critical appraisal. Neuroimage Clin. **1**(1), 164–178 (2012)
25. Seghier, M.L., Ramlackhansingh, A., Crinion, J., Leff, A.P., Price, C.J.: Lesion identification using unified segmentation-normalisation models and fuzzy clustering. Neuroimage **41**(4–3), 1253–1266 (2008)
26. Wilke, M., de Haan, B., Juenger, H., Karnath, H.O.: Manual, semi-automated, and automated delineation of chronic brain lesions: a comparison of methods. Neuroimage **56**(4), 2038–2046 (2011)
27. Zikic, D., Glocker, B., Konukoglu, E., Criminisi, A., Demiralp, C., Shotton, J., Thomas, O.M., Das, T., Jena, R., Price, S.J.: Decision forests for tissue-specific segmentation of high-grade gliomas in multi-channel MR. In: Ayache, N., Delingette, H., Golland, P., Mori, K. (eds.) MICCAI 2012, Part III. LNCS, vol. 7512, pp. 369–376. Springer, Heidelberg (2012)

# Deep Convolutional Neural Networks for the Segmentation of Gliomas in Multi-sequence MRI

Sérgio Pereira[1,2(✉)], Adriano Pinto[1], Victor Alves[2], and Carlos A. Silva[1]

[1] CMEMS-UMinho Research Unit, Guimarães, Portugal
id5692@alunos.uminho.pt, csilva@dei.uminho.pt
[2] Centro Algoritmi, Universidade do Minho, Braga, Portugal

**Abstract.** In their most aggressive form, the mortality rate of gliomas is high. Accurate segmentation is important for surgery and treatment planning, as well as for follow-up evaluation. In this paper, we propose to segment brain tumors using a Deep Convolutional Neural Network. Neural Networks are known to suffer from overfitting. To address it, we use Dropout, Leaky Rectifier Linear Units and small convolutional kernels. To segment the High Grade Gliomas and Low Grade Gliomas we trained two different architectures, one for each grade. Using the proposed method it was possible to obtain promising results in the 2015 Multimodal Brain Tumor Segmentation (BraTS) data set, as well as the second position in the on-site challenge.

**Keywords:** Magnetic Resonance Imaging · Brain tumor · Glioma · Segmentation · Deep learning · Deep Convolutional Neural Network

## 1 Introduction

Gliomas are brain tumors originated from the glial cells, and can be divided into Low Grade Gliomas (LGG) and High Grade Gliomas (HGG). Although the former are less aggressive, the mortality rate of the later is high [4,19]. In fact, the most aggressive gliomas are called Glioblastoma Multiforme, with most patients not surviving more than fourteen months, on average, even when under treatment [29]. The accurate segmentation of the tumor and its sub-regions is important for treatment and surgery planning, but also for follow-up evaluation [4,19].

Over the years, several approaches were proposed for brain tumor segmentation [4,19]. Some probabilistic methods explicitly model the underlying data [9,12,20,23]. In these approaches, besides the model for the tissue intensities, it is possible to include priors on the neighborhood through Markov Random Field models [20], estimate a tumor atlas at segmentation time [9,12,20] and take advantage of biomechanical tumor growth models [9,12]. Agn et al. [1] used a generative method based on Gaussian Mixture Models and probabilistic atlases, extended with a prior on the tumor shape learned by convolutional Restricted Boltzmann Machines.

A. Crimi et al. (Eds.): BrainLes 2015, LNCS 9556, pp. 131–143, 2016.
DOI: 10.1007/978-3-319-30858-6_12

Other approaches learn a model directly from the data in a supervised way [3, 14, 17, 22, 27, 30]. In their core, all of these supervised methods have classifiers that learn how to classify each individual voxel into a tissue type, which may result in isolated voxels, or small clusters, misclassified inside another tissue; however, it is possible to regularize the segmentation by taking the neighborhood into account using Conditional Random Fields [3, 14, 17, 18]. Among the classifiers, Random Forests obtained some of the most promising results [17, 27, 30]. Bakas et al. [2] employed a hybrid generative-discriminative approach. The method is semi-automatic, requiring the user to select some seed points in the image. These points will be used in a modified version of Glistr [9] to obtain a first segmentation; then, it is refined with the gradient boosting algorithm. Lastly, a probabilistic refinement based in intensity statistics is used to obtain the final segmentation.

All the previous supervised methods require the computation of hand-crafted features, which may be difficult to design, or require specialized knowledge on the problem. On the other hand, Deep Learning methods automatically extract features [13]. In Convolutional Neural Networks (CNNs), a set of filters is optimized and convolved with the input image to compute certain characteristics; so, CNNs can deal with the raw data directly. Those filters represent weights of the neural network. Since the filters are convolved over the features, the weights are shared across neural units in the resulting feature maps. In this way, the number of weights in these networks is lower than in neural networks constituted by only fully-connected (FC) layers, making them less prone to overfitting [13]. Overfitting can be a severe problem in neural networks; so, Dropout appears as a regularization method that removes nodes of the network according to some probability in each training step, thus enforcing all nodes to learn good features [25]. Some methods employing CNN for brain tumor segmentation were already proposed [8, 10, 15, 28]. Havaei et al. [10] used a complex architecture of parallel branches and two cascaded CNNs; training of the network was accomplished in two stages: first with balanced classes and, then, a refinement of the last layer was accomplished using a number of samples of each class closer to the observed in brain tumors. Lyksborg et al. [15] trained a CNN in each of the three orthogonal planes of the Magnetic Resonance Imaging (MRI) images, using them as an ensemble of networks for segmentation. Dvořák and Menze [8] used CNNs for structured predictions.

Inspired by Simonyan and Zisserman [24], we developed CNN architectures using small $3 \times 3$ kernels. In this way, we can have more convolutional layers, with the opportunity to apply more non-linear transformations of the data. Additionally, we use data augmentation to increase the amount of training data and Leaky Rectifier Linear Units (LReLU) as non-linear activation function. This approach and architecture obtained the second position in the 2015 BraTS challenge.

## 2    Materials and Methods

The processing pipeline has three main stages: pre-processing, classification through CNNs and post-processing; Fig. 1 presents an overview of the proposed method and interactions between the Training and Testing stages.

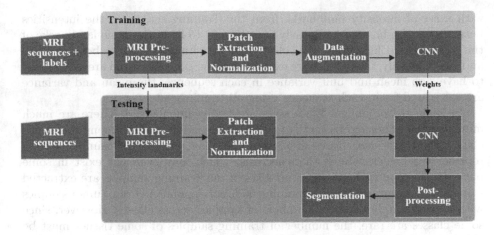

**Fig. 1.** Overview of the processing pipeline. During training, we artificially augment the data, but at test time we use just the original version of patches.

## 2.1 Data

BraTS 2015 [11,19] includes two data sets: Training and Challenge. The Training data set comprises 220 acquisitions from patients with HGG and 54 from patients with LGG. Four MRI sequences are available for each patient: T1-, T1- post contrast (T1c), T2- and FLAIR-weighted. In this data set, the manual segmentations are publicly available. In the Challenge data set, both the manual segmentations and tumor grade are unknown. This set contains 53 subjects with the same MRI sequences as the Training set. All images were already rigidly aligned with the T1c and skull stripped; the resolution was guaranteed to be coherent among all MRI sequences and patients by interpolation of the sequences with thickest slices to 1 mm × 1 mm × 1 mm voxels.

## 2.2 Method

Given the differences between HGG and LGG, a model was trained for each grade. Thus, when segmenting a data set where the tumor grade is unknown, we require the user to visually inspect the images and identify the grade beforehand. After this procedure, the remaining pipeline is automatic, without requiring further intervention of the user, for example, to select parameters, seed points or regions of interest.

**Pre-processing.** The bias field in each MRI sequence was corrected using the N4ITK method [26]. This procedure was similar for all sequences, using 20, 20, 20 and 10 iterations, a shrink factor of 2 and a B-spline fitting distance of 200. After that, the intensities of each individual MRI sequence were normalized [21]. The method for this normalization procedure learns a standardized histogram with a set of intensity landmarks from the Training set, then, the intensities between two landmarks are linearly transformed to fit in the same landmarks of the standardized histogram; we selected 12 matching landmarks both in LGG and HGG. Finally, the patches are extracted in the axial slices and are normalized to have zero mean and unit variance in each sequence; the mean and variance are calculated for in each sequence using all training patches.

In brain tumor images the classes are highly imbalanced. There are much more samples of normal tissue than tumor tissue; additionally, among the tumor classes there are also classes more common than others, for example, edema represents a bigger volume than necrosis, which may even not exist in some patients. To cope with this, around 40 % of our training samples are extracted from normal tissue, while the remaining 60 % corresponds to brain tumor samples with approximately balanced numbers of samples across classes. However, since some classes are rare, the number of training samples of some tissues must be reduced to keep the classes balanced; so, during training each patch is rotated on the fly (in a parallel process) by 90, 180 and 270 to artificially augment the training data; at test time the patches are not rotated and we classify just the central voxel.

**Convolutional Neural Network.** In convolutional layers of CNNs the features are extracted by convolving a set of weights, organized as kernels, with the input. These weights are optimized during training to enhance different features of the images. The computation of the $i^{th}$ feature map in layer $l$ ($F_i^l$) is defined as

$$F_i^l = f\left(b_i^l + \sum_j W_{i,j}^l * X_j^{l-1}\right) \tag{1}$$

where $f$ denotes the activation function, $b$ represents the bias, $j$ indexes the input channel, $W$ denotes the kernels and $X^{l-1}$ the output of the previous layer.

The architectures of the CNNs were developed following [24] and are described in Table 1; several variations were experimented, but these were found to obtain better results in the validation set. By using small kernels, we can stack more layers and have a deeper architecture, while maintaining the same effective receptive field of bigger kernels. For example, two layers with $3 \times 3$ filters have the same receptive field of one layer with $5 \times 5$ kernels, but we have fewer weights to train and we can apply two non-linear transformations to the data. We trained a deeper architecture for HGG than for LGG; adding more layers to the LGG architecture did not improve results, possibly because of the nature of LGG, such as its lower contrast in the core, when compared to HGG. The input consists in $33 \times 33$ axial patches in each of the 4 MRI sequences. Max-pooling consists in downsampling the features maps by only keeping the maximum inside a neighborhood of units in the feature maps; in this way, the computational load of the next layers decrease and small irrelevant details can be discarded. However, segmentation must also detect fine details in the image, thus, in our architectures, max-pooling is performed with some overlapping of the receptive fields, to keep important details

**Table 1.** Architecture of the CNN for HGG (left) and LGG (right). All non-linearities were LReLU, with the exception of the last FC layer, where softmax was used.

| Layer | Receptive Field | Stride | # of feat. maps/FC units | | Layer | Receptive Field | Stride | # of feat. maps/FC units |
|---|---|---|---|---|---|---|---|---|
| Input: 33 X 33 X 4 | | | | | Input: 33 X 33 X 4 | | | |
| Conv. | 3X3 | 1X1 | 64 | | | | | |
| Conv. | 3X3 | 1X1 | 64 | | Conv. | 3X3 | 1X1 | 64 |
| Conv. | 3X3 | 1X1 | 64 | | Conv. | 3X3 | 1X1 | 64 |
| Max-Pool. | 3X3 | 2X2 | - | | Max-Pool. | 3X3 | 2X2 | - |
| Conv. | 3X3 | 1X1 | 128 | | Conv. | 3X3 | 1X1 | 128 |
| Conv. | 3X3 | 1X1 | 128 | | Conv. | 3X3 | 1X1 | 128 |
| Conv. | 3X3 | 1X1 | 128 | | Max-Pool. | 3X3 | 2X2 | - |
| Max-Pool. | 3X3 | 2X2 | - | | FC | - | - | 256 |
| FC | - | - | 256 | | FC | - | - | 256 |
| FC | - | - | 256 | | FC | - | - | 5 |
| FC | - | - | 5 | | | | | |

for segmentation. In all the FC layers we use Dropout with $p = 0.5$ as regularization, in order to reduce overfitting. Besides preventing nodes to co-adapt to each other, Dropout works as an extreme case of bagging and ensemble of networks, since in each mini-batch there are different nodes exposed to a small and different portion of the training data [25]. LReLU was the activation function in almost all layers, expressed as

$$f(x) = \max(0, x) + \alpha \min(0, x) \qquad (2)$$

where $\alpha$ denotes the leakyness parameter defined as $\alpha = \frac{1}{3}$. Contrasting with ReLU, which imposes a constant 0 in the negative part of the function, LReLU has a small negative slope in that part of the function. This is useful for training, since imposing a constant forces the back-propagated gradient to become 0 in the negative values [16]. The loss function was defined as the Categorical Cross-entropy

$$H = - \sum_{j \in voxels} \sum_{k \in classes} c_{j,k} \log(\hat{c}_{j,k}) \qquad (3)$$

where $\hat{c}$ denotes the probabilistic predictions (after the softmax activation function) and $c$ denotes the target. Training is accomplished by optimizing the loss function through Stochastic Gradient Descent using Nesterov's Momentum with momentum coefficient of 0.9. The learning rate $\epsilon$ was initialized with $\epsilon = 0.003$ and linearly decreased after each epoch during the first 25 epochs until $\epsilon = 0.00003$. All convolutional layers operate over padded inputs to maintain its sizes in the output.

The CNNs were implemented using Theano [5] and Lasagne [7].

**Post-processing.** A morphological filter was applied to impose volumetric constrains. Consequently, the clusters are identified and we remove those with less than 10,000 voxels in HGG and 3,000 voxels in LGG.

## 2.3   Evaluation

Although we segment each image into five classes (normal tissue, necrosis, edema, non-enhancing tumor and enhancing tumor), the evaluation appraises three tumor regions: Enhancing tumor, Core (necrosis + non-enhancing tumor + enhancing tumor) and the Complete tumor (all tumor classes). To evaluate the segmentations, the following metrics were computed: Dice Similarity Coefficient (DSC), Positive Predictive Value (PPV), Sensitivity and Robust Hausdorff Distance. The DSC [6] measures the overlap between the manual and the automatic segmentation. It is defined as,

$$DSC = \frac{2TP}{FP + 2TP + FN},$$

(4)

where TP, FP and FN denote the numbers of true positive, false positive and false negative detections, respectively. PPV represents the proportion of detected positive results that are really positive and is defined as,

$$PPV = \frac{TP}{TP + FP}.$$

(5)

Sensitivity measures the proportion of positive detections that are correctly identified as such and is useful to evaluate the number of true positive and false negative detections, being defined as

$$Sensitivity = \frac{TP}{TP + FN}.$$

(6)

The metrics provided by the organizers for the Challenge set were DSC and robust Hausdorff Distance. The Hausdorff Distance measures the distance between the surface of computed ($\partial P$) and manual ($\partial T$) segmentation, as

$$Haus(\partial P, \partial T) = \max\{ \sup_{p \in \partial P} \inf_{t \in \partial T} d(p,t), \sup_{t \in \partial T} \inf_{p \in \partial P} d(t,p)\}$$

(7)

In the robust version of this measure, instead of calculating the maximum distance between the surface of the computed and manual segmentation, it is taken into account the 95 % quantile.

## 3   Results and Discussion

Some segmentation examples obtained in the Training data set are illustrated in Fig. 2, where we can observe the necrosis, edema, non-enhanced and enhanced tumor classes; quantitative results in the same set are presented in Table 2 and Fig. 3. These results were obtained by 2-fold cross-validation and 3-fold cross-validation in HGG and LGG, respectively. Observing Table 2, metrics in the Core and Enhanced regions of LGG are lower than in HGG, which may be due to the lower contrast of the former. In fact, the contrast in the Core region is lower in LGG [19] than in HGG. Additionally, although brain tumors are very heterogeneous, LGG tend to be smaller than HGG, with less Core tissues, as observed from the first and third rows of Fig. 2b. Another issue with LGG is the smaller number of training patients, when compared to HGG. From the boxplots in Fig. 3, we can observe the higher dispersion in the Core region of LGG compared to HGG; in the enhanced tumor in LGG the boxplots range almost the full scale of the metrics, possibly because some of these tumors do not possess enhancing tumor. However, the results for the Complete region are similar in

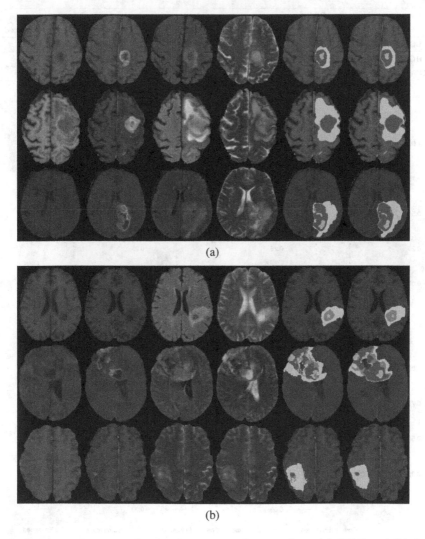

(a)

(b)

**Fig. 2.** Segmentation examples on the training data set from (a) HGG and (b) LGG. From left to right: T1, T1c, FLAIR, T2, manual segmentation and obtained segmentation. Colors in the segmentations represent: blue - necrosis, green - edema, yellow - non-enhanced tumor, red - enhanced tumor (Color figure online).

LGG and HGG, with similar dispersion as observed in the boxplots. There are some outliers in Fig. 3, mainly in HGG, which may be due to the high variability of brain tumors and to the bigger amount of patients with HGG. Following the results in Table 2, in Fig. 2 the boundaries of the complete tumor seem well defined, both in LGG and HGG. However, from the second and third rows in

**Table 2.** Results (mean) obtained with BraTS 2015 training data set.

|  | DSC | | | PPV | | | Sensitivity | | |
|---|---|---|---|---|---|---|---|---|---|
|  | Complete | Core | Enhanced | Complete | Core | Enhanced | Complete | Core | Enhanced |
| LGG | 0.86 | 0.64 | 0.40 | 0.86 | 0.67 | 0.39 | 0.88 | 0.71 | 0.51 |
| HGG | 0.87 | 0.75 | 0.75 | 0.89 | 0.76 | 0.80 | 0.86 | 0.79 | 0.75 |
| LGG + HGG | 0.87 | 0.73 | 0.68 | 0.89 | 0.74 | 0.72 | 0.86 | 0.77 | 0.70 |

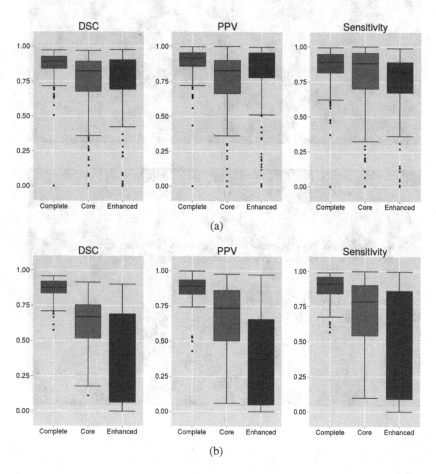

**Fig. 3.** Boxplot of the results in each of the evaluated brain tumor regions using the Training data set in (a) HGG and (b) LGG; black dots represent outliers

Fig. 2b it seems that we are over-segmenting the Core classes in LGG; nevertheless, the second example looks particularly difficult with a big portion of tumor
Core tissues in a very heterogeneous distribution, sharp shapes and details.

Figure 4 presents segmentation examples obtained in the Challenge data set,
while Table 3 and Fig. 5 present the quantitative results. In this case, all subjects

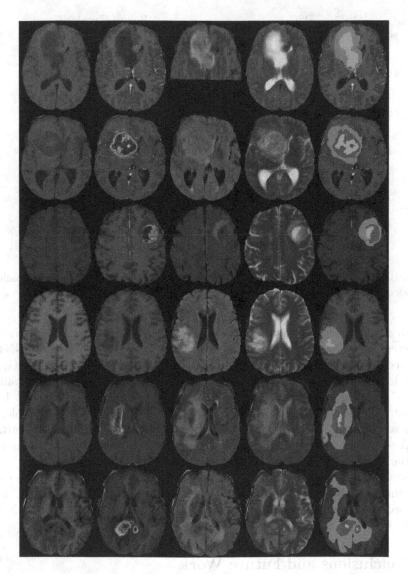

**Fig. 4.** Segmentation examples on the challenge data set. From left to right: T1, T1c,
FLAIR, T2 and obtained segmentation. Colors in the segmentations represent: blue -
necrosis, green - edema, yellow - non-enhanced tumor, red - enhanced tumor (Color
figure online).

**Table 3.** Results (mean) using the challenge data set of BraTS 2015.

| | DSC | | | Robust Hausdorff | | |
| --- | --- | --- | --- | --- | --- | --- |
| | Complete | Core | Enh. | Complete | Core | Enh. |
| | 0.78 | 0.65 | 0.75 | 15.83 | 26.54 | 6.99 |

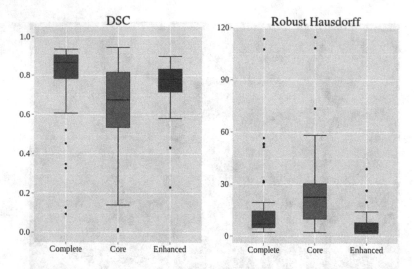

**Fig. 5.** Boxplots of DSC and Robust Hausdorff Distance obtained using the challenge data set of BraTS 2015.

in each grade of the Training data set were used for training the CNN, with the exception of six validation patients in each grade. To train the CNNs we extracted around 4,000,000 training patches of HGG and 1,800,000 of LGG, and we used mini-batches of 128 training samples. However, the number of training patches was 4 times bigger due to the data augmentation. Observing Fig. 4, the segmentations seem coherent with the expected tumor tissues, for example, the enhanced tumor portions appear delineated following the enhancing parts in T1c. Also, the complete tumor appears to be well delineated, when comparing with the FLAIR and T2 sequences, where the edema is hyperintense.

The training stage of each CNN took around one week. However, the entire processing pipeline takes approximately 8 min to segment each patient, using GPU processing on a Intel Core i7 3.5 GHz CPU, 32 GB of RAM, with a Nvidia Geforce GTX 980 computer running Ubuntu 14.04 OS.

## 4    Conclusions and Future Work

In this paper, we presented a CNN to segment brain tumors in MRI. Excluding when the user needs to identify the tumor grade, all steps in the processing pipeline are automatic. Although simple, this architecture shows promising results, with space for further developments, especially in the Core region and segmentation of LGG; in the Challenge data set the proposed method was ranked in the second position. As future work, we want to make a totally grade independent method, possibly through a joint LGG/HGG training or an automatic grade identification procedure before segmentation.

**Acknowledgments.** This work is supported by FCT with the reference project UID/EEA/04436/2013, by FEDER funds through the COMPETE 2020 Programa Operacional Competitividade e Internacionalização (POCI) with the reference project POCI-01-0145-FEDER-006941. Sérgio Pereira was supported by a scholarship from Fundação para a Ciência e Tecnologia (FCT), Portugal (scholarship number PD/BD/105803/2014). Brain tumor image data used in this article were obtained from the MICCAI 2013 Challenge on Multimodal Brain Tumor Segmentation. The challenge database contain fully anonymized images from the Cancer Imaging Archive.

# References

1. Agn, M., Puonti, O., Law, I., af Rosenschöld, P.M., van Leemput, K.: Brain tumor segmentation by a generative model with a prior on tumor shape. In: Proceeding of the Multimodal Brain Tumor Image Segmentation Challenge, pp. 1–4 (2015)
2. Bakas, S., Zeng, K., Sotiras, A., Rathore, S., Akbari, H., Gaonkar, B., Rozycki, M., Pati, S., Davazikos, C.: Segmentation of gliomas in multimodal magnetic resonance imaging volumes based on a hybrid generative-discriminative framework. In: Proceeding of the Multimodal Brain Tumor Image Segmentation Challenge, pp. 5–12 (2015)
3. Bauer, S., Nolte, L.-P., Reyes, M.: Fully automatic segmentation of brain tumor images using support vector machine classification in combination with hierarchical conditional random field regularization. In: Fichtinger, G., Martel, A., Peters, T. (eds.) MICCAI 2011, Part III. LNCS, vol. 6893, pp. 354–361. Springer, Heidelberg (2011)
4. Bauer, S., Wiest, R., Nolte, L.P., Reyes, M.: A survey of mri-based medical image analysis for brain tumor studies. Phys. Med. Biol. **58**(13), R97 (2013)
5. Bergstra, J., Breuleux, O., Bastien, F., Lamblin, P., Pascanu, R., Desjardins, G., Turian, J., Warde-Farley, D., Bengio, Y.: Theano: a CPU and GPU math expression compiler. In: Proceedings of the Python for Scientific Computing Conference (SciPy), June 2010
6. Dice, L.R.: Measures of the amount of ecologic association between species. Ecology **26**(3), 297–302 (1945)
7. Dieleman, S., Schlter, J., Raffel, C., Olson, E., Snderby, S.K., Nouri, D., Maturana, D., Thoma, M., Battenberg, E., Kelly, J., Fauw, J.D., Heilman, M., diogo149, McFee, B., Weideman, H., takacsg84, peterderivaz, Jon, instagibbs, Rasul, D.K., CongLiu, Britefury, Degrave, J.: Lasagne: First release, August 2015. http://dx.doi.org/10.5281/zenodo.27878
8. Dvorák, P., Menze, B.: Structured prediction with convolutional neural networks for multimodal brain tumor segmentation. In: Proceeding of the Multimodal Brain Tumor Image Segmentation Challenge, pp. 13–24 (2015)
9. Gooya, A., Pohl, K.M., Bilello, M., Cirillo, L., Biros, G., Melhem, E.R., Davatzikos, C.: Glistr: glioma image segmentation and registration. IEEE Trans. Med. Imaging **31**(10), 1941–1954 (2012)

10. Havaei, M., Davy, A., Warde-Farley, D., Biard, A., Courville, A., Bengio, Y., Pal, C., Jodoin, P.M., Larochelle, H.: Brain tumor segmentation with deep neural networks. arXiv preprint (2015). arXiv:1505.03540
11. Kistler, M., Bonaretti, S., Pfahrer, M., Niklaus, R., Büchler, P.: The virtual skeleton database: an open access repository for biomedical research and collaboration. J. Med. Internet Res. **15**(11), e245 (2013). http://www.jmir.org/2013/11/e245/
12. Kwon, D., Shinohara, R.T., Akbari, H., Davatzikos, C.: Combining generative models for multifocal glioma segmentation and registration. In: Golland, P., Hata, N., Barillot, C., Hornegger, J., Howe, R. (eds.) MICCAI 2014, Part I. LNCS, vol. 8673, pp. 763–770. Springer, Heidelberg (2014)
13. LeCun, Y., Bengio, Y., Hinton, G.: Deep learning. Nature **521**(7553), 436–444 (2015)
14. Lee, C.-H., Wang, S., Murtha, A., Brown, M.R.G., Greiner, R.: Segmenting brain tumors using pseudo–conditional random fields. In: Metaxas, D., Axel, L., Fichtinger, G., Székely, G. (eds.) MICCAI 2008, Part I. LNCS, vol. 5241, pp. 359–366. Springer, Heidelberg (2008)
15. Lyksborg, M., Puonti, O., Agn, M., Larsen, R.: An ensemble of 2D convolutional neural networks for tumor segmentation. In: Paulsen, R.R., Pedersen, K.S. (eds.) SCIA 2015. LNCS, vol. 9127, pp. 201–211. Springer, Heidelberg (2015)
16. Maas, A.L., Hannun, A.Y., Ng, A.Y.: Rectifier nonlinearities improve neural network acoustic models. In: Proceedings of the ICML, vol. 30 (2013)
17. Meier, R., Bauer, S., Slotboom, J., Wiest, R., Reyes, M.: Appearance-and context-sensitive features for brain tumor segmentation. In: BraTS Challenge Manuscripts, pp. 20–26 (2014)
18. Meier, R., Karamitsou, V., Habegger, S., Wiest, R., Reyes, M.: Parameter learning for crf-based tissue segmentation of brain tumors. In: Proceeding of the Multimodal Brain Tumor Image Segmentation Challenge, pp. 48–51 (2015)
19. Menze, B., Jakab, A., Bauer, S., Kalpathy-Cramer, J., Farahani, K., Kirby, J., Burren, Y., Porz, N., Slotboom, J., Wiest, R., Lanczi, L., Gerstner, E., Weber, M.A., Arbel, T., Avants, B., Ayache, N., Buendia, P., Collins, D., Cordier, N., Corso, J., Criminisi, A., Das, T., Delingette, H., Demiralp, C., Durst, C., Dojat, M., Doyle, S., Festa, J., Forbes, F., Geremia, E., Glocker, B., Golland, P., Guo, X., Hamamci, A., Iftekharuddin, K., Jena, R., John, N., Konukoglu, E., Lashkari, D., Mariz, J., Meier, R., Pereira, S., Precup, D., Price, S., Riklin Raviv, T., Reza, S., Ryan, M., Sarikaya, D., Schwartz, L., Shin, H.C., Shotton, J., Silva, C., Sousa, N., Subbanna, N., Szekely, G., Taylor, T., Thomas, O., Tustison, N., Unal, G., Vasseur, F., Wintermark, M., Ye, D.H., Zhao, L., Zhao, B., Zikic, D., Prastawa, M., Reyes, M., Van Leemput, K.: The multimodal brain tumor image segmentation benchmark (brats). IEEE Trans. Med. Imaging **34**(10), 1993–2024 (2015)
20. Menze, B.H., van Leemput, K., Lashkari, D., Weber, M.-A., Ayache, N., Golland, P.: A generative model for brain tumor segmentation in multi-modal images. In: Jiang, T., Navab, N., Pluim, J.P.W., Viergever, M.A. (eds.) MICCAI 2010, Part II. LNCS, vol. 6362, pp. 151–159. Springer, Heidelberg (2010)
21. Nyúl, L.G., Udupa, J.K., Zhang, X.: New variants of a method of mri scale standardization. IEEE Trans. Med. Imaging **19**(2), 143–150 (2000)
22. Pinto, A., Pereira, S., Correia, H., Oliveira, J., Rasteiro, D.M., Silva, C.A.: Brain tumour segmentation based on extremely randomized forest with high-level features. In: 2015 37th Annual International Conference of the IEEE Engineering in Medicine and Biology Society (EMBC), pp. 3037–3040. IEEE (2015)
23. Prastawa, M., Bullitt, E., Ho, S., Gerig, G.: A brain tumor segmentation framework based on outlier detection. Med. Image Anal. **8**(3), 275–283 (2004)

24. Simonyan, K., Zisserman, A.: Very deep convolutional networks for large-scale image recognition. arXiv preprint. (2014). arXiv:1409.1556
25. Srivastava, N., Hinton, G., Krizhevsky, A., Sutskever, I., Salakhutdinov, R.: Dropout: a simple way to prevent neural networks from overfitting. J. Mach. Learn. Res. **15**(1), 1929–1958 (2014)
26. Tustison, N.J., Avants, B.B., Cook, P.A., Zheng, Y., Egan, A., Yushkevich, P.A., Gee, J.C.: N4itk: improved n3 bias correction. IEEE Trans. Med. Imaging **29**(6), 1310–1320 (2010)
27. Tustison, N.J., Shrinidhi, K., Wintermark, M., Durst, C.R., Kandel, B.M., Gee, J.C., Grossman, M.C., Avants, B.B.: Optimal symmetric multimodal templates and concatenated random forests for supervised brain tumor segmentation (simplified) with antsr. Neuroinformatics pp. 1–17 (2014)
28. Urban, G., Bendszus, M., Hamprecht, F., Kleesiek, J.: Multi-modal brain tumor segmentation using deep convolutional neural networks. In: MICCAI Brain Tumor Segmentation Challenge (BraTS), pp. 1–5 (2014)
29. Van Meir, E.G., Hadjipanayis, C.G., Norden, A.D., Shu, H.K., Wen, P.Y., Olson, J.J.: Exciting new advances in neuro-oncology: the avenue to a cure for malignant glioma. CA Cancer J. Clin. **60**(3), 166–193 (2010)
30. Zikic, D., Glocker, B., Konukoglu, E., Criminisi, A., Demiralp, C., Shotton, J., Thomas, O.M., Das, T., Jena, R., Price, S.J.: Decision Forests for Tissue-Specific Segmentation of High-Grade Gliomas in Multi-channel MR. In: Ayache, N., Delingette, H., Golland, P., Mori, K. (eds.) MICCAI 2012, Part III. LNCS, vol. 7512, pp. 369–376. Springer, Heidelberg (2012)

# GLISTRboost: Combining Multimodal MRI Segmentation, Registration, and Biophysical Tumor Growth Modeling with Gradient Boosting Machines for Glioma Segmentation

Spyridon Bakas$^{(\boxtimes)}$, Ke Zeng, Aristeidis Sotiras, Saima Rathore,
Hamed Akbari, Bilwaj Gaonkar, Martin Rozycki, Sarthak Pati,
and Christos Davatzikos$^{(\boxtimes)}$

Section of Biomedical Image Analysis,
Center for Biomedical Image Computing and Analytics, Perelman School of
Medicine, University of Pennsylvania, Philadelphia, USA
{S.Bakas,Ke.Zeng,Aristeidis.Sotiras,Saima.Rathore,Hamed.Akbari,B.Gaonkar,
Martin.Rozycki,Sarthak.Pati,Christos.Davatzikos}@uphs.upenn.edu

**Abstract.** We present an approach for segmenting low- and high-grade gliomas in multimodal magnetic resonance imaging volumes. The proposed approach is based on a hybrid generative-discriminative model. Firstly, a generative approach based on an Expectation-Maximization framework that incorporates a glioma growth model is used to segment the brain scans into tumor, as well as healthy tissue labels. Secondly, a gradient boosting multi-class classification scheme is used to refine tumor labels based on information from multiple patients. Lastly, a probabilistic Bayesian strategy is employed to further refine and finalize the tumor segmentation based on patient-specific intensity statistics from the multiple modalities. We evaluated our approach in 186 cases during the training phase of the BRAin Tumor Segmentation (BRATS) 2015 challenge and report promising results. During the testing phase, the algorithm was additionally evaluated in 53 unseen cases, achieving the best performance among the competing methods.

**Keywords:** Segmentation · Brain tumor · Glioma · Multimodal MRI · BRATS challenge · Gradient boosting · Expectation maximization · Brain tumor growth model · Probabilistic model

## 1 Introduction

Gliomas comprise a group of primary central nervous system (CNS) tumors of neuroglial cells (*e.g.*, astrocytes and oligodendrocytes) that have different degrees of aggressiveness. They are mainly divided into low- and high-grade gliomas (LGGs and HGGs) according to their progression rate and histopathology. LGGs and HGGs exhibit distinct pathophysiological phenotypes and are subject to different treatment options. LGGs are less common than HGGs, constitute approximately 20 % of CNS glial tumors, and almost all of them eventually progress to

© Springer International Publishing Switzerland 2016
A. Crimi et al. (Eds.): BrainLes 2015, LNCS 9556, pp. 144–155, 2016.
DOI: 10.1007/978-3-319-30858-6_13

HGGs [15]. HGGs are rapidly progressing malignancies, divided based on their histopathologic features into anaplastic gliomas and glioblastomas (GBMs) [21].

Gliomas consist of various parts, each of which shows a different imaging phenotype in multimodal magnetic resonance imaging (MRI). Typically, the core of HGGs consists of enhancing, non-enhancing and necrotic parts, whereas the core of LGGs does not necessarily include an enhancing part. Another critical feature, for both understanding and treating gliomas, is the peritumoral edematous region. Edema occurs from infiltrating tumor cells, as well as a biological response to the angiogenic and vascular permeability factors released by the spatially adjacent tumor cells [1].

Quantification of the various parts of gliomas, in multimodal MRI, has an important role in treatment decisions, planning, as well as monitoring in longitudinal studies. The accurate segmentation of these regions is required to allow this quantification. However, tumor segmentation is extremely challenging due to the tumor regions being defined through intensity changes relative to the surrounding normal tissue, and such intensity information being disseminated across various modalities for each region. Additional factors that contribute to the difficulty of brain tumor segmentation task is the motion of the patient during the examination, as well as the magnetic field inhomogeneities. Hence, the manual annotation of such boundaries is time-consuming, prone to misinterpretation, human error and observer bias [3], with intra- and inter-rater variability up to 20 % and 28 %, respectively [16]. Computer-aided segmentation of brain tumor images would thus be an important advancement. Towards this end, we present a computer-aided segmentation method that aims to accurately segment such tumors and eventually allow for their quantification.

The remainder of this paper is organized as follows: Sect. 2 details the provided data, while Sect. 3 presents the proposed segmentation strategy. The experimental validation setting is described in Sect. 4 along with the obtained results. Finally, Sect. 5 concludes the paper with a short discussion and potential future research directions.

## 2  Materials

The data used in this study comprise 186 preoperative multimodal MRI scans of patients with gliomas (54 LGGs and 132 HGGs) that were provided as the training set for the multimodal BRATS 2015 challenge, from the Virtual Skeleton Database (VSD) [12]. Specifically, these data are a combination of the training set (10 LGGs and 20 HGGs) used in the BRATS 2013 challenge [17], as well as 44 LGG and 112 HGG scans provided from the National Institutes of Health (NIH) Cancer Imaging Archive (TCIA). The data of each patient consists of native and contrast-enhanced (CE) T1-weighted, as well as T2-weighted and T2 Fluid-attenuated inversion recovery (FLAIR) MRI volumes. The volumes of the various modalities were, co-registered to the same anatomical template and interpolated to 1 mm$^3$ voxel resolution. In addition to the training set, 53 multimodal volumetric images were provided as the testing set for the challenge, comprising both preoperative and after initial therapy scans.

Finally, ground truth (GT) segmentations for the training set were also provided. Specifically, the data from BRATS 2013 were manually annotated, whereas data from TCIA were automatically annotated by fusing the approved by experts results of the segmentation algorithms that ranked high in the BRATS 2012 and 2013 challenges [17]. The GT segmentations comprise the enhancing part of the tumor (ET), the tumor core (TC), which is described by the union of necrotic, non-enhancing and enhancing parts of the tumor, and the whole tumor (WT), which is the union of the TC and the peritumoral edematous region. Note that the testing sets have been segmented manually by one to four rates, but the GT segmentations were not provided to the participating teams, allowing for their evaluation only by the challenge organizers.

## 3   Methods

The provided skull-stripped and co-registered MRI volumes were initially smoothed using a low-level image processing method, namely Smallest Univalue Segment Assimilating Nucleus (SUSAN) [20], to reduce intensity noise in regions of uniform intensity profile. The intensity histograms of all modalities of all patients were then matched to the corresponding modality of a single reference patient.

A modified version of the GLioma Image SegmenTation and Registration (GLISTR) software [10] was subsequently used to delineate the boundaries of healthy tissues (*i.e.*, white and gray matter, cerebrospinal fluid, vessels and cerebellum), as well as tumor tissues (*i.e.*, edema, necrosis, non-enhancing and enhancing parts of the tumor). Although GLISTR was inspired by a sequential approach of segmentation of the input brain scans followed by the registration of the outcome to a given healthy atlas [8], it was originally proposed in [9,10] as a tool that jointly performs segmentation and registration, but handles only scans with solitary HGGs. It was then conceptually improved in [14] to target broader brain tumor appearances, including multifocal masses and complex shapes with heterogeneous textures (*e.g.*, LGGs), enabling it to also participate in the BRATS 2014 challenge [13]. The version of GLISTR used here, was modified in terms of using multiple seed-points for each brain tissue label, in order to model the exact intensity distribution (*i.e.*, mean and variance) of each, whereas [14] uses a single seed-point for each label, assuming it is representative of each label's mean intensity value, and the variance is described by a fixed value for all labels. Note that both previous and current versions of GLISTR do not depend on the coordinates of the initialization seed-points, but on the intensity value of the corresponding voxel on each modality. Therefore, even if different seed-points are initialized across two independent segmentation attempts, GLISTR output segmentation results should be identical, if the intensity distributions modeled during these attempts are the same. The whole framework of GLISTR is based on a probabilistic generative model that relies on Expectation-Maximizaton (EM), to recursively refine the estimates of the posteriors for all tissue labels, the deformable mapping to the atlas, and the parameters of the incorporated brain tumor growth model [11].

This modified version of GLISTR requires as input a single seed-point and a radius for each apparent tumor, as well as multiple seed-points for each brain tissue label. These seed-points were initialized using BrainTumorViewer[1], which has been primarily developed for this purpose. Given the single seed-point and the radius inputs, the center and the bulk volume of each tumor are approximated by a sphere (Fig. 1). The parametric model of the sphere is used to initiate the tumor growth model for each apparent tumor. This growth model is used to modify the healthy atlas into one with tumor and edema tissues matching the input scans, whilst it approximates the deformation occurred to the surrounding brain tissues, due to the effect of the tumors' mass. A tumor shape prior is also estimated separately, by a random-walk-based generative model, which uses multiple tumor seed-points as initial foreground cues. This tumor shape prior is systemically incorporated into the EM framework via an empirical Bayes model, as described in [14]. Furthermore, a minimum of three seed-points are initialized for each brain tissue label, with the intention of capturing the intensity variation of each tissue label, and modeling each label's intensity distribution. This provides a better initialization to the EM framework, resulting to more accurate delineation of all tissue labels, when compared to [14] that uses a single seed-point for each label. The output of GLISTR is a posterior probability map for each tissue label, as well as a label map, which is a very good initial segmentation of all different tissues within a patient's brain.

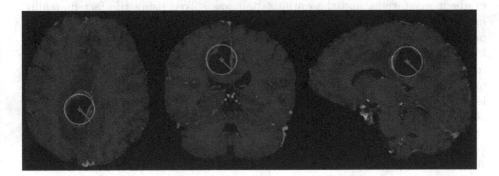

**Fig. 1.** Example of using a single seed-point and a radius to approximate the center and the bulk volume of a tumor by a sphere. The figures illustrate (from left to right) the axial, coronal and sagittal view of the same patient.

A machine-learning approach was then used to refine GLISTR results by utilizing information across multiple patients. Specifically, the gradient boosting algorithm [5] is employed for voxel-level multi-label classification. Gradient boosting is an ensemble method that produces a prediction model by combining weak learners in a stage-wise fashion. It generalizes other boosting techniques by allowing the optimization of an arbitrary differentiable loss function. We used

---

[1] Available on: https://www.cbica.upenn.edu/sbia/software/braintumorviewer/.

the Python package scikit-learn [18] for the implementation, choosing deviance as the loss function. At each iteration, a weak learner, specifically a decision tree of maximum depth 3, was added to the decision function, approximating the current negative gradient of the objective. Randomness was introduced when constructing each tree [6]. Each decision tree was fit to a sub-sample of the training set, with the sampling rate set equal to 0.6. The split was also determined stochastically by sampling a subset of features at each node, with the number of sampled features set equal to the square root of the total number of features. The algorithm was terminated after 100 such iterations.

The features used for training our model consist of five components; image intensity, image derivative, geodesic information, texture features, and the GLISTR posterior probability maps. The intensity component comprises the raw intensity value of each voxel $(I(v_i))$, as well as their differences among all four modalities (*i.e.*, T1, T1-CE, T2, T2-FLAIR). The image derivative component comprises the Laplacian of Gaussian and the image gradient magnitude. Note that prior to calculating any intensity-based feature, intensity normalization was performed based on the median intensity value of the GLISTR segmented cerebrospinal fluid. The geodesic information at voxel $v_i$ was given by the geodesic distance from the seed-point used in GLISTR as the tumor center, at voxel $v_s$. Specifically, the geodesic distance between $v_i$ and $v_s$ was defined as $\min_\gamma \int_\gamma P(\gamma(s))ds$, where $\gamma$ is a path connecting $v_i$ to $v_s$. Similar to the approach taken in [7], we set the weight $P$ at each voxel to be proportional to its gradient magnitude, and the optimization was solved using the fast marching method [4,19]. Furthermore, the texture features describe the first and second order texture statistics computed from a gray-level co-occurrence matrix. Specifically, the first order statistics comprise the mean and variance of the intensities from each modality within a radius of 2 voxels for each voxel. For the second order statistics, the image volumes were firstly normalized to 64 different gray levels, and then a bounding box of 5-by-5 pixels was used for all the pixels of each image slice. Subsequently, a graylevel co-occurrence matrix was filled with the intensity values within a radius of 2 pixels for all eight main directions (*i.e.*, $\{0°, 45°, 90°, 135°, 180°, 225°, 270°, 315°\}$) to extract the energy, entropy, dissimilarity, homogeneity (*i.e.*, inverse difference moment of order 2), and inverse difference moment of order 1. It should also be mentioned that our model was trained using both LGG and HGG training samples simultaneously using a 54-fold cross-validation setting (given that 54 LGGs were present in the training data, *i.e.*, allowing for using a single LGG within each fold). The cross-validation setting is necessary in order to avoid over-fitting.

Finally, a patient-wise refinement was performed by assessing the local intensity distribution of the current segmentation labels and updating their spatial configuration based on a probabilistic model, inspired by [2]. Firstly, the intensity distribution of voxels with GLISTR posterior probability equal to 1 for the tissue classes of white matter, edema, necrosis, non-enhancing and enhancing tumor, were populated separately. Note that in the current segmentation goal, there is no distinction between the non-enhancing and the necrotic parts of the tumor.

A normalization to the histograms of pair-wise distributions was then applied. The class-conditional probability densities $(Pr(I(v_i)|Class_1)$ and $Pr(I(v_i)|Class_2))$ were modeled by fitting distinct Gaussian models, using Maximum Likelihood Estimation to find the mean and standard deviation for each class. There are three pair-wise distributions considered here; the edema voxels opposed to the white matter voxels in the T2-FLAIR volume, the ET voxels opposed to the edema voxels in the T1-CE volume, and the ET voxels opposed to the union of the necrosis and the non-enhancing tumor in the T1-CE volume. In all cases, the former intensity population is expected to have much higher (*i.e.*, brighter) values. Hence, voxels of each class with small spatial proximity (namely 3 voxels) to the opposing tissue class were evaluated based on their intensity. Specifically, the intensity $I(v_i)$ of each of these voxels was assessed and $Pr(I(v_i)|Class_1)$ was compared with $Pr(I(v_i)|Class_2)$. The voxel $v_i$ was then classified into a tissue class according to the larger of the two conditional probabilities. This is equivalent to a classification based on Bayes' Theorem with equal priors for the two classes, *i.e.*, $Pr(Class_1) = Pr(Class_2) = 0.5$.

Note that our challenge winning methodology has been made publicly available on the Online Image Processing Portal (IPP)[2] of the Center for Biomedical Image Computing and Analytics (CBICA), of the University of Pennsylvania. CBICA's IPP allows users to perform their data analysis using the integrated algorithms, without any software installation, whilst also using CBICA's High Performance Computing resources.

## 4   Experiments and Results

In order to assess the segmentation performance of our method, we evaluated the overlap between the proposed tumor labels and the GT in three regions, *i.e.*, WT, TC and ET, as suggested in [17]. Figure 2 showcases example segmentation results along with the respective GT segmentations for eight patients (four HGGs and four LGGs). These correspond to the two most and least successful segmentation results for each glioma grade. We observe high agreement between the generated results and the provided labels. We note that the highest overlap is observed for edema, while there is some disagreement between the segmentations of the enhancing and non-enhancing parts of the tumor.

To further appraise the performance of the proposed method, we quantitatively validated the per-voxel overlap between respective regions, in the training set, using the DICE coefficient (see Fig. 3 and Table 1). This metric takes values between 0 and 1, with higher values corresponding to increased overlap. Moreover, aiming to understand fully the obtained results, we stratified them based on the labeling protocol of the GT segmentation. In particular, data with manually annotated GT (*i.e.*, BRATS 2013 data) was evaluated separately from data with automatically defined GT (*i.e.*, TCIA data). The reason behind this distinction is twofold. First, only manual segmentation can be considered as gold standard, thus allowing us to evaluate the potential of our approach when

---

[2] Available on: https://ipp.cbica.upenn.edu/.

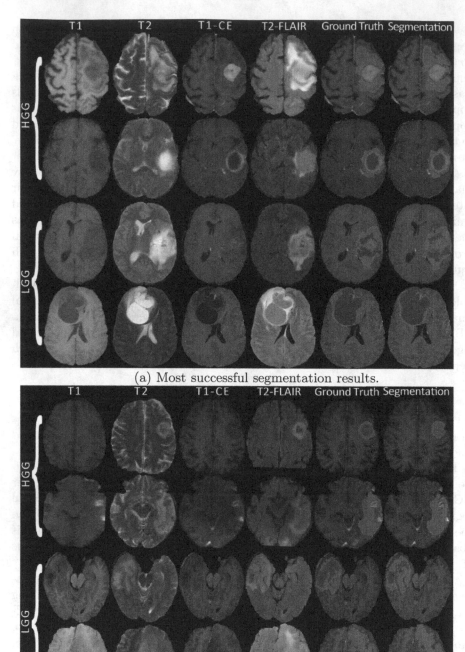

(a) Most successful segmentation results.

(b) Least successful segmentation results.

**Fig. 2.** Examples for four LGG and four HGG patients. Green, red and blue masks denote the edema, the enhancing tumor and the union of the necrotic and non-enhancing parts of the tumor, respectively (Color figure online).

targeting an interactive clinical work-flow. Second, results validated using auto-matically defined GT should be interpreted with caution because of the inher-ently introduced bias towards the employed automated methods, which also influences visually inspecting experts [3]. As a consequence, our method may be negatively impacted since it may learn to reproduce the systematic mistakes of the provided annotations. Furthermore, since LGGs are characterized by a distinct pathophysiological phenotype (*i.e.*, lack of enhancing tumor part), we also divided the obtained results in terms of the tumors' grade (*i.e.*, LGG and HGG). This allows the performance assessment of the proposed approach on the distinct imaging phenotype of each grade separately.

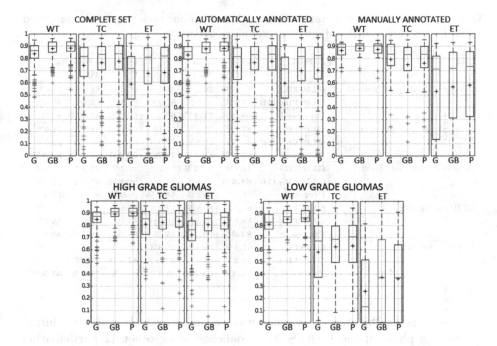

**Fig. 3.** Distributions of the DICE score across patients for each step (G: GLISTR, GB: gradient boosting, P: proposed) of the proposed method, each tissue label and different groupings of data. The black cross and the red line inside each box denote the mean and median values, respectively (Color figure online).

Figure 3 reports the distributions of the cross-validated DICE score across patients of the training set, for each step of the proposed method and for each tissue label (WT, TC and ET) while Table 1 reports the respective mean and median values. The results are presented following the previously described strat-ifications. Figure 3 shows a clear step-wise improvement in both the mean and median values of all tissue labels when considering the complete set of data, the automatically annotated, the LGGs and the HGGs. On the contrary, we observe a step-wise deterioration of both the mean and median values for the TC label when assessing the manually annotated subset of the data (see Table 1 for the exact values). This is probably the effect of learning systematically mislabeled voxels present in the automatically generated GT annotations (see mislabeled ET in GT of the second HGG in Fig. 2(a)). Furthermore, we note the segmentation results for the ET label to vary significantly between LGGs and HGGs, with the former showing lower and less consistent results. This seems to be the effect of training our learning model using both classes simultaneously, when LGGs typically show a different pathophysiological phenotype marked by the lack of an enhancing part. Nevertheless, the segmentation of the WT label in the LGGs is comparable to this of the HGGs.

**Table 1.** Mean and median values of the DICE score for each step of the proposed method, each tissue label and different groupings of data.

| Data | Method | Dice score (mean) | | | Dice score (median) | | |
|---|---|---|---|---|---|---|---|
| | | WT | TC | ET | WT | TC | ET |
| Complete training set (n=186) | GLISTR | 83.7% | 74.2% | 58.6% | 86.4% | 81.6% | 71.6% |
| | GLISTR+GB | 87.9% | 76.5% | 67.6% | 89.9% | 83.3% | 80.9% |
| | Proposed | **88.4%** | **77.4%** | **68.2%** | **90.3%** | **83.7%** | **82%** |
| Automatically annotated (n=156) | GLISTR | 83.1% | 73.2% | 60.1% | 85.8% | 81.6% | 71.6% |
| | GLISTR+GB | 87.9% | 76.8% | 70.5% | 89.9% | 83.5% | 82.6% |
| | Proposed | **88.5%** | **77.7%** | **71%** | **90.3%** | **83.7%** | **82.8%** |
| Manually annotated (n=30) | GLISTR | 86.7% | **79.2%** | 52.9% | 89.2% | **83.6%** | 71.3% |
| | GLISTR+GB | **88.3%** | 74.8% | 56.7% | **90.8%** | 83.2% | 72.6% |
| | Proposed | 87.6% | 76.1% | **58.1%** | 90.5% | 83.4% | **75.7%** |
| All HGGs (n=132) | GLISTR | 84.7% | 80.8% | 72.2% | 87.3% | 85.3% | 76.2% |
| | GLISTR+GB | 89.1% | 82.3% | 80.5% | 91% | 86.7% | 85.7% |
| | Proposed | **89.6%** | **83.2%** | **82%** | 91% | **87.2%** | **86.5%** |
| All LGGs (n=54) | GLISTR | 81.1% | 58.1% | 25.8% | 82.8% | 67.3% | 12.8% |
| | GLISTR+GB | 85.2% | 62.4% | **37.3%** | **87.2%** | 68.6% | 36.9% |
| | Proposed | **85.4%** | **63.2%** | 35.9% | 86.9% | **70.7%** | **37.3%** |

Lastly, the hereby proposed method was also quantitatively evaluated during the testing phase of the BRATS 2015 challenge along other 12 participating teams, using the DICE score and the robust Hausdorff distance (95 % quantile), similar to [17]. Each team had only 48 hours for producing their segmentation labels, from the time the testing set was made available, until the submission of the results to VSD. The limited time of the testing phase was considered essential to minimize the chance of optimizing the proposed algorithms on the given data. According to the results presented during the challenge, our semi-automatic approach performed best when compared to the other competing methods.

## 5    Discussion

We presented an approach that combines generative and discriminative methods towards providing a reliable and highly accurate segmentation of LGGs and

HGGs in multimodal MRI volumes. Our proposed approach is built upon the brain segmentation results provided by a modified version of GLISTR. GLISTR segments the brain into tumor and healthy tissue labels by means of a generative model encompassing a tumor growth model and a probabilistic atlas of healthy individuals. GLISTR tumor labels are subsequently refined taking into account population-wide tumor label appearance statistics that were learned by employing a gradient boosting multi-class classifier. The final results are produced by adapting the segmentation labels based on patient-specific label intensity distributions from the multiple modalities.

Our approach was able to deliver high quality tumor segmentation results, eventually performing best among the competing methods in BRATS 2015 challenge, by significantly improving GLISTR results [13] through the adopted post-processing strategies. This improvement was evident for both manually and automatically segmented data, as well as for both LGGs and HGGs. The only case where the post-processing resulted in a decrease of the performance is for the TC label when considering only the manually segmented data. This could be probably attributed to the fact that the supervised gradient boosting model learned consistent errors present in the automatically generated segmentations and propagated them when refining GLISTR results. While pooling information for more patients seems to be benefiting the learning algorithm, it also introduces a bias towards the more numerous automatically generated data. Accounting for this bias by weighting accordingly manually and automatically segmented samples could possible allow for harnessing the additional information without compromising quality. Moreover, the proposed approach performed best in the WT label, which is clinically considered of the highest importance since it allows for: (i) assessment and evaluation of the heterogeneity of the peritumoral edematous region [1], (ii) estimates of diffuse tumor infiltration, rather than a binary tumor/no-tumor classification, and (iii) guidance to spatially-precise treatment decisions.

The proposed approach segmented the whole tumor and the tumor core with high accuracy for both LGGs and HGGs. However, the segmentation results for the enhancing tumor varied importantly between the two classes of tumors, with the performance of our method in the case of LGGs being significantly lower and less consistent. This is due to the fact that LGGs are characterized by a distinct pathophysiological phenotype that is often marked by the lack of an enhancing part, hence not having the same imaging phenotype with the HGGs. In addition, the segmentation of the enhancing tumor could be further improved considering that gliomas can be distinguished into two distinct imaging phenotypes, which are not necessarily consistent with their clinical grade (i.e., LGG/HGG). These distinct imaging signatures could be possibly exploited in a machine learning framework that considers separately radiologically defined HGGs and LGGs, i.e., tumors with and without a distinctive enhancing part. By modeling separately these distinct imaging phenotypes, it is possible to capture better the imaging heterogeneity and improve label prediction.

# References

1. Akbari, H., Macyszyn, L., Da, X., Wolf, R.L., Bilello, M., Verma, R., O'Rourke, D.M., Davatzikos, C.: Pattern analysis of dynamic susceptibility contrast-enhanced MR imaging demonstrates peritumoral tissue heterogeneity. Radiology **273**(2), 502–510 (2014)
2. Bakas, S., Chatzimichail, K., Hunter, G., Labbe, B., Sidhu, P.S., Makris, D.: Fast semi-automatic segmentation of focal liver lesions in contrast-enhanced ultrasound, based on a probabilistic model. Comput. Methods Biomech. Biomed. Eng.: Imaging Vis., 1–10 (2015). doi:10.1080/21681163.2015.1029642
3. Deeley, M.A., Chen, A., Datteri, R., Noble, J.H., Cmelak, A.J., Donnelly, E.F., Malcolm, A.W., Moretti, L., Jaboin, J., Niermann, K., Yang, E.S., Yu, D.S., Yei, F., Koyama, T., Ding, G.X., Dawant, B.M.: Comparison of manual and automatic segmentation methods for brain structures in the presence of space-occupying lesions: a multi-expert study. Phy. Med. Biol. **56**(14), 4557–4577 (2011)
4. Deschamps, T., Cohen, L.D.: Fast extraction of minimal paths in 3D images and applications to virtual endoscopy. Med. Image Anal. **5**(4), 281–299 (2001)
5. Friedman, J.H.: Greedy function approximation: a gradient boosting machine. Ann. Stat. **29**(5), 1189–1232 (2001)
6. Friedman, J.H.: Stochastic gradient boosting. Comput. Stat. Data Anal. **38**(4), 367–378 (2002)
7. Gaonkar, B., Macyszyn, L., Bilello, M., Sadaghiani, M.S., Akbari, H., Attiah, M.A., Ali, Z.S., Da, X., Zhan, Y., O'Rourke, D., Grady, S.M., Davatzikos, C.: Automated tumor volumetry using computer-aided image segmentation. Acad. Radiol. **22**(5), 653–661 (2015)
8. Gooya, A., Biros, G., Davatzikos, C.: Deformable registration of glioma images using EM algorithm and diffusion reaction modeling. IEEE Trans. Med. Imaging **30**(2), 375–390 (2011)
9. Gooya, A., Pohl, K.M., Bilello, M., Biros, G., Davatzikos, C.: Joint segmentation and deformable registration of brain scans guided by a tumor growth model. Med. Image Comput. Comput.-Assist. Interv. **14**(2), 532–540 (2011)
10. Gooya, A., Pohl, K.M., Bilello, M., Cirillo, L., Biros, G., Melhem, E.R., Davatzikos, C.: GLISTR: glioma image segmentation and registration. IEEE Trans. Med. Imaging **31**(10), 1941–1954 (2012)
11. Hogea, C., Davatzikos, C., Biros, G.: An image-driven parameter estimation problem for a reaction diffusion glioma growth model with mass effects. J. Math. Biol. **56**(6), 793–825 (2008)
12. Kistler, M., Bonaretti, S., Pfahrer, M., Niklaus, R., Büchler, P.: The virtual skeleton database: an open access repository for biomedical research and collaboration. J. Med. Internet Res. **15**(11), e245 (2013)
13. Kwon, D., Akbari, H., Da, X., Gaonkar, B., Davatzikos, C.: Multimodal brain tumor image segmentation using GLISTR. MICCAI Brain Tumor Segmentation (BraTS) Challenge Manuscripts, pp. 18–19 (2014)
14. Kwon, D., Shinohara, R.T., Akbari, H., Davatzikos, C.: Combining generative models for multifocal glioma segmentation and registration. Med. Image Comput. Comput.-Assist. Interv. **17**(1), 763–770 (2014)
15. Louis, D.N.: Molecular pathology of malignant gliomas. Annu. Rev. Pathol. - Mech. Dis. **1**, 97–117 (2006)

16. Mazzara, G.P., Velthuizen, R.P., Pearlman, J.L., Greenberg, H.M., Wagner, H.: Brain tumor target volume determination for radiation treatment planning through automated MRI segmentations. Int. J. Radiat. Oncol. - Biol. - Phy. **59**(1), 300–312 (2004)
17. Menze, B.H., Jakab, A., Bauer, S., Kalpathy-Cramer, J., Farahani, K., Kirby, J., Burren, Y., Porz, N., Slotboom, J., Wiest, R., Lanczi, L., Gerstner, E., Weber, M.A., Arbel, T., Avants, B.B., Ayache, N., Buendia, P., Collins, D.L., Cordier, N., Corso, J.J., Criminisi, A., Das, T., Delingette, H., Demiralp, C., Durst, C.R., Dojat, M., Doyle, S., Festa, J., Forbes, F., Geremia, E., Glocker, B., Golland, P., Guo, X., Hamamci, A., Iftekharuddin, K.M., Jena, R., John, N.M., Konukoglu, E., Lashkari, D., Mariz, J.A., Meier, R., Pereira, S., Precup, D., Price, S.J., Riklin-Raviv, T., Reza, S.M.S., Ryan, M., Sarikaya, D., Schwartz, L., Shin, H.-C., Shotton, J., Silva, C.A., Sousa, N., Subbanna, N.K., Szekely, G., Taylor, T.J., Thomas, O.M., Tustison, N.J., Unal, G., Vasseur, F., Wintermark, M., Ye, D.H., Zhao, L., Zhao, B., Zikic, D., Prastawa, M., Reyes, M., Van Leemput, K.: The multimodal brain tumor image segmentation benchmark (BRATS). IEEE Trans. Med. Imaging **34**(10), 1993–2024 (2015). doi:10.1109/TMI.2014.2377694
18. Pedregosa, F., Varoquaux, G., Gramfort, A., Michel, V., Thirion, B., Grisel, O., Blondel, M., Prettenhofer, P., Weiss, R., Dubourg, V., Vanderplas, J., Passos, A., Cournapeau, D., Brucher, M., Perrot, M., Duchesnay, E.: Scikit-learn: machine learning in python. J. Mach. Learn. Res. **12**, 2825–2830 (2011)
19. Sethian, J.A.: A fast marching level set method for monotonically advancing fronts. Proc. Nat. Acad. Sci. U.S.A. **93**(4), 1591–1595 (1996)
20. Smith, S.M., Brady, J.M.: SUSAN - a new approach to low level image processing. Int. J. Comput. Vis. **23**(1), 45–78 (1997)
21. Wen, P.Y., Kesari, S.: Malignant gliomas in adults. N. Engl. J. Med. **359**(5), 492–507 (2008)

# Parameter Learning for CRF-Based Tissue Segmentation of Brain Tumors

Raphael Meier[1]([⊠]), Venetia Karamitsou[1], Simon Habegger[2,3], Roland Wiest[2,3], and Mauricio Reyes[1]

[1] Institute for Surgical Technologies and Biomechanics, University of Bern, Bern, Switzerland
raphael.meier@istb.unibe.ch
[2] Support Center for Advanced Neuroimaging – Institute for Diagnostic and Interventional Neuroradiology, University Hospital, Augusta, USA
[3] University of Bern, Bern, Switzerland

**Abstract.** In this work, we investigated the potential of a recently proposed parameter learning algorithm for Conditional Random Fields (CRFs). Parameters of a pairwise CRF are estimated via a stochastic subgradient descent of a max-margin learning problem. We compared the performance of our brain tumor segmentation method using parameter learning to a version using hand-tuned parameters. Preliminary results on a subset of the BRATS2015 training set show that parameter learning leads to comparable or even improved performance. In addition, we also performed experiments to study the impact of the composition of training data on the final segmentation performance. We found that models trained on mixed data sets achieve reasonable performance compared to models trained on stratified data.

**Keywords:** Brain tumor segmentation · Structured learning · Decision forest · Conditional random field

## 1 Introduction

The diagnosis and treatment of brain tumor patients requires the interplay of different disciplines such as neuroradiology, neurooncology (radiation therapy) and neurosurgery. All of these different disciplines rely on accurate and reproducible measurements of tumor size. Assessment of tumor response to therapy is standardized (RANO [1]) and employs usually bi-dimensional measures for estimating tumor size. Several limitations of bi-dimensional measures have been exposed in the past, e.g., a high sensitivity to imaging quality [2] or the inadequacy in assessing residual enhancing tumor burden after surgery [3]. Consequently, clinicians desire a volumetric analysis of the tumor. This is commonly achieved via manually segmenting the tumor. Subsequently, information about the volume of a tumor and its position relative to neighboring possibly eloquent brain areas can be obtained. However, manual segmentation is a time-consuming

© Springer International Publishing Switzerland 2016
A. Crimi et al. (Eds.): BrainLes 2015, LNCS 9556, pp. 156–167, 2016.
DOI: 10.1007/978-3-319-30858-6_14

procedure and prone to subjectivity. In contrast, fully-automatic segmentation methods perform segmentation of a brain tumor within a fraction of the usual amount of time and provide objective and reproducible measurements. Furthermore, it has been shown in clinical studies that fully-automatic segmentation methods can generate segmentations comparable to human raters in terms of spatial overlap/volume [4] and association to patient survival [5].

The development of new brain tumor segmentation methods has been fostered through the MICCAI Brain Tumor Segmentation (BRATS) Challenge [6], which was held for the first time during MICCAI 2012. The majority of the best performing methods use techniques from machine learning in order to realize brain tumor segmentation. The segmentation problem is usually posed as a classification task. Machine learning-based methods utilize information extracted from a set of training images. Recently, it has been shown that a more directed use of the training data can lead to improved performance [7]. Furthermore, several previously published segmentation methods rely on the use of structured prediction including approaches such as Markov or Conditional Random Fields (CRFs) (e.g., [8,9]). However, parameters for those models are often hand-tuned rather than estimated from training data. Recently, an efficient method for parameter learning in CRFs applicable to volumetric imaging data was proposed [11]. The approach relies on linearizing the CRF energy function and posing the problem of parameter learning as a maximum margin learning problem [12,13]. Efficient learning is implemented via optimization of a quadratic program with a stochastic subgradient descent algorithm.

In this article, we propose a modification of our previous segmentation method [9,10] employing the learning algorithm of [11]. A comparison between CRF-based brain tumor tissue segmentation using parameter learning and segmentation using hand-tuned parameters is drawn. In addition, we investigate the impact of the composition of training data on the final segmentation performance when pre- and (immediate) postoperative images as well as images from low- and high-grade glioma are available. The remainder of the paper is organized as follows. We first introduce in Sect. 2 a set of preliminaries necessary to understand the proposed fully-automatic segmentation algorithm. Subsequently, we present our segmentation framework and describe the employed parameter learning method. In Sect. 4, we present experimental results on the composition of training data on a separate data set and for the proposed parameter learning method on the BRATS2015 data set. Finally, we discuss our findings, limitations and propose future work in Sect. 5.

## 2 Preliminaries

**Glioma.** Glioma can be categorized into low- and high-grade glioma depending on their degree of malignancy. A glioma can be compartmentalized into four different parts: necrosis, edema, contrast-enhancing and non-enhancing tumor. We refer to such a compartmentalization as *labeling*. A labeling is acquired through segmentation. The automatic segmentation of these four different tissues is of primary interest in the present work.

**Structural MRI.** Our approach relies on four different MRI sequences that are routinely used in clinical acquisiton protocols, namely $T_1$-, $T_1$ post-contrast-, $T_2$-, $FLAIR$-weighted images. We assume that these images are co-registered and organized as a vector image, where every voxel contains the four different MR intensity values. We refer to this image as $X = \{\mathbf{x}^{(i)}\}_{i \in V}$, where voxel $i$ is represented by a feature vector $\mathbf{x}^{(i)} \in \mathbb{R}^4$ and $V$ denotes the set of all voxels in $X$. The corresponding labeling of $X$ is denoted by $Y = \{y^{(i)}\}_{i \in V}$ with $y^{(i)}$ being a scalar tissue label (e.g., $1 =$ necrosis, $2 =$ edema, etc.).

**Classification.** We pose the problem of brain tumor segmentation as a structured classification problem (structured prediction). Thus, we seek a hypothesis (classifier) $H$ that relates an image $X$ to a corresponding tissue label map $Y$ (i.e. $H(X) : X \rightarrow Y$). We consider seven possible tissue classes: three unaffected (gray matter, white matter, csf) and four tumor tissues (necrosis, edema, enhancing and non-enhancing tumor). The seven different labels are contained in the set $\mathcal{L}$. Based on a given fully-labeled training set $\mathcal{S} = \{(X^{(i)}, Y^{(i)}) : i = 1, ..., m\}$, we estimate $H$ (supervised learning). All possible labelings for an image $X$ are contained in the set $\mathcal{Y}$, i.e., $Y \in \mathcal{Y}$.

**Conditional Random Field.** We are given a graph $G = (V, E)$, where $V$ denotes the set of nodes and $E$ the set of edges. Furthermore, a labeling $Y$ is indexed by $V$. A pair $(X, Y)$ is a Conditional random field (CRF) iff. the random variables $y^{(i)}$ obey the Markov property with respect to the graph $G$ when conditioned on $X$. Consequently, a CRF models a parametrized conditional probability

$$p(Y|X, \mathbf{w}) = \frac{1}{Z(X, \mathbf{w})} \exp(-E(X, Y, \mathbf{w})) \tag{1}$$

where $Z(X, \mathbf{w})$ is the partition function. The energy $E(X, Y, \mathbf{w})$ depends linearly on the unknown parameters $\mathbf{w}$. In general, given the parameter vector $\mathbf{w}$, a CRF can predict the labeling $Y$ of a given input image $X$ by minimizing the energy, i.e., $Y^* = H(X) = \arg\min_{Y \in \mathcal{Y}} E(X, Y, \mathbf{w})$.

**Structural Risk Minimization.** We define $\Delta : \mathcal{Y} \times \mathcal{Y} \longrightarrow \mathbb{R}_+$ to be a loss function that is used to specify the cost of predicting $\tilde{Y} = H(X)$ when the correct labeling is $Y$. Estimation of a good hypothesis $H$ can then be achieved by the minimization of the regularized empirical risk [14]:

$$\sum_{n=1}^{m} \Delta(Y^{(n)}, H(X^{(n)})) + \mathcal{R}(H) \tag{2}$$

with $\mathcal{R}(H)$ being the regularizer. Optimization of Eq. (2) is complicated by the piece-wise constant term $\Delta(Y^{(n)}, H(X^{(n)}))$. However, one can resort to the minimization of a convex upper bound to the loss (surrogate loss function).

## 3    Methods

Our current segmentation method (proposed in [9]) encompasses a preprocessing, a feature extraction step followed by a voxel-wise classification and a spatial regularization. The features try to capture visual cues of appearance and image context relevant for discriminating the different tissue classes. Classification is performed by a decision forest. Spatial regularization is formulated as an energy-minimization problem of a CRF. The hand-tuned CRF is described in more detail in [10]. A schematic overview of the method is shown in Fig. 1. In the remainder of this paper, we present a modification of the spatial regularization used so far.

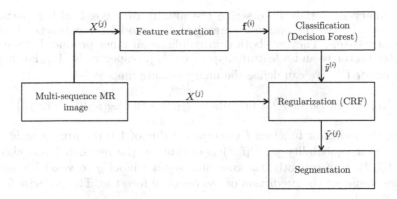

**Fig. 1.** Overview of segmentation pipeline.

### 3.1    Feature Extraction

For every voxel $i$ a number of different features are extracted which are stacked in a feature vector $\mathbf{f}^{(i)}$. The extracted features can be grouped in two different groups: appearance- and context-sensitive features. The former try to capture contrast information and include voxel-wise intensity values and differences, first-order texture features and gradient texture features. The latter aim at capturing spatial context information and include atlas-normalized coordinates, symmetric intensity differences (where the midsagittal plane serves as symmetry axis) and ray features. In the end, we obtain a 237-dimensional feature vector. A more detailed description of the different features can be found in [9].

### 3.2    Decision Forest

After feature extraction, a decision forest classifier [15] is used to perform a voxel-wise tissue label classification. We employ the information gain as split criterion and axis-aligned weak learner for performing the splits. The prediction model stored in the leaf nodes corresponds to the histogram of class labels. The final prediction for a given voxel $i$ of the decision forest is obtained via the Maximum-A-Posteriori rule, i.e., $\tilde{y}^{(i)} = \arg\max_y p(y^{(i)}|\mathbf{f}^{(i)})$, where $p(y^{(i)}|\mathbf{f}^{(i)}) = \frac{1}{T}\sum_{t=1}^T p_t(y^{(i)}|\mathbf{f}^{(i)})$. Our implementation is an adaptation of the Sherwood library [16]. The probability distribution $p(y|\mathbf{f})$ is used in order to define the unary potentials of the conditional random field.

### 3.3   Energy Function

We employ an energy function associated with a pairwise CRF:

$$E(X, Y, \mathbf{w}) = \sum_{i \in V} D_i(\mathbf{x}^{(i)}, y^{(i)}) + \sum_{(i,j) \in E} B_{i,j}(\mathbf{x}^{(i)}, y^{(i)}, \mathbf{x}^{(j)}, y^{(j)}). \qquad (3)$$

The unary potentials $D_i$ describe the affinity of a voxel with a particular tissue class whereas the pairwise potentials $B_{i,j}$ model the coherence between neighboring voxels. They are both expressible as an inner product between the parameter vector $\mathbf{w}$ and a feature map $\psi_i$ or $\psi_{i,j}$, respectively [11]. For a given feature vector $\mathbf{f}^{(i)}$, we can define the unary feature map

$$\psi_i = \left[I(y^{(i)} = 1)(-\log(p(y^{(i)} = 1|\mathbf{f}^{(i)}))), \cdots, I(y^{(i)} = 7)(-\log(p(y^{(i)} = 7|\mathbf{f}^{(i)})))\right]^T \qquad (4)$$

by using the indicator function $I$ (returns a value of 1 if the argument is true). The posterior probability $p(y^{(i)}|\mathbf{f}^{(i)})$ is output by the decision forest classifier (cf. Sect. 3.2). Consequently, the cost of assigning label $y$ to voxel $i$ is smaller the more confident the prediction of the decision forest is. The pairwise feature map is given by

$$\psi_{i,j} = \left[I(y^{(i)} = a, y^{(i)} = b)(1 - I(y^{(i)} = y^{(j)})) \exp\left(-\left\|\mathbf{x}^{(i)} - \mathbf{x}^{(j)}\right\|_\infty\right)\right]_{(a,b) \in \mathcal{L}^2} \qquad (5)$$

which is defined for all possible label pairs in $\mathcal{L}$. The term $1 - I(y^{(i)} = y^{(j)})$ establishes a Potts-like model. The exponential term penalizes large intensity discontinuities between neighboring voxels. We use the $\ell_\infty$-norm based on the fact that the transitions between different tumor tissues show up more prominent in particular sequences, whereas in other sequences they do not. Potentials can now be expressed as an inner product between parameter vector and feature map, i.e., $\langle \mathbf{w}, \psi \rangle$. Furthermore, let $\Psi^D = \sum_{i \in V} \psi_i$ and $\Psi^B = \sum_{(i,j) \in E} \psi_{i,j}$. Given the parameter vector $\mathbf{w} = [(\mathbf{w}^D)^T, (\mathbf{w}^B)^T]^T$, the energy function can then be rewritten as $E(X, Y, \mathbf{w}) = \langle \mathbf{w}^D, \Psi^D \rangle + \langle \mathbf{w}^B, \Psi^B \rangle$.

### 3.4   Parameter Learning

For estimating the parameter vector $\mathbf{w}$, we use the recently proposed method by Lucchi et al. [11] which builds on the max-margin formulation for parameter learning [13]. Essentially, learning is formulated within the framework of structural risk minimization and is posed as a quadratic program with soft margin constraints. We aim to identify $\mathbf{w}$ via

$$\mathbf{w}^\star = \arg\min_{\mathbf{w}} \sum_{n=1}^{m} \ell(X^{(n)}, Y^{(n)}, \mathbf{w}) + \frac{1}{2C} \|\mathbf{w}\|^2 \qquad (6)$$

where $\ell$ is defined to be the hinge loss:

$$\ell(Y^{(n)}, Y^\star, \mathbf{w}) = [E(X^{(n)}, Y^{(n)}, \mathbf{w}) + \Delta(Y^{(n)}, Y^\star) - E(X^{(n)}, Y^\star, \mathbf{w})]_+. \qquad (7)$$

The most violated constraint of all possible labelings $Y^\star$ is obtained via loss-augmented inference [17], i.e., $Y^\star = \arg\min_{Y \in \mathcal{Y}}(E(X, Y, \mathbf{w}) - \Delta(Y^{(n)}, Y))$. The objective function in Eq. (6) can be minimized via stochastic subgradient descent in which iteratively a training example $(X^{(n)}, Y^{(n)})$ is chosen, the subgradient with respect to this example computed and the weight vector updated accordingly (see Algorithm 1). The objective function for a single training example $(X^{(n)}, Y^{(n)})$ is then defined as $f(\mathbf{w}, n) = \ell(Y^{(n)}, Y^\star, \mathbf{w}) + \frac{1}{2C} \|\mathbf{w}\|^2$. The task-specific loss is defined as $\Delta(Y^{(n)}, Y) = \sum_{i \in V} I(y^{(n),(i)} \neq y^{(i)})$ and measures the dissimilarity between a labeling $Y$ and its ground truth $Y^{(n)}$. In contrast to [18], the method of Lucchi et al. aims at an increased reliability in the computation of the subgradient by the use of working sets of constraints $\mathcal{A}^n$. For every iteration, loss-augmented inference is performed to obtain a current estimate of the labeling $Y^\star = \arg\min_{Y \in \mathcal{Y}} (E(X, Y, \mathbf{w}) - \Delta(Y^{(n)}, Y))$ (step 4). The set $\mathcal{A}^{n'}$ contains all labelings (constraints) $Y$ which are violated (i.e., $\ell(Y, Y^{(n)}, \mathbf{w}) > 0$) (step 7). The subgradient is then computed as an average subgradient over all violated constraints (step 8).

---

**Algorithm 1.** Subgradient Method with Working Sets [11]

---

1: Training data $\mathcal{S} = \left\{ (X^{(i)}, Y^{(i)}) : i = 1, ..., m \right\}, \beta := 1, \mathbf{w}^{(1)} := \mathbf{0}, t := 1$
2: **while** $(t < T)$ **do**
3:      Pick randomly an example $(X^{(n)}, Y^{(n)})$ from $\mathcal{S}$
4:      $Y^\star = \arg\min_{Y \in \mathcal{Y}}(E(X, Y, \mathbf{w}) - \Delta(Y^{(n)}, Y))$
5:      $\mathcal{A}^n := \mathcal{A}^n \cup \{Y^\star\}$
6:      $\mathcal{A}^{n'} := \left\{ Y \in \mathcal{A}^n : \ell(Y, Y^{(n)}, \mathbf{w}^{(t)}) > 0 \right\}$
7:      $\eta^{(t)} := \frac{\beta}{t}$
8:      $\mathbf{g}^{(t)} := \frac{1}{\mathcal{A}^{n'}} \sum_{Y \in \mathcal{A}^{n'}} \left( \Psi^D(Y^{(n)}) + \Psi^B(Y^{(n)}) - (\Psi^D(Y) + \Psi^B(Y)) + \frac{1}{C}\mathbf{w} \right)$
9:      $\mathbf{w}^{(t+1)} := \mathcal{P} \left[ \mathbf{w}^{(t)} - \eta^{(t)} \mathbf{g}^{(t)} \right]$
10:      $t := t + 1$
11: **end while**

---

For performing loss-augmented inference, we employed the Fast-PD algorithm proposed by Komodakis and Tziritas [19]. Fast-PD requires $B_{i,j}(\cdot, \cdot) \geq 0$.[1] The update of the weights (step 9) can potentially violate this constraint. Thus, we apply a projection $\mathcal{P}$ to ensure the compatibility of the weights $\mathbf{w}$ with Fast-PD.

# 4    Results

## 4.1    Composition of Training Data

**Pre- and Immediate Postoperative Images.** This experiment was performed previous to the BRATS2015 challenge. However, it influenced the way we used the given training data to build our model. The aim was to investigate the impact of changing the composition of the training data on the final performance of our (baseline) model. In contrast to the BRATS2013 data set, the BRATS2015 data set contains longitudinal imaging data. Hence, we decided to investigate the combined use of pre- and postoperative imaging data to perform segmentation in postoperative MR images. The experiment was performed on a separate data set of 24 patients retrieved retrospectively at the Inselspital, University Hospital Bern. The imaging data encompassed for each patient pre- and immediate (acquired within 72 hours after surgery) postoperative MR images (including $T_1$-, $T_1$ post-contrast-, $T_2$- and FLAIR-weighted images). Except for the FLAIR-images, all of the MR sequence were acquired with isotropic resolution, whereas the FLAIR-images showed a resolution of $1\,\text{mm}\times1\,\text{mm}\times3\,\text{mm}$. Evaluated performance metrics were Dice-coefficient and absolute volume error in $[\text{mm}^3]$. We performed a 6-fold cross-validation. Four training data compositions were formed: only preoperative images (20 images, PRE), only postoperative images (20 images, POST), equal amount of randomly chosen pre- and postoperative images ($2\times10$ images, PREPOST-rand) and equal amount of pre- and postoperative images from the same patients ($2\times10$ images, PREPOST-same). The results in terms of Dice-coefficient and absolute volume error are shown in Figs. 2 and 3, respectively. The Dice-coefficients for enhancing tumor are rather small due to the fact that residuals in immediate postoperative images are very small making overlap measures overly sensitive.

**Low- and High-Grade Glioma.** We performed a second experiment similar to the previous one, in which we studied the influence of the composition of the training data for segmenting high-grade glioma when data of low-grade glioma patients is available. We randomly split the 20 high-grade glioma cases of the BRATS2013 training set in two equal subsets (10 cases each). We used one of the subsets as testing and the other as training set. For the training set, we added 10 low-grade glioma cases of the BRATS2013 training set. We ended up with three different compositions: 10 high-grade glioma (HGG), 10 low-grade glioma (LGG), both sets combined (HGG-LGG). We evaluated the performance

---

[1] Fast-PD requires $B_{i,j}$ to define a semi-metric.

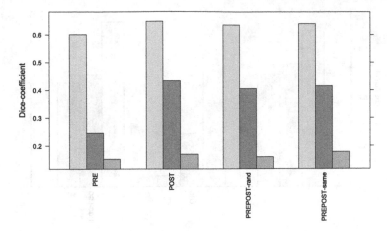

**Fig. 2.** Results in terms of Dice-coefficient (mean values). Segmentation of complete tumor (cyan), segmentation of tumor core (magenta) and segmentation of enhancing tumor (green) (Color figure online).

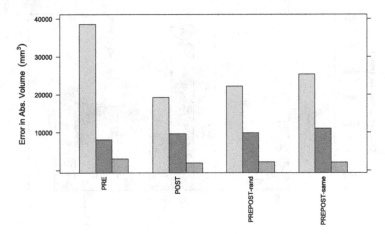

**Fig. 3.** Results in terms of absolute volume error (mean values). Segmentation of complete tumor (cyan), segmentation of tumor core (magenta) and segmentation of enhancing tumor (green) (Color figure online).

in terms of Dice coefficient and absolute volume error on the remaining 10 high-grade cases. The results for the different training set compositions are shown in Figs. 4 and 5, respectively.

## 4.2 Parameter Learning

We evaluated our method using parameter learning via a 5-fold cross-validation on a subset of the BRATS2015 training data, encompassing 20 high-grade glioma cases (part of the former BRATS2013 training set). The performance of the

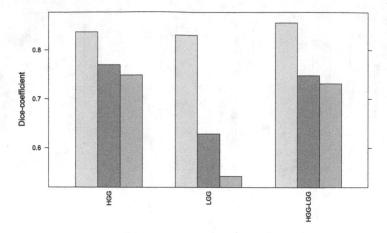

**Fig. 4.** Results in terms of Dice-coefficient (mean values). Segmentation of complete tumor (cyan), segmentation of tumor core (magenta) and segmentation of enhancing tumor (green) (Color figure online).

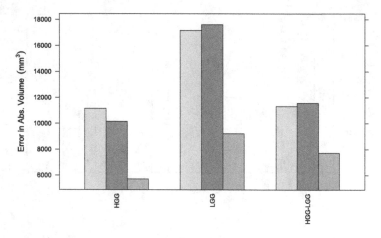

**Fig. 5.** Results in terms of absolute volume error (mean values). Segmentation of complete tumor (cyan), segmentation of tumor core (magenta) and segmentation of enhancing tumor (green) (Color figure online).

presented method was compared against our previous approach using hand-tuned CRF parameters (baseline). Quantitative results are presented in Table 1.

### 4.3 Performance on BRATS2015 Testing Set

The BRATS2015 testing set encompassed 53 patient cases including both low- and high-grade glioma as well as pre- and postoperative images. We aimed at having a fully-automatic segmentation pipeline and thus did not separate the testing set into different sub-categories (e.g., low- and high-grade glioma). Based

**Table 1.** Results of evaluation on subset of BRATS2015 training set. Performance measures are given as (median, range = max-min). Left tuple: Results for all 20 cases. Right tuple: Results after removal of outlier "brats_2013_pat0012_1".

| Region | Dice coefficient | Absolute volume error [mm$^3$] |
|---|---|---|
| Complete tumor (CRF+Learning) | $(0.887, 0.35)/(0.885, 0.35)$ | $(10276, 41871)/(11078, 41257)$ |
| Complete tumor (CRF Baseline) | $(0.888, 0.353)/(0.886, 0.353)$ | $(9029, 42199)/(9029, 42001)$ |
| Tumor core (CRF+Learning) | $(0.784, 0.912)/(0.793, 0.538)$ | $(6504, 29505)/(6472, 29505)$ |
| Tumor core (CRF Baseline) | $(0.789, 0.915)/(0.79, 0.58)$ | $(6057, 32954)(6017, 32954)$ |
| Enhancing tumor (CRF+Learning) | $\mathbf{(0.811, 0.918)/(0.812, 0.827)}$ | $(2784, 29875)/(2825, 29875)$ |
| Enhancing tumor (CRF Baseline) | $(0.767, 0.942)/(0.768, 0.852)$ | $(2485, 36986)/(2041, 36986)$ |

on our experience from the experiments in Sect. 4.1, we decided to train a model on a mixed subset ($n = 65$) of the BRATS2015 training set containing low- ($\sim \frac{1}{3}$, $n = 20$) and high-grade glioma ($\sim \frac{2}{3}$ of the selected data, $n = 45$). The results were automatically evaluated on the Virtual Skeleton Database (VSD, https://www.smir.ch/). The performance of the proposed method using parameter learning in terms of Dice-coefficient is 0.83 (complete tumor), 0.69 (tumor core) and 0.63 (enhancing tumor).

## 5   Discussion and Future Work

The work at hand focused on two different aspects: The influence of the composition of training data and the impact of parameter learning in CRFs on the final segmentation performance. We found that in the context of postoperative segmentation and segmentation including low- and high-grade glioma cases a reasonable performance can be achieved with models trained on mixed data sets. In case of the postoperative segmentation task, it emerged that the best performance can be achieved by training only on postoperative images. Interestingly, for the case of segmenting (preoperative) high-grade glioma cases with a model trained on a data set including also low-grade glioma the complete tumor segmentation improved. A possible explanation for this finding is the fact that for both low- and high-grade glioma the complete outline is mainly defined by its $T_2$-hyperintensity visible in $T_2$- and FLAIR-weighted sequences. Consequently, the model profited from the additional 10 low-grade cases which convey information also relevant for segmenting the complete tumor in high-grade glioma. Regarding parameter learning, our preliminary results indicate that learning CRF parameters from data instead of hand-tuning them can lead to comparable or even improved performance. We observed that wrongly labeled non-enhancing tumor was correctly classified as enhancing tumor after parameter learning, which led to the aforementioned performance increase. The main limitation of our implementation is the fact that we performed CRF learning as well as inference slice-wise instead over the complete volume image. The reason for this simplification was to lower the memory consumption.

In the future, it would be certainly interesting to investigate more elaborate approaches to effectively use the available training data (as e.g., in [7]). Furthermore, we plan to investigate task-specific loss functions for CRF parameter learning as well as CRFs with a higher connectivity.

**Acknowledgments.** This project has received funding from the European Unions Seventh Framework Programme for research, technological development and demonstration under grant agreement No. 600841.

# References

1. Wen, P.Y., Macdonald, D.R., Reardon, D.A., Cloughesy, T.F., Sorensen, A.G., et al.: Updated response assessment criteria for high-grade gliomas: response assessment in neuro-oncology working group. J. Clin. Oncol. **28**(11), 1963–1972 (2010)
2. Reuter, M., Gerstner, E.R., Rapalino, O., et al.: Impact of MRI head placement on glioma response assessment. J. Neuro-Oncol. **118**, 123–129 (2014)
3. Kanaly, C.W., Ding, D., Mehta, A.I., Waller, A.F., Crocker, I., Desjardins, A., Reardon, D.A., Friedman, A.H., Bigner, D.D., Sampson, J.H.: A novel method for volumetric MRI response assessment of enhancing brain tumors. PLoS ONE **6**(1), e16031 (2011)
4. Porz, N., Bauer, S., Pica, A., Schucht, P., Beck, J., Verma, R.K., Slotboom, J., Reyes, M., Wiest, R.: Multi-modal glioblastoma segmentation: man versus machine. PLoS ONE **9**(5), e96873 (2014)
5. Velazquez, E.R., Meier, R., Dunn Jr., W.D., Alexander, B., Bauer, S., Gutman, D.A., Reyes, M., Aerts, H.J.W.L.: Fully automatic GBM segmentation in the TCGA-GBM dataset : prognosis and correlation with VASARI features. Nat. Sci. Rep. **5**, 16822 (2015)
6. Menze, B.H., Jakab, A., Bauer, S., Kalpathy-Cramer, J., Farahani, K., et al.: The multimodal brain tumor image segmentation benchmark (BRATS). In: TMI (2014)
7. Lombaert, H., Zikic, D., Criminisi, A., Ayache, N.: Laplacian forests: semantic image segmentation by guided bagging. In: Golland, P., Hata, N., Barillot, C., Hornegger, J., Howe, R. (eds.) MICCAI 2014, Part II. LNCS, vol. 8674, pp. 496–504. Springer, Heidelberg (2014)
8. Zhao, L., Wu, W., Corso, J.J.: Semi-automatic brain tumor segmentation by constrained MRFs using structural trajectories. In: Mori, K., Sakuma, I., Sato, Y., Barillot, C., Navab, N. (eds.) MICCAI 2013, Part III. LNCS, vol. 8151, pp. 567–575. Springer, Heidelberg (2013)
9. Meier, R., Bauer, S., Slotboom, J., Wiest, R., Reyes, M.: Appearance-and context-sensitive features for brain tumor segmentation. In: MICCAI BRATS Challenge (2014)
10. Bauer, S., Nolte, L.-P., Reyes, M.: Fully automatic segmentation of brain tumor images using support vector machine classification in combination with hierarchical conditional random field regularization. In: Fichtinger, G., Martel, A., Peters, T. (eds.) MICCAI 2011, Part III. LNCS, vol. 6893, pp. 354–361. Springer, Heidelberg (2011)
11. Lucchi, A., Marquez-Neila, P., Becker, C., Li, Y., Smith, K., Knott, G., Fua, P.: Learning Structured Models for Segmentation of 2D and 3D Imagery. In: IEEE TMI, p. 1, March 2014

12. Taskar, B., Guestrin, C., Koller, D.: Max margin Markov networks. Neural Inf. Process. Syst. (2003)
13. Tsochantaridis, I., Hofmann, T., Joachims, T., Altun, Y.: Support vector machine learning for interdependent and structured output spaces. In: ICML (2004)
14. Nowozin, S., Lampert, C.H.: Structured learning and prediction in computer vision. Found. Trends Comput. Graph. Vis. **6**(3–4), 185–365 (2010)
15. Breiman, L.: Random forests. Mach. Learn. **45**, 5–32 (2001)
16. Criminisi, A., Shotton, J.: Decision Forests for Computer Vision and Medical Image Analysis. Springer, Heidelberg (2013)
17. Ben Taskar, V., Chatalbashev, D.K., Guestrin, C.: Learning structured prediction models: a large margin approach. In: ICML (2005)
18. Ratliff, N.D., Andrew Bagnell, J., Zinkevich, M.A.: (Online) subgradient methods for structured prediction. Artif. Intell. Stat. (2007)
19. Komodakis, N., Tziritas, G.: Approximate labeling via graph cuts based on linear programming. IEEE TPAMI **29**(8), 1436–1453 (2007)

# Brain Tumor Segmentation Using a Generative Model with an RBM Prior on Tumor Shape

Mikael Agn[1(✉)], Oula Puonti[1], Per Munck af Rosenschöld[2], Ian Law[3], and Koen Van Leemput[1,4]

[1] Department of Applied Mathematics and Computer Science, Technical University of Denmark, Kongens Lyngby, Denmark
miag@dtu.dk
[2] Department of Oncology, Rigshospitalet, Copenhagen University Hospital, Copenhagen, Denmark
[3] Department of Clinical Physiology, Nuclear Medicine and PET, Rigshospitalet, Copenhagen University Hospital, Copenhagen, Denmark
[4] Martinos Center for Biomedical Imaging, MGH, Harvard Medical School, Boston, USA

**Abstract.** In this paper, we present a fully automated generative method for brain tumor segmentation in multi-modal magnetic resonance images. The method is based on the type of generative model often used for segmenting healthy brain tissues, where tissues are modeled by Gaussian mixture models combined with a spatial atlas-based tissue prior. We extend this basic model with a tumor prior, which uses convolutional restricted Boltzmann machines (cRBMs) to model the shape of both tumor core and complete tumor, which includes edema and core. The cRBMs are trained on expert segmentations of training images, without the use of the *intensity information* in the training images. Experiments on public benchmark data of patients suffering from low- and high-grade gliomas show that the method performs well compared to current state-of-the-art methods, while not being tied to any specific imaging protocol.

## 1  Introduction

Brain tumor segmentation from multi-modal magnetic resonance (MR) images is of high value in radiotherapy planning. Automatic tumor segmentation is challenging since tumor location, shape and appearance vary greatly across patients. Moreover, brain tumor images often exhibit significant intensity inhomogeneity as well as large intensity variations between subjects, particularly when they are acquired with different scanners or at different imaging facilities.

Most current state-of-the-art methods in brain tumor segmentation use a *discriminative* approach, which exploits the specific intensity contrast information of annotated training images, e.g., [1–3]. This may hinder their applicability to images acquired at different centers, because the intensity contrast depends

© Springer International Publishing Switzerland 2016
A. Crimi et al. (Eds.): BrainLes 2015, LNCS 9556, pp. 168–180, 2016.
DOI: 10.1007/978-3-319-30858-6_15

on the scanner and the imaging protocol that has been used. Many discriminative methods have been based on the random forest (RF) classification scheme, which predicts segmentation labels from user-engineered image features. One such a method is the winner of the 2013 brain tumor segmentation (BRATS) challenge [4], developed by Tustison et al. [1]. Another large group of discriminative methods are based on deep convolutional neural networks (CNNs) that are capable of automatically learning features from image intensity information. CNNs have recently proved successful in many segmentation tasks. At the 2015 BRATS challenge, two such methods achieved a high segmentation accuracy: Havaei et al. [2] developed a two-way architecture of CNNs that captures both local details and larger contexts; whereas Pereira et al. [3] trained one CNN for high-grade gliomas and another for low-grade gliomas, which proved useful because of the differences between these two types of tumors. However, the latter method requires the user to manually select one of the CNNs.

In contrast to these discriminative methods, Kwon et al. [5] developed a successful semi-automatic *generative* method, which does not use intensity information from training images. This method, however, requires the user to manually assign tumor seed points and radii to initialize the tumor growth model used in the method. For the 2015 BRATS challenge, the same group extended a version of this generative method with a discriminative post-processing step using a gradient boosting multi-class classification scheme followed by a patient-wise refinement step, which increased the segmentation accuracy [6]. Some fully automated generative approaches have previously been proposed, such as [7,8], but with generally lower segmentation accuracy.

In this paper we propose a fully automated generative method that achieves segmentation accuracy comparable to state-of-the-art discriminative methods while being contrast-adaptive. To achieve this, we incorporate a prior on tumor shape into an atlas-based probabilistic model for healthy tissue segmentation. The prior models tumor shape by convolutional restricted Boltzmann machines (cRBMs), which are higher-order Markov random fields (MRFs) capable of modeling more complex interactions than traditionally used first-order MRFs. The features of the cRBMs are learned automatically from expert segmentations of training data without the use of the *intensity information* corresponding to these segmentations. This allows the model to adapt to varying intensity contrasts during the segmentation phase. Experiments on the test data sets of the 2013 and 2015 BRATS challenges show that the method compares well to the current state-of-the-art.

## 2   Generative Modeling Framework

Let $\mathbf{D} = (\mathbf{d}_1, ..., \mathbf{d}_I)$ denote the multi-contrast MR data of a subject, where $I$ is the number of voxels and $\mathbf{d}_i$ contains the (log-transformed) intensities at voxel $i$. We aim to segment each voxel $i$ into either one of $K$ healthy tissue labels $l_i \in \{1, ..., K\}$ or tumor tissue $z_i \in \{0, 1\}$, and within tumor tissue into either edema or core $y_i \in \{0, 1\}$. We also aim to segment the voxels in the core that are enhanced in T1c (see [4] for a description of the tumor tissue labels). For this purpose we build a generative model that describes the image formation process, illustrated in Fig. 1. We then use this model to obtain a fully automated segmentation algorithm by focusing on the posterior of the segmentation variables given the data:

$$p(\mathbf{l}, \mathbf{z}, \mathbf{y} | \mathbf{D}) \propto p(\mathbf{D} | \mathbf{l}, \mathbf{z}, \mathbf{y}) p(\mathbf{l}) p(\mathbf{z}, \mathbf{y}) \quad \text{with} \tag{1}$$

$$p(\mathbf{D} | \mathbf{l}, \mathbf{z}, \mathbf{y}) = \int_{\boldsymbol{\theta}} p(\mathbf{D} | \mathbf{l}, \mathbf{z}, \mathbf{y}, \boldsymbol{\theta}) p(\boldsymbol{\theta}) \mathrm{d}\boldsymbol{\theta},$$

where $\mathbf{l} = (l_1, ..., l_I)$, $\mathbf{z} = (z_1, ..., z_I)$ and $\mathbf{y} = (y_1, ..., y_I)$; and $\boldsymbol{\theta}$ contains free model parameters. The model consists of the likelihood function $p(\mathbf{D} | \mathbf{l}, \mathbf{z}, \mathbf{y}, \boldsymbol{\theta})$, which links labels to MR intensities; and the priors $p(\mathbf{l})$, $p(\mathbf{z}, \mathbf{y})$ and $p(\boldsymbol{\theta})$.

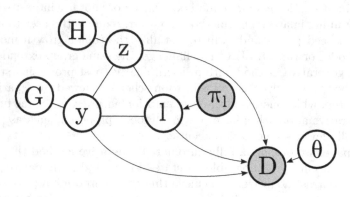

**Fig. 1.** Graphical representation of the model. The atlas-based prior $\pi_l$ models healthy tissue labels l. The complete tumor label z and core label y are connected to the hidden units of their RBM models **H** and **G**, respectively. The labels l, z and y jointly predict the multi-contrast data **D** according to the model parameters $\boldsymbol{\theta}$. Shading indicates observed variables.

For the likelihood $p(\mathbf{D} | \mathbf{l}, \mathbf{z}, \mathbf{y}, \boldsymbol{\theta})$, we use Gaussian mixture models (GMMs) to model the relationships between tissue labels and image intensities. Furthermore, we model bias fields corrupting the MR scans as linear combinations of spatially smooth basis functions added to the scans [9]. Specifically, we define the likelihood as

$$p(\mathbf{D} | \mathbf{l}, \mathbf{z}, \mathbf{y}, \boldsymbol{\theta}) = \prod_i \begin{cases} p_i(\mathbf{d}_i | \boldsymbol{\theta}_{l_i}, \mathbf{C}) & \text{if } z_i = 0 \text{ and } y_i = 0, \text{ (healthy)} \\ p_i(\mathbf{d}_i | \boldsymbol{\theta}_e, \mathbf{C}) & \text{if } z_i = 1 \text{ and } y_i = 0, \text{ (edema)} \\ p_i(\mathbf{d}_i | \boldsymbol{\theta}_c, \mathbf{C}) & \text{if } z_i = 1 \text{ and } y_i = 1, \text{ (core)} \\ (y_i = 1 \text{ and } z_i = 0 \text{ prohibited by prior, see Eq. 11}) \end{cases} \tag{2}$$

where $\boldsymbol{\theta}_x$ denotes the parameters of the GMM connected to tissue $x$ and $\mathbf{C} = (\mathbf{c}_1, ..., \mathbf{c}_N)$, where $\mathbf{c}_n$ denotes the parameters of the bias field model for MR contrast $n$. All GMM and bias field parameters are collected in $\boldsymbol{\theta}$. We define a Gaussian mixture model, with $G_x$ Gaussian components, as $p_i(\mathbf{d}_i|\boldsymbol{\theta}_x, \mathbf{C}) = \sum_{g=1}^{G_x} \gamma_{xg} \mathcal{N}(\mathbf{d}_i - \mathbf{C}^T \boldsymbol{\phi}^i|\boldsymbol{\mu}_{xg}, \boldsymbol{\Sigma}_{xg})$, where subscript $g$ denotes a Gaussian component within the Gaussian mixture model; $\mathcal{N}(\cdot)$ denotes a normal distribution; and the parameters $\gamma_{xg}$, $\boldsymbol{\mu}_{xg}$ and $\boldsymbol{\Sigma}_{xg}$ are the weight, mean and covariance of the corresponding Gaussian. Furthermore, $\boldsymbol{\phi}^i$ evaluates the basis functions of the bias field model at voxel $i$. We assume that one of the Gaussian components of the core will correspond to the enhanced parts of the core.

For the healthy tissue prior $p(\mathbf{l})$, we use a probabilistic affine atlas computed from segmented healthy subjects [10], defined as $p(\mathbf{l}) = \prod_i \pi_{l_i}^i$. In the $i$th voxel, $\pi_{\mathrm{WM}}^i$, $\pi_{\mathrm{GM}}^i$, $\pi_{\mathrm{CSF}}^i$ and $\pi_{\mathrm{BG}}^i$ denote the prior probability for white matter (WM), gray matter (GM), cerebrospinal fluid (CSF) and background (BG) respectively. Note that the atlas does not include a vessel label, i.e., vessels are not directly handled by the model. However, they do not typically affect the final tumor segmentation due to their small size. The affine registration of the atlas is often insufficient for capturing the displacement of healthy tissues seen in many tumor patients due to the so-called mass effect of tumors. We therefore add an extra healthy label OTHER to the atlas with a constant prior probability $\pi_{\mathrm{OTHER}}^i = 0.1$, to put some probability mass in otherwise unexpected places. We then re-normalize the probability maps to ensure that they sum to one.

For the prior $p(\boldsymbol{\theta})$ on the distribution parameters, we use uniform priors on $\mathbf{C}$ and most mean vectors. However, we found it beneficial to use a prior with a linear constraint for edema and WM. We model these two tissues with just one Gaussian component each, and define a prior over their mean vectors as

$$p(\boldsymbol{\mu}_e, \boldsymbol{\mu}_{WM}) = \begin{cases} \propto 1 & \text{if } \mu_{e,\mathrm{FLAIR}} \geq \alpha\,\mu_{\mathrm{WM,FLAIR}} \\ 0 & \text{otherwise} \end{cases}, \tag{3}$$

to encode our prior knowledge that edema appears brighter than WM in FLAIR. Here, the scalar $\alpha$ defines the limit of how close $\mu_{e,\mathrm{FLAIR}}$ can be to $\mu_{\mathrm{WM,FLAIR}}$.

For each GMM's mixture weights, collected in vector $\boldsymbol{\gamma}_x$, we use the conjugate prior

$$p(\boldsymbol{\gamma}_x) = \mathrm{Dir}(\boldsymbol{\gamma}_x|\boldsymbol{\beta}), \tag{4}$$

which is Dirichlet distributed [11, Ch. 3.4]. Each element of $\boldsymbol{\beta}$ is set to 1000 to discourage the removal of Gaussian components. For each GMM's covariances, we use the conjugate prior

$$p(\boldsymbol{\Sigma}_{xg}) = \mathcal{W}^{-1}(\boldsymbol{\Sigma}_{xg} \,|\, v_{xg}^0 \boldsymbol{\Sigma}_0, \, v_{xg}^0), \tag{5}$$

which is inverse-Wishart distributed [11, Ch. 4.6]. The matrix $\boldsymbol{\Sigma}_0$ is our prior belief of the covariance structure. We set off-diagonal elements in $\boldsymbol{\Sigma}_0$ to zero and diagonal elements to the variances of the intensities in the whole brain divided by the number of Gaussians in the full model. The scalar $v_{xg}^0$ defines the strength of the prior. As healthy tissues are rather well-defined, we set $v_{xg}^0$ to zero for the healthy Gaussians to obtain uniform priors. For the tumor Gaussians, we set $v_{xg}^0$ to 20 % of their estimated volumes (cf. Sect. 3.1 for details).

Finally, for $p(\mathbf{z}, \mathbf{y})$ we use a convolutional RBM model, defined below.

## 2.1   Tumor Prior

We model tumor shape by RBMs, which are higher-order MRFs that are capable of modeling higher-order interactions. An RBM is a graphical model with a set of visible units and a set of hidden units, where connections exist between the two sets but not between the units within each set. This restriction facilitates inference with the model. To allow for more efficient inference over large images without a predefined size, we use *convolutional* RBMs (cRBMs), where the connection weights are shared among all locations [12]; see Fig. 2 for an example. In particular, for modeling tumor label $\mathbf{z}$ we use a binary cRBM of the form $p(\mathbf{z}) = \sum_{\mathbf{H}} p(\mathbf{z}, \mathbf{H})$, with $p(\mathbf{z}, \mathbf{H}) \propto e^{-E(\mathbf{z}, \mathbf{H})}$ and the energy term

$$E(\mathbf{z}, \mathbf{H}) = -\sum_k \mathbf{h}_k \bullet (\mathbf{w}_k * \mathbf{z}) - \sum_k b_k \sum_j h_{kj} - a \sum_i z_i, \qquad (6)$$

where $\bullet$ denotes element-wise product followed by summation and $*$ denotes convolution. Here the model is defined in 1D to avoid cluttered equations; it is trivial to extend it to 3D images. Each hidden group $\mathbf{h}_k \in \mathbf{H}$ is connected to the visible units in $\mathbf{z}$ with a convolutional filter $\mathbf{w}_k$, which models interactions between the hidden and visible units, effectively detecting specific features in $\mathbf{z}$. Furthermore, each hidden group has a bias $b_k$ and visible units have a bias $a$, encouraging units to be enabled or disabled.

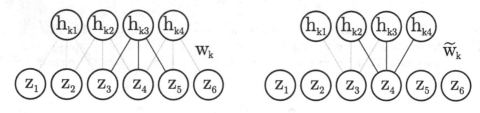

**Fig. 2.** A small 1D example of a cRBM. Visible units in $\mathbf{z}$ are connected to hidden units in a hidden group $\mathbf{h}_k$ through a convolutional filter $\mathbf{w}_k$ of size 3. The first illustration shows the model from the hidden layer's perspective. The second shows the model from the visible layer's perspective, where $\tilde{\mathbf{w}}_k$ is a mirror-reversed version of the filter. Note that boundary units in the visible layer are set to 0.

We train a cRBM for the complete tumor label $\mathbf{z}$, where we learn the filters and bias terms from expert segmentations of the complete tumor obtained from training data. This is done by stochastic gradient ascent with the contrastive divergence (CD) approximation of the log-likelihood gradients with one block-Gibbs sampling step (persistent CD was also tried as an alternative to standard CD, but yielded inferior results in our experiments) [13]. We use the so-called enhanced gradient together with the CD approximation to obtain more distinct filters [14]. Due to the structure of the cRBM model, the conditional distributions needed for block-Gibbs sampling are easily obtained as $p(\mathbf{z}|\mathbf{H}) = \prod_i p(z_i|\mathbf{H})$ and $p(\mathbf{H}|\mathbf{z}) = \prod_k \prod_j p(h_{kj}|\mathbf{z})$, where

$$p(z_i = 1|\mathbf{H}) = \sigma((\sum_k \tilde{\mathbf{w}}_k * \mathbf{h}_k)_i + a) \tag{7}$$

$$\text{and} \quad p(h_{kj} = 1|\mathbf{z}) = \sigma((\mathbf{w}_k * \mathbf{z})_j + b_k). \tag{8}$$

Here, $\sigma(t) = 1/(1 + e^{-t})$ and tilde denotes a mirror-reversal of the filter in each direction. Similarly, we train a cRBM for the tumor core label $\mathbf{y}$, with conditional distributions

$$p(y_i = 1|\mathbf{G}) = \sigma((\sum_k \tilde{\mathbf{u}}_k * \mathbf{g}_k)_i + c) \tag{9}$$

$$\text{and} \quad p(g_{kj} = 1|\mathbf{y}) = \sigma((\mathbf{u}_k * \mathbf{y})_j + d_k), \tag{10}$$

where $\mathbf{G}$ denotes the hidden units connected to $\mathbf{y}$; $\mathbf{u}$ the filters; and $c$ and $d$ the bias terms. After the training phase we combine the two cRBMs to form the joint tumor shape prior:

$$p(\mathbf{z}, \mathbf{y}) = \sum_{\mathbf{H}, \mathbf{G}} p(\mathbf{z}, \mathbf{y}, \mathbf{H}, \mathbf{G}) \tag{11}$$

$$\text{with} \quad p(\mathbf{z}, \mathbf{y}, \mathbf{H}, \mathbf{G}) \propto e^{-E(\mathbf{z}, \mathbf{H}) - E(\mathbf{y}, \mathbf{G}) - \sum_i f(z_i, y_i)},$$

which models both edema and core simultaneously. Here, $f(z_i, y_i) = \infty$ if $z_i = 0$ and $y_i = 1$, and otherwise 0, restricting tumor core to only exist within the complete tumor.

## 2.2    Inference

Exact inference of $p(\mathbf{l}, \mathbf{z}, \mathbf{y}|\mathbf{D})$ requires an intractable integration over all possible combinations of model parameters. Moreover, even if the model parameters were known the model does not factorize over the voxels, as the cRBM introduces non-local dependencies between them. Therefore, we resort to Markov chain Monte Carlo sampling (MCMC) to generate samples of $\mathbf{l}$, $\mathbf{z}$ and $\mathbf{y}$ from $p(\mathbf{l}, \mathbf{z}, \mathbf{y}|\mathbf{D})$, and perform a voxel-wise majority voting across the collected samples to obtain the final segmentation. In particular, we generate samples of $\mathbf{l}, \mathbf{z}, \mathbf{y}, \mathbf{H}, \mathbf{G}$ and $\boldsymbol{\theta}$ by block-Gibbs sampling from the distribution $p(\mathbf{l}, \mathbf{z}, \mathbf{y}, \mathbf{H}, \mathbf{G}, \boldsymbol{\theta}|\mathbf{D})$, and ignore the samples of $\mathbf{H}, \mathbf{G}$ and $\boldsymbol{\theta}$ as they are of no interest to us.

Block-Gibbs sampling is straightforward to implement as each of the conditional distributions factorizes over its components: the labels $\mathbf{l}$, $\mathbf{z}$ and $\mathbf{y}$ are sampled simultaneously from the conditional distribution $p(\mathbf{l}, \mathbf{z}, \mathbf{y} | \mathbf{D}, \mathbf{H}, \mathbf{G}, \boldsymbol{\theta})$, for each voxel independently:

$$p(l_i, z_i, y_i | \mathbf{d}_i, \mathbf{H}, \mathbf{G}, \boldsymbol{\theta}) \propto \begin{cases} p_i(\mathbf{d}_i | \boldsymbol{\theta}_{l_i}, \mathbf{C})\, p(z_i = 0 | \mathbf{H})\, p(y_i = 0 | \mathbf{G})\, \pi_{l_i}^i & \text{if } z_i = 0, y_i = 0 \\ p_i(\mathbf{d}_i | \boldsymbol{\theta}_e, \mathbf{C})\, p(z_i = 1 | \mathbf{H})\, p(y_i = 0 | \mathbf{G})\, \pi_{l_i}^i & \text{if } z_i = 1, y_i = 0 \\ p_i(\mathbf{d}_i | \boldsymbol{\theta}_c, \mathbf{C})\, p(z_i = 1 | \mathbf{H})\, p(y_i = 1 | \mathbf{G})\, \pi_{l_i}^i & \text{if } z_i = 1, y_i = 1 \\ 0 & \text{if } z_i = 0, y_i = 1 \end{cases}.$$

The hidden layers $\mathbf{H}$ and $\mathbf{G}$ are sampled from the conditional distributions $p(\mathbf{H}|\mathbf{z})$ and $p(\mathbf{G}|\mathbf{y})$, given by Eqs. (8) and (10). For the GMM parameters, we iteratively assign voxels to individual GMM components and sample the parameters accordingly ([11, p. 840]). We use rejection sampling to satisfy the constraint of Eq. (3). Note that we could also easily sample from the bias field model, since its conditional distribution is a multi-variate Gaussian. However, this was not implemented. Instead, we use the point estimates of the bias field model parameters $\mathbf{C}$ obtained with the initialization algorithm described below.

We initialize the MCMC sampler with the *maximum a posteriori* segmentation obtained with a generalized expectation-maximization algorithm (GEM) [9]. Since we are only interested in a good parameter initialization at this stage, we temporarily replace the combined cRBM's energy with a simple energy of the form: $-\sum_i [l_i \neq BG](z_i \log w + (1 - z_i) \log(1 - w))$, where $w$ represents the probability of a voxel to be tumor. This reduces the model to the same form as in [9] (with the addition of $p(\boldsymbol{\mu}_e, \boldsymbol{\mu}_{WM})$). We set $w$ to the average fraction of tumor tissue within brain tissue in the training data. At this stage we simply use uniform priors on all covariance matrices.

## 3    Experiments

We demonstrate the performance of our method on the data of the BRATS brain tumor segmentation challenges. The data sets include high- and low-grade gliomas and consist of four MR-sequences: FLAIR, T2, T1 and contrast-enchanced T1 (T1c). The data are publicly available at the virtual skeleton online platform [15]. Previous to the release of the data sets, all data were skull-stripped and resampled to 1 mm isotropic resolution and the four MR-sequences of each subject were co-registered.

To learn the parameters of the cRBM model, we used the expert segmentations of the BRATS 2013 training data, consisting of 20 high-grade gliomas (HGGs) and 10 low-grade gliomas (LGGs). To internally test our method, we used the 2015 training data with available ground truth segmentations. This data set contains 200 HGGs and 44 LGGs (we excluded the subset of BRATS 2013 training subjects). We then tested the method on two independent test data sets from 2013: the data set used in the 2013 on-site challenge with 10 HGGs, and the leaderboard data set with 25 subjects used for an off-site evaluation including both HGGs and LGGs [4]. Furthermore, we participated in the 2015 challenge where the test data set consisted of 53 subjects, including both HGGs and LGGs. Note that the ground truth segmentations and tumor grades of the test data sets were not publicly available. Instead, we evaluated our method and compared to other methods by uploading segmentations to the online platform.

## 3.1  Implementation

We used 40 filters of size $(7 \times 7 \times 7)$ for each cRBM, corresponding to 40 hidden groups. Each cRBM was trained with 9600 gradient steps of size 0.1. A subset of 10 training examples was used to compute the gradient at each step. As the training data set is small, we augmented it by flipping the tumor segmentations in 8 different directions. Furthermore, to reduce the number of parameters to be estimated, we let each element in an cRBM filter model two neighboring elements in $z$ or $y$, i.e., a filter of size 7 will span over 14 visible units.

We registered the healthy tissue atlas by an affine transformation and log-transformed the MR intensities, to account for the additive bias field model [9]. The number of components in each GMM was chosen as follows: we represented the core label $y$ with one Gaussian during GEM initialization, and three during MCMC: one for enhanced core and two for unenhanced core. Before starting the MCMC procedure, the unenhanced core Gaussians were initialized by randomly setting $y_i = 1$ to a fraction of the voxels with $z_i = 1$ and $y_i = 0$ in the GEM segmentation. The fraction was chosen so that the total fraction of core within the complete tumor equaled the average fraction in the training data set. All other labels were represented by one Gaussian each, except CSF and BG that were represented by two Gaussians each.

The healthy tissues' GMM parameters were initialized based on the atlas, except for the label OTHER's mean values which were initialized as the 30th percentile of the brain intensities in each MR-contrast. For tumor tissue, we used the knowledge that edema is always brighter than healthy tissue in FLAIR and T2, and additionally that enhanced core is brighter than any other label in T1c. We therefore initialized the mean values to the percentiles $\{90, 70, 50, 50\}$ and $\{90, 70, 50, 95\}$ in FLAIR, T2, T1 and T1c for edema and core respectively. When validating the method, we found that this initialization is adequate in most cases, i.e., the algorithm is able to adapt to the intensity distribution of a subject. However, the method might fail if e.g., the intensity distribution of tumor tissue is not sufficiently different from healthy tissue due to a bias field.

Due to the large size variation of tumors, we found it necessary to individualize the bias term $a$ connected to $z$ in Eq. (7) to better represent the tumor to be segmented. We therefore added $\log\left(\frac{p_{zs}(1-p_{zt})}{p_{zt}(1-p_{zs})}\right)$ to $a$, where $p_{zs}$ denotes the fraction of tumor within the GEM-segmented brain and $p_{zt}$ denotes the average tumor size in the data used to train the cRBM. We did the same for the bias term connected to $y$ in Eq. (9), matching it with the average fraction of core within complete tumor in the training data set.

As discussed previously for the Gaussians modeling tumor tissue, we set the strength of the covariance priors ($v_{xg}^0$ in Eq. 6) to 20 % of the number of voxels belonging to each Gaussian in the initial segmentation. However, due to the large changes of tumor size during sampling, we found it necessary to re-estimate $v_{xg}^0$ to 20 % of the volumes in the updated segmentations during sampling. Note that this is non-standard and a more proper use of the priors is left for future work.

Finally, we estimated the limit parameter $\alpha$ (in Eq. 3) to 1.08 by estimating the means on the BRATS 2013 training subjects using the described GEM, but with tumor labels fixed to the ground truth, and subsequently building statistics of the FLAIR mean values in edema and WM.

All computations were done on a i7-5930K CPU and a GeForce GTX Titan Black GPU in MATLAB 2014b. The training phase of each cRBM took around 3 days on the GPU. The full segmentation algorithm takes approximately 30 min per subject, including atlas registration (CPU), GEM-initialization (CPU) and sampling (GPU). The sampling is the most time consuming part, taking 25 min on average, mainly due to the many convolutions that are involved. We generated 15 samples after a burn-in period of 200 samples and obtained the final segmentation by majority voting on these 15 samples.

## 3.2   Results

In Table 1, we compare our method on the three test data sets described in the beginning of this section to the five state-of-the-art methods discussed in the introduction. The evaluated labels are the complete tumor (which includes tumor core and edema), the core region of the tumor, as well as the enhancing regions within the core. Our method performed comparably well on complete tumor and core, but not as well on enhanced core. When comparing average Dice scores in the 2015 challenge, out of 13 participants we ranked 2nd for complete tumor, 1st for core and 6th for enhanced core. The lower performance on enhanced core

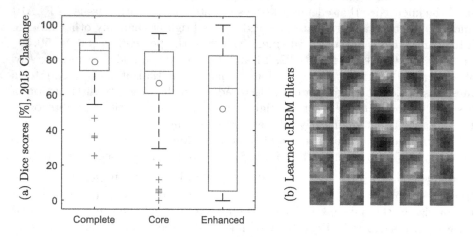

**Fig. 3.** (a) Box plot of Dice scores, 2015 challenge. Circles show mean values, central lines show medians, edges of boxes show the 25th and 75th percentiles, and outliers are marked with '+'. (b) 5 learned cRBM filters for complete tumor.

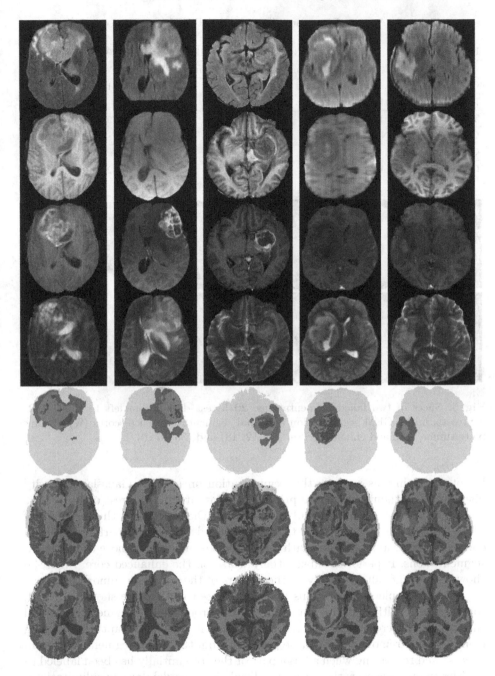

**Fig. 4.** Slices of five exemplary subjects, 2015 training data. The last subject has a low-grade tumor and the rest high-grade tumors. From top to bottom: MR-contrasts: FLAIR, T1, T1c and T2; ground-truth segmentation; initial GEM-segmentation; and final segmentation. Healthy labels are in blue to cyan, edema is in lilac and core is in different shades of yellow (Color figure online).

**Table 1.** Average Dice scores (%) for the BRATS test data sets [15].

| Data set: | 2013 Challenge | | | 2013 Leaderboard | | | 2015 Challenge | | |
|---|---|---|---|---|---|---|---|---|---|
| | Comp | Core | Enh | Comp | Core | Enh | Comp | Core | Enh |
| Our method | 87 | 82 | 70 | 83 | 71 | 54 | 81 | 68 | 65 |
| Random forest method [1] | 87 | 78 | 74 | 79 | 65 | 53 | – | – | – |
| Two-way CNN method [2] | 88 | 78 | 73 | 81 | 67 | 55 | 79 | 62 | 72 |
| Grade-specific CNN method [3] | 88 | 83 | 77 | 84 | 72 | 62 | 78 | 65 | 75 |
| Generative method [5] | 88 | 83 | 72 | 86 | 79 | 59 | – | – | – |
| Generative-Discriminative [6] | – | – | – | – | – | – | 82 | 59 | 74 |

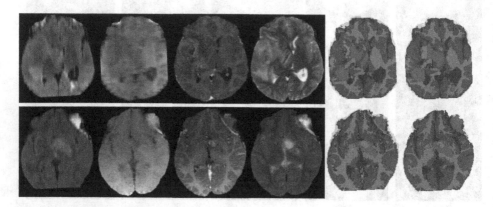

**Fig. 5.** Slices of two failed segmentations, 2015 test data. From left to right: MR-contrasts, initial GEM segmentation and final segmentation. Dice scores (%) of complete tumor, core and enhanced core: (54, 12, 18) and (36, 87, 0).

is not surprising, as we base this segmentation on a single Gaussian intensity distribution without any spatial prior to separate it from the rest of the core.

Figure 3a shows a box plot of the resulting Dice scores for the test data of the 2015 challenge. We can see that the method on average performs well on complete tumor and core, but with a considerable amount of more or less failed segmentations. It performs substantially worse on the enhanced core. Figure 3b shows five of the automatically learned filters of the complete tumor cRBM.

A few example segmentations by the proposed method are shown in Fig. 4, together with initial GEM-segmentations, the ground truth segmentations and the MR data. Here we can see that the method is capable of capturing varying tumor shapes, removing many false positives from the initial segmentation (e.g., vessels) and recovering when a large part of the core initially has been labeled as healthy tissue. However, the rather localized shape model does have limitations, e.g., it has difficulties to remove sizable ventricular CSF flow artifacts and it tends to oversmooth the tumor border. Furthermore, the intensity difference between edema and core is not always clear; the last subject has a typical low-grade tumor appearance, where this difference is almost non-existent.

Figure 5 shows two failed subjects. In the first subject, large parts of the core exhibit a similar intensity distribution to GM, mainly due to a bias field in FLAIR combined with low enhancement in T1c. The interaction between the strong edge detecting cRBM filters and the smooth affine healthy atlas is not ideal in this case. For the second subject, a large part of non-tumor tissue is better explained by the intensity distribution of tumor than the healthy labels.

## 4   Discussion

In this paper, we have proposed a fully automated generative method for brain tumor segmentation, with a tumor prior that uses convolutional restricted Boltzmann machines to model tumor shape. We have shown that the method's performance compares well to current state-of-the-art methods on public benchmark data sets. Moreover, it is not tied to any specific imaging protocol as the optimal parameters of the tumor model are estimated only from expert *segmentations* of annotated training images, without using intensity information.

Described here is a work in progress with many potential paths of improvement still to be explored. The structure of healthy tissues could probably be better explained by a deformable atlas. Furthermore, it was observed that the proposed sampling method only explores a small part of the total space of possible configurations. This is due to the Gibbs sampling framework and the fairly strong edge detecting filters obtained by training the cRBM model, which result in a slow mixing of the MCMC chain. Although the method is effective in the sense that just a few sampling steps are needed to produce competitive segmentations, it could be more efficient and less dependent on initialization when using a better sampling framework. Future work will involve further experimentation with different filter configurations and deformable atlases, exploration of more efficient sampling frameworks and simultaneous segmentation of important healthy structures for radiotherapy.

**Acknowledgments.** This research was supported by NIH NCRR (P41-RR14075), NIBIB (R01EB013565) and the Lundbeck Foundation (R141-2013-13117).

## References

1. Tustison, N., et al.: ANTs and Árboles. In: Proceedings of the MICCAI-BRATS 2013 (2013)
2. Havaei, M., et al.: A convolutional neural network approach to brain tumor segmentation. In: Proceedings of the MICCAI-BRATS 2015 (2015)
3. Pereira, S., et al.: Deep convolutional neural networks for the segmentation of gliomas in multi-sequence MRI. In: Proceedings of the MICCAI-BRATS 2015 (2015)
4. Menze, B.H., et al.: The multimodal brain tumor image segmentation benchmark (BRATS). IEEE Trans. Med. Imaging **34**(10), 1993–2024 (2015)

5. Kwon, D., Shinohara, R.T., Akbari, H., Davatzikos, C.: Combining generative models for multifocal glioma segmentation and registration. In: Golland, P., Hata, N., Barillot, C., Hornegger, J., Howe, R. (eds.) MICCAI 2014, Part I. LNCS, vol. 8673, pp. 763–770. Springer, Heidelberg (2014)
6. Bakas, S., et al.: Segmentation of gliomas in multimodal magnetic resonance imaging volumes based on a hybrid generative-discriminative framework. In: Proceedings of the MICCAI-BRATS 2015 (2015)
7. Menze, B.H., et al.: Segmenting glioma in multi-modal images using a generative model for brain lesion segmentation. In: Proceedings of the MICCAI-BRATS 2012 (2012)
8. Haeck, T., et al.: Automated model-based segmentation of brain tumors in MR images. In: Proceedings of the MICCAI-BRATS 2015 (2015)
9. Leemput, V., et al.: Automated model-based tissue classification of MR images of the brain. IEEE Trans. Med. Imaging 18(10), 897–908 (1999)
10. Ashburner, J., et al.: Statistical Parametric Mapping. The Wellcome Department Cognitive Neurology, University College London, London, UK. http://www.fil.ion.ucl.ac.uk/spm/
11. Murphy, K.P.: Machine learning: a probabilistic perspective. MIT Press, Cambridge (2012)
12. Lee, H., et al.: Unsupervised learning of hierarchical representations with convolutional deep belief networks. Commun. ACM 54(10), 95–103 (2011)
13. Fischer, A., et al.: Training restricted boltzmann machines: an introduction. Pattern Recogn. 47(1), 25–39 (2014)
14. Melchior, J., et al.: How to center binary restricted boltzmann machines. arXiv preprint (2013). arXiv:1311.1354
15. Kistler, M., et al.: The virtual skeleton database: an open access repository for biomedical research and collaboration. J. Med. Internet Res 15(11), e245 (2013)

# Multi-modal Brain Tumor Segmentation Using Stacked Denoising Autoencoders

Kiran Vaidhya, Subramaniam Thirunavukkarasu,
Varghese Alex, and Ganapathy Krishnamurthi(✉)

Indian Institute of Technology Madras, Chennai, India
gankrish@iitm.ac.in

**Abstract.** Accurate Segmentation of Gliomas from Magnetic Resonance Images (MRI) is required for treatment planning and monitoring disease progression. As manual segmentation is time consuming, an automated method can be useful, especially in large clinical studies. Since Gliomas have variable shape and texture, automated segmentation is a challenging task and a number of techniques based on machine learning algorithms have been proposed. In the recent past, deep learning methods have been tested on various image processing tasks and found to outperform state of the art techniques. In our work, we consider stacked denoising autoencoder (SDAE), a deep neural network that reconstructs its input. We trained a three layer SDAE where the input layer was a concatenation of fixed size 3D patches ($11 \times 11 \times 3$ voxels/neurons) from multiple MRI sequences. The 2nd, 3rd and 4th layers had 3000, 1000 and 500 neurons respectively. Two different networks were trained one with high grade glioma (HGG) data and other with a combination of high grade and low grade gliomas (LGG). Each network was trained with 35 patients for pre-training and 21 patients for fine tuning. The predictions from the two networks were combined based on maximum posterior probability. For HGG data, the whole tumor dice score was .81, tumor core was .68 and active tumor was .64 ($n = 220$ patients). For LGG data, the whole tumor dice score was .72, tumor core was .42 and active tumor was .29 ($n = 54$ patients).

**Keywords:** Gliomas · MRI · SDAE · Unsupervised learning · Supervised learning

## 1 Introduction

Gliomas affect the glial cells in the brain and are the most common brain tumors. Based on their severity, Gliomas can be classified as either HGG or LGG, with most low grade Gliomas progressing to high grade malignancy. The treatment regimen in clinical practice as outlined in [18] may consist of chemotherapy, radiation therapy and surgery with treatment monitoring and progression done by

---

K. Vaidhya et al.—All authors have contributed equally.

© Springer International Publishing Switzerland 2016
A. Crimi et al. (Eds.): BrainLes 2015, LNCS 9556, pp. 181–194, 2016.
DOI: 10.1007/978-3-319-30858-6_16

multi-sequence MRI. Tumor volumes obtained from segmentation of MR images are used as a marker of disease progression and the segmentation itself can be used for treatment planning for e.g. surgical planning and radiation therapy. For large clinical trials, automated segmentation of Gliomas from MR images is desirable but is a challenging task due to its complex shapes, diffuse boundaries and heterogeneous intensity distribution within the tumor. Further difficulties arise due to multi foci tumor and non-standard pixel values of MR images, which can vary depending the scanner and scan center. To facilitate automated segmentation, the tumor is divided into 4 major regions; Edema, Necrotic core, enhancing and non-enhancing tumor regions, which takes into account the heterogeneity of tumor tissue. These regions are identified by inspecting multiple MR imaging sequences, namely T1, T1c, T2 and FLAIR. For instance, T1 and T1c together can be used to detect contrast enhancing regions, while FLAIR and T2 can be used for delineating edema. An expert radiologist would have to consider all the four sequences together to identify each region. Thus, an automatic segmentation tool would improve processing time and provide consistent quantification of tumor progression.

In this paper, we describe our entry in the BRATS 2015 challenge using Stacked Denosing Autoencoders. The paper is further divided as: Related work in Sect. 2, Autoencoders and Stacked Denosing Autoencoders in Sect. 3, Materials and Methods in Sect. 4, Results and Discussion in Sect. 5.

## 2    Related Work

Techniques used for Automatic segmentation of Gliomas can be broadly classified as generative or discriminative [14]. Generative techniques make use of prior spatial information of each tissue in the brain obtained using an atlas. The atlas itself is derived from normal brain images and comprises of Gray matter, White Matter and CSF. However, patients with Glioma, apart from the aforementioned structures, have an additional structure i.e. tumor and its constituents. The test data is registered to the atlas and each voxel in the image is assigned as Gray Matter, White Matter or CSF with a certain probability. Tumor and its constituents are also assigned as normal tissue but with a small probability. Following this, outlier voxels are further analyzed to obtain the segmented tumor volume. In a typical approach, techniques based on active contours are used to figure regions with probability values below a certain threshold [10,15]. Aligning the atlas with data having large lesions or resection cavities is challenging as the presence of the large lesions can alter the structure of brain considerably. Overall, Generative techniques exhibit good generalisation on unseen data.

Discriminative techniques learn intensity based features to differentiate between lesion and normal tissues. Discriminative techniques require large amount of training data to learn features for voxel classification. Over the past few years, the best performing techniques in the BRATS challenge have been Convolutional Networks (CNN's) [3,19,23] and Random Forests [4,6,11]. Random Forests require hand-crafted low level features, such as edge filters, difference between sequences, mean or median over a small neighbourhood etc. The final results of the algorithm is dependent heavily on these hand-crafted features. Techniques such as CNNs and SDAEs automatically learn high order features like edges, texture and patterns present in the images to differentiate between lesion and normal tissue. Since discriminative techniques makes use of intensity based features, it is required that test images have the same intensity range as that of the training data.

Our entry, SDAE, has shown promising results in digit recognition and natural image classification tasks [5,22]. The use of SDAE for medical image analysis has been limited. It has been used in organ detection [17] and for characterizing the skin from OCT images [16]. A variant of Autoencoder has been used for detecting various stages of dementia [12].

## 3   Autoencoder

Autoencoders are fully connected neural networks that are trained to reconstruct the given input. The traditional autoencoder consists of an encoder and a decoder. The encoder (Fig. 1a) is basically an affine mapping followed by a non-linearity $f$ that takes the input to its hidden representation. The encoding function $g$ is given by (Eq. 1), where $x$ is the input, $f$ is the non linearity applied, $W$, $b$ are parameters of the affine mapping referred to as weights and biases.

$$g = f(W * x + b) \tag{1}$$

The decoder (Fig. 1b) maps the hidden representation back to an estimate of the input $x$. The decoder function is again a composition of affine mapping and a squashing non-linearity. The decoding function $g'$ is given by (Eq. 2), where $f$ is the non linearity applied, $W'$, $b'$ are weights and biases connecting the hidden and the output layer.

$$g' = f(W' * g + b') \tag{2}$$

The parameters to be determined are the weights and biases; $W$, $b$, $b'$ and $W'$. For real valued inputs, parameter estimation is done by minimizing the least square error (Eq. 3) between the actual input and the reconstructed input.

$$Loss = (x - g')^2 \tag{3}$$

The reconstruction is not exact but the intuition is that the hidden representation is a higher level representation of the original data that allows one to complete 'missing data' in the input. The cost function is trivially optimized by learning the identity transform and without additional constraints, no useful representation will be learnt. The often used approach is to learn the undercomplete representation where the dimensionality of data is reduced or the over-complete but sparse representation. Both of these constraints help in learning useful representations of data. Traditional autoencoders can be stacked to form deep neural networks as shown in Fig. 1f.

In addition to these techniques Vincent et al. [21] proposed the denoising autoencoder (DAE) where the representation is learnt by denoising the partially

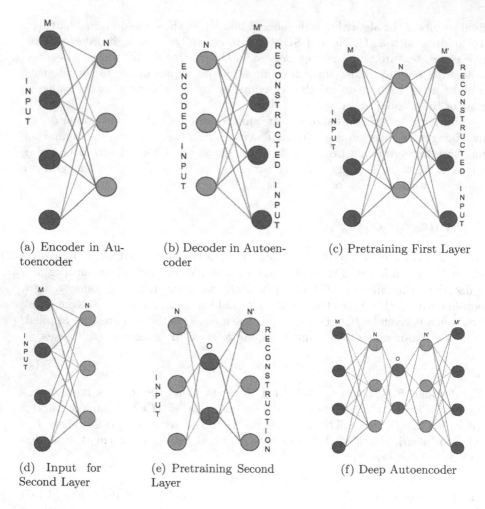

(a) Encoder in Autoencoder

(b) Decoder in Autoencoder

(c) Pretraining First Layer

(d) Input for Second Layer

(e) Pretraining Second Layer

(f) Deep Autoencoder

**Fig. 1.** Traditional autoencoder

corrupted input. The representation learnt by the DAE is expected to be robust to noisy input and since the training itself involves denoising, significant features of the data will be captured by the representation.

The input is corrupted either by Gaussian, masking or salt and pepper noise. In masking noise, a small fraction of neurons in the input are set to zero, while Gaussian noise corrupts all the neurons in the input layer. The input is corrupted by (Eq. 4) where $C$ is the function applied on the input $x$ to generate the corrupted input $x'$.

$$x' = C(x) \tag{4}$$

The encoding function $g$ is then given by (Eq. 5) as:

$$g = f(W * x' + b) \tag{5}$$

The decoding function $g'$ is then given by (Eq. 6) :

$$g' = f(W' * g + b')  \hspace{2cm} (6)$$

The parameters $W$, $b$, $W'$ and $b'$ are estimated by minimising the loss equation (Eq. 7).

$$Loss = (x - g')^2  \hspace{2cm} (7)$$

DAEs can also be stacked to form deep neural networks (SDAE) and the training proceeds layer by layer (Figs. 2 and 1d-e). Briefly, the learned representation from the first layer is used as input to the second layer and the representation itself is estimated by using uncorrupted inputs. This process of learning layer-wise representation is referred to as pre-training and has been shown to improve the generalization performance of deep neural networks. The stacked DAEs have the added advantage that no data labels are necessary for the pre-training. Once the pre-training is complete, the uppermost layer of learnt representation can be used as input to a generic classifier or a MLP. In this stage, labeled data is used to further train or 'fine tune' the network to improve prediction performance.

For a segmentation task, individual voxels in the image have to be labeled. It is not feasible to provide the entire patient volume as input to the encoder because of the dimensionality of the data, equal to the number of voxels in the image. Consequently, training and testing are done using small patches extracted from the images (2D and 3D), with class labels corresponding to the center pixel of the patch. The number of input neurons to the SDAE is then equal to the number of voxels in each patch times the number of MR sequences.

The advantage of using SDAE lies in pre-training which can be done using unlabeled data. One can expect the repository of medical images to grow manifold in the future, apart from unlabeled images currently available. It would

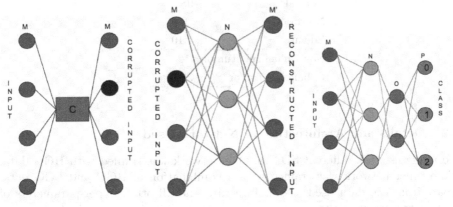

(a) Corruption of Input using Masking Noise  (b) Pretraining a Layer using Corrupted Input  (c) FineTuning of SDAE

**Fig. 2.** Denosing autoencoder

not be feasible for expert radiologists to label pixels in every image for training machine learning algorithms and since images would be obtained from different centers, a large inter-rater variability can be expected. In this situation, an auto-encoder based deep network can be pre-trained using unlabeled or partially labeled images, with a smaller number of expert segmented images for the fine-tuning step. In our work, we use SDAEs that are pre-trained and fine tuned using a small subset of the training data made available for the challenge.

## 4  Materials and Methods

### 4.1  Pre-processing

Patient image dataset made available for BRATS 2015 was minimally pre-processed as described in [19,20]. The pre-processing includes histogram matching all the images to a reference image and dividing each sequence by the mean value of the brain and removing outliers. The above steps ensures that the dynamic range of all sequences falls within the same range. Representative results of pre-processing are shown in Fig. 3.

3D Patches from the preprocessed volumes were extracted and used as input to the network. Since the Gliomas occupy a small volume ($<2\%$) [7] of the brain, the number of patches corresponding to the tumor regions is significantly lower compared to patches from healthy tissue, leading to class imbalance (Table 1). The severity of the class imbalance was reduced by extracting patches only from in and around the tumor.

**Table 1.** Amount of class imbalance

| Labels | Percentage |
| --- | --- |
| Normal | 98 |
| Necrotic | .18 |
| Edema | 1.10 |
| Non Enhancing Tumor | .12 |
| Enhancing Tumor | .38 |

### 4.2  Details and Architecture of Network Used

We made use of 2 different SDAEs. One network was trained with HGG data, while other network was trained with a combination of HGG and LGG data. Apart from the data used, the architecture and all other hyper-parameters of both networks were the same. The network training proceeds in two stages, pre-training and fine tuning described in the next two sections.

**PreTraining:** The network was pre-trained with 35 patients. 3D patches were extracted from all four sequences and concatenated to form the input layer of

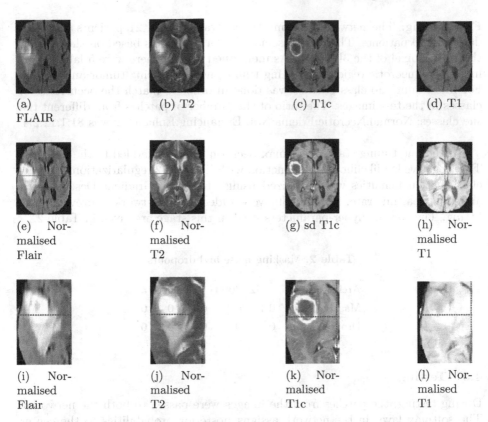

(a) FLAIR

(b) T2

(c) T1c

(d) T1

(e) Normalised Flair

(f) Normalised T2

(g) sd T1c

(h) Normalised T1

(i) Normalised Flair

(j) Normalised T2

(k) Normalised T1c

(l) Normalised T1

**Fig. 3.** (a-d) Raw images, (d-f) Normalised images, (i-l) Area from where patches are extracted.

the SDAE. The size of patch was 11*11*3 voxels with a fixed overlap between patches. We experimented with various other patch sizes like $7 \times 7 \times 7$, $5 \times 5 \times 5$, $3 \times 3 \times 3$ and 2D patch sizes like $11 \times 11$, $9 \times 9$, $21 \times 21$, $15 \times 15$, $13 \times 13$, for a range of over-complete and under-complete architectures, with varying levels of masking noise and the prediction performance on a limited data set was used to decide the optimal architecture. As pre-training is completely unsupervised, labels associated with patches were never used other than to determine pixel coordinates for extracting patches. To ensure that network learns features from all classes, the network was pre-trained with equal number of patches from each class.

Masking noise of 10 % was added to each layer. Sigmoid activation function was used for encoding while linear activation function was used for decoding. The loss function used was mean squared error. L2 regularization was added to the cost function to prevent over-fitting. The pre-training was optimized using RmsProp [8] with annealing learning rate.

**FineTuning:** The network was fine tuned trained with 21 patients and validated on 10 patients. The label associated to a patch was based on the label of the center pixel of the 3D patch. As mentioned earlier, there were 5 labels, normal tissue, necrotic region, enhancing tumor, non-enhancing tumor and edema. For fine tuning, no class balance was done in order to match the occurrence of classes in the test images. The ratio of the number of patches from different tissue classes; Normal:Necrotic:Edema:Non-Enhancing:Enhancing was 81:1:12:2:4

In the fine tuning stage, a softmax decision layer was added to the network. The Negative log likelihood cost function with L1 and L2 regularization and misclassification penalties was optimized using Stochastic Gradient Descent with annealing learning rate. Dropouts [9] were added to the network to prevent overfitting. The various hyper-parameters used in this stage are given in Table 2.

**Table 2.** Masking noise and dropouts

| Architecture | 1452 | 3000 | 1000 | 500 | 5 |
|---|---|---|---|---|---|
| Masking Noise | 0.1 | 0.1 | 0.1 | 0 | 0 |
| Dropouts | 0 | 0 | 0.3 | 0.3 | 0 |

### 4.3 Testing

During testing, the patches from the images were passed to both the networks. The softmax layer in the network assigns posterior probabilities to the center pixel in a patch (Eq. 8). The posterior probabilities from both the networks are compared, and the patch is assigned the label which has highest probability value (Eq. 11).

$$P(y = c|X) = \frac{e^{X^T W_c}}{\sum_{k=1}^{k=K} e^{X^T W_k}} \tag{8}$$

$$Output1 = [C0 : p0, C1 : p1, C2 : p2, C3 : p3, C4 : p4] \tag{9}$$

$$Output2 = [C0 : q0, C1 : q1, C2 : p2, C3 : q3, C4 : q4] \tag{10}$$

$$Final\ label = argmax[p0, p1, p2, p3, p4, q0, q1, q2, q3, q4] \tag{11}$$

In Eqs. 9 and 10, Output1 corresponds to the output from the first network, while Output2 corresponds output from the second Network. C0,C1,C2,C3,C4 stands for class 0, class1, class2, class3, class4 respectively while p0,p1,p2,p3,q0,q1,q2,q3,q4 are the probability assigned to the class.

### 4.4   Post Processing

Post Processing helps in reducing the number of false positives in the Image. It was found that large number of false positives were generated at the ventricles, cerebellum and brain stem. The likelihood of occurrence of Gliomas in cerebellum and brain stem is very minimal [13]. The post processing pipeline comprises of,

- Multiplying the predicted output with ventricles, cerebellum and brain-stem masks.
- Connected Component Analysis
- Discard connected components lesser than a size threshold.

The masks were obtained through Atropos segmentation [4]. Figure 4 shows the how the post processing helps in reducing the False positives.

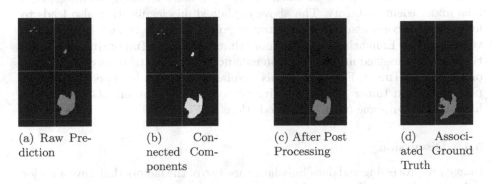

(a) Raw Prediction

(b)    Connected Components

(c) After Post Processing

(d)    Associated Ground Truth

**Fig. 4.** Post processing

## 5   Results and Discussion

Our network performs better on High grade Glioma than on Low Grade. Table 3 gives performance of the current network on HGG and LGG. For evaluating the prediction performance, dice scores and other metrics were calculated for whole tumor, active tumor (enhancing tumor) and the tumor core consisting of the necrotic core, non-enhancing tumor and enhancing tumor. The network achieves a mean whole tumor dice score of $81.52\% \pm 14.07\%$, mean active tumor dice score of $64.36\% \pm 23.33\%$ and a mean tumor core dice score of $68.00\% \pm 21.61\%$ on HGG data. While on LGG data, network achieves a mean whole tumor dice score of $72.02\% \pm 21.0\%$, mean active tumor dice score of $29.00\% \pm 26.\%$and a mean tumor core dice score of $42.00\% \pm 22.10\%$. The dice scores were calculated using Advanced Normalisation Toolkit software [1]. It takes approximately 30 min per patient to complete the pipeline (pre-processing, generation of mask, prediction and post processing).

For tumor core and active tumor classification tasks on HGG data, the algorithm performed below par for certain patients, for example, patient ID 374

**Table 3.** Performance on entire BRATS data

| TYPE | Whole Tumor | | Tumor Core | | Active Tumor | |
|------|------|-----|------|-----|------|-----|
| | Dice | STD | Dice | STD | Dice | STD |
| HGG | .81 | .14 | .68 | .21 | .64 | .23 |
| LGG | .72 | .21 | .42 | .22 | .29 | .26 |

shown in Fig. 5(a-b). A possible explanation for such a result would be that the amount of pixels corresponding to enhancing tumor were very low, hence, missing out on them would have a huge impact on the mean active and tumor core dice scores. Similarly in some of ground truth supplied in the training data, small blobs of non enhancing tumor are surrounded by edema. The algorithm classifies these small blobs as edema (Fig. 5(j)), since the neighbouring pixels falls under edema category. The above explained misclassification also leads to lowered dice scores associated with tumor core and active tumor. In LGG, the volume of Non Enhancing Tumor is more than Enhancing Tumor. In some cases, the network classified most of the Non enhancing tumor patches as either edema or Enhancing Tumor, Fig. 5(e-h). This misclassification leads to poor prediction performance in tumor core and active tumor classification on LGG data. We have also shown some of the best predictions in Fig. 5(i-t)

## 5.1 Discussion

Image pre-processing and data imbalance are two of the factors that have a major influence on the prediction performance. In our case, image pre-processing leads to saturation in several sequence resulting in large false positive predictions. As stated in [7], we found data imbalance to be the another major issue as the ratio of necrotic core and non-enhancing tumor voxels was lower than that of edema. We implemented a penalty in the cost function for the respective classes and found the mean dice scores to improve. However, there were a few patients where the dice scores have dropped and we are currently working on determining appropriate penalties for misclassification (Table 4).

**Table 4.** Sensitivity and Specificity

| Metric | Whole Tumor | Tumor Core | Active Tumor |
|--------|-------------|------------|--------------|
| Sensitivity | 0.79 | 0.66 | 0.74 |
| Specificity | 0.84 | 0.71 | 0.53 |

The network architecture i.e. the number of input neurons or patch size, number of hidden layers and the number of neurons in the hidden layers, were determined empirically by experimenting with various configurations and choosing the best network based on the prediction performance on a limited data set.

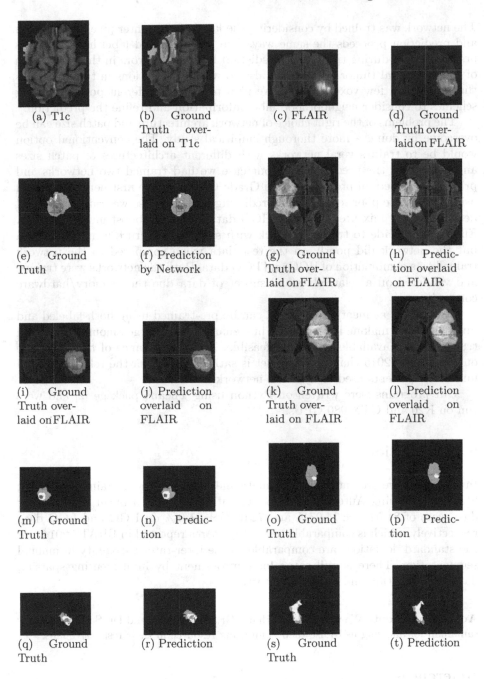

**Fig. 5.** (a) and (b) - Worst Performing image, as amount of enhancing tumor is low. (c) and (d) - Presence of blobs of Non-Enhancing Tumor. (e)-(f) - Misclassification of Non Enhancing Tumor as Edema or Enhancing Tumor in LGG. (g)-(h) - Performance of network on LGG. (i)-(l)-Performance on HGG data. (m)-(t)- Best performing Images (Dice>.85) For all Images, Orange - Edema, Yellow- Non Enhancing Tumor, White - Enhancing Tumor, Red - Necrotic core (Color figure online)

The network was trained by considering the label of the center pixel of the patch and prediction proceeds the same way. The neighborhood label information is not considered during training or prediction leading to errors in the boundaries of the individual tumor regions and also to wrong predictions in tumor regions that are only a few voxels in size. We plan to explore different post-processing schemes to consider neighborhood label information and refine the prediction.

The problems of the right choice of network architecture and patch size can be overcome by doing a more thorough empirical study. The conventional option would be to train several networks with different architectures & patch sizes and combining the predictions. In our case we had trained two networks and primarily focused on predicting High Grade Gliomas. The first network trained using HGG gave poor results when predicting LGG data, so we trained a second network with a mixture of LGG & HGG data and got a boost in performance. Efforts were made to train a network with same architecture using LGG data but the network did poorly on the test data when compared to the network trained on a combination of HGG and LGG data. Both the networks were trained and validated on a relatively small subset of data due the memory/hardware constraints.

The SDAE, as mentioned earlier, can be pre-trained using both labeled and unlabeled data making it very useful in scenarios where large amounts of ground truths are not available or are not feasible. The performance of the technique on the BRATS2015 challenge data set is satisfactory given the relatively small number of patients used to train the network.

Our programs were written on Python using Theano package [2] and were run on K20 and GTX-980 GPUs.

## 6   Conclusion

In this paper, we present a fully automatic method to segment brain tumor using Stacked Denoising Autoencoder. The algorithm achieves a mean whole tumor dice score of 81.52 % ± 14.07 % and 72.02 % ± 21.0 % on HGG and LGG data respectively, which is comparable to the top scores reported in BRATS 2014 and the standard deviations are comparable to the inter-rater variability in manual segmentation. There is still scope for improvement by implementing sparsity, data augmentation and deeper architectures.

**Acknowledgment.** We would like to thank Dr.Sandipan B. and Dr. Sankara J. Subramanian for allowing us to use their computing resource in their respective labs.

## References

1. Tustison, N., Gee, J.: Introducing Dice, Jaccard, and Other Label Overlap Measures To ITK (December 2009)

2. Bergstra, J., Breuleux, O., Bastien, F., Lamblin, P., Pascanu, R., Desjardins, G., Turian, J., Warde-Farley, D., Bengio, Y.: Theano: A CPU and GPU math expression compiler. In: Proceedings of the Python for Scientific Computing Conference, SciPy 2010, Austin, TX, June 30 - July 3 (2010)

3. Davy, A., Havaei, M., Warde-Farley, D., Biard, A., Tran, L., Jon, P., Courville, A., Larochelle, H., Pal, C., Bengio, Y.: Brain tumor segmentation with deep neural networks. In: Proceedings of the MICCAI-BRATS (2014)

4. Durst, C., Tustison, N., Wintermark, M., Avants, B.: Ants and arboles (2013)

5. Glorot, X., Bordes, A., Bengio, Y.: Deep sparse rectifier neural networks. In: International Conference on Artificial Intelligence and Statistics, pp. 315–323 (2011)

6. Gotz, M., Weber, C., Blocher, J., Stieltjes, B., Meinzer, H.P., Maier-Hein, K.: Extremely randomized trees based brain tumor segmentation. In: Proceedings of the BRATS Challenge-MICCAI (2014)

7. Havaei, M., Davy, A., Warde-Farley, D., Biard, A., Courville, A.C., Bengio, Y., Pal, C., Jon, P., Larochelle, H.: Brain tumor segmentation with deep neural networks. CoRR abs/1505.03540 (2015). http://arxiv.org/abs/1505.03540

8. Hinton, G., Srivastava, N., Swersky, K.: Neural networks for machine learning lecture 6e rmsprop : divide the gradient by a running average of its recent magnitude

9. Hinton, G.E., Srivastava, N., Krizhevsky, A., Sutskever, I., Salakhutdinov, R.R.: Improving neural networks by preventing co-adaptation of feature detectors. arXiv preprint (2012). arXiv:1207.0580

10. Khotanlou, H., Colliot, O., Atif, J., Bloch, I.: 3d brain tumor segmentation in mri using fuzzy classification, symmetry analysis and spatially constrained deformable models. Fuzzy Sets Syst. **160**(10), 1457–1473 (2009)

11. Kleesiek, J., Biller, A., Urban, G., Köthe, U., Bendszus, M., Hamprecht, F.A.: ilastik for multi-modal brain tumor segmentation

12. Liu, S., Liu, S., Cai, W., Pujol, S., Kikinis, R., Feng, D.: Early diagnosis of alzheimer's disease with deep learning. In: 2014 IEEE 11th International Symposium on Biomedical Imaging (ISBI), pp. 1015–1018, April 2014

13. Meier, R., Bauer, S., Slotboom, J., Wiest, R., Reyes, M.: Appearance-and context-sensitive features for brain tumor segmentation

14. Menze, B., Reyes, M., Van Leemput, K.: The multimodal brain tumor image segmentation benchmark (brats). IEEE Trans. Med. Imaging **34**(10), 1993–2024 (2014)

15. Popuri, K., Cobzas, D., Murtha, A., Jägersand, M.: 3d variational brain tumor segmentation using dirichlet priors on a clustered feature set. Int. J. Comput. Assist. Radiol. Surg. **7**(4), 493–506 (2012)

16. Sheet, D., Karri, S.P.K., Katouzian, A., Navab, N., Ray, A.K., Chatterjee, J.: Deep learning of tissue specific speckle representations in optical coherence tomography and deeper exploration for in situ histology, pp. 777–780 (2015)

17. Shin, H.C., Orton, M., Collins, D., Doran, S., Leach, M.: Stacked autoencoders for unsupervised feature learning and multiple organ detection in a pilot study using 4d patient data. IEEE Trans. Pattern Anal. Mach. Intell. **35**(8), 1930–1943 (2013)

18. Stupp, R., Brada, M., van den Bent, M., Tonn, J.C., Pentheroudakis, G., Group, E.G.W., et al.: High-grade glioma: esmo clinical practice guidelines for diagnosis, treatment and follow-up. Ann. Oncol. **25**(3), iii93–iii101 (2014)

19. Urban, G., Bendszus, M., Hamprecht, F., Kleesiek, J.: Multi-modal brain tumor segmentation using deep convolutional neural networks. In: MICCAI BraTS (Brain Tumor Segmentation) Challenge. Proceedings, Winning Contribution, pp. 31–35 (2014)

20. Vaidya, S., Chunduru, A., Muthuganapathy, R., Krishnamurthi, G.: Longitudinal multiple sclerosis lesion segmentation using 3d convolutional neural networks
21. Vincent, P., Larochelle, H., Lajoie, I., Bengio, Y., Manzagol, P.A.: Stacked denoising autoencoders: learning useful representations in a deep network with a local denoising criterion. J. Mach. Learn. Res. **11**, 3371–3408 (2010)
22. Wang, N., Yeung, D.Y.: Learning a deep compact image representation for visual tracking. In: Advances in Neural Information Processing Systems, pp. 809–817 (2013)
23. Zikic, D., Ioannou, Y., Brown, M., Criminisi, A.: Segmentation of brain tumor tissues with convolutional neural networks. In: Proceedings MICCAI-BRATS 2014, pp. 36–39 (2014)

# A Convolutional Neural Network Approach to Brain Tumor Segmentation

Mohammad Havaei[1]([✉]), Francis Dutil[1], Chris Pal[2],
Hugo Larochelle[1], and Pierre-Marc Jodoin[1]

[1] Université de Sherbrooke, Sherbrooke, QC, Canada
mohammad.havaei@gmail.com
[2] École Polytechnique de Montréal, Montréal, Canada

**Abstract.** We consider the problem of fully automatic brain focal pathology segmentation, in MR images containing low and high grade gliomas and ischemic stroke lesion. We propose a Convolutional Neural Network (CNN) approach which is amongst the top performing methods while also being extremely computationally efficient, a balance that existing methods have struggled to achieve. Our CNN is trained directly on the image modalities and thus learns a feature representation directly from the data. We propose a cascaded architecture with two pathways: one which focuses on small details in gliomas and one on the larger context. We also propose a two-phase patch-wise training procedure allowing us to train models in a few hours. Fully exploiting the convolutional nature of our model also allows us to segment a complete brain image in 25 s to 3 min. Experimental results on BRain Tumor Segmentation challenges (BRATS'13, BRATS'15) and Ischemic Stroke Lesion Segmentation challenge (ISLES'15) reveal that our approach is among the most accurate in the literature, while also being computationally very efficient.

## 1 Introduction

The goal of brain focal pathology segmentation is to identify areas of the brain whose texture and/or intensity configuration deviates from normal tissues. We consider two pathologies namely gliomas and ischemic stroke lesions. Segmentation methods typically look for the pathologic area by exploiting several magnetic resonance imaging (MRI) modalities, such as T1, T2, T1 post-contrast (T1C) and Flair.

Recently, Convolutional Neural Networks (CNNs) have proven particularly successful in many computer vision applications. For instance, the so-called AlexNet architecture [10] was the first to establish CNNs as the *de facto* state-of-the-art methodology for object recognition in natural images. The main appeal of convolutional networks is the ability of extracting a deep hierarchy of increasingly complex features. In terms of image segmentation, Ciresan et al. [4] exploblack deep CNNs using a fairly standard architecture which yielded impressive results for Neuronal Membrane segmentation in Electron Microscopy Images. Other work has exploblack alternatives to standard CNN architectures and training

A. Crimi et al. (Eds.): BrainLes 2015, LNCS 9556, pp. 195–208, 2016.
DOI: 10.1007/978-3-319-30858-6_17

procedures [9] for segmentation. However, the potential of CNNs for tumor and lesion segmentation is currently poorly understood, and has only been the subject of preliminary investigations [5,12,13].

In this paper, we propose one of the top performing CNN architectures for brain focal pathology segmentation. We report results on the MICCAI BRATS'13, BRATS'15 and ISLES'15 challenge datasets [1] and confirm that our approach is among the fastest and most accurate ones currently available. The work presented here is built on our previous work [8]. In this work we extend the experiments on larger datasets (i.e. BRATS'15 and ISLES'15).

## 2    Convolutional Neural Network Architecture

We approach the problem of brain focal pathology segmentation by solving it slice by slice, from the axial view. Let $\mathbf{X}$ be one such 2D image (slice), where each pixel is associated with multiple channels, one for each image modality. We treat the problem of segmentation as predicting the label of the center pixel of all overlapping patches. The problem is thus converted into an image classification problem.

In the context of this work, we tested a large number of CNN architectures. Figure 1 (top) shows our base model which we refer to as TwoPathCNN. As can be seen, our method uses a two-pathway architecture in which each pathway is responsible for learning about either the local details or the larger context of tissue appearances (e.g. whether or not it is close to salient regions of the brain like the skull or the CSF. The pathways are joined by concatenating their feature maps immediately before the output layer. Finally, a prediction of the class label is made by stacking a final output layer, which is fully convolutional to the last convolutional hidden layer. The number of feature maps in this layer matches the number of class labels and uses the so-called *softmax* non-linearity.

Since CNNs perform pixel classification without taking into account the local dependencies of labels, one can model label dependencies by considering the pixel-wise probability estimates of an initial CNN as additional input to a second CNN, forming a cascaded architecture. This is illustrated in Fig. 1 (bottom) which we refer to as InputCascadeCNN.

### 2.1    Efficient Two-Phase, Patch-Wise Training

By interpreting the output of our CNN as a model for the distribution over segmentation labels, a natural training criteria is to maximize the probability of all labels in our training set or, equivalently, to minimize the negative log-probability $-\log p(\mathbf{Y}|\mathbf{X}) = \sum_{ij} -\log p(Y_{ij}|\mathbf{X})$ for each labeled brain where $Y$ is the preticted label field and $X$ is the input image. To do this, we follow a stochastic gradient descent approach by repeatedly selecting labels $Y_{ij}$ at a random subset of positions (i.e. patches) within each brain, computing the average negative log-probabilities for this mini-batch of positions and performing a gradient descent step on the CNNs parameters.

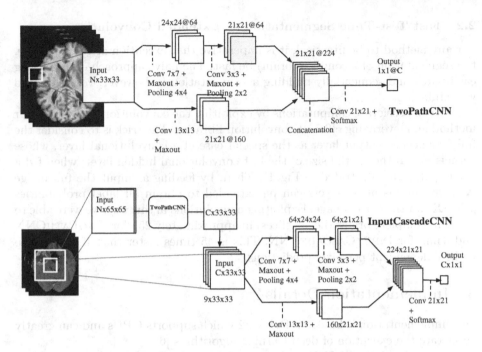

**Fig. 1.** Our implemented models. Top: TwoPathCNN model, where the input patch goes through two streams; a local stream and a global stream. Bottom:InputCascadeCNN model, where the outputs of the first TwoPathCNN is concatenated with the inputs of the second TwoPathCNN.

Care must be taken however to ensure efficient training. Since the distribution of labels is very imbalanced (e.g. most of the brain is healthy and even within the non-healthy classes, the number of voxels belonging to each non-healthy subclasses varies a lot) selecting patches from the true distribution would cause the model to be overwhelmed by healthy patches. It is well known that neural network training algorithms such as stochastic gradient descent perform poorly in cases of strong class imbalances. To avoid these issues, we initially construct our training dataset such that all labels are equiprobable (equal number of patches from each class). This is what we call the *first* training phase. Then, in a *second* phase, we account for the unbalanced nature of the data and re-train only the output layer (i.e. keeping the kernels of all other layers fixed) with a more representative distribution over the labels. Using this approach, we were able to train the TwoPathCNN and InputCascadeCNN models in 6 h and 12 h on Nvidia TITAN black GPU respectively.

## 2.2 Fast Test-Time Segmentation as Extended Convolution

For any method to be practical, it is imperative that execution at test time (i.e. the segmentation of a complete brain) be fast. The naive approach of extracting each patch and sequentially building a segmentation is, however, very slow and wasteful.

We can accelerate computations by exploiting the convolutional nature of our method and leveraging efficient convolution libraries. The trick is to consider the fully connected output layer as the special case of a convolutional layer, whose kernels match the spatial size of the last convolutional hidden layer, when fed a single patch (as illustrated in Fig. 1). Then, by feeding as input the full image $\mathbf{X}$, convolutions at all layers can be extended to obtain all label probabilities $p(Y_{ij}|\mathbf{X})$ for the entire image. Exploiting convolutions in this way, we were able to segment complete brains (i.e. all slices) in approximately 25 s for TwoPathCNN and 3 min for InputCascadeCNN. This is 45 times faster than if we were to make independent per pixel predictions.

## 3 Implementation Details

Our implementation is based on Pylearn2 which supports GPUs and can greatly accelerate the execution of deep learning algorithms [6].

To test the ability of CNNs to learn useful features from scratch, we employed only minimal pre-processing. We truncate the 1 % highest and lowest intensities, as done in [11] and applied N4ITK bias correction [3]. These choices were found to work best in our experiments. The input data was normalized within each input channel, by subtracting the channel mean and dividing by its standard deviation.

The hyper-parameters (kernel and pooling size for each layer) of the model are illustrated in Fig. 1. Dropout, momentum and weight decay is used as described in [7]. The learning rate $\alpha$ is decreased by a factor $\gamma = 10^{-1}$ at every epoch. The initial learning rate was set to $\alpha = 0.005$. The models are trained about 70 to 100 epochs before being stopped by the early stopping criteria.

A post-processing method based on connected components was also implemented to remove flat blobs which might appear in the predictions due to bright corners of the brains close to the skull.

## 4 Experiments and Results

We conducted our experiments on BRATS13, BRATS15, sub-acute ischemic stroke lesion segmentation (SISS) and acute stroke outcome/penumbra estimation (SPES) datasets. BRATS is a challenge on brain tumor segmentation while SISS and SPES are datasets for the Ischemic Stroke Lesion Segmentation (ISLES) challenge. Both BRATS and ISLES are in conjunction with Brain Lesion workshop as part of the Medical Image Computing and Computer-Assisted Intervention (MICCAI'15) conference. In the following we briefly describe these datasets.

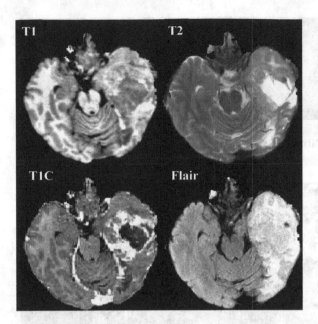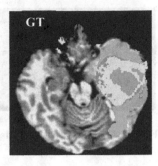

**Fig. 2.** Four MRI modalities used as input channels to our CNN model as well as the ground truth labels: ▨ edema, ▨ enhanced tumor, ▨ necrosis, ▨ non-enhanced tumor (Color figure online).

## 4.1   Datasets

*BRATS'13* contains 20 brains with high grade and 10 brains with low grade gliomas for training and 10 brains with high grade gliomas for testing. For each brain, there exists 4 modalities, namely T1,T1 post-contrast (T1C), T2 and Flair. These modalities are co-registeblack to the T1 post-contrast image, skull stripped, and interpolated to 1 mm isotropic resolution. The training brains come with a *hand-labeled* ground truth of 5 segmentation labels, namely *healthy, necrosis, edema, non-enhancing tumor* and *enhancing tumor*. Figure 2 shows an example of the data as well as the ground truth.

BRATS'15 contains 220 brains with high grade and 54 brains with low grade gliomas for training and 53 brains with mixed high and low grade gliomas for testing. Similar to BRATS'13, each brain from the training data comes with a 5 class segmentation ground truth. BRATS'15 contains the training data of 2013. The ground truth for the rest of the training brains is generated by a voted average of segmented results of the top performing methods in BRATS'13 and BRATS'12. Some of these automatically generated ground truths have been refined manually by a user. For evaluation purposes the tumor regions in both BRATS challenges are categorized as follows: the *complete* (including all four tumor subclasses), the *core* (including all tumor subclasses except "edema") and the *enhancing* (comprising the "enhanced tumor" subclass). The evalua-

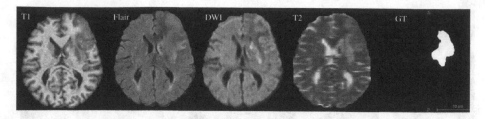

**Fig. 3.** Four SISS MRI modalities used as input channels to our CNN model as well as ground truth (GT).

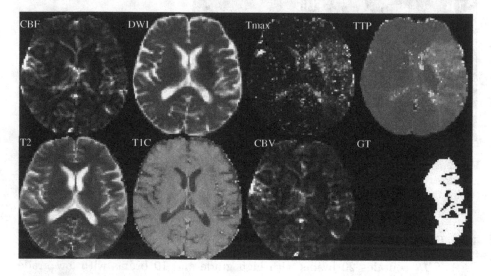

**Fig. 4.** Seven SPES MRI modalities used as input channels to the CNN model as well as ground truth (GT).

tion measures consist of the *Dice* measure (which is identical to the F score), *Specificity* and *Sensitivity* [11].

SISS contains 28 brains with four modalities namely: Flair, Diffusion Weighted Image (DWI) and T1. Figure 3 shows an example of this dataset. The challenge dataset consists of 36 subjects. The evaluation measures used for the ranking were the Dice's coefficient, the Average symmetric surface distance, and the Hausdorf distance.

SPES dataset contains 30 brains with 7 modalities namely: CBF (Cerebral blood flow), CBV (cerebral blood volume), DWI (diffusion weighted images), T1c, T2, Tmax and TTP (time to peak). The challenge data set contains 20 subjects. Both datasets provide pixel-accurate level ground truth of the abnormal areas (2 class segmentation).

Since ground truth segmentations are not available for the challenge data (i.e. test data), a quantitative evaluation is only possible through the online evaluation system [2] (Fig. 4).

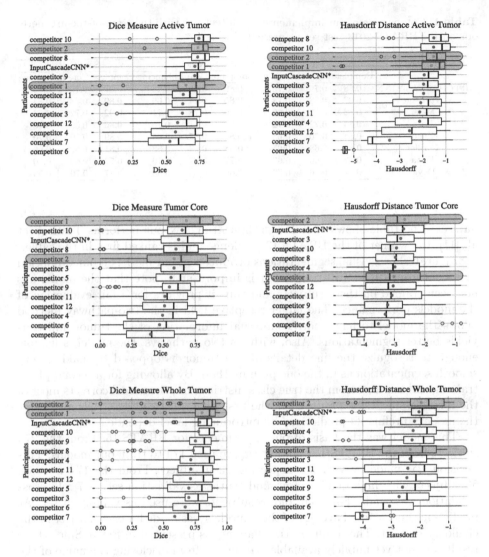

**Fig. 5.** Brats'15 challenge results. Dice score and Hausdorff distance are presented for the three tumor categories. Since the results of the challenge are not yet publicly available, we are unable to disclose the name of the participants. The semi-automatic methods are highlighted in gray. In each sub-figure, the methods are ranked based on the mean value which is shown in black.

## 4.2  Results on BRATS

According to our validation set, on the BRATS datasets, INPUTCASCADECNN* performed superior to TWOPATHCNN*. Table 1 shows how this architecture compares to the currently published state-of-the-art methods on BRATS13

**Table 1.** Comparison of our implemented architectures with the state-of-the-art methods on the BRATS-2013 test set as presented in [11].

| Method | Dice | | | Specificity | | | Sensitivity | | |
|---|---|---|---|---|---|---|---|---|---|
| | Complete | Core | Enhancing | Complete | Core | Enhancing | Complete | Core | Enhancing |
| INPUTCASCADECNN | 0.88 | 0.79 | 0.73 | 0.89 | 0.79 | 0.68 | 0.87 | 0.79 | 0.80 |
| Tustison | 0.87 | 0.78 | 0.74 | 0.85 | 0.74 | 0.69 | 0.89 | 0.88 | 0.83 |
| Meier | 0.82 | 0.73 | 0.69 | 0.76 | 0.78 | 0.71 | 0.92 | 0.72 | 0.73 |
| Reza | 0.83 | 0.72 | 0.72 | 0.82 | 0.81 | 0.70 | 0.86 | 0.69 | 0.76 |
| Zhao | 0.84 | 0.70 | 0.65 | 0.80 | 0.67 | 0.65 | 0.89 | 0.79 | 0.70 |
| Cordier | 0.84 | 0.68 | 0.65 | 0.88 | 0.63 | 0.68 | 0.81 | 0.82 | 0.66 |
| Festa | 0.72 | 0.66 | 0.67 | 0.77 | 0.77 | 0.70 | 0.72 | 0.60 | 0.70 |
| Doyle | 0.71 | 0.46 | 0.52 | 0.66 | 0.38 | 0.58 | 0.87 | 0.70 | 0.55 |

dataset. The table shows that INPUTCASCADECNN out performs Tustison et al. [11], the winner of the BRATS'13 challenge and is ranked first in the table.

Figure 6 shows visual segmentations produced by our model on our validation set taken from BRATS'13 trainset. It is important to note that the model has not been trained on these subjects and thus it provides for a fair evaluation of the models performance. The larger receptive field in the two-pathway method allows the model to have more contextual information of the tumor and thus yields better segmentations. Also, with its two pathways, the model is flexible enough to recognize the fine details of the tumor as opposed to making very smooth segmentation as in the one path method. By allowing for a second phase training and learning from the true class distribution, the model corrects most of the miss-classifications produced in the first phase. Cascading CNNs also helps the model to refine its predictions by introducing label dependencies.

This model was the basis of our experiments for BRATS'15. From the 274 subjects from the BRATS'15 training set, we used 174 to train our models. This decision was made by visually inspecting each subject. From the 174 we took 56 subjects with high quality of ground truths as validation set. A 7 fold cross validation was made. For each fold, 8 subjects were used as validation set. At prediction time, a voted average of these models was made for each subject in the challenge dataset. The results of the challenge is presented in Fig. 5. Since these results are not yet publicly available, we refrain from disclosing the name of the participants. In this figure the semi-automatic methods are highlighted in gray. As seen from the figure, our method ranks either first or second on Complete tumor and tumor Core categories and gets competitive results on active tumor category. Our method has also less outliers than most other approaches.

### 4.3   Results on ISLES

For the ISLES challenge, TWOPATHCNN seemed to outperform INPUTCASCADECNN. Tables 2 and 3 show the results on the training data obtained from the virtualskeleton webpage on both SISS and SPES datasets and how we compare with other methods applied on these datasets. As one can see, our method (TWOPATHCNN*) is well in front the other methods. On the training data, our

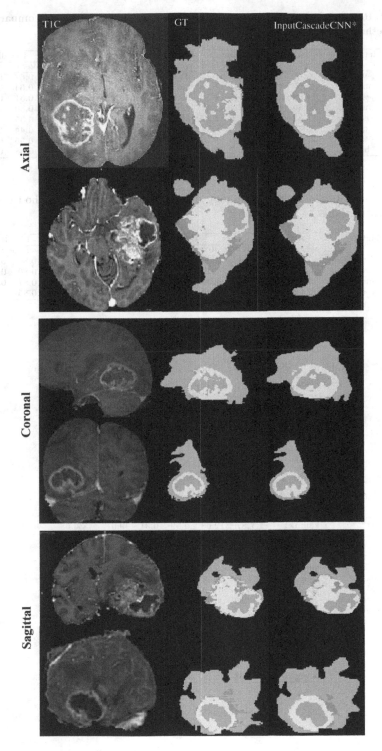

**Fig. 6.** Results obtained by our model on BRATS'13 dataset shown from top to down in Axial, Coronal and Sagittal views.

**Table 2.** Results on the SISS training dataset showing how our method compares with other methods.

| Method | ASSD | | Dice | | Hausdorff Distance | | Precision | | Recall | |
|---|---|---|---|---|---|---|---|---|---|---|
| | average | std | average | std | average | std | average | std | average | std |
| TwoPathCNN* | 8.92 | 19.23 | 0.69 | 0.30 | 31.75 | 28.52 | 0.72 | 0.31 | 0.67 | 0.31 |
| mh1 | 6.77 | 13.17 | 0.63 | 0.23 | 36.16 | 36.46 | 0.68 | 0.24 | 0.64 | 0.26 |
| jessa1 | 11.59 | 18.34 | 0.45 | 0.24 | 39.23 | 30.70 | 0.52 | 0.26 | 0.51 | 0.31 |
| mq2 | 10.30 | 11.11 | 0.54 | 0.26 | 82.78 | 23.95 | 0.67 | 0.33 | 0.50 | 0.25 |
| eo1 | 12.36 | 12.30 | 0.36 | 0.25 | 56.94 | 40.98 | 0.65 | 0.41 | 0.35 | 0.21 |
| cj1 | 56.77 | 79.90 | 0.48 | 0.38 | 76.88 | 81.77 | 0.57 | 0.43 | 0.44 | 0.37 |
| ta1 | 12.18 | 22.59 | 0.50 | 0.31 | 43.21 | 30.50 | 0.61 | 0.34 | 0.55 | 0.33 |
| bd1 | 9.36 | 13.85 | 0.57 | 0.28 | 53.88 | 34.58 | 0.58 | 0.33 | 0.68 | 0.21 |

**Table 3.** Results on the SPES training dataset showing how our method compares with other methods.

| Method | ASSD | | Dice | | Hausdorff Distance | | Precision | | Recall | |
|---|---|---|---|---|---|---|---|---|---|---|
| | average | std | average | std | average | std | average | std | average | std |
| TwoPathCNN* | 1.76 | 0.94 | 0.85 | 0.08 | 23.28 | 14.13 | 0.83 | 0.11 | 0.88 | 0.08 |
| haect1 | 3.51 | 2.13 | 0.78 | 0.08 | 46.31 | 25.17 | 0.78 | 0.11 | 0.80 | 0.12 |
| mckir1 | 1.42 | 1.01 | 0.85 | 0.06 | 30.71 | 18.91 | 0.84 | 0.10 | 0.87 | 0.07 |
| robbd1 | 2.03 | 1.35 | 0.82 | 0.07 | 44.29 | 27.59 | 0.81 | 0.14 | 0.85 | 0.07 |

**Table 4.** Results on the ISLES valid datasets.

| Method | ASSD | | Dice | | Hausdorff Distance | |
|---|---|---|---|---|---|---|
| | average | std | average | std | average | std |
| SISS | 8.23 | 13.15 | 0.59 | 0.27 | 45.80 | 29.23 |
| SPES | 2.55 | 1.47 | 0.77 | 0.12 | 29.87 | 16.71 |

**Table 5.** Results on the SISS challenge datasets.

| Method | ASSD | | Dice | | Hausdorff Distance | |
|---|---|---|---|---|---|---|
| | average | std | average | std | average | std |
| kamnk1 | 7.87 | 12.63 | 0.59 | 0.31 | 39.61 | 30.68 |
| fengc1 | 8.13 | 15.15 | 0.55 | 0.30 | 25.02 | 22.02 |
| halmh1 | 14.61 | 20.17 | 0.47 | 0.32 | 46.26 | 34.81 |
| chenl2 | 13.33 | 11.95 | 0.44 | 0.30 | 72.61 | 25.51 |
| muscj1 | 13.56 | 13.65 | 0.43 | 0.32 | 64.22 | 28.79 |
| rezas1 | 11.90 | 20.50 | 0.43 | 0.28 | 46.38 | 29.32 |
| robbd1 | 14.22 | 14.41 | 0.43 | 0.30 | 62.58 | 30.61 |
| maieo1 | 17.36 | 20.29 | 0.42 | 0.33 | 53.90 | 30.15 |
| mahmq2 | 13.96 | 13.77 | 0.40 | 0.27 | 71.25 | 17.02 |
| haect1 | 17.36 | 19.27 | 0.37 | 0.33 | 63.59 | 31.68 |
| TwoPathCNN* | 18.74 | 20.64 | 0.35 | 0.31 | 55.99 | 35.09 |
| goetm2 | 15.97 | 15.07 | 0.34 | 0.29 | 60.37 | 31.14 |
| jessa3 | 17.15 | 21.96 | 0.33 | 0.26 | 47.46 | 32.36 |
| doyls2 | 19.66 | 23.23 | 0.30 | 0.34 | 52.01 | 31.86 |
| wangc2 | 31.88 | 25.88 | 0.17 | 0.26 | 60.38 | 29.38 |

**Table 6.** Results on the SPES challenge datasets.

| Method | ASSD | | Dice | | Hausdorff Distance | |
|--------|------|-----|------|-----|----------|-----|
| | average | std | average | std | average | std |
| mckir1 | 1.65 | 1.40 | 0.82 | 0.08 | 29.02 | 16.29 |
| maieo1 | 1.36 | 0.74 | 0.81 | 0.09 | 23.62 | 12.99 |
| robbd1 | 2.77 | 3.27 | 0.78 | 0.09 | 40.27 | 25.10 |
| fengc1 | 2.29 | 1.76 | 0.76 | 0.09 | 30.65 | 16.49 |
| kelle1 | 2.44 | 1.93 | 0.73 | 0.13 | 28.79 | 16.39 |
| haect1 | 5.18 | 6.13 | 0.67 | 0.24 | 42.29 | 19.42 |
| TwoPathCNN* | 5.53 | 7.59 | 0.54 | 0.26 | 36.10 | 19.41 |

approach provides the best score on 4 of the 5 metrics on the SISS dataset, and on 3 of the 5 metrics on the SPES dataset. Overall, we are ranked either first or second on each metric. Let us underline the fact that since the Hausdorff distances of our method (31.75 and 23.28) is significantly lower than the ones obtained by the other methods, we may conclude that our approach has a higher precision rate compablack to other methods. Table 4 shows the results on the validation set. It is important to note that there is no training performed on this data and thus is can be a fair estimate of how the model is expected to perform on an unseen data set like the challenge data.

Figure 7 shows visual segmentation maps produced by our model on subjects from the validation sets of both SISS and SPES datasets. The first two rows show segmentation results on SPES dataset and the two bottom rows show segmentation results on SISS dataset. It takes on average 25 s to produce a segmentation result.

Although performing well on validation set, the model did not perform well on challenge data from these datasets. Tables 5 and 6 show the challenge results for these two datasets. As seen from this table, our method does not rank well compared to other methods. We strongly believe this is due in part to high degree of variation in the challenge data compared to the training data. The challenge data contains a high degree of noise, which is different from the training set. In addition, the challenge data contains subjects with very small lesions. The final evaluation is an average over all subject which does not take into account the size of the lesion and equal weight is given to subjects with large lesions and subjects with small lesions. This way of evaluation would significantly penalize a method if it fails to recognize small lesions or if small lesions are removed due to post-processing. In our case our post-processing did not account for small lesions. We aim to improve our results by having a better post-processing step. For the SPES dataset we get a good score on our validation set which indicates the model does not overfit to the training data. After fixing the implementation defect in our pre-processing script our results improve significantly and is now second best in terms of the Hausdorff distance and third best in terms of the ASSD. The updated results are presented in Table 7.

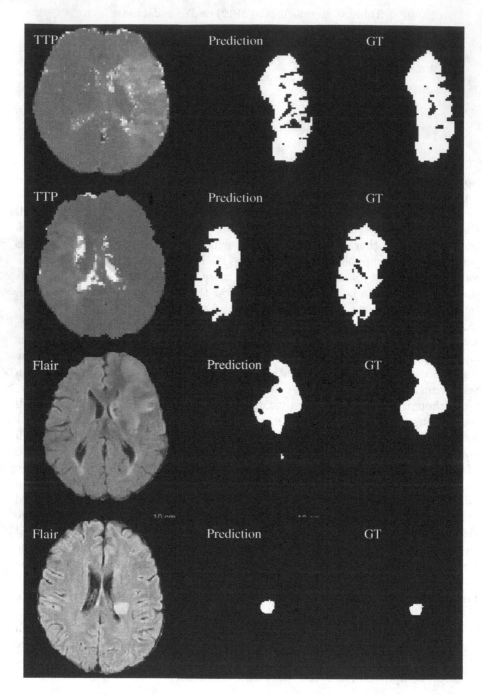

**Fig. 7.** Results obtained by our model on SPES (top row) and SISS (bottom row) datasets. The subjects are chosen from the validation set.

**Table 7.** Results on the SPES challenge datasets, with corrected pre-processing.

| Method | ASSD | | Dice | | Hausdorff Distance | |
|---|---|---|---|---|---|---|
| | average | std | average | std | average | std |
| mckir1 | 1.65 | 1.40 | 0.82 | 0.08 | 29.02 | 16.29 |
| maieo1 | 1.36 | 0.74 | 0.81 | 0.09 | 23.62 | 12.99 |
| robbd1 | 2.77 | 3.27 | 0.78 | 0.09 | 40.27 | 25.10 |
| TwoPathCNN* | 2.24 | 0.79 | 0.76 | 0.10 | 24.16 | 12.62 |
| fengc1 | 2.29 | 1.76 | 0.76 | 0.09 | 30.65 | 16.49 |
| kelle1 | 2.44 | 1.93 | 0.73 | 0.13 | 28.79 | 16.39 |
| haect1 | 5.18 | 6.13 | 0.67 | 0.24 | 42.29 | 19.42 |

## 5 Conclusion

In this paper, we proposed a focal brain pathology segmentation method based on deep convolutional neural networks. In BRATS challenges our method is among the most accurate methods available, while being computationally very efficient. The high performance is achieved with the help of a novel two-pathway architecture (which can model both the local details and global context) as well as modeling local label dependencies by stacking two CNNs. As for the lesion segmentation, our approach yielded competitive results on the SPES dataset but didn't perform as well on the SISS dataset. We think that one underlying factor for inferior performance compablack with BRATS is the comparatively lower amount of training data available. It also appears that the underlying distribution of the challenge data may be different from the training distribution.

## References

1. Brats challenge manuscripts (2014). http://www.braintumorsegmentation.org
2. Virtual skeleton database. http://www.virtualskeleton.ch/
3. Avants, B.B., Tustison, N., Song, G.: Advanced normalization tools (ants). Insight J. **2**, 1–35 (2009). http://papers.nips.cc/paper/4741-deep-neural-networks-segment-neuronal-membranes-in-electron-microscopy-images.pdf
4. Ciresan, D., Giusti, A., Gambardella, L.M., Schmidhuber, J.: Deep neural networks segment neuronal membranes in electron microscopy images. In: Pereira, F., Burges, C., Bottou, L., Weinberger, K. (eds.) Advances in Neural Information Processing Systems, vol. 25, pp. 2843–2851. Curran Associates, Inc (2012)
5. Davy, A., Havaei, M., Warde-Farley, D., Biard, A., Tran, L., Jon, P.M., Courville, A., Larochelle, H., Pal, C., Bengio, Y.: Brain tumor segmentation with deep neural networks. In: Proceedings of the BRATS-MICCAI (2014)
6. Goodfellow, I.J., Warde-Farley, D., Lamblin, P., Dumoulin, V., Mirza, M., Pascanu, R., Bergstra, J., Bastien, F., Bengio, Y.: Pylearn2: a machine learning research library. arXiv preprint (2013). arxiv:1308.4214
7. Havaei, M., Jon, P.M., Larochelle, H.: Efficient interactive brain tumor segmentation as within-brain knn classification. In: International Conference on Pattern Recognition (ICPR) (2014)
8. Havaei, M., Davy, A., Warde-Farley, D., Biard, A., Courville, A., Bengio, Y., Pal, C., Jodoin, P.M., Larochelle, H.: Brain tumor segmentation with deep neural networks. arXiv preprint (2015). arxiv:1505.03540

9. Huang, G.B., Jain, V.: Deep and wide multiscale recursive networks for robust image labeling. ICLR (2014). arxiv:1310.0354
10. Krizhevsky, A., Sutskever, I., Hinton, G.E.: Imagenet classification with deep convolutional neural networks. In: Advances in Neural Information Processing Systems, pp. 1097–1105 (2012)
11. Menze, B., Jakab, A., Bauer, S., Kalpathy-Cramer, J., Farahani, K., Kirby, J., et al.: The multimodal brain tumor image segmentation benchmark (brats). IEEE Trans. Med. Imaging **34**(10), 1993–2024 (2015)
12. Urban, G., Bendszus, M., Hamprecht, F., Kleesiek, J.: Multi-modal brain tumor segmentation using deep convolutional neural networks. In: Proceedings of the BRATS-MICCAI (2014)
13. Zikic, D., Ioannou, Y., Brown, M., Criminisi, A.: Segmentation of brain tumor tissues with convolutional neural networks. In: Proceedings of the BRATS-MICCAI (2014)

# Ischemic Stroke Lesion Image Segmentation

# ISLES Introduction

**Ischemic Stroke Lesion Segmentation (ISLES)** is a medical image processing challenge[1] aiming to provide a platform for a fair and direct comparison of methods for ischemic stroke lesion segmentation from multi-spectral MRI images. A public dataset of diverse ischemic stroke cases and a suitable automatic evaluation procedure was made available. Researchers working in the field can download the data, apply their methods and then upload the results for an automatic on-line evaluation. A continuously updated table allows to directly compare each algorithms against all other submission.

The challenge comprises of two distinct sub-challenge:

**SISS:** Sub-acute ischemic stroke lesion segmentation
**SPES:** Acute stroke perfusion lesion estimation

This third part of the volume contains contributions to the ISLES opening event held at the International Conference on Medical Image Computing and Computer Assisted Intervention (MICCAI) on October the 5th 2015. The articles describe the methods of 14 teams who submitted to SISS and another 7 who submitted to SPES in detail.

For the ranking table of the participating methods and further information, see the official homepage http://www.isles-challenge.org. The data repository, evaluation system and ongoing rankings are hosted at https://www.smir.ch/ISLES/Start2015.

We sincerely hope that our contribution promotes the development of new methods in and general visibility of the clinically important field of stroke lesion segmentation.

January 2016

Oskar Maier
Mauricio Reyes
Björn Menze
Heinz Handels

---

[1] A comprehensive collection of medical image processing challenges: http://grand-challenge.org.

# ISLES (SISS) Challenge 2015: Segmentation of Stroke Lesions Using Spatial Normalization, Random Forest Classification and Contextual Clustering

Hanna-Leena Halme[1,2]([✉]), Antti Korvenoja[1], and Eero Salli[1]

[1] HUS Medical Imaging Center, Radiology, University of Helsinki
and Helsinki University Hospital, P.O. Box 340, 00029 HUS, Helsinki, Finland
`hanna.halme@hus.fi`
[2] Department of Neuroscience and Biomedical Engineering NBE,
Aalto University School of Science, P.O. Box 12200, 00076 Aalto, Espoo, Finland

**Abstract.** Automated methods for segmentation of ischemic stroke lesions could significantly reduce the workload of radiologists and speed up the beginning of patient treatment. In this paper, we present a method for subacute ischemic stroke lesion segmentation from multispectral magnetic resonance images (MRI). The method involves classification of voxels with a Random Forest algorithm and subsequent classification refinement with contextual clustering. In addition, we utilize the training data to build statistical group-specific templates and use them for calculation of individual voxel-wise differences from the global mean. Our method achieved a Dice coefficient of 0.61 for the leave-one-out cross-validated training data and 0.47 for the testing data of the ISLES challenge 2015.

## 1 Introduction

Ischemic stroke is the most common neurological disorder in industrial countries and a major cause of both human suffering and economical loss. Stroke is usually diagnosed in the acute phase using computed tomography (CT) and in many cases also using magnetic resonance imaging (MRI). While CT remains the mainstay of stroke diagnosis due to its high availability, MRI is more sensitive in detection of very early acute brain ischemia as well as ischemic changes in infratentorial brain. Both acute and subacute lesions can be seen with diffusion weighted (DWI) MRI. As the tissue ischemia progresses to the stage of infarction signal changes in T1-weighted images, T2-weighted and fluid attenuated inversion recovery (FLAIR) images appear. The temporal sequence of this signal evolution forms the basis of determining the stage of pathological tissue changes and choice of therapeutic strategy.

In order to predict the patient's outcome and plan appropriate treatment, it is important to accurately define the stage, location and extent of the ischemic lesion. Spatial extent of ischemic changes have been shown to correlate with clinical outcome and a scoring system for CT has been introduced [1].

© Springer International Publishing Switzerland 2016
A. Crimi et al. (Eds.): BrainLes 2015, LNCS 9556, pp. 211–221, 2016.
DOI: 10.1007/978-3-319-30858-6_18

However, manual segmentation of the lesioned area from healthy brain tissue is time-consuming. Ischemic stroke is a common incidence and due to this, all cases of stroke are not always reviewed by expert radiologists and especially small lesions could go undetected. Automated segmentation methods could offer aid in lesion detection and most importantly, reduce the time spent on manual segmentations. Quick and robust lesion segmentation would be of importance especially when used as diagnostic aid in acute cases, when treatment decisions must be done within minutes. Automated methods could facilitate large scale studies where manual segmentation approach is very soon overwhelmed by the amount of lesions to be segmented.

Several automated segmentation methods have been proposed [2,3], but none of the presented methods has yet reached accuracy equal to the professional radiologists' manual segmentations, which leaves room for improvement. Ischemic Stroke Lesion Segmentation (ISLES) challenge is devoted to the development of an automated lesion segmentation method. In this paper, we present an approach for segmentation of stroke lesions from multispectral MR images as part of the ISLES sub-acute ischemic stroke lesion segmentation (SISS) challenge 2015.

## 2    Materials and Methods

The proposed method is a combination of Random Forest classification and subsequent contextual clustering. Contextual clustering is based on a Markov random fields (MRF) prior and iterated conditional modes (ICM, [7]) algorithm, and it was previously used for analysis of detection of activated regions in functional magnetic resonance imaging (fMRI) [8]. Furthermore, we generate statistical template images utilizing the healthy brain tissue of all patients on the training dataset. The template images are used for calculation of individual voxel-wise differences from the global mean. An overview of the method is presented in Figs. 1 and 2.

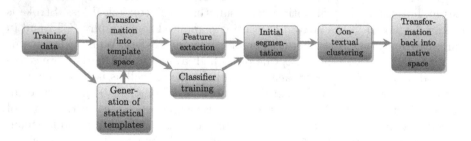

**Fig. 1.** Overview of the classifier training process.

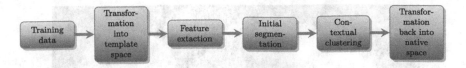

**Fig. 2.** Overview of the segmentation process for the test data.

## 2.1  Statistical Template

In order to enable voxel-wise comparisons across subjects, all T1, T2, FLAIR and DWI volumes, as well as the volumes containing manual segmentations, were warped to a common template space. The template was generated by the Advanced Normalization Tools (ANTs) software version 2.1.0rc3 [4] using *buildtemplateparallel* script, greedy SyN transformation model, cross-correlation similarity metric, 30 × 90 × 20 iterations and the T1 images of the training dataset. All T1 images were deformed to this template with ANTs software using Affine transformation model for rigid registration and SyN transformation model for warping. The detailed parameters are given in Appendix. This defined a transformation which was applied to T2, FLAIR, DWI and manually segmented volumes. All MR images were masked with a volume containing only in-brain voxels to minimize the effect of background to the automatic segmentation of ischemic stroke lesion volumes.

Images in the common template space representing mean and standard deviation (std) of voxel intensities over subjects were calculated voxel-by-voxel, separately for T1, T2, FLAIR and DWI images. The mean images are shown in Fig. 3. We call these images *statistical* templates from now on. Note that the lesion voxels were not included in the calculation of average and std. Because most subjects in the training dataset had lesions in the left hemisphere, there were fewer voxels contributing to the mean and std on the left; as a result, the left hemisphere appeared slightly distorted in the template images. In order to compensate for this left-right bias, average images of left and right hemisphere were calculated. Furthermore, the images were smoothed with a 3D Gaussian kernel (FWHM 3 mm) to decrease the effect of registration inaccuracies.

## 2.2  Random Forest Classification Algorithm

The initial segmentation was predicted with an ensemble learning method. A set of features was derived from the training data and fed to a Random Forest [5] classification algorithm implemented in Scikit-learn version 0.16.dev [6]. The Random Forest algorithm combines classification results from a number of decision trees. Several trees are constructed and fitted to the data during training phase, using a random subset of features to train each tree. The final classification is the mode of the classes obtained from all individual trees. Random Forest classification greatly reduces overfitting, which is a common problem for simple decision tree classifiers [5].

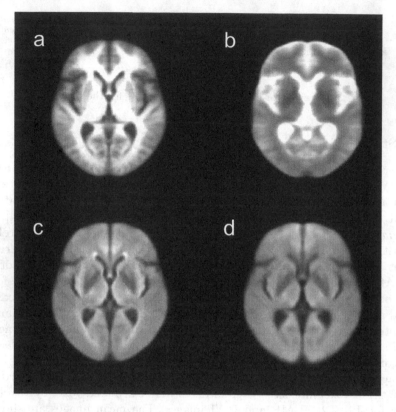

**Fig. 3.** Statistical templates representing the mean of (a) T1, (b) T2, (c) FLAIR, and (d) DWI images.

In the training phase, the performance of the classifier was tested and optimized with leave-one-out cross-validation, in which one subject from the training dataset was used for testing and the rest for training the classifier, and the procedure was repeated for all subjects. In the testing phase, the trained classifier was applied to a different dataset. The classifier returned both the binary classifications (lesion/non-lesion) and probabilities in range 0–1 that a voxel belonged to the lesion area.

## 2.3    Classifier Training

Sixteen features were extracted from the MR images for subsequent classification. Z-score normalized voxel intensities of T1, T2, FLAIR and DWI images constituted features 1–4. Features 5–8 represented the voxelwise Z-score deviations from global average images, calculated separately for each sequence by subtracting the global mean and dividing with the global std. The purpose of these features was to find regions showing large deviations from the normal brain, which likely indicates presence of a lesion. Features 9–12 were voxel intensities obtained by smoothing the original images with a 3D Gaussian kernel (FWHM 3 mm), thus including information from the local neighborhood of each voxel. Smoothing was expected to improve classification since it may reduce the effect of registration inaccuracies. Features 13–16 represented local asymmetry, obtained by comparing voxel intensities on one hemisphere to the corresponding voxel intensities on the other hemisphere. The motivation for calculating local asymmetry was the fact that lesions rarely occur symmetrically on both hemispheres. As the transformed images were left-right symmetric, the asymmetry measure could be calculated simply by subtracting the original smoothed image from the left-right -mirrored smoothed image.

In order to decrease computational time and avoid classifier overfitting, we only collected the aforementioned features from a randomly selected subset of voxels. The maximum number of lesion voxels sampled from each subject was set to 300, and the ratio of lesion and non-lesion voxels per subject was kept constant, such that twice as many voxels were sampled from non-lesion area as from lesion area. Thus, if the lesion extended over 300 voxels, we sampled 300 lesion and 600 non-lesion voxels, and if the lesion size $n$ was smaller that 300 voxels, $n$ lesion and $2n$ non-lesion voxels were sampled. In order to investigate whether increasing $n$ improves the results, we also tested $n = 400$ and $n = 500$ and calculated the quality of segmentations obtained with these sample sizes.

For the Random Forest classifier, the training set was resampled to train a total of 300 decision trees. 4 features were used to obtain the best split at each individual node. The quality of each split was described by Gini impurity [5]. The trees were grown unlimitedly, i.e. until each leaf contained only samples of a single class. All parameters and default values used by Scikit-learn's Random Forest classification algorithm are listed in Appendix.

## 2.4   Contextual Clustering

The segmentation results obtained with the Random Forest classifier were further improved with contextual clustering (CC). The basic assumption in contextual clustering is that neighboring voxels tend to belong to the same class. Furthermore, it is assumed that the intensity distribution of background voxels (in present case, non-lesion voxels) is transformed to be standard normal. In the derivation, the intensity distribution of object (lesion) voxels is modeled to be normal too, but experiments have shown that this is not required in practice.

The MRF model takes the neighborhood of a voxel into account by stating that the prior probability distribution for a voxel label is defined conditionally on the labels of the neighboring voxels. The optimal image segmentation is thus achieved by maximizing the *a posteriori* probability globally. The ICM algorithm is used to find local maximum *a posteriori* probabilities by utilizing Bayes' rule and MRF prior. The initial classification is obtained such that the class probability is maximized for each voxel separately, and the classification is updated to maximize the conditional probability at each voxel, given the class of the voxel and the classes of the neighboring voxels. The algorithm converges when the classification no longer changes. Oscillation between two states is also possible in our implementation based on synchronous updating.

The CC algorithm modified for this study consisted of the following steps:

1. Fit a gamma distribution to all nonzero voxels of the lesion probability map given by the Random Forest classifier. Fitting is done using MATLABs (R2015a) function *fitdist* with default parameters.
2. Transform the probability map values to standard normal distribution by calculating the inverse normal distribution function (MATLAB function *norminv*) from the cumulative distribution function (MATLAB function *cdf*) of gamma distribution. This gives image $N$ with voxel values $r_i$.
3. Define the parameter $T$ for contextual clustering [8] using the fitted gamma distribution: $T = -norminv(cdf(gamma, D))$, where *gamma* is the fitted gamma distribution, and $D$ some threshold. Decision parameter T is used to tune sensitivity and specificity in contextual clustering like thresholds in thresholding. In this study we used empirically chosen $D = 0.6$, which gave reasonable sensitivity and specificity with the training data.
4. Apply the CC rule (1) to all voxels $r_i$ belonging to image $N$:

$$r_i + \frac{\beta}{T}[u_i(1) - 13] \begin{cases} <T \to k_i = 1 \\ \geq T \to k_i = 0 \end{cases} \tag{1}$$

where neighborhood weight coefficient $\beta = T^2/6$ and $u_i(1)$ is the number of neighboring voxels (26 connectivity) belonging to class 1 (lesion). The CC rule is repeated iteratively until none of the voxel labels changes anymore.
5. Repeat steps 1–4 with only the voxels classified as non-lesion in the first run of CC.

Finally, all automatically segmented images were transformed back to each subject's native space using inverse transformation and nearest neighbor interpolation. After transformation it was possible to compare the automatic segmentations with the manual lesion segmentations. The classification accuracy was evaluated with the script provided at ISLES web page (http://www.isles-challenge. org), including measurements for Dice coefficient, average symmetric surface distance (ASSD), Hausdorff distance, precision and recall. For comparison, we calculated these metrics also for the segmentations obtained with only the Random Forest classification and probability map thresholding at 0.5, 0.7 and 0.8.

## 2.5    Testing Phase

The test data was spatially normalized to the common template generated from the training data. We used the parameters listed in Appendix, but without the lesion images (–x option). After that, the trained Random Forest classifier and contextual clustering were applied to the test data. The classifier was trained using all patients from the training dataset.

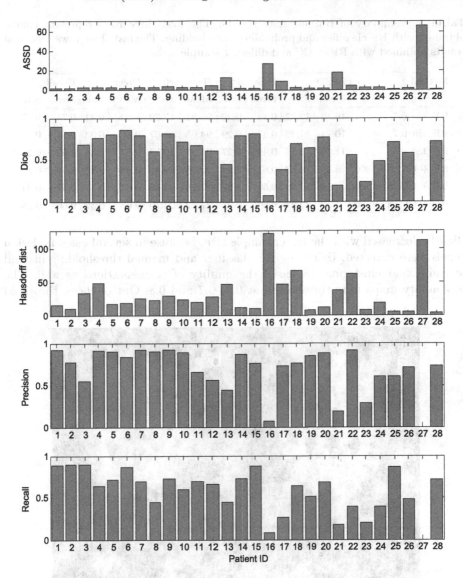

**Fig. 4.** ASSD, Dice coefficient, Hausdorff distance, precision and recall for each patient in the training dataset.

## 3    Results

### 3.1    Training Data

The results for the training data were obtained using leave-one-out cross-validation. Our method achieved a Dice coefficient of 0.61 and ASSD of 6.44. Increasing the sample number $n$ from 300 to 400 or 500 did not significantly improve the results. In fact, the average Dice coefficient, precision and recall

**Table 1.** Summary of training data results. The first three rows represent results obtained with RF classifier and probability thresholding. The last three rows represent results obtained with RF + CC and different sample sizes.

| Method | ASSD | | Dice | | Hausdorff | | Precision | | Recall | |
|---|---|---|---|---|---|---|---|---|---|---|
| | Mean | Std | Mean | Std | Mean | Std | Mean | Std | Mean | Std |
| RF, thr 0.5 | 16.13 | 12.77 | 0.38 | 0.30 | 98.31 | 17.70 | 0.33 | 0.31 | 0.74 | 0.17 |
| RF, thr 0.7 | 10.74 | 11.42 | 0.47 | 0.29 | 94.65 | 18.67 | 0.46 | 0.33 | 0.64 | 0.19 |
| RF, thr 0.8 | 11.16 | 12.86 | 0.49 | 0.27 | 91.36 | 20.23 | 0.54 | 0.34 | 0.57 | 0.21 |
| RF + CC, n = 300 | 6.44 | 12.93 | 0.61 | 0.24 | 30.96 | 29.40 | 0.68 | 0.26 | 0.58 | 0.25 |
| RF + CC, n = 400 | 4.49 | 12.36 | 0.59 | 0.27 | 27.76 | 23.45 | 0.67 | 0.31 | 0.57 | 0.31 |
| RF + CC, n = 500 | 4.50 | 12.27 | 0.59 | 0.27 | 27.72 | 22.70 | 0.66 | 0.32 | 0.56 | 0.28 |

slightly decreased with the larger sample size, because in several cases no lesion voxels were detected. Using the RF classifier and manual thresholding instead of contextual clustering decreased the quality of segmentations as well. The probability maps were thresholded at 0.5, 0.7 and 0.8. Out of these, threshold

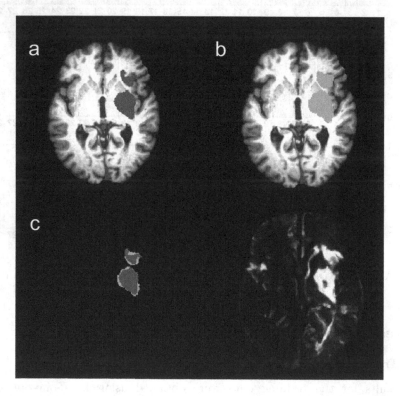

**Fig. 5.** For a single patient from the training dataset: (a) predicted lesion, (b) ground truth lesion, (c) predicted and ground truth lesions overlaid, and (d) lesion probability image given by the Random Forest classifier.

0.8 yielded the best results, although the differences were not significant. The summary of all results is shown in Table 1. The results for individual patients, obtained with RF + CC and $n = 300$, are shown in Fig. 4. The corresponding segmentation results for a single patient are illustrated in Fig. 5.

## 3.2   Testing Data

A summary of the testing data results is presented in Table 2.

**Table 2.** Summary of testing data results.

| Method | ASSD | | Dice | | Hausdorff | | Precision | | Recall | |
|---|---|---|---|---|---|---|---|---|---|---|
| | Mean | Std | Mean | Std | Mean | Std | Mean | Std | Mean | Std |
| RF + CC, n = 300 | 14.61 | 20.17 | 0.47 | 0.32 | 46.26 | 34.81 | 0.47 | 0.34 | 0.56 | 0.33 |

# 4   Discussion

In this paper, we proposed an approach for sub-acute ischemic stroke lesion segmentation. Our method was able to detect lesions with a good accuracy in most patients of the training dataset. It was also ranked as the third best method in the ISLES challenge 2015, implying that the method's generalizability to an unknown dataset was reasonable as well. Contextual clustering significantly improved the initial results obtained with Random Forest classifier and probability thresholding. The total computation time of our method was roughly 3–5 min per patient, which is sufficient for a clinical application even in case of acute patients, when data processing needs to be very quick. Fast computation is one of the benefits of Random Forest classifiers compared to e.g. neural networks. In clinical context this means the ability to quickly train the classifier again as new data becomes available. This was our main motivation for using Random Forest instead of neural networks or deep learning in the current approach.

Despite the fitness of our approach compared to most of the proposed methods in the ISLES challenge, significant improvements are needed before the segmentation algorithm can be developed into a fully functional clinical software. Our method mostly failed to detect very small lesions, especially when located in subcortical regions. A likely reason for this result is that contextual clustering considers the close neighborhood of voxel in classification. Since small lesions can comprise only a few voxels, they are easily misclassified according to the surrounding healthy tissue. In future, the neighborhood weight coefficient of CC algorithm should be optimized such that it would not completely discard the small lesions. The effect of other CC parameters on segmentation accuracy should be more carefully evaluated as well.

We sampled at most $n = 300$ voxels from lesion and $2n$ voxels from non-lesion areas of each patient in the training data. The main reason for sample size limitation was to speed up computation, and our results also show that increasing the number of samples did not improve the segmentation results. When the sample size was increased, no lesion voxels were detected in several patients. This probably happened due to overfitting; more voxels were collected from large lesions, and therefore the features of large lesions contributed more to the classification than features of small lesions. It would be beneficial to collect more data from patients having small lesions in order to improve the generalizability of the classifier.

In further development of the method, we should also account for the varying image quality. First, both the intensity inhomogeneity (bias field) and the susceptibility artefact present in many DWI images should be corrected. This would probably improve the detection of frontal lesions, since the intensity bias and distortions are usually most prominent in frontal areas. Second, the statistical templates must be matched to each dataset separately. We generated the template images solely based on the ISLES training dataset, which was collected from a single imaging site. However, in case of multi-site datasets, such as the ISLES testing data, it would be more appropriate to generate templates for each site separately, because the scanner properties and imaging parameters may vary significantly between sites.

In future, the current method could be modified and used for several clinical applications in addition to subacute ischemic stroke. Since acute stroke is usually diagnosed with CT, it would be relevant to modify and study the current method for segmentation of stroke lesions from CT images. Put simply, this means adjusting the features fed to the Random Forest classifier; instead of MR image features one should draw a number of features from CT images. The exact features and their optimal number remain to be investigated. Another possible clinical application is segmentation of focal cortical dysplasias (FCD), i.e. malformations of cortical development which are common causes of medically refractory epilepsy, from multi-spectral MRI. In order to validate the method for these two applications, training data for both stroke patients' CT images and FCD patients' MR images should be collected and manually labeled.

We are planning to continue the research at HUS Medical Imaging Center by collecting new clinical data, improving the current method and implementing the aforementioned new applications.

## Appendix

### Generation of Templates
The common template was done in two phases. First, the initial template was formed:

```
buildtemplateparallel.sh -d 3 -m 1 × 0 × 0 -n 0 -r 1 -t GR -s CC
-o [initial template image] -c 0 -j 1 [T1 images]
```

After that, the final template was built using the initial template:

```
buildtemplateparallel.sh -d 3 -m 30 × 90 × 20 -n 0 -r 0 -t GR -s
CC -o [template image] -z [initial template image] -c 0 [T1
images]
```

Warping of T1 images to common template was done using `antsRegistration` tool and the following parameters:
`--metric MI[template image, T1 image,1,32]`
`--transform affine[0.25] --convergence 10000 × 10000 × 10000 × 10000 × 10000 --shrink factors 5 × 4 × 3 × 2 × 1 --smoothing-sigmas 4 × 3 × 2 × 1 × 0 --metric CC[template image, T1 image,1,5] --transform SyN[0.25,3.0,0.0] --convergence 50 × 35 × 15 --shrink factors 3 × 2 × 1 --smoothing-sigmas 2 × 1 × 0 --use-histogram-matching 1 --x [lesion image]`

**Parameters for Random Forest Classifier**
Scikit-learn's function `sklearn.ensemble.RandomForestClassifier` was used with the following parameters:
   `n_estimators=300, criterion='gini', max_depth=None, min_samples_split=2, min_samples_leaf=1, min_weight_fraction_leaf=0.0, max_features=4, max_leaf_nodes=None, bootstrap=True, oob_score=False, n_jobs=1, random_state=None, verbose=0, warm_start=False, class_weight=None`

# References

1. Pexman, J.H., Barber, P.A., Hill, M.D., Sevick, R.J., Demchuk, A.M., Hudon, M.E., Hu, W.Y., Buchan, A.M.: Use of the Alberta Stroke Program Early CT Score (ASPECTS) for assessing CT scans in patients with acute stroke. Am. J. Neuroradiol. **22**(8), 1534–1542 (2001)
2. Maier, O., Wilms, M., von der Gablentz, J., Krämer, U.M., Münte, T.F., Handels, H.: Extra Tree forests for sub-acute ischemic stroke lesion segmentation in MR sequences. J. Neurosci. Methods **240**, 89–100 (2015)
3. Kabir, Y., Dojat, M., Scherrer, B., Garbay, C., Forbes, F.: Multimodal MRI segmentation of ischemic stroke lesions. In: 29th Annual International Conference of the IEEE Engineering in Medicine and Biology Society, 2007. EMBS 2007, pp. 1595–1598. IEEE, August 2007
4. Avants, B.B., Tustison, N.J., Song, G., Cook, P.A., Klein, A., Gee, J.C.: A reproducible evaluation of ANTs similarity metric performance in brain image registration. Neuroimage **54**(3), 2033–2044 (2011)
5. Breiman, L.: Random forests. Mach. Learn. **45**(1), 5–32 (2001)
6. Pedregosa, F., Varoquaux, G., Gramfort, A., Michel, V., Thirion, B., Grisel, O., Blondel, M., Prettenhofer, P., Weiss, R., Dubourg, V., Vanderplas, J., Passos, A., Cournapeau, D., Brucher, M., Perrot, M., Duchesnay, E.: Scikit-learn: machine learning in Python. J. Mach. Learn. Res. **12**, 2825–2830 (2011)
7. Besag, J.: On the statistical analysis of dirty pictures. J. R. Stat. Soc. Series B (Methodological) **48**(3), 259–302 (1986)
8. Salli, E., Aronen, H.J., Savolainen, S., Korvenoja, A., Visa, A.: Contextual clustering for analysis of functional MRI data. IEEE Trans. Med. Imaging **20**(5), 403–414 (2001)

# Stroke Lesion Segmentation of 3D Brain MRI Using Multiple Random Forests and 3D Registration

Ching-Wei Wang[✉] and Jia-Hong Lee

Graduate Institute of Biomedical Engineering,
National Taiwan University of Science and Technology, Taipei City, Taiwan
cweiwang@mail.ntust.edu.tw

**Abstract.** Stroke is a common cause of sudden death and disability worldwide. In clinical practice, brain magnetic resonance (MR) scans are used to assess the stroke lesion presence. In this work, we have built a fully automatic stroke lesion segmentation system using 3D brain magnetic resonance (MR) data. The system contains a 3D registration framework and a 3D multi-random forest model trained from the data provided by the Ischemic Stroke Lesion Segmentation (ISLES) challenge of the 18th International Conference on Medical Image Computing and Computer Assisted Intervention. The preliminary test results show that the presented system is capable to detect stroke lesion from 3D brain MRI data.

## 1 Introduction

Stroke is a common cause of sudden death and disability worldwide. In clinical practice, brain magnetic resonance (MR) scans are used to assess the stroke lesion presence. A fully automatic random forest based stroke lesion 3D segmentation approach is built. A 3D segmentation framework with backward registration and forward registration is developed for processing the 3D brain data. A machine learning model is trained using the training data provided by the Ischemic Stroke Lesion Segmentation (ISLES) challenge of the 18th International Conference on Medical Image Computing and Computer Assisted Intervention. The results section show that the presented system is capable to detect stroke lesion from 3D brain MRI data. The outline of this paper is as follows. Section 2 presents our proposed method, Sect. 3 demonstrates the evaluation result of our proposed method and Sect. 4 concludes the paper.

## 2 Methodology

A fully automatic machine learning based stroke lesion three-dimensions segmentation system is built, which consists of a feature selection method, a multi-level random forest model and a simple 3D registration approach.

© Springer International Publishing Switzerland 2016
A. Crimi et al. (Eds.): BrainLes 2015, LNCS 9556, pp. 222–232, 2016.
DOI: 10.1007/978-3-319-30858-6_19

## 2.1   Data Preparation

Three-dimensional brain magnetic resonance images are acquired from the VSD system of the Ischemic Stroke Lesion Segmentation (ISLES) challenge held in the 18th International Conference on Medical Image Computing and Computer Assisted Intervention 2015. The challenge organizers provide the four different kinds of MRI sequences for individual the three-dimensional Brain MR datasets, as illustrated in Fig. 1.

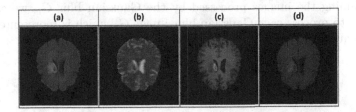

**Fig. 1.** Stacks of four kinds of a 3D brain MRI dataset. From left to right: (a) Fluid-attenuated inversion recovery (FLAIR), (b) T2w TSE, (c) T1w TFE/TSE and (d) Diffusion MRI (DWI)

In the preliminary tests using the training data, we compare the prediction results of the proposed system with the ground truth data using four kinds of MRI sequences, and it is found that the model using the *FLAIR* MRI datasets outperforms other models using three other kinds of MRI sequences. Therefore, we select the *FLAIR* MRI sequence images to use as the training data.

## 2.2   Feature Extraction

275 features, which can be categorized into 24 types as shown in Fig. 2, are extracted for building random forests models. Below, eight types of features are described in details.

| No. | Features | Attributes | | | |
|-----|----------|-----------|-----|------|-----|
| 1 | Original | 1 | 13 | Maximum | 5 |
| 2 | Hue | 1 | 14 | Median | 5 |
| 3 | Saturation | 1 | 15 | Anisotropic diffusion | 10 |
| 4 | Brightness | 1 | 16 | Bilateral | 4 |
| 5 | Gaussian blur | 5 | 17 | Lipschitz | 5 |
| 6 | Sobel filter | 6 | 18 | Kuwahara | 3 |
| 7 | Hessian | 48 | 19 | Gabor | 44 |
| 8 | Difference of gaussians | 10 | 20 | Derivatives | 20 |
| 9 | Membrane projections | 6 | 21 | Laplacian | 5 |
| 10 | Variance | 5 | 22 | Structure | 20 |
| 11 | Mean | 5 | 23 | Entropy | 20 |
| 12 | Minimum | 5 | 24 | Neighbors | 40 |
| | | | | Total Feature | 275 |

**Fig. 2.** Features selected for training

**Sobel Filter** [1]. To extract six Sobel features for each image, we combine the Gaussian blur and Sobel filter. We define the parameter sigma of the Gaussian blur $\sigma = 1$, the masks of the Sobel filter $Mx$ and $My$ and the input image $I$, and we first process the input image by Gaussian blur which is represented by the following equation:

$$G_i = g(I_x, I_y) = \frac{1}{2\pi(2^{i-1}\sigma)^2} \exp^{-\frac{I_x^2+I_y^2}{2(2^{i-1}\sigma)^2}}, \ i = \{0,1,2,3,4,5\}.$$

After obtaining the images processed by the Gaussian blur $G_i$, we apply the Sobel filter to process each Gaussian blur image $G_i$ which is represented by the following equations:

$$Mx = \begin{pmatrix} -1 & 0 & 1 \\ -2 & 0 & 2 \\ -1 & 0 & 1 \end{pmatrix}, My = \begin{pmatrix} -1 & -2 & -1 \\ 0 & 0 & 0 \\ 1 & 2 & 1 \end{pmatrix},$$

$$S_ix(the \ Sobel \ image \ of \ the \ x-coordinate) = Mx * G_i$$

$$S_iy(the \ Sobel \ image \ of \ the \ y-coordinate) = My * G_i,$$

$$SF_i(the \ Sobel \ image) = \sqrt{S_ix^2 + S_iy^2}$$

**where ∗ denotes** the two-dimensional signal processing convolution operation and $i = \{0,1,2,3,4,5\}$.

**Hessian** [2]. To generate forty eight image features of the Hessian in each input image, we combine the Gaussian blur and Hessian. **We set the parameter $\sigma$ of the Gaussian blur to be 1 and first process** the input image $I$ by Gaussian blur which is represented by the following equation:

$$G_i = g(I_x, I_y) = \frac{1}{2\pi(2^{i-1}\sigma)^2} \exp^{-\frac{I_x^2+I_y^2}{2(2^{i-1}\sigma)^2}}, \ i = \{0,1,2,3,4,5\}.$$

When obtaining the images processed by the Gaussian blur $G_i$, we calculate the Hessian matrix of each Gaussian blur image as the mask $HM_i$. Suppose $f_i : \mathbb{R}^2 \to \mathbb{R}$ is function which is taken as input vectors $G_ix$ , $G_iy \in \mathbb{R}^2$ and is outputting a scalar $f_i(G_ix, G_iy) \in \mathbb{R}$. If all second partial derivatives of $f_i$ exist and are continuous over the domain of the function, then the Hessian matrix $HM_i$ of $f_i$ is a square $2 \times 2$ matrix defined as follows:

$$HM_i = f_i''(G_ix, G_iy) = \begin{pmatrix} \frac{\partial^2 f_i}{G_i\partial x^2} & \frac{\partial^2 f_i}{G_i\partial x \cdot G_i\partial y} \\ \frac{\partial^2 f_i}{G_i\partial x \cdot G_i\partial y} & \frac{\partial^2 f_i}{G_i\partial y^2} \end{pmatrix} = \begin{pmatrix} A_i & B_i \\ C_i & D_i \end{pmatrix},$$

$$where \ A_i = \frac{\partial^2 f_i}{G_i\partial x^2}, \ B_i = C_i = \frac{\partial^2 f_i}{G_i\partial x \cdot G_i\partial y}, \ D_i = \frac{\partial^2 f_i}{G_i\partial y^2}$$

$$and \ i = \{0,1,2,3,4,5\}.$$

When we obtain the Hessian matrix $HM_i$ of each Gaussian blur image, we apply the Hessian matrix $HM_i$ to calculate the value of the Module, the Trace, the Determinant, the First Eigenvalue, the Second Eigenvalue, the Orientation, the Gamma Normalized Square Eigenvalue Difference and the Square of Gamma Normalized Eigenvalue Difference to become image features, so the number of total image features of the Hessian are 6×8, is equal to 48,which are generated using the following equations:

$$Module_i = \sqrt{A_i{}^2 + B_iC_i + D_i{}^2}, \ Trace_i = A_i + D_i, \ Determinant_i = A_iD_i - C_iD_i,$$

$$Orientation_i = \frac{1}{2}\arccos(4B_i{}^2 + (A_i - D_i)^2),$$

$$First\ Eigenvalue_i = \frac{A_i + D_i}{2} + \sqrt{\frac{4B_i{}^2 + (A_i - D_i)^2}{2}},$$

$$Second\ Eigenvalue_i = \frac{A_i + D_i}{2} - \sqrt{\frac{4B_i{}^2 + (A_i - D_i)^2}{2}},$$

$$Gamma - Normalized\ Square\ Eigenvalue\ Difference_i$$
$$= T^4(A_i - D_i)^2((A_i - D_i)^2 + 4B_i{}^2),$$

$$Square\ of\ Gamma - Normalized\ Eigenvalue\ Difference_i$$
$$= T^2((A_i - D_i)^2 + 4B_i{}^2),$$

$$where\ T = 1^{\frac{3}{4}}\ and\ i = \{0, 1, 2, 3, 4, 5\}.$$

**Membrane Projection.** To generate six image features of the Membrane Projection in each image, we define the initial mask $m$ which is the $19 \times 19$ zeros matrix with the middle column entries set to 1 and the input image $I$, and obtain the set of masks $M = \{m_1, m_2, ..., m_{30}\}$ by rotating the initial mask $m$ 6 degrees up to a total rotation of 180 degrees. After obtaining the set of masks $M$, we apply the set of masks $M$ to process the input image $I$ using the convolution operation $*$ that is represented by the following equation:

$$O = M * I, where\ the\ set\ of\ the\ processed\ images\ O = \{o_1, o_2, ..., o_{30}\}$$

Then, we calculate the sum of the pixels $O_{sum}$, the mean of the pixels $O_{mean}$, the standard deviation of the pixels $O_{std}$, the median of the pixels $O_{median}$, the maximum of the pixels $O_{max}$ and the minimum of the pixels $O_{min}$ in the set of processed images $O$. Each equation can generate thirty processed images,and we combine these processed images to become one image features. Therefore, we can obtain six image features.

**Gabor Filter** [3]. To generate forty four image features of the Gabor in each input image, we apply the Fourier transform of the impulse response of the Gabor filter which is the convolution of the Fourier transform of the harmonic function and the Fourier transform of the Gaussian function, and define the input image $I$, the frequency of the sinusoidal factor $f$, the orientation of the Fourier transform $\theta$, the phase offset $\psi$, the standard deviation of the Gaussian envelope $\sigma$, the spatial aspect ratio $\gamma$ and the number of the angle $n$, is represented by the following equation:

$$Gabor_{\sigma,\gamma,\psi,f,n}(I_x, I_y) = \cos(2\pi f X + \psi) \times e^{-\frac{X^2 + \gamma^2 Y^2}{2\sigma^2}},$$

$$where\ X = x\cos\theta + y\sin\theta,\ Y = -x\sin\theta + y\cos\theta,$$

$$\theta_i = (\pi \div n) \times i, \psi_j = (\pi \div 2) \times j, i = \{0, 1, 2..., n\}, j = \{0, 1, 2\},$$

$$\sigma = \{1.0, 2.0, 4.0\}, \gamma = \{0.25, 0.5, 1.0, 2.0\}, f = \{2.0, 3.0\}, n = 10.$$

**Derivatives Filter** [4,5]. To generate twenty image features of the Derivatives in each input image, we combine the Gaussian blur and Derivatives Filter. We define the parameters sigma of the Gaussian blur $\sigma = 1$, the $n - derivative$ filter $n = \{2, 3, 4, 5\}$ and the input image $I$, and **we first process the input image by Gaussian blur which is represented by the following equation:**

$$G_i = g(I_x, I_y) = \frac{1}{2\pi(2^{i-1}\sigma)^2} \exp^{-\frac{I_x^2 + I_y^2}{2(2^{i-1}\sigma)^2}}, \ i = \{1, 2, 3, 4, 5\}.$$

Then, we apply the $n - derivative$ filter to process the $G_i$ image to generate twenty image features that is represented by the following equation:

$$DF_n = \frac{d^{2n}G_i}{G_i dx^n G_i dy^n}, where\ i = \{1, 2, 3, 4, 5\}\ and\ n = \{2, 3, 4, 5\}.$$

**Laplacian Filter** [6,7]. To obtain five image features of the Laplacian in each input image, we combine the Gaussian blur and Laplacian filter. We define the parameter sigma of the Gaussian blur $\sigma = 1$, the mask of the Laplacian filter $M$ and the input image $I$, and **we first process the input image by Gaussian blur which is represented by the following equation:**

$$G_i = g(I_x, I_y) = \frac{1}{2\pi(2^{i-1}\sigma)^2} \exp^{-\frac{I_x^2 + I_y^2}{2(2^{i-1}\sigma)^2}}, \ i = \{1, 2, 3, 4, 5\}.$$

After obtaining the images processed by the Gaussian blur $G_i$, we apply the Laplacian filter to process each Gaussian blur image $G_i$ which is represented by the following equations:

$$M = \begin{pmatrix} 0 & 1 & 0 \\ 1 & -4 & 1 \\ 0 & 1 & 0 \end{pmatrix}$$

$$LF_i(the\ Laplacian\ image) = M * G_i,$$

*where∗ denotes the two−dimensional signal processing convolution operation*

$$and\ i = \{1, 2, 3, 4, 5\}.$$

**Structure Filter** [8,9]. To obtain twenty image features of the Structure Filter in each three-dimensional brain magnetic resonance imaging image, we apply the Structure Tensor to analyze the each stack of the three-dimensional brain magnetic resonance imaging image. Consider an three-dimensional image domain $\Omega := (0, d_1) \times (0, d_2) \times (0, d_3)$, and make a image $I(x)$ be represented by a bounded mapping $I :\to \mathbb{R}$. A structure descriptor for applying to three-dimensional space is given by $\nabla I_\sigma$ which the gradient of the Gaussian-smoothed version of $I$ are represented by the following equations:

$$G_\sigma(x) := \frac{1}{(2\pi\sigma^2)^{\frac{3}{2}}} \times \exp(-\frac{|x|^2}{2\sigma^2}),\ I_\sigma(x, t) := (G_\sigma * \tilde{I}(., t))(x).$$

The standard deviation $\sigma$ are represented the *noise scale* and the sign $*$ means that convolution between $G_\sigma$ and $\tilde{I}$ on $\mathbb{R}$ and $\mathbb{R}^3$, where $\tilde{I}$ denotes an extension of $I$ by mirroring. The $\nabla I_\sigma$ is unsuitable for detecting parallel structures despite the fact that it is useful for detecting edges. In order to solve the deficiency, we may replace $\nabla I_\sigma$ by its tensor product that is represented by the following equation:

$$Junction(\nabla T_\sigma) := \nabla I_\sigma \bigotimes \nabla I_\sigma := \nabla I_\sigma \nabla I_\sigma{}^T.$$

After we have replaced directions by orientations, we can average the orientations by applying the convolution with the Gaussian $G_\rho$ what is represented by the following equation which the junction matrix is named *Structure Tensor*:

$$Junction_{\sigma,\rho}(\nabla I_\sigma) := G_\rho * (\nabla I_\sigma \bigotimes \nabla I_\sigma),$$

$$where\ \sigma = \{1, 2, 4, 8, 16\}\ and\ \rho = \{1, 2\}.$$

**Entropy.** To obtain twenty image features of the Entropy in each image, we define the mask which is the circle of radius $r$ around each pixel, calculate the histogram of the mask which we only select the pixel value $H = \{31, 63, 127, 255\}$ and apply the following equation:

$$Entropy_{r,H} = \sum_{p\ in\ H} -p * \log_2(p),$$

*where p is the probability of each mask in the histogram*

$$and\ r = \{1, 2, 4, 8, 16\}.$$

After finishing to describe the equation of the eight higher effective feature types, we demonstrate them by processing the original images, as being represented in Fig. 3.

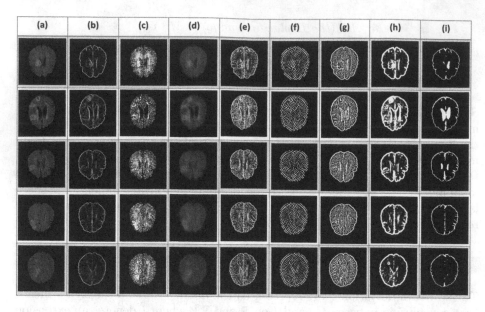

**Fig. 3.** The original images are processed by using the filters which can produce lots of features. The above figures are from left to right: (a) Original image, (b) The features are obtained by using the Sobel Filter $SF_1$, (c) The features are obtained by using the Hessian $First\ Eigenvalue_1$, (d) The features are obtained by using the Membrane Projection $O_{mean}$, (e) The features are obtained by using the Gabor Filter $Gabor_{2.0,1.0,\psi_0,3.0,10}$, (f) The features are obtained by using the Derivatives Filter $DF_2$, (g) The features are obtained by using the Laplacian Filter $LF_1$, (h) The features are obtained by using the Structure Filter $Junction_{1,1}(\nabla I_1)$ and (i) The features are obtained by using the Entropy $Entropy_{1,255}$.

## 2.3   Machine Learning Using Multiple Random Forests

**After generating** the features of the brain magnetic resonance imaging images, we apply this features of this image, the region of interest class of this image and the foreground class of this image to be trained **using a Random Forests classifier** [10]. Random Forests are an ensemble of tree predictors, and each tree is built based on the values of a random vector generated independently. The parameters of the random forest model is present in Table 1.

To deal with the three dimensional data, a multi-random forest model is developed, and for every five stacks in the Z direction, a random forest model is built (see Table 2 and Fig. 4). Training each random forest model takes 4.75 h to finish this procedure using the desktop with the CPU processors $Intel\ Xeon\ CPU\ E5 - 2650$ 2.60 Hz, the 32 GB memory and the operation system $Window$ 7. In testing, as illustrated in Fig. 5, the system generates probability maps and takes 0.67 h to finish this procedure using the same equipment.

**Table 1.** The parameters designed for the random forests classifier

| | |
|---|---|
| The maximum depth of the trees to be built | 50 |
| The number of trees to be generated | 50 |
| The number of features to be applied | 275 |
| The random number seed to be applied | 1 |

**Table 2.** The parameters designed for generating the multiple random forests classifiers

| | |
|---|---|
| The number of stack images to be used to train one random forests classifier | 5 |
| The total number of random forests classifier to be built | $N/5$ |

N: The maximum number of stack images in the Z direction

## 2.4  Post-processing Using Three-Dimensional Registration

After obtaining the potential candidates from the random forests models mention above, we build a three-dimensional registration [11] framework with backward and forward searching. The three-dimensional registration framework is applied to generate optimal three-dimensional predictions and removes larger noises. In Fig. 6, the system finds the largest object among all stacks and uses the stack with the largest object as the referenced stack $T$. Then, the system preforms backward and forward registration to maintain spatial consistency and removes the objects with no overlap to the detected objects in the neighboring stacks.

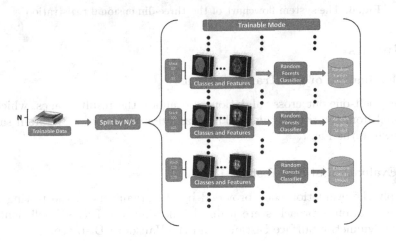

**Fig. 4.** The system flowchart for generating the multiple random forests models.

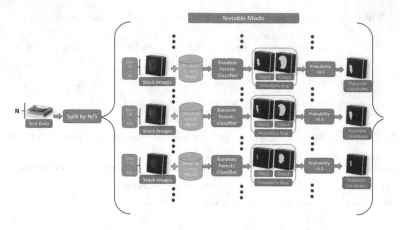

**Fig. 5.** The system flowchart for generating the potential candidates.

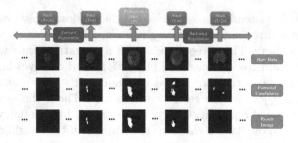

**Fig. 6.** The system flowchart of the three-dimensional registration.

## 3    Results

### 3.1    Evaluation of the Training Data

We apply left-one-out cross validation to evaluate the result images, which are generated from the training data. The evaluation results of a 3D brain sample are shown in the Fig. 7.

### 3.2    Evaluation of the Testing Data

We apply the evaluation code provided by the organizers to the testing data. Three evaluation approaches are utilized, inlcuding the Dice's Coefficient, the Average Symmetric Surface Distance and the Hausdorff Distance.

**Dice's Coefficient (DC).** Measures the similarity between two images. Considering two sets of volume voxels $X$ and $Y$, the equation of the $DC$ value is given as:

$$DC = \frac{2\,|X \cap Y|}{|X| + |Y|}, \ DC = \begin{cases} 0, \ no\ overlap \\ 1, \ perfect\ similarity \end{cases}$$

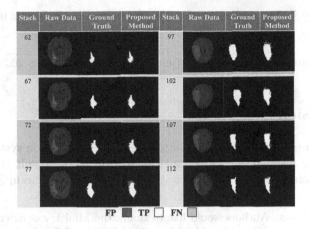

**Fig. 7.** Eight stacks of the evaluation results on a 3D brain MRI sample.

**Average Symmetric Surface Distance (ASSD).** Represents the average distance between the volumes which surface points are averaged over both directions. Defining two sets of surface points $X$ and $Y$, the average surface distance ($ASD$) is represented the following equation:

$$ASD(X,Y) = \frac{\sum_{x \in X} \min_{y \in Y} D(x,y)}{|X|},$$

*where $D(x,y)$ is the Euclidean distance between the points $x$ and $y$.*

After we obtain the equation of the average surface distance, we can apply this equation to calculate the average symmetric surface distance ($ASSD$) which is represented the following equation:

$$ASSD(x,y) = \frac{ASD(x,y) + ASD(y,x)}{2}, \quad ASD(x,y) \neq ASD(y,x).$$

**Hausdorff Distance (HD).** Represents the maximum distance or outlier between two volumes $X$ and $Y$ when multiple objects are considered. It is represented the following equation:

$$HD(x,y) = \max \left\{ \max_{x \in X} \min_{y \in Y} D(x,y), \max_{y \in Y} \min_{x \in X} D(y,x) \right\}.$$

In the Table 3, our proposed method successfully detect 15 three-dimensional Brain MR images in the testing data which have 36 three-dimensional Brain MR images, and the evaluation value of the $ASSD$, $DC$ and $HD$ are $7.59 \pm 6.24$ (mm), $0.16 \pm 0.26$ and $38.54 \pm 20.36$ (mm).

**Table 3.** The evaluation of the result images for the testing data

| Data | Cases | ASSD | DC | HD |
|------|-------|------|-----|-----|
| Testing data | 15/36 | 7.59 ± 6.24 (mm) | 0.16 ± 0.26 | 38.54 ± 20.36 (mm) |

# 4    Conclusion

We have presented a fully automatic stroke lesion segmentation system using 3D brain magnetic resonance (MR) data. The section of the result show that the presented system is capable to detect stroke lesion from 3D brain MRI data.

**Acknowledgments.** Authors would like to thank the Ministry of Science and Technology of Taiwan under Grant No. MOST104-2221-E-011-085 for the financial support.

# References

1. Burger, W., Burge, M.J.: Digital Image Processing - An Algorithmic Introduction Using Java. Springer, Heidelberg (2008)
2. Binmore, K., Davies, J.: Calculus Concepts and Methods. Cambridge University Press, Cambridge (2007)
3. Feichtinger, H.G., Strohmer, T.: Gabor Analysis Algorithms: Theory and Applications. Birkhuser, Basel (1999)
4. Koenderink, J.J., van Doorn, A.J.: Representation of local geometry in the visual system. Biol. Cybern. **55**(6), 367–375 (1987)
5. Lindeberg, T.: Scale-Space Theory in Computer Vision. Kluwer Academic Publishers, Berlin (1994)
6. Marr, D.C., Hildreth, E.: Theory of edge detection. In: Proceedings of the Royal Society of London, vol. B-207, no. 1167, pp. 187–217. February 1980
7. Sonka, M., Hlavac, V., Boyle, R.: Image Processing Analysis, and Machine Vision, 2nd edn. PWS Publishing, Boston (1999)
8. Rao, A.R., Schunck, B.G.: Computing oriented texture fields. CVGIP: Graph. Models Image Process. **53**(2), 157–185 (1991)
9. Weickert, J.: Coherence-enhancing diffusion filtering. Int. J. Comput. Vision **31**(2/3), 111–127 (1999)
10. Breiman, L.: Random forests. Mach. Learn. **45**(1), 5–32 (2001)
11. Wang, C.-W., Gosno, E., Li, Y.: Fully automatic, robust 3D registration of serial-section microscopic images. Sci. Rep. **5**, 15051 (2015)

# Segmentation of Ischemic Stroke Lesions in Multi-spectral MR Images Using Weighting Suppressed FCM and Three Phase Level Set

Chaolu Feng[1,2]([✉]), Dazhe Zhao[1,2], and Min Huang[1,3]

[1] School of Computer Science and Engineering, Northeastern University,
Shenyang 110819, Liaoning, China
[2] Key Laboratory of Medical Image Computing of Ministry of Education,
Northeastern University, Shenyang 110819, Liaoning, China
fengchl@ise.neu.edu.cn
[3] State Key Laboratory of Synthetical Automation for Process Industries,
Northeastern University, Shenyang 110819, Liaoning, China

**Abstract.** Accurate segmentation of ischemic lesions is still a challenging task. In this paper, we propose a framework to extract ischemic lesions from multi-spectral MR images. In the proposed framework, MR images of each modality are first segmented into brain tissues and ischemic lesions by weighting suppressed fuzzy c-means. Preliminary lesion segmentation results are then fused among all the imaging modalities by majority voting. The fused segmentation results are finally refined by a three phase level set method. The level set formulation is defined on multi-spectral images with the capability of dealing with intensity inhomogeneities. The proposed framework has been applied to the MICCAI 2015 ISLES challenge. According to the ranking rules of the challenge, the proposed framework took the second place and the fourth place in sub-acute lesion segmentation and acute stroke estimation, respectively.

**Keywords:** Lesion segmentation · Fuzzy c-means · Label fusion · Level set

## 1 Introduction

Ischemic stroke generally manifests as a loss of neurological brain function due to the sudden loss of blood circulation to an area of the brain [15]. It is by far the most common type of stroke and has become to be the most frequent cause of permanent disability in adults worldwide and the third leading cause of death in industrialized countries [17]. Magnetic resonance imaging (MRI) has become the modality of choice for diagnosing and evaluating ischemic stroke in clinic due to its excellent soft tissue contrast and multi-spectral imaging capability [11]. As ischemic stroke lesions usually change over time and remote and secondary changes may also occur in response to the injury, it is therefore necessary to characterize the injury and changes with different acquisition parameters and distinctive spectral signatures [4].

© Springer International Publishing Switzerland 2016
A. Crimi et al. (Eds.): BrainLes 2015, LNCS 9556, pp. 233–245, 2016.
DOI: 10.1007/978-3-319-30858-6_20

In clinical practice, diffusion weighted imaging (DWI), T1-weighted (T1w) and T2-weighted (T2w) images, and fluid attenuated inversion recovery (FLAIR) images are often used to diagnose ischemic stroke, locate the lesions and monitor their progression [15]. In the acute phase of stroke, DWI is particularly sensitive to detect the anatomical location and infarcted territory of the lesions and reveal differentiation of brain tissues with hyperintense signal [5]. The lesions appear slightly to strongly hyperintense in T2w and FLAIR images for stroke in sub-acute stage, whereas they are decreasingly hyperintense in DWI images and hypointense in T1w images [13]. For chronic ischemic stroke, lesions appear as hyperintense in FLAIR images with some heterogeneity within the lesion due to ongoing gliosis and demyelination [14]. In contrast, intensities of ischemic lesions are hypointense in T1w images for stroke in the more chronic phase [9]. Figure 1 shows an example of intensity characteristics of ischemic stroke lesions that are in the sub-acute phase.

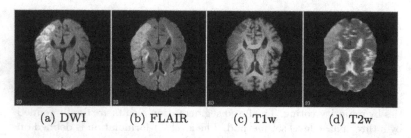

(a) DWI        (b) FLAIR        (c) T1w        (d) T2w

**Fig. 1.** Intensity characteristics of ischemic stroke lesion in different imaging modalities. Images come from http://www.isles-challenge.org/.

Above all, early diagnosis of ischemic lesions in multi-spectral magnetic resonance images is particularly important for ischemic stroke prevention and treatment [13]. But it is really challenging for neuro-radiologists to read the images slice-by-slice [18]. Although lesion segmentation is able to rescue radiologists from the labor of image reading, manual segmentation is tedious, time consuming, and prone to intraobserver and interobserver variability [11]. Therefore, a few semi-automatic or automatic segmentation methods have been proposed in the literature [6,7,11,16]. However, due to varieties of possible shapes and locations of ischemic lesions, and noise and intensity inhomogeneity in MR images, segmentation of ischemic lesions is still a challenging task [8].

In this paper, we propose a framework to automatically segment ischemic stroke lesions in multi-spectral images (e.g. DWI, T1w, T2w, and FLAIR). The rest of this paper is organized as follows. The proposed framework is described in Sect. 2. Experimental results and quantitative evaluation are given in Sect. 3. This paper is finally summarized and discussed in Sect. 4.

## 2    Method

In this paper, we suppose that the input images of different modalities have already been rigidly registered in the same coordinate system and non-brain tissues have already been removed from the images. Lesion segmentation is then performed by the proposed framework which consists of three major steps: (1) preliminary segmentation, (2) segmentation fusion, and (3) boundary refinement. More details will be given in the following subsections.

### 2.1    Preliminary Segmentation of Lesions and Normal Tissues

Given an image $I_i$ from the $i$-th imaging modality, the image characterizes an intrinsic physical property of human brain, which ideally takes a specific intensity for each type of brain tissue (white matter (WM), gray matter (GM), and cerebrospinal fluid (CSF)) and lesion. That is to say, the image $I_i$ approximately takes distinct constant values $c_{i1}$, $c_{i2}$, ..., and $c_{iN}$ for $N - 1$ brain tissues and the lesions in disjoint regions $\Omega_1$, $\Omega_2$, ..., and $\Omega_N$, i.e.

$$I_i(\mathbf{x}) \approx c_{ij} \quad \text{for} \quad \mathbf{x} \in \Omega_j. \tag{1}$$

where $j = 1, 2, ..., N$. Note that the variable $i$ takes all integers in the interval of $[1, L]$ where $L$ is the total number of imaging modalities. It is obvious that intensities in the set $I_{ij} = \{I_i(\mathbf{x}) : \mathbf{x} \in \Omega_j\}$ form a cluster with the cluster centroid $m_{ij} \approx c_{ij}$. This clustering property indicates that intensities in the image domain $\Omega$ can be classified into $N$ clusters.

To classify these intensities, we define

$$\mathcal{F}_i = \int_\Omega \sum_{j=1}^N \lambda_{ij} \parallel I_i(\mathbf{x}) - c_{ij} \parallel^2 u_{ij}^q(\mathbf{x}) d\mathbf{x} \tag{2}$$

where $\parallel * \parallel$ is the Euclidean distance between measured intensity $I_i(\mathbf{x})$ and the cluster centroid $c_{ij}$, $q$ is any real number that is not less than 1, $\lambda_{i1}$, $\lambda_{i2}$, ..., $\lambda_{iN}$ are positive weighting coefficients for the $N$ clusters, and $u_{ij}(\mathbf{x})$ is the membership function that indicates whether voxel $\mathbf{x}$ belongs to the $j$-th tissue. In fact, the smaller parameter $\lambda_{ij}$ is, the greater the $j$-cluster is, and vice versa.

It is obvious that the proposed method, which we call *weighting suppressed fuzzy c-means*, is a generalization of the standard fuzzy c-means. Note that the objective function defined above is the same with standard fuzzy c-means if $\lambda_{i1}$, $\lambda_{i2}$, ..., $\lambda_{iN}$ are all set to be 1. This objective function is minimized when high membership values are assigned to voxels, intensities of which are close to the centroid, and low membership values are assigned to the voxels if they are far from the centroids under the condition $\sum_{j=1}^N u_{ij}(\mathbf{x}) = 1$ where $u_{ij}(\mathbf{x}) \in [0, 1]$. For convenience, we represent the constants $c_{i1}$, $c_{i2}$, ..., and $c_{iN}$ with a vector $\mathbf{c}_i = (c_{i1}, c_{i2}, ..., c_{iN})$, the member functions $u_{i1}$, $u_{i2}$, ..., and $u_{iN}$ with a vector $\mathbf{u}_i = (u_{i1}, u_{i2}, ..., u_{iN})$. Thus, the vectors $\mathbf{c}_i$ and $\mathbf{u}_i$ are the variables of the energy function $\mathcal{F}_i$, which can therefore be written as $\mathcal{F}_i(\mathbf{c}_i, \mathbf{u}_i)$.

Energy minimization of $\mathcal{F}_i(\mathbf{c}_i, \mathbf{u}_i)$ can be achieved by alternately minimizing it with respect to each of its variables $\mathbf{c}_i$ and $\mathbf{u}_i$. For fixed $\mathbf{u}_i$, we minimize $\mathcal{F}_i(\mathbf{c}_i, \mathbf{u}_i)$ with respect to $\mathbf{c}_i$ by resolving $\frac{\partial \mathcal{F}_i(\mathbf{c}_i, \mathbf{u}_i)}{\partial \mathbf{c}_i} = \mathbf{0}$ where $\mathbf{0}$ is the constant vector with value 0. It is obvious that $\mathcal{F}_i(\mathbf{c}_i, \mathbf{u}_i)$ is minimized at $\hat{\mathbf{c}}_i = (\hat{c}_{i1}, \hat{c}_{i2}, ..., \hat{c}_{iN})$, given by

$$\hat{c}_{ij} = \frac{\int_\Omega I_i(\mathbf{x}) u_{ij}^q(\mathbf{x})}{\int_\Omega u_{ij}^q(\mathbf{x})} \tag{3}$$

where $j = 1, 2, ..., N$.

For the case $q > 1$, it can be shown that $\mathcal{F}_i(\mathbf{c}_i, \mathbf{u}_i)$ is minimized at $\hat{\mathbf{u}}_i(\mathbf{x}) = (\hat{u}_{i1}(\mathbf{x}), \hat{u}_{i2}(\mathbf{x}), ..., \hat{u}_{iN}(\mathbf{x}))$ for fixed $\mathbf{c}_i$, given by

$$\hat{u}_{ij}(\mathbf{x}) = \frac{\left(\lambda_{ij} \| I_i(\mathbf{x}) - c_{ij} \|^2\right)^{\frac{1}{1-q}}}{\sum_{k=1}^N \left(\lambda_{ik} \| I_i(\mathbf{x}) - c_{ik} \|^2\right)^{\frac{1}{1-q}}} \tag{4}$$

where $j = 1, 2, ..., N$.

For the case $q = 1$, it can be shown that the minimizer $\hat{\mathbf{u}}_i(\mathbf{x}) = (\hat{u}_{i1}(\mathbf{x}), \hat{u}_{i2}(\mathbf{x}), ..., \hat{u}_{iN}(\mathbf{x}))$ is given by

$$\hat{u}_{ij}(\mathbf{x}) = \begin{cases} 1, & j = j_{min}(\mathbf{x}) \\ 0, & j \neq j_{min}(\mathbf{x}) \end{cases} \quad j = 1, 2, ..., N \tag{5}$$

where

$$j_{min}(\mathbf{x}) = \underset{j}{argmin}\left(\lambda_{ij} \| I_i(\mathbf{x}) - c_{ij}\|^2\right). \tag{6}$$

In fact, segmentation of WM, GM, CSF, and stroke lesions in this step is performed in an iterative process, which will be described in detail in Sect. 2.4.

## 2.2 Fusion of Preliminary Segmentation Results of Lesions

Label fusion is one of the most important steps for multi-spectral segmentation due to its significance in merging useful knowledge of different labels [3]. In the literature, many efforts have already been devoted to developing effective and accurate label fusion strategies [2,3,12]. As one of the well known label fusion strategies, majority voting is much more straightforward and concise [1]. Therefore, majority voting is used in the proposed framework to fuse segmentation results of ischemic stroke lesions obtained by the above described fuzzy c-means method. The judge rule is that candidate voxels are regarded as lesions only if (1) they are considered as brain lesions in FLAIR images, and (2) they are viewed as brain lesions in more than 1 imaging modality beside FLAIR.

## 2.3 Boundary Refinement of Brain Lesions Using 3-Phase Level Set

Since miss- and over- segmentations may arise in the above mentioned two steps. A three phase level set method is proposed in this subsection as the third step to

refine segmentation boundaries of the lesions. The proposed method can be seen
as an extension of the local intensity clustering (LIC) model with the capability
of segmenting ischemic stroke lesions from multi-spectral MR images [10].

Before defining the energy formulation of the proposed level set method, we
first view inhomogeneous intensities of an observed MR brain image $I_i$ coming
from the $i$-th imaging modality, which is defined on a continuous domain $\Omega \subset R^3$,
as a product of the true image $J_i$ and the bias field $b_i$, i.e.,

$$I_i(\mathbf{x}) = b_i(\mathbf{x})J_i(\mathbf{x}) + n_i(\mathbf{x}) \tag{7}$$

where $\mathbf{x} \in \Omega$ and $n_i$ is the zero-mean additive noise.

Consider a relatively small spherical neighborhood with a radius $\rho$ centered
at a given point $\mathbf{y} \in \Omega$, defined by $\mathcal{O}_\mathbf{y} \triangleq \{\mathbf{x} : \mid \mathbf{x} - \mathbf{y} \mid \leq \rho\}$. The bias field
$b_i$ in the neighborhood can be ignored due to its slowly and smoothly varying
property. Taking into account the constant intensity $c_{ij}$ of the true image $J_i$ in
$\Omega_j$ as mentioned in Sect. 2.1, we obtain

$$b_i(\mathbf{x})J_i(\mathbf{x}) \approx b_i(\mathbf{y})c_{ij} \quad \text{for} \quad \mathbf{x} \in \Omega_j \cap \mathcal{O}_\mathbf{y}. \tag{8}$$

This local intensity clustering property allows us to apply the standard K-means
algorithm in the following continuous form to classify these local inhomogeneous
intensities in the neighborhood $\mathcal{O}_\mathbf{y}$. Taking all images of the $L$ imaging modalities
into account, we define

$$\mathcal{E}_y = \sum_{j=1}^{N} \gamma_j \int_{\mathcal{O}_y} \left( \sum_{i=1}^{L} \chi_i \parallel I_i(\mathbf{x}) - b_i(\mathbf{y})c_{ij} \parallel^2 \right) u_j(\mathbf{x})d\mathbf{x} \tag{9}$$

where $\gamma_j$ is a weighting coefficient used to control size of the $j$-th tissue, $\chi_i$ is
a weighting coefficient for images from the $i$-th imaging modality, and $u_j$ is the
binary membership function of $\Omega_j$. On account of the inherent property of the
membership function $u_j$ in representing $\Omega_j$, $\mathcal{E}_y$ can be rewritten as

$$\mathcal{E}_\mathbf{y} = \sum_{j=1}^{N} \gamma_j \int_{\Omega_j} K_\sigma(\mathbf{x} - \mathbf{y}) \left( \sum_{i=1}^{L} \chi_i \parallel I_i(\mathbf{x}) - b_i(\mathbf{y})c_{ij} \parallel^2 \right) d\mathbf{x} \tag{10}$$

where $K_\sigma$ is a nonnegative kernel function with the property $\int_{|\mathbf{u}|\leq\rho} K_\rho(\mathbf{u}) = 1$
and $K_\rho(\mathbf{u}) = 0$ for $\mathbf{u} \notin \mathcal{O}_y$.

To ensure the partition $\{\Omega_j\}_{j=1}^{N}$ of the entire domain $\Omega$ to be the one such
that $\mathcal{E}_y$ is minimized for all $\mathbf{y}$ in $\Omega$, we minimize the integral of $\mathcal{E}_y$ with respect
to $\mathbf{y}$ over the entire image domain $\Omega$ and define

$$\mathcal{E} = \int_\Omega \left( \sum_{j=1}^{N} \gamma_j \int_{\Omega_j} K_\sigma(\mathbf{x} - \mathbf{y}) \left( \sum_{i=1}^{L} \chi_i \parallel I_i(\mathbf{x}) - b_i(\mathbf{y})c_{ij} \parallel^2 \right) d\mathbf{x} \right) d\mathbf{y}. \tag{11}$$

As our goal is to segment brain lesions, we consider the lesions as one region,
brain tissues (WM, GM, and CSF) as the second region, and the background as

the third region. Let $H$ be the Heaviside function and $\phi_1$ and $\phi_2$ be two level set functions both defined on $\Omega$. We therefore use $M_1(\phi_1, \phi_2) = (1 - H(\phi_1))(1 - H(\phi_2))$, $M_2(\phi_1, \phi_2) = H(\phi_1)(1 - H(\phi_2))$, and $M_3(\phi_1, \phi_2) = H(\phi_2)$ to represent these three regions, respectively, and rewrite $\mathcal{E}$ as

$$\mathcal{E} = \int_\Omega \left( \sum_{j=1}^N \gamma_j e_j(\mathbf{x}) M_j(\phi_1(\mathbf{x}), \phi_2(\mathbf{x})) \right) d\mathbf{x} \tag{12}$$

where

$$e_j(\mathbf{x}) = \int_\Omega K_\sigma(\mathbf{x} - \mathbf{y}) \left( \sum_{i=1}^L \chi_i \parallel I_i(\mathbf{x}) - b_i(\mathbf{y}) c_{ij} \parallel^2 \right) d\mathbf{y} \tag{13}$$

For convenience, we represent the bias field $b_1$, $b_2$, ..., $b_L$ with a vector $\mathbf{b} = (b_1, b_2, ..., b_L)$ and further rewrite $\mathbf{c}_1$, $\mathbf{c}_2$, ..., and $\mathbf{c}_L$ into a new vector $\mathbf{c} = (\mathbf{c}_1, \mathbf{c}_2, ..., \mathbf{c}_L)$. Thus, the level set functions $\phi_1$ and $\phi_2$ and the vectors $\mathbf{b}$ and $\mathbf{c}$ are variables of the energy $\mathcal{E}$, which can therefore be written as $\mathcal{E}(\phi_1, \phi_2, \mathbf{b}, \mathbf{c})$.

The energy $\mathcal{E}(\phi_1, \phi_2, \mathbf{b}, \mathbf{c})$ defined above is used as the data term of the final energy functional of the proposed level set formulation, defined by

$$\mathcal{F}(\phi_1, \phi_2, \mathbf{b}, \mathbf{c}) = \mathcal{E}(\phi_1, \phi_2, \mathbf{b}, \mathbf{c}) + \mathcal{P}(\phi_1, \phi_2) + \mathcal{L}(\phi_1, \phi_2). \tag{14}$$

where $\mathcal{P}(\phi_1, \phi_2)$ and $\mathcal{L}(\phi_1, \phi_2)$ are the regularization term and arc length term. These two terms are introduced to maintain the regularity of the level set functions and smooth the 0-level set contours of the level set functions, defined by

$$\mathcal{P}(\phi_1, \phi_2) = \mu_1 \int \frac{1}{2} (\mid \nabla\phi_1(\mathbf{x}) \mid -1)^2 d\mathbf{x} + \mu_2 \int \frac{1}{2} (\mid \nabla\phi_2(\mathbf{x}) \mid -1)^2 d\mathbf{x} \tag{15}$$

and

$$\mathcal{L}(\phi_1, \phi_2) = \nu_1 \int \mid \nabla H(\phi_1(\mathbf{x})) \mid d\mathbf{x} + \nu_2 \int \mid \nabla H(\phi_2(\mathbf{x})) \mid d\mathbf{x} \tag{16}$$

where $\mu_1$, $\mu_2$, $\nu_1$ and $\nu_2$ are weighting coefficients.

Energy minimization of $\mathcal{F}(\phi_1, \phi_2, \mathbf{b}, \mathbf{c})$ can be achieved by alternately minimizing it with respect to each of its variables. For fixed $\mathbf{b}$ and $\mathbf{c}$, we minimize the final energy functional $\mathcal{F}$ using standard gradient descent method and obtain

$$\frac{\partial \phi_1}{\partial t} = \delta(\phi_1)(1 - H(\phi_2))(\lambda_1 e_1 - \lambda_2 e_2)$$
$$+ \mu_1 \left( \nabla^2 \phi_1 - \text{div}\left( \frac{\nabla\phi_1}{\mid \nabla\phi_1 \mid} \right) \right) + \nu_1 \delta(\phi_1) \text{div}\left( \frac{\nabla\phi_1}{\mid \nabla\phi_1 \mid} \right) \tag{17}$$

and

$$\frac{\partial \phi_2}{\partial t} = \delta(\phi_2)(\lambda_1 e_1(1 - H(\phi_1)) + \lambda_2 e_2 H(\phi_1) - \lambda_3 e_3)$$
$$+ \mu_2 \left( \nabla^2 \phi_2 - \text{div}\left( \frac{\nabla\phi_2}{\mid \nabla\phi_2 \mid} \right) \right) + \nu_2 \delta(\phi_2) \text{div}\left( \frac{\nabla\phi_2}{\mid \nabla\phi_2 \mid} \right). \tag{18}$$

For fixed $\phi_1$, $\phi_2$, and $\mathbf{b}$, the optimal $\tilde{\mathbf{c}} = (\tilde{\mathbf{c}}_1, \tilde{\mathbf{c}}_2, ..., \tilde{\mathbf{c}}_L)$ where $\tilde{\mathbf{c}}_i = (\tilde{c}_{i1}, \tilde{c}_{i2}, ..., \tilde{c}_{iN})$ and $i = 1, 2, ..., L$ minimizes the final energy functional $\mathcal{F}(\phi_1, \phi_2, \mathbf{b}, \mathbf{c})$, given by

$$c_{ij} = \frac{\int I_i(\mathbf{x}) M_j(\phi_1(\mathbf{x}), \phi_2(\mathbf{x}))(b_i * K_\sigma)(\mathbf{x}) dx}{\int M_j(\phi_1(\mathbf{x}), \phi_2(\mathbf{x}))(b_i^2 * K_\sigma)(\mathbf{x}) dx}, \quad j = 1, 2, ..., N. \tag{19}$$

For fixed $\phi_1$, $\phi_2$, and $\mathbf{c}$, the optimal $\tilde{\mathbf{b}} = (\tilde{b}_1, \tilde{b}_2, ..., \tilde{b}_L)$ that minimizes the final energy functional $\mathcal{F}(\phi_1, \phi_2, \mathbf{b}, \mathbf{c})$ is given by

$$\tilde{b}_i = \frac{\left( I_i \sum_{j=1}^{N} c_{ij} M_j(\phi_1, \phi_2) \right) * K_\sigma}{\sum_{j=1}^{N} c_{ij}^2 M_j(\phi) * K_\sigma}, \quad i = 1, 2, ..., L. \tag{20}$$

## 2.4 Implementation

In the implementation of the proposed framework, the choice of $K$ is important but flexible as long as it is a normalized even function and satisfies the property that $K(\mathbf{u}) \geq K(\mathbf{v})$, if $| \mathbf{u} | < | \mathbf{v} |$, and $\lim_{|\mathbf{u}| \to \infty} K(\mathbf{u}) = 0$. In this paper, an averaging filter with size of $\rho$ is chosen as $K$. In our numerical implementation, the stepped Heaviside function $H$ is approximated by a smoothed Heaviside function $H_\epsilon$ with $\epsilon = 1$, defined by $H_\epsilon(x) = \frac{1}{2} \left[ 1 + \frac{2}{\pi} \arctan \left( \frac{x}{\epsilon} \right) \right]$. The derivative of $H_\epsilon$ is used to approximate the Dirac delta function $\delta$, which can be written as $\delta_\epsilon(x) = H'_\epsilon(x) = \frac{1}{\pi} \frac{\epsilon}{\epsilon^2 + x^2}$.

The implementation of the proposed framework can be straightforwardly expressed in the following steps.

- Step 1. Segment images of each modality separately using the weighting suppressed fuzzy c-means as described in Sect. 2.1. Update each variable of the energy function defined in Eq. (2) iteratively until the iteration number exceeds a predetermined maximum number or convergence criterion has been reached.
- Step 2. Fuse segmentation results of different modalities using the voting strategy as described in Sect. 2.2.
- Step 3. Refine fused segmentation results using the three phase level set method as described in Sect. 2.3 where the level set functions $\phi_1$ and $\phi_2$ are initialized to the results of Step 2. Update each variables of energy functional defined in Eq. (14) iteratively until the solution is stable or the iteration number exceeds a predetermined maximum number.

## 3 Results

To evaluate the proposed framework, we participated in the ischemic stroke lesion segmentation (ISLES) challenge of MICCAI 2015 and applied it to images of the challenge. Figure 2 shows a segmentation example of the proposed framework.

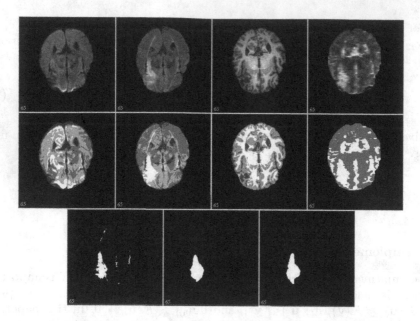

**Fig. 2.** Segmentation results of the proposed framework on images from four different imaging modalities (http://www.isles-challenge.org/). Orignal images and corresponding preliminary segmentations are given in the 1st and 2nd rows. Fusion result, final segmentation, and the ground truth are given from left to right in the 3rd row.

### 3.1    Dataset and Parameter Set

The ISLES challenge consists of two sub-challenges: sub-acute ischemic stroke lesion segmentation (SISS) and acute stroke outcome/penumbra estimation (SPES). Dataset of the former includes 28 training cases and 36 testing cases, whereas there are 30 training and 20 testing cases in the latter one. The images are all from MRI and modalities DWI, T1w, T2w, and FLAIR are adopted by the first sub-challenge SISS. In contrast, T1c, T2, DWI, CBF, CBV, TTP, Tmax images are provided by the second sub-challenge SPES. The images are all skull-stripped and have been re-sampled to an isotropic spacing of $1^3$ mm (SISS) and $2^3$ mm (SPES) and have also been co-registered to the FLAIR (SISS) and T1w contrast (SPES) sequences, respectively.

For SISS, the number of imaging modalities $L$ are set to be 4 with DWI, T1w, T2w, and FLAIR as viewed as the 1st, 2nd, 3rd, and 4th imaging modalities, respectively. When the images are segmented by the proposed weighting suppressed fuzzy c-means separately, we set $N = 4, 3, 2, 4$, respectively. For each imaging modality, e.g., the $i$-th modality, elements of the cluster centroid vector $\mathbf{c}_i$ are initialized with equally spaced intensities. The other weighting coefficients of the proposed weighting suppressed fuzzy c-means are set to $\lambda_{11} = \lambda_{12} = \lambda_{13} = \lambda_{14} = 1.0$, $\lambda_{21} = 1.0, \lambda_{22} = 0.4, \lambda_{23} = 1.5, \lambda_{31} = 1.0, \lambda_{32} = 0.5$, and $\lambda_{41} = \lambda_{42} = \lambda_{43} = \lambda_{44} = 1.0$. The level set function in the third step was initialized as a binary step function, defined by $\phi(\mathbf{x}) = -c$ for $\mathbf{x}$ inside the initial zero-level contour of $\phi$ and $\phi(\mathbf{x}) = c$ otherwise. Unless otherwise specified, we set $c = 10$, $\gamma_1 = \dots = \gamma_L = 1.0$, $\chi_1 = \dots = \chi_L = 1.0$, $\mu_1 = \dots = \mu_L = 1.0$, $\nu_1 = \dots = \nu_L = 0.1 \times 255 \times 255$, $\Delta t = 0.1$, and $\rho = 6$ in this paper. Note that these parameters can be set to be values learning from training sets.

We have also applied the proposed framework to sub-challenge SPES. We set $N = 3, 5, 3$ for preliminarily segmenting images of modalities CBF, TTP, Tmax, respectively. All weighting coefficients of the proposed weighting suppressed fuzzy c-means are set to be 1.0. As the ground truth provided by the organizers are not smooth enough and there are holes in the lesion-like regions, fusion results obtained by the proposed framework are considered as final segmentation results.

## 3.2 Evaluation Measures

To evaluate segmentation accuracy of automatic methods that participated in the challenge quantitatively, segmentation results are compared with the reference ground-truth in terms of Dice's coefficient (DC), average symmetric surface distance (ASSD), and Hausdorff distance (HD).

It is well known that the DC is defined as twice of the quotient between intersection size of a pairwise variable and sum of their sizes where the variables are a segmentation result $B$ and the ground truth $A$ for image segmentation, which can therefore be written as

$$DC = \frac{2\,|\,A \cap B\,|}{|\,A\,| + |\,B\,|} \tag{21}$$

where $\cap$ is the intersection operator. It is obvious that values of $DC$ are in the interval of $[0, 1]$ with a higher value indicating a better match between $A$ and $B$.

Considering two sets of surface points that constitute the segmentation result $B$ and the ground truth $A$, the average surface distance (ASD) is given by

$$ASD(A, B) = \frac{\sum_{a \in A} min_{b \in B}\, d(a, b)}{|\,A\,|} \tag{22}$$

where $d(a, b)$ is the Euclidean distance between the points of $a$ and $b$. Since $ASD(A, B) \neq ASD(B, A)$, the ASSD can be then defined by

$$ASD(A, B) = \frac{ASD(A, B) + ASD(B, A)}{2}. \tag{23}$$

Note that that ASSD is given in $mm$, a lower value indicating a better match between the ground truth $A$ and the segmentation result $B$.

The HD denotes the maximum distance between the obtained volume surface points $B$ and corresponding points in the ground truth $A$. It can be defined by

$$HD(A, B) = max\{\max_{a \in A}(\min_{b \in B} d((a, b))), \max_{b \in B}(\min_{a \in A} d((b, a)))\}. \tag{24}$$

Thus, HD is given in $mm$ and a smaller HD value indicates a better agreement of the segmentation result with the ground truth.

### 3.3   Quantitative Evaluation of the Proposed Framework

As shown in Table 1, 16 teams from all over the world participated in the challenge, where our team information are emphasized in bold font.

Quantitative comparison of the proposed framework with the other participants' methods on images from sub-challenges SISS and SPES are given in Tables 2 and 3, respectively. It is obvious that the proposed framework is the

**Table 1.** Participants of the ISLES challenge of MICCAI 2015.

| Team name | Team leader | Affiliation |
|---|---|---|
| UK-Imp1 | Chen, Liang | Biomedical Image Analysis Group, Imperial College London |
| CA-USher | Dutil, Francis | Université de Sherbrooke, Sherbrooke |
| **CN-Neu** | **Feng, Chaolu** | **College of Inform. Science and Engineering, Northeastern University, Shenyang** |
| DE-Dkfz | Goetz, Michael | Junior Group Medical Image Computing, German Cancer Research Center (DKFZ), Heidelberg |
| BE-Kul1 | Haeck, Tom | ESAT/PSI, Department of Electrical Engineering, KU Leuven |
| FI-Hus | Halme, Hanna | HUS Medical Imaging Center, University of Helsinki and Helsinki University Hospital |
| CA-McGill | Jesson, Andrew | Centre for Intelligent Machines, McGill University |
| UK-Imp2 | Kamnitsas, Konstantinos | Biomedical Image Analysis Group, Imperial College London |
| SE-Cth | Mahmood, Qaiser | Signals and Systems, Chalmers University of Technology, Gothenburg |
| DE-UzL | Maier, Oskar | Institute of Medical Informatics, Universität zu Lübeck |
| US-Jhu | Muschelli, John | Johns Hopkins Bloomberg School of Public Health |
| US-Odu | Reza, Syed | Vision Lab, Old Dominion University, Norfolk |
| BE-Kul2 | Robben, David | ESAT/PSI, Department of Electrical Engineering, KU Leuven |
| TW-Ntust | Wang, Ching-Wei | Graduate Institute of Biomedical Engineering, National Taiwan University of Science and Technology |
| DE-Ukf | Kellner, Elias | Department of Radiology, Medical Physics, University Medical Center Freiburg |
| CH-Insel | McKinley, Richard | Department of Diagnostic and Interventional Neuroradiology, Inselspital, Bern University Hospital |

**Table 2.** Accuracy comparison of segmentation results of the proposed framework with the other participants' methods on images from sub-challenge SISS.

| Place | Rank | Team | Cases | ASSD | DC | HD |
|---|---|---|---|---|---|---|
| 1st | 3.25 | UK-Imp2 (Kamnitsas, Konstantinos) | 34/36 | 5.96 ± 9.38 | 0.59 ± 0.31 | 37.88 ± 30.06 |
| **2nd** | **3.82** | **CN-Neu (Feng, Chaolu)** | **32/36** | **3.27 ± 3.62** | **0.55 ± 0.30** | **19.78 ± 15.65** |
| 3rd | 5.63 | FI-Hus (Halme, Hanna) | 31/36 | 8.05 ± 9.57 | 0.47 ± 0.32 | 40.23 ± 33.17 |
| 4th | 6.40 | US-Odu (Reza, Syed) | 33/36 | 6.24 ± .21 | 0.43 ± 0.27 | 41.76 ± 25.11 |
| 5th | 6.67 | BE-Kul2 (Robben, David) | 33/36 | 11.27 ± 10.17 | 0.43 ± 0.30 | 60.79 ± 31.14 |
| 6th | 6.70 | DE-UzL (Maier, Oskar) | 31/36 | 10.21 ± 9.44 | 0.42 ± 0.33 | 49.17 ± 29.6 |
| 7th | 7.07 | US-Jhu (Muschelli, John) | 33/36 | 11.54 ± 11.14 | 0.42 ± 0.32 | 62.43 ± 28.64 |
| 8th | 7.54 | UK-Imp1 (Chen, Liang) | 34/36 | 11.71 ± 10.12 | 0.44 ± 0.30 | 70.61 ± 24.59 |
| 9th | 7.66 | CA-USher (Dutil, Francis) | 27/36 | 9.25 ± 9.79 | 0.35 ± 0.32 | 44.91 ± 32.53 |
| 10th | 7.92 | BE-Kul1 (Haeck, Tom) | 30/36 | 12.24 ± 13.49 | 0.37 ± 0.33 | 58.65 ± 29.99 |
| 11th | 7.97 | CA-McGill (Jesson, Andrew) | 31/36 | 11.04 ± 13.68 | 0.32 ± 0.26 | 40.42 ± 26.98 |
| 12th | 9.18 | SE-Cth (Mahmood, Qaiser) | 30/36 | 10.00 ± 6.61 | 0.38 ± 0.28 | 72.16 ± 17.32 |
| 13th | 9.21 | DE-Dkfz (Goetz, Michael) | 35/36 | 14.20 ± 10.41 | 0.33 ± 0.28 | 77.95 ± 22.13 |
| 14th | 10.99 | TW-Ntust (Wang, Ching-Wei) | 15/36 | 7.59 ± 6.24 | 0.16 ± 0.26 | 38.54 ± 20.36 |

**Table 3.** Accuracy comparison of segmentation results of the proposed framework with the other participants' methods on images from sub-challenge SPES.

| Place | Rank | Team | Cases | ASSD | DC |
|-------|------|------|-------|------|-----|
| 1st | 2.02 | CH-Insel (McKinley, Richard) | 20/20 | $1.65 \pm 1.40$ | $0.82 \pm 0.08$ |
| 2nd | 2.20 | DE-UzL (Maier, Oskar) | 20/20 | $1.36 \pm 0.74$ | $0.81 \pm 0.09$ |
| 3rd | 3.92 | BE-Kul2 (Robben, David) | 20/20 | $2.77 \pm 3.27$ | $0.78 \pm 0.09$ |
| **4th** | **4.05** | **CN-Neu (Feng, Chaolu)** | **20/20** | **$2.29 \pm 1.76$** | **$0.76 \pm 0.09$** |
| 5th | 4.60 | DE-Ukf (Keller, Elias) | 20/20 | $2.44 \pm 1.93$ | $0.73 \pm 0.13$ |
| 6th | 5.15 | BE-Kul1 (Haeck, Tom) | 20/20 | $4.00 \pm 3.39$ | $0.67 \pm 0.24$ |
| 7th | 6.05 | CA-USher (Dutil, Francis) | 20/20 | $5.53 \pm 7.59$ | $0.54 \pm 0.26$ |

best in terms of ASSD and HD and the second best in DC for sub-challenge SISS. According to the ranking rules of the challenge, which can be found on the website http://www.isles-challenge.org/, the proposed framework finally took the second and fourth places for SISS and SPES, respectively.

## 4   Conclusion and Discussions

An ischemic lesion segmentation framework has been proposed, which consists of preliminary segmentation, label fusion, and boundary refinement. As most of level set methods are usually time consuming and sensitive to initialization, an improved fuzzy c-means method is first used to coarsely extract ischemic lesions from normal brain tissues. The preliminary segmentation results are only used as initialization of the level set method. Therefore, there is no need to introduce bias correction rules in the first step in consideration of saving time. Quantitative evaluation and comparison with methods that participated in the ISLES challenge have demonstrated advantages of the proposed framework in terms of accuracy.

Note that as the zero level contour of $\phi_2$ is used to represent boundaries between brain tissues and the background, update of $\phi_2$ is not important for seeking lesion boundaries. Therefore, $\phi_2$ can be fixed in the evolution of $\phi_1$ to improve computational efficiency. In addition, narrow band implementation can be used to further improve time performance of the proposed level set method.

In the future, we will further improve and validate the proposed method on more datasets, such as MICCAI 2008 lesion segmentation data.

**Acknowledgement.** This work was supported by the Fundamental Research Funds for the Central Universities of China under grant N140403006, N140402003, and N140407001, the Postdoctoral Scientific Research Funds of Northeastern University under grant No. 20150310, the National Science Foundation for Distinguished Young Scholars of China under Grant Nos. 71325002 and 61225012, the Chinese National Natural Science Foundation under grant Nos. 61172002 and 71071028, the National Key

Technology Research and Development Program of the Ministry of Science and Technology of China under grant 2014BAI17B01, and the Fundamental Research Funds for State Key Laboratory of Synthetical Automation for Process Industries under Grant No. 2013ZCX11.

# References

1. Artaechevarria, X., Munoz-Barrutia, A., Ortiz-de Solórzano, C.: Combination strategies in multi-atlas image segmentation: application to brain MR data. IEEE Trans. Med. Imaging **28**(8), 1266–1277 (2009)
2. Asman, A.J., Landman, B.A.: Non-local statistical label fusion for multi-atlas segmentation. Med. Image Anal. **17**(2), 194–208 (2013)
3. Chakravarty, M.M., Steadman, P., Eede, M.C., Calcott, R.D., Gu, V., Shaw, P., Raznahan, A., Collins, D.L., Lerch, J.P.: Performing label-fusion-based segmentation using multiple automatically generated templates. Hum. Brain Mapp. **34**(10), 2635–2654 (2013)
4. Chyzhyk, D., Dacosta-Aguayo, R., Mataró, M., Graña, M.: An active learning approach for stroke lesion segmentation on multimodal MRI data. Neurocomputing **150**, 26–36 (2015)
5. DeIpolyi, A.R., Wu, O., Macklin, E.A., Schaefer, P.W., Schwamm, L.H., Gilberto Gonzalez, R., Copen, W.A.: Reliability of cerebral blood volume maps as a substitute for diffusion-weighted imaging in acute ischemic stroke. J. Magn. Reson. Imaging **36**(5), 1083–1087 (2012)
6. Feng, C., Li, C., Zhao, D., Davatzikos, C., Litt, H.: Segmentation of the left ventricle using distance regularized two-layer level set approach. In: Mori, K., Sakuma, I., Sato, Y., Barillot, C., Navab, N. (eds.) MICCAI 2013, Part I. LNCS, vol. 8149, pp. 477–484. Springer, Heidelberg (2013)
7. Feng, C., Zhao, D., Huang, M.: Image segmentation using CUDA accelerated non-local means denoising and bias correction embedded fuzzy c-means (BCEFCM). Signal Process. **122**, 164–189 (2015). http://dx.doi.org/10.1016/j.sigpro.2015.12.007
8. de Haan, B., Clas, P., Juenger, H., Wilke, M., Karnath, H.O.: Fast semi-automated lesion demarcation in stroke. NeuroImage Clin. **9**, 69–74 (2015)
9. Lee, W.J., Choi, H.S., Jang, J., Sung, J., Kim, T.W., Koo, J., Shin, Y.S., Jung, S.L., Ahn, K.J., Kim, B.S.: Non-stenotic intracranial arteries have atherosclerotic changes in acute ischemic stroke patients: a 3T MRI study. Neuroradiology **57**, 1007–1013 (2015)
10. Li, C., Huang, R., Ding, Z., Gatenby, J.C., Metaxas, D.N., Gore, J.C.: A level set method for image segmentation in the presence of intensity inhomogeneities with application to MRI. IEEE Trans. Image Process. **20**(7), 2007–2016 (2011)
11. Lladó, X., Oliver, A., Cabezas, M., Freixenet, J., Vilanova, J.C., Quiles, A., Valls, L., Ramió-Torrentà, L., Rovira, À.: Segmentation of multiple sclerosis lesions in brain MRI: a review of automated approaches. Inf. Sci. **186**(1), 164–185 (2012)
12. Magon, S., Chakravarty, M.M., Amann, M., Weier, K., Naegelin, Y., Andelova, M., Radue, E.W., Stippich, C., Lerch, J.P., Kappos, L., et al.: Label-fusion-segmentation and deformation-based shape analysis of deep gray matter in multiple sclerosis: the impact of thalamic subnuclei on disability. Hum. Brain Mapp. **35**(8), 4193–4203 (2014)

13. Maier, O., Wilms, M., von der Gablentz, J., Krämer, U.M., Münte, T.F., Handels, H.: Extra tree forests for sub-acute ischemic stroke lesion segmentation in MR sequences. J. Neurosci. Methods **240**, 89–100 (2015)
14. Mitra, J., et al.: Classification forests and markov random field to segment chronic ischemic infarcts from multimodal MRI. In: Shen, L., Liu, T., Yap, P.-T., Huang, H., Shen, D., Westin, C.-F. (eds.) MBIA 2013. LNCS, vol. 8159, pp. 107–118. Springer, Heidelberg (2013)
15. Mitra, J., Bourgeat, P., Fripp, J., Ghose, S., Rose, S., Salvado, O., Connelly, A., Campbell, B., Palmer, S., Sharma, G., et al.: Lesion segmentation from multimodal MRI using random forest following ischemic stroke. NeuroImage **98**, 324–335 (2014)
16. Mortazavi, D., Kouzani, A.Z., Soltanian-Zadeh, H.: Segmentation of multiple sclerosis lesions in MR images: a review. Neuroradiology **54**(4), 299–320 (2012)
17. Rekik, I., Allassonnière, S., Carpenter, T.K., Wardlaw, J.M.: Medical image analysis methods in MR/CT-imaged acute-subacute ischemic stroke lesion: segmentation, prediction and insights into dynamic evolution simulation models. A critical appraisal. Neuroimage Clin. **1**(1), 164–178 (2012)
18. Sridharan, R., et al.: Quantification and analysis of large multimodal clinical image studies: application to stroke. In: Shen, L., Liu, T., Yap, P.-T., Huang, H., Shen, D., Westin, C.-F. (eds.) MBIA 2013. LNCS, vol. 8159, pp. 18–30. Springer, Heidelberg (2013)

# ISLES Challenge 2015: Automated Model-Based Segmentation of Ischemic Stroke in MR Images

Tom Haeck[1,2](✉), Frederik Maes[1,2], and Paul Suetens[1,2,3]

[1] Department of Electrical Engineering, ESAT/PSI, KU Leuven, Leuven, Belgium
tom.haeck@esat.kuleuven.be
[2] Medical Imaging Research Center, UZ Leuven, Leuven, Belgium
[3] Medical Information Technologies Department, IMinds, Ghent, Belgium

**Abstract.** We present a novel fully-automated generative ischemic stroke lesion segmentation method that can be applied to individual patient images without need for a training data set. An Expectation Maximization-approach is used for estimating intensity models for both normal and pathological tissue. The segmentation is represented by a level-set that is iteratively updated to label voxels as either normal or pathological, based on which intensity model explains the voxels' intensity the best. A convex level-set formulation is adopted, that eliminates the need for manual initialization of the level-set. The performance of the method for segmenting the ischemic stroke is summarized by an average Dice score of $0.78 \pm 0.08$ and $0.53 \pm 0.26$ for the SPES and SISS 2015 training data set respectively and $0.67 \pm 0.24$ and $0.37 \pm 0.33$ for the test data set.

## 1 Introduction

In ischemic stroke, blood supply to the brain is lowered due to an artery occlusion [1]. Depending on the severity and the duration of the blood supply deficiency, damage to the brain tissue is reversible (penumbral tissue) or irreversible (infarctic core tissue). MR image analysis techniques can be used to measure the extent of the lesion and to distinguish between core and penumbral tissue. The MICCAI Ischemic Stroke Lesion Segmentation (ISLES) challenge comprises the automatic segmentation of ischemic stroke lesions acquired in the sub-acute stroke development stage (SISS) and automatic segmentation of acute ischemic stroke lesions for stroke outcome prediction (SPES).

Discriminative segmentation methods require a set of manually annotated training images from which the appearance of the brain structures of interest is implicitly learned by the algorithm. Generative models on the other hand do not require a set of annotated training images. Explicit prior knowledge of anatomy or intensity appearance is directly incorporated into the algorithm [2]. Although it is clear that existing methods need to be improved in terms of accuracy, practical usability of the methods on clinical data needs to be considered as well. In clinical practice the availability of annotated training data may be limited or

© Springer International Publishing Switzerland 2016
A. Crimi et al. (Eds.): BrainLes 2015, LNCS 9556, pp. 246–253, 2016.
DOI: 10.1007/978-3-319-30858-6_21

non-existent, such that a generative method that does not rely on training data may be preferred.

We present a novel fully-automated generative ischemic stroke lesion segmentation method that only makes use of a probabilistic brain atlas of white matter (WM), grey matter (GM) and cerebrospinal fluid (CSF) and for which no manual initialization is needed. The probabilistic prior guides the global search for voxel outliers that cannot be explained by the normal tissue model and likely should be labelled as lesion. The lesion boundary is represented as a level-set that spatially regularizes the segmentation. The method is outlined in Sect. 2 and results are presented in Sect. 3.

## 2  Method

A level-set is used to represent the boundary between the normal region and the pathological region. By means of an Expectation Maximization (EM)-approach, an intensity model for the normal region is built as well as a separate intensity model for the pathological region. The level-set is subsequently updated such that a voxel is assigned to the region of which the intensity model best explains the voxel's intensity. The intensity models are then rebuilt, based on the current estimate of the normal and pathological region. This process is repeated until convergence (Fig. 1).

*Prior Registration.* Spatial priors indicate for every voxel the prior probability of encountering WM, GM and CSF and they are widely available for healthy adults in the form of brain atlases. These spatial priors of WM, GM and CSF are non-rigidly registered to the patient image. Although registration of a healthy atlas to a patient image is still an active field of research, this problem is ignored for now and standard intensity-based non-rigid registration methods are used. The prior information is relaxed by smoothing the spatial priors with a Gaussian kernel.

*Intensity Models and the Expectation-Maximization Algorithm.* Normal and pathological tissue intensities are modelled separately. Let $G_{\Sigma_j}$ be a zero-mean multivariate Gaussian with covariance matrix $\Sigma_j$, then normal and pathological tissue are both modelled by a Gaussian mixture model

$$p(\mathbf{y_i}|\theta) = \sum_{j}^{K} G_{\Sigma_j}(\mathbf{y_i} - \mu_j)p(\Gamma_i = j),\qquad(1)$$

with $\mathbf{y_i} = (y_{i_1},\ldots,y_{i_N})$ the (raw) intensity of voxel $i$ and $\Gamma_i = \{j|j = 1\ldots K\}$ the tissue class. The intensity model parameters $\theta = \{(\mu_j,\Sigma_j)|j \in 1\ldots K\}$ are iteratively updated using an EM-approach [2]. For normal tissue, $K = 3$ and $p(\Gamma = j) = \pi_j$ are the spatial priors for WM, GM and CSF. For pathological tissue, the weights of the Gaussians are updated according to the volume fraction of each of the tumor classes.

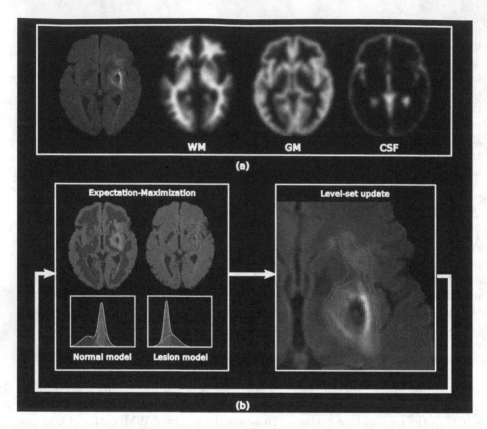

**Fig. 1.** (a) Spatial priors are non-rigidly registered to the patient image. (b) A full EM-estimation of the normal and pathological intensity models is done, after which a level-set is updated. This process is repeated until convergence.

*Convex Level-Set Formulation.* The image $I$ is subdivided into regions labelled $\Omega_{in}$ (pathological tissue) and $\Omega_{out}$ (normal tissue) for which the intensities are modelled by the probability distributions described in the previous paragraph [3]. The regions are separated by a boundary $\partial\Omega$ that is implicitly represented by a level-set function $u$. The boundary and intensity model parameters are found by minimizing the energy functional

$$\underset{\theta_{in},\theta_{out},\partial\Omega}{\operatorname{argmin}} \quad \lambda_1 \int_{\Omega_{in}} -\log p_{in}(I|\Omega_{in},\theta_{in})\,d\mathbf{x}$$
$$+ \lambda_2 \int_{\Omega_{out}} -\log p_{out}(I|\Omega_{out},\theta_{out})\,d\mathbf{x} \tag{2}$$
$$+ \kappa \, \text{length}(\partial\Omega),$$

where length(.) is the length of the boundary. The first two terms penalize the negative loglikelihood of the image $I$ evaluated in respectively the pathological and normal region. Voxels in a region that are unlikely according to the Gaussian mixture model for that region will have a high contribution to the energy function. The third term penalizes the length of the boundary and acts as a regularization term. Parameters $\lambda_1$, $\lambda_2$ and $\kappa$ determine the relative importance of the energy terms. For each iteration to update the level-set, a full EM-estimation of the parameters $\theta_{in}$ and $\theta_{out}$ is done.

The energy functional is non-convex and the gradient flow on the level-set function $u$ finds a solution that depends on a manual initialization of the level-set [4]. This initialization typically has significant impact on the segmentation result. In this work, this problem is overcome by using a convex level-set formulation that performs a global search over the image and makes a manual initialization superfluous. A global minimum is guaranteed by replacing the gradient flow by another gradient flow with the same steady-state solution and by restricting the level-set to lie in a finite interval [5]. The problem is thus reformulated as an $L_1$-minimization problem that is solved by the Split Bregman-numerical scheme, which is an iterative technique that was recently proposed for solving this kind of convex problem in a fast and efficient way [6]. As a result, given a set of intensity parameters, our method will search for tumorous voxels in a global way and independently of a manual initialization. The energy functional equals

$$\operatorname*{argmin}_{0 \le u \le 1} \quad \|\nabla u\|_{L_1} + \lambda \langle u, r \rangle \tag{3}$$

with $\langle .,. \rangle$ the summation over the voxel-wise products of the arguments, $u$ is the level-set function and $r$ is the data-fitting term,

$$r = \log p_{out}(I | \Omega_{out}, \theta_{out}) - \log p_{in}(I | \Omega_{in}, \theta_{in}). \tag{4}$$

To solve this minimization problem, the split Bregman iteration technique introduces an auxiliary variable $\mathbf{d} = \nabla u$ and the Bregman variable $\mathbf{b}$ and solves a sequence of unconstrained problems

$$(u^{n+1}, \mathbf{d}^{n+1}) = \operatorname*{argmin}_{0 \le u \le 1, \mathbf{d}} \quad \|\mathbf{d}\|_{L_1} + \lambda \langle u, r^n \rangle + $$

$$\frac{\mu}{2} \|\mathbf{d} - \nabla u - \mathbf{b}^n\|^2, \tag{5}$$

$$\mathbf{b}^{n+1} = \mathbf{b}^n + \nabla u^n - \mathbf{d}^n, \tag{6}$$

where $u^{n+1}$ is found by a Gauss-Seidel sweep and $\mathbf{d}$ is found by vectorial shrinkage. The superscript $n$ denotes the iteration index. A more detailed description on the split Bregman iteration technique can be found in [6]. It is important to note that, by using spatial priors of WM, GM and CSF, the global optimum coincides with the clinically meaningful notion of normal and pathological regions.

*Overall Algorithm.* The overall algorithm is summarized in Algorithm 1. With the Gaussian mixture model parameters from a previous iteration, the loglikelihoods of the image for both normal and pathological region are combined into the data-fitting term $r^n$. Consequently, based on this data-fitting term an update of the level-set $u$ is done by performing one iteration of the split Bregman scheme. This gives rise to a new estimate of the normal region $\Omega_{out}$ and a new estimate of the pathological region $\Omega_{in}$. Within these regions, a full EM-estimation of the parameters $\theta_{in}$ and $\theta_{out}$ is done. This process is repeated until the change of the level-set is below a threshold.

Initialize $\mathbf{d} = 0$, $\mathbf{b} = 0$, $u = 0.5$
**while** $\|u^{n+1} - u^n\|_{L_2} > \epsilon$  **do**

> // data-fitting term
> $r^n = \log p_{out}(I|\Omega_{out}^n, \Theta_{out}^n) - \log p_{in}(I|\Omega_{in}^n, \Theta_{in}^n)$
>
> // update level-set from Eq. 5 en 6
> Solve $u^{n+1}$
> Solve $d^{n+1}$
> $\mathbf{b}^{n+1} = \mathbf{b}^n + \nabla u^n - \mathbf{d}^n$
>
> // update regions
> $\Omega_{in}^{n+1} = \{\mathbf{x} : u^{n+1}(\mathbf{x}) > 0.5\}$
> $\Omega_{out}^{n+1} = \{\mathbf{x} : u^{n+1}(\mathbf{x}) < 0.5\}$
>
> **while** *EM not converged* **do**
>
> > // update intensity models
> > $\Theta_{in}^{n+1}$ from region $\Omega_{in}^{n+1}$
> > $\Theta_{out}^{n+1}$ from region $\Omega_{out}^{n+1}$
>
> **end**

**end**

**Algorithm 1.** Split Bregman tumor segmentation method

## 3    Experiments and Results

The patient volumes in the SPES and SISS training data set are already skull-stripped and registered intra-patient. No further pre-processing is done. Prior registration is based on the T1-weighted MNI-Colin27 atlas (2008) that is registered to the patient volume with a cross-correlation similarity measure (radius 4 voxels) by the Advanced Normalization Tools (ANTs) toolbox [7]. The spatial priors are relaxed by a Gaussian kernel with $\sigma = 3$ voxels.

For segmentation of the SPES data, we use the T2-weighted and TTP-weighted MR images and for SISS the diffusion weighted and FLAIR-weighted MR images. For SPES, the modalities are used in a completely multivariate way, i.e. with bivariate Gaussian models. For SISS, the modalities are segmented separately and a voxel is only labelled as lesion if it is a lesion in both modalities.

The number of Gaussians for modelling the lesion intensities is set to 1. The energy functional hyperparameters are $\lambda_1 = \lambda_2 = 1e1$ and $\kappa = 1e1$. For each update of the level-set, a full EM-estimation for both the pathological and normal intensity model is performed.

The computation time for a single patient volume is about 15 min on a $2 \times 2.66$ GHz Quad-Core CPU, out of which 10 min are spent for the non-rigid registration of the priors to the patient volume. Example segmentations for the test data set are visualized in Fig. 3. Performance of the algorithm for SPES and SISS is evaluated by means of the ASSD, Dice overlap coefficient, Hausdorff distance and precision and recall for both the training data set and test data set (Table 1). The median Dice scores for the SPES and SISS training data sets are 0.79 and 0.60 respectively (Fig. 2).

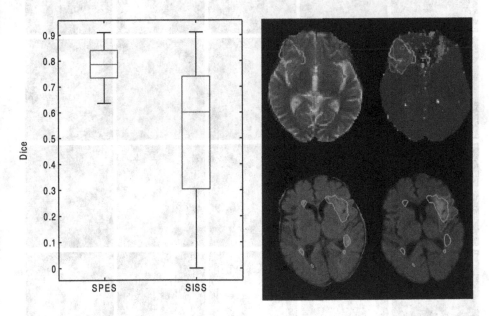

**Fig. 2. Left:** Dice score boxplots for SPES and SISS training data sets. **Right:** T2- and TTP-weighted MR example image from SPES (**top**) and FLAIR- and diffusion weighted MR example image from SISS (**bottom**) with ground truth segmentations (red) and the resulting segmentations (green) for a typical segmentation (Dice score 0.79 and 0.50).

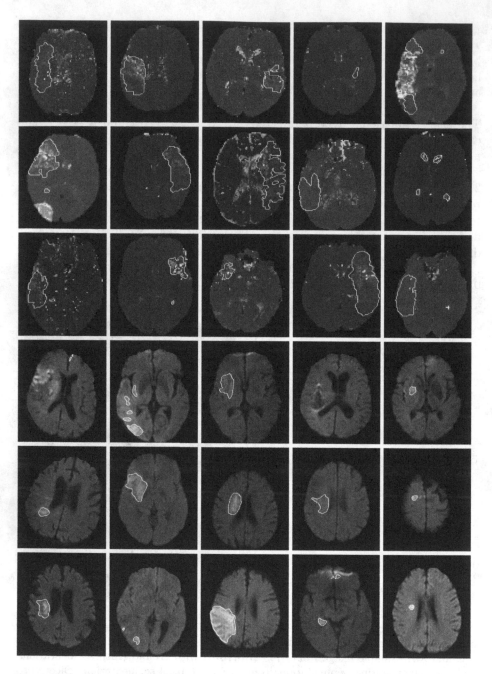

**Fig. 3. Row 1–3:** Resulting segmentations overlayed on the TTP-weighted MR images (patient nr. 1–15), as found by the presented method for the SPES test data set. **Row 4–6:** Example segmentations overlayed on the diffusion weighted MR images (patient nr. 1–15), as found by the presented method for the SISS test data set. Since the challenge is ongoing, the ground truth for the test data set is not publicly available.

**Table 1.** Performance of the presented method on the SPES and SISS data

|          | ASSD  |       | Dice |      | Hausdorff |       | Precision |      | Recall |      |
|----------|-------|-------|------|------|-----------|-------|-----------|------|--------|------|
|          | Avg   | Std   | Avg  | Std  | Avg       | Std   | Avg       | Std  | Avg    | Std  |
| Training |       |       |      |      |           |       |           |      |        |      |
| SPES     | 3.51  | 2.13  | 0.78 | 0.08 | 46.31     | 25.17 | 0.78      | 0.11 | 0.80   | 0.12 |
| SISS     | 14.43 | 25.88 | 0.53 | 0.26 | 69.67     | 30.77 | 0.62      | 0.31 | 0.56   | 0.29 |
| Testing  |       |       |      |      |           |       |           |      |        |      |
| SPES     | 5.18  | 6.13  | 0.67 | 0.24 | 42.29     | 19.42 | 0.74      | 0.22 | 0.67   | 0.27 |
| SISS     | 17.36 | 19.27 | 0.37 | 0.33 | 63.59     | 31.68 | 0.49      | 0.40 | 0.40   | 0.33 |

## 4 Discussion and Conclusion

In plenty of clinical settings only a handful of patient images needs to be processed without the availability of an annotated training set. Generative methods have therefore an enormous practical value. We have presented a generative method for segmenting the ischemic stroke lesion in the SPESS and SISS training set. The method is abundantly flexible to detect any intensity abnormality, and therefore also suitable to detect other lesions like tumor or MS.

## References

1. Rekik, I., Allassonnière, S., Carpenter, T.K., Wardlaw, J.M.: Medical image analysis methods in MR/CT-imaged acute-subacute ischemic stroke lesion: segmentation, prediction and insights into dynamic evolution simulation models. A critical appraisal. NeuroImage Clin. **1**(1), 164–178 (2012)
2. Van Leemput, K., Maes, F., Vandermeulen, D., Suetens, P.: Automated model-based tissue classification of MR images of the brain. IEEE Trans. Med. Imaging **18**, 897–908 (1999)
3. Rousson, M., Deriche, R.: A variational framework for active and adaptative segmentation of vector valued images. In: Proceedings of the Workshop on Motion and Video Computing, MOTION 2002. IEEE Computer Society (2002)
4. Riklin-Raviv, T., Van Leemput, K., Menze, B.H., Wells, W.M., Golland, P.: Segmentation of image ensembles via latent atlases. Med. Image Anal. **14**(5), 654–665 (2010)
5. Chan, T.F., Esedoglu, S., Nikolova, M.: Algorithms for finding global minimizers of image segmentation and denoising models. SIAM J. Appl. Math. **66**(5), 1632–1648 (2006)
6. Goldstein, T., Bresson, X., Osher, S.: Geometric applications of the split Bregman method: segmentation and surface reconstruction. J. Sci. Comput. **45**(1–3), 272–293 (2010)
7. Avants, B.B., Tustison, N.J., Song, G., Cook, P.A., Klein, A., Gee, J.C.: A reproducible evaluation of ants similarity metric performance in brain image registration. Neuroimage **54**(3), 2033–2044 (2011)

# A Voxel-Wise, Cascaded Classification Approach to Ischemic Stroke Lesion Segmentation

David Robben[1,3(✉)], Daan Christiaens[1,3], Janaki Raman Rangarajan[1,3],
Jaap Gelderblom[1,3], Philip Joris[1,3], Frederik Maes[1,3], and Paul Suetens[1,2,3]

[1] Department of Electrical Engineering, KU Leuven, ESAT/PSI, Leuven, Belgium
david.robben@kuleuven.be
[2] Medical IT Department, iMinds, Ghent, Belgium
[3] UZ Leuven, Medical Imaging Research Center,
Herestraat 49 – 7003, 3000 Leuven, Belgium

**Abstract.** Automated localisation and segmentation of stroke lesions in patients is of great interest to clinicians and researchers alike. We propose a supervised method based on cascaded extremely randomised trees for lesion segmentation, working on a per voxel basis in native subject space. The proposed pipeline is evaluated in the MICCAI Ischemic Stroke Lesion Segmentation (ISLES) challenge, both with nested cross-validation on the training data as well as on independent, multi-centre test data. We obtained good performance although inter-subject variability is large, and reached 3rd place in the SPES sub-challenge.

## 1 Introduction

In ischemic stroke, reduced blood flow to part of the brain results in localised tissue damage and eventual necrosis. Automated localisation and segmentation of the stroke lesion in patients is of great interest to clinicians and researchers alike. Ultimately, this would enable them to differentiate potentially salvageable and permanently damaged tissue, identify effective treatments, and follow progression of the ischemic lesion [9].

Segmentation of ischemic stroke lesion is often marred by the complexity of shape, lack of ground truth, ambiguity and heterogeneity of the lesion size, location and contrast [4]. There is growing interest to move from subjective thresholding based techniques to automated methods that allow not only objective lesion segmentation but also insight on critical sub-regions that characterise the onset and evolution of stroke. The multi-modal MR images with diffusion and perfusion information provide complimentary image features to make such classification.

An overview of ischemic stroke lesion segmentation methods based on MR/CT images has been well discussed in Rekik et al. [9]. More recently, a number of fully automated approaches have been introduced, based on supervised learning [5,7]. Mitra et al. [7] combine Bayesian-Markov random fields and random decision forests. Maier et al. [5] use Extra Tree forests for voxel-wise classification into two classes: the stroke lesion and healthy brain tissue. Likewise, the benefit of randomness during training phase when using Extremely

© Springer International Publishing Switzerland 2016
A. Crimi et al. (Eds.): BrainLes 2015, LNCS 9556, pp. 254–265, 2016.
DOI: 10.1007/978-3-319-30858-6_22

randomized trees (ExtraTrees) over random foresets for tumour segmentation has been recently demonstrated [2].

In this paper, we propose a novel, supervised method based on cascaded extremely randomised trees and optimal thresholding for stroke lesion segmentation in a single pipeline. This method is then evaluated in the MICCAI Ischemic Stroke Lesion Segmentation (ISLES) challenge on two multi-modal MRI datasets for sub-acute ischemic stroke lesion segmentation (SISS) and for acute stroke outcome and penumbra estimation (SPES).

## 2   Method

Our processing pipeline first preprocessed all data for field inhomogeneity and intensity standardization, and registers the resulting images to MNI reference space. Subsequently, features are extracted at different spatial scales. Finally, a cascaded Extra Trees classifier is trained on a dataset in which the stroke lesions were manually delineated. Independent test data is processed identically and passed to the classifier, generating a lesion probability map. Those maps are then thresholded for optimal Dice score, to obtain the final segmentation.

### 2.1   Preprocessing

At first, the non-parametric images in both datasets were corrected for RF inhomogeneity. We estimated the bias field on the T1w-images using FSL FAST [3], using a 3-tissue model and a bias field smoothing filter of 40 mm full-width half maximum. The elevated smoothing parameter (default is 20 mm) was chosen to improve robustness to the pathology. The estimated bias field was subsequently applied to correct all T1w- and T2w-images, as well as the Flair and DWI images in the SISS dataset. The ADC images and the perfusion measures in the SPES dataset were not corrected, as these images are already normalised or assumed to be in physical units.

Secondly, cross-subject histogram normalisation was done for each dataset and each modality. To this end, we used a linear intensity rescaling based on two percentile intensities of the histogram. These were heuristically determined based on the histogram profile of a given modality across all subjects of each dataset. For SISS we used 20 % and 99 % for T1, T2, and DWI, and 30 % and 90 % for Flair. For SPES we used 30 % and 90 % for T1, 20 % and 99 % for T2, 20 % and 90 % for DWI (ADC), and 20 % and 50 % for TTP. No intensity normalisation was applied to Tmax, CBF, and CBV.

Additionally, we wish to include spatial features in the classifier as well. Therefore, we registered all subjects T1w-images to the MNI152 template using a 12 degrees of freedom affine transformation and normalised mutual information, as implemented in FSL FLIRT [3]. The resulting transformation matrices are converted to (affine) deformation fields which provide, for each voxel in native space, the corresponding coordinate in MNI space. As such, no image interpolation is needed and the subsequent classifier training can be done in native space.

## 2.2  Classifier

We decided to use a voxel-wise classification approach for both segmentation tasks. That is, we build a classifier that, given a set of features of a voxel, estimates the probability that this voxel is part of a lesion. To increase computational efficiency and spatial consistency, we use a cascaded approach. First, the to-be-classified voxel is given to a classifier that uses a limited set of features. If this classifier decides with very high probability that the voxel is non-lesion, then this probability is the final answer. Else, the voxel is given to the second classifier that uses a large set of features. Then, the voxels which were not classified as non-lesion with very high probability, are given to a third classifier. This last classifier uses the same features as the second classifier and additionally the earlier computed probabilities of that voxel and its neighbouring voxels.

We use extremely randomised trees [1] as a base classifier. This classifier builds an ensemble of decision trees, but by randomising the selection of cut-point in the decision tree nodes, its training is significantly faster than the training of random forests while achieving comparable accuracy. We use the implementation provided by scikit-learn [8].

## 2.3  Features

Since the classifier is the same for both challenges, the features are constructed in a similar fashion.

For the SPES sub-challenge, the first cascade uses the T1c intensity. The second cascade uses the intensity of the T1c, T2, TTP, Tmax and DWI images smoothed with a sigma of 0 – 6 mm. It also has for TTP and Tmax the 0.5, 0.75 and 0.9 percentiles and for DWI the 0.1 and 0.25 percentiles of its neighbourhood for varying radii (4 – 12 mm). Finally, it has the MNI-coordinates. The third cascade uses the same features as the latter and additionally it has the earlier estimated probabilities smoothed with a sigma of 0 – 8 mm and the 0.5, 0.75 and 0.9 percentiles of it neighbourhood for varying radii (4 – 8 mm).

For the SISS sub-challenge, the first cascade uses the T1 intensity. The second cascade uses the intensity of the T1, T2, Flair and DWI images smoothed with a sigma of 0 – 8 mm. It also has for Flair and DWI the 0.5, 0.75 and 0.9 percentiles of its neighbourhood for varying radii (4 – 8 mm). Finally, it uses the MNI-coordinates. The third cascade uses the same features as the latter and additionally it has the earlier estimated probabilities smoothed with a sigma of 0 – 8 mm and the 0.5, 0.75 and 0.9 percentiles of it neighbourhood for varying radii (4 – 8 mm).

## 2.4   Hyper Parameters

The extremely randomized trees classifier has a few hyper parameters that have to be determined. We use 100 trees per classifier, and the number of features considered at each cut-point is set to the square root of the number of features. The most important hyper parameter is the size of the trees as it controls the tendency of the classifier to under-/overfit. This can be constrained by either enforcing a maximum depth of the trees or by requiring a minimum number of samples in each leaf of the trees. We don't have a preference for one over the other and used the first for the SISS and the second for the SPES sub challenge. Since the optimal value of this hyper parameter is strongly dependent on the specific dataset, we define a range of considered values and use cross validation to select the best performing one. We use 5-fold cross validation, meaning we split the images in 5 folds, and each time leave one fold out for testing and use the other four for training. The optimal hyper parameter value is the one that results in the lowest mean log loss. The considered leaf sizes for SPES are 50, 100, 200 and 400. The considered tree depths for SISS are 12, 14, 16 and 18.

## 2.5   Probability Threshold for an Optimal Dice

Following the voxel-wise classification, we have for every voxel a probability of belonging to a lesion. However, the ISLES challenge requires a binary segmentation and hence we need to threshold the resulting probabilities. Instead of using a fixed threshold for all images, we use a novel technique to find for every image its optimal threshold, that is, the one that will give the highest dice score. This threshold is estimated for each image independently using the estimated probabilities.

The dice score of a segmentation $S$ and the ground truth $G$ is defined as:

$$DICE(S, G) = \frac{2|S \cap G|}{|S| \cup |G|}, \tag{1}$$

where both S and G are sets of voxels. Our classifier gives for every voxel $x$ a probability $P(x)$ that it is part of the lesion. Hence, our segmentation $S$ will depend on the probability threshold $P_t$:

$$S(P_t) = \{x | P(x) > P_t\}, \tag{2}$$

and thus:

$$|S(P_t)| = \sum_x I[P(x) > P_t]. \tag{3}$$

Assuming that the probability estimates are correct and voxels are independent from each other, we can calculate the expected value of $|G|$:

$$\mathbb{E}[\,|G|\,] = \mathbb{E}\Big[\sum_x \mathbb{1}_G(\boldsymbol{x})\Big] = \sum_x \mathbb{E}\big[\mathbb{1}_G(\boldsymbol{x})\big] = \sum_x P(\boldsymbol{x}), \qquad (4)$$

with $\mathbb{1}$ the indicator function. The expected value of $|S \cap G|$ is:

$$\mathbb{E}[\,|S(P_t) \cap G|\,] = \mathbb{E}\Big[\sum_x I[P(\boldsymbol{x}) > P_t]\mathbb{1}_G(\boldsymbol{x})\Big] \qquad (5)$$

$$= \sum_x I[P(\boldsymbol{x}) > P_t]P(x). \qquad (6)$$

Hence the expected dice score obtained with threshold $P_t$ will be:

$$D(P_t) = \frac{2\sum_x I[P(\boldsymbol{x}) > P_t]P(x)}{\sum_x P(\boldsymbol{x}) + \sum_x I[P(x) > P_t]}, \qquad (7)$$

To speed up the computation, we first calculate the histogram of the probability image $P(\boldsymbol{x})$. For each bin $i$ we have the left bin edge $b_i$, its center $c_i$ and its number of voxels $f_i$. With $b_i$ used as threshold, the expected dice score is:

$$D(b_i) = \frac{2\sum_{j\geq i} f_j c_j}{\sum_j f_j c_j + \sum_{j\geq i} f_j}, \qquad (8)$$

We exhaustively search for the optimal threshold $P_t$, considering all the left bin edges $b_i$. We use 1000 bins; the considered $P_t$ are thus $[0, 1e{-}3, 2e{-}3, ..., 999e{-}3]$.

## 3   Results

The performance of the proposed segmentation method is evaluated in the online submission system of the challenge, and relies on the average symmetric surface distance (ASSD), the Dice overlap coefficient (DC), and the Hausdorff distance (HD). Additionally, precision and recall are reported to discriminate between over- and under-segmentation respectively. The results of cross-validation on the training data, and of independent evaluation in the testing data, are reported in Table 1. ISLES did not report precision and recall on the testing data, and because the ground truth is hidden we have no means to compute them ourselves. Similarly, the challenge organisers decided to eliminate the Hausdorff distance from the SPES evaluation due to many outliers.

The proposed lesion segmentation method is visually compared to expert segmentations in training set cases of median and maximum overlap in Fig. 1. These images show that the presented method produces acceptable results in both SISS and SPES datasets. The lesion boundary is delineated accurately

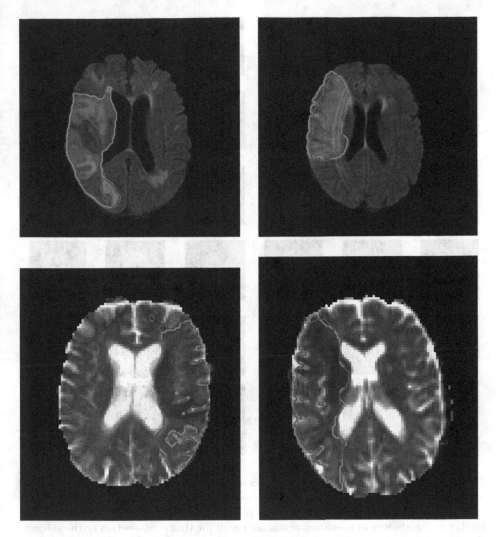

**Fig. 1.** Comparison between the ground-truth labels (*green*) and the predicted segmentation (*red*), shown for selected examples with median (*left*) and maximum (*right*) Dice coefficient in the training set. SISS Flair dataset on the *top*; SPES DWI (ADC) dataset on the *bottom* (Color figure online).

in regions where intensities are elevated, but deviates if intensity differences are inconclusive while an expert anatomical knowledge is more informative. Leukoaraiosis in the contralateral hemisphere are correctly labelled as not part of the ischemic lesion. Cases with a small lesion in the cerebellum remain challenging, particularly in the SISS dataset.

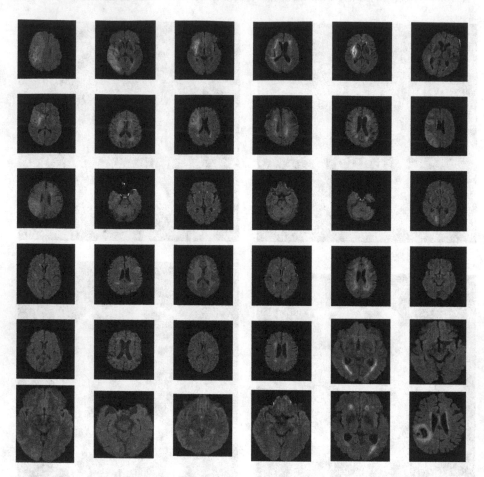

**Fig. 2.** Segmentation results (*red*) in the 36 test subjects of the SISS dataset, overlaid onto their FLAIR images. Representative cross-sections from individual subjects correspond to the mid-slice of the segmentation result. No overlay in some cases may likely be due to the absence of lesion segmentation result for that cross-section or the subject themselves. The last eight images (rows 7-8) possibly corresponds to the second center, whose data was not part of the training set (Color figure online).

Performance in the testing data is on par with the cross-validation results in the training data, except for the lower Dice score in the SISS sub-challenge. We attribute this decrease of DC to the multi-centre nature of the SISS testing data, as can be seen in Fig. 2. Similarly, Fig. 3 shows the segmentation of the test cases in the SPES dataset.

**Table 1.** Segmentation metrics on the training and testing data, reported as the average symmetric surface distance (ASSD), Dice coefficient (DC), Hausdorff distance (HD), precision, and recall, between the predicted segmentation and the ground truth.

|      |          | ASSD (mm)      | DC            | HD (mm)        | Precision     | Recall        |
|------|----------|----------------|---------------|----------------|---------------|---------------|
| SISS | Training | 9.36 ± 13.85   | 0.57 ± 0.28   | 53.88 ± 34.58  | 0.58 ± 0.33   | 0.68 ± 0.21   |
|      | Testing  | 11.27 ± 10.17  | 0.43 ± 0.30   | 60.79 ± 31.14  | -             | -             |
| SPES | Training | 2.03 ± 1.35    | 0.82 ± 0.07   | 44.29 ± 27.59  | 0.81 ± 0.14   | 0.85 ± 0.07   |
|      | Testing  | 2.77 ± 3.27    | 0.78 ± 0.09   | -              | -             | -             |

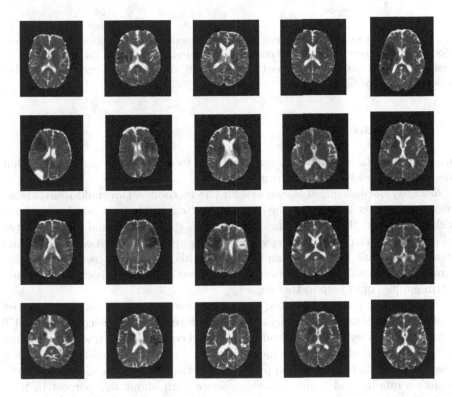

**Fig. 3.** Segmentation results (*red*) in the 20 test subjects of the SPES dataset, overlaid onto their DWI (ADC) images (Color figure online).

Compared to other participants in the challenge, our method performed above average on the testing data, as shown in Fig. 4. Given the simplicity of our approach, these results are satisfying.

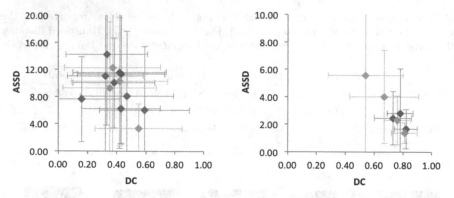

**Fig. 4.** Plots of the Dice coefficient (DC) and average symmetric surface distance (ASSD) performance metrics of all challenge participants. *Red:* the presented method, *green:* other methods that took part in both SISS and SPES challenges, *blue* other participants (Color figure online).

## 4    Discussion

Our method is fairly standard, but we'd like to address the components that have a large impact on our performance.

*Intensity normalization* is essential for the method: a threshold-based classifier such as ours is sensitive to the intensity scaling. Without it, results degraded quickly. However, the current linear approach is still sub-optimal. As illustrated in Fig. 5, intensity differences between subjects are still present after histogram correction. Future work may improve upon this method by revising the histogram normalisation. More advanced, non-linear approaches such as Meier and Guttmann [6] could help in this regard.

*The cascaded approach* showed strong improvement over a single voxel-wise classifier, and allows to take neighbourhood information into account while still limiting the number of features and the required computation time. Even though the third cascade uses the same image features as the second cascade, the additional features that describe the prediction of the second cascade, increase the prediction quality and improve the dice score with about five percent in both subchallenges. In retrospect, this approach is very similar to Auto-Context [10]. In our opinion, there are two big differences between our approach and Auto-Context. First, only our last cascade uses predictions of the previous cascade. They keep adding cascades that use the previous predictions until the predicted probabilities are stable. Their experiments demonstrate that this improves results and in future work we would follow this approach. Secondly, our context features are the smoothed probability estimates and percentiles of the local neighborhood. Auto-Context uses the probability estimates of sparsely sampled neighboring voxels. It would be interesting to compare both approaches in future work.

(a) Before intensity normalisation      (b) After intensity normalisation

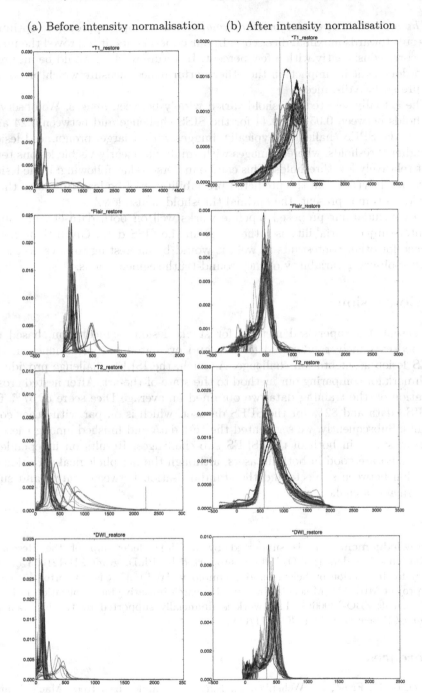

**Fig. 5.** Histograms of SISS Test cases, before and after intensity normalisation. The vertical lines in red corresponds to the lower and upper percentile intensities of the histogram, as defined on the training data set. Residual inter-subject intensity variations appears to remain even after normalization, especially for multi-center data (Color figure online).

*The probability threshold for an optimal dice* is a simple approach to optimize the result towards maximal dice score. In our experiments, it improved the mean dice scores consistently with a few percent. In future work, it would be interesting to document its impact on the other performance measure which primarily measure surface distance.

The actually selected threshold varied widely between images. We observed thresholds between 0.05 and 0.44 for the SISS challenge and between 0.24 and 0.43 for the SPES challenge. Typically, images with a large, pronounced lesion get higher thresholds, whereas images with small, not clearly visible lesions tend to get relatively low thresholds. This can be understood as following: if the lesion is not clearly visible, all the predicted probabilities will be low. But since there is always a tumor present, the optimal threshold is also low.

To conclude, our proposed pipeline works well on both datasets, although the inter-subject variability is rather large in the SISS data. Given that this is the case for other contestants as well, it would be interesting to have access to the inter-observer variability of the ground-truth segmentations.

## 5    Conclusion

We presented a supervised method for stroke lesion segmentation, based on cascaded extremely randomised forests, and evaluated its performance in the ISLES lesion segmentation challenge. As such, the ISLES challenge provides a benchmark for comparing our method to the state-of-the-art. After nested cross-validation on the training data, we obtained an average Dice score of 57 % for the SISS data and 82 % for the SPES dataset, which is on par with other contestants. Subsequently, we segmented the test data and finished among the top five contestants in both of the ISLES sub-challenges. Results on independent testing data are good in both datasets, although the morphological variation of the lesion between subjects and the standardisation between centres and subjects remains a challenge.

**Acknowledgement.** DR is supported by a Ph.D. fellowship of the Research Foundation - Flanders (FWO). DC is supported by Ph.D. grant SB 121013 of the Agency for Innovation by Science and Technology (IWT). JRR is supported by IWT SBO project MIRIAD (Molecular Imaging Research Initiative for Application in Drug Development, SBO-130065). This work is financially supported by the KU Leuven Concerted Research Action GOA/11/006.

## References

1. Geurts, P., Ernst, D., Wehenkel, L.: Extremely randomized trees. Mach. Learn. **63**(1), 3–42 (2006)
2. Goetz, M., Weber, C., Bloecher, J., Stieltjes, B., Meinzer, H., Maier-Hein, K.: Extremely randomized trees based brain tumor segmentation. In: MICCAI 2014 Brats Workshop (2014)

3. Jenkinson, M., Beckmann, C.F., Behrens, T.E., Woolrich, M.W., Smith, S.M.: FSL. NeuroImage **62**(2), 782–790 (2012)
4. Kabir, Y., Dojat, M., Scherrer, B., Forbes, F., Garbay, C.: Multimodal MRI segmentation of ischemic stroke lesions. In: Conference Proceedings, pp. 1595–1598 (2007)
5. Maier, O., Wilms, M., von der Gablentz, J., Krämer, U.M., Münte, T.F., Handels, H.: Extra tree forests for sub-acute ischemic stroke lesion segmentation in MR sequences. J. Neurosci. Methods **240**, 89–100 (2015)
6. Meier, D.S., Guttmann, C.R.: Time-series analysis of MRI intensity patterns in multiple sclerosis. NeuroImage **20**(2), 1193–1209 (2003)
7. Mitra, J., Bourgeat, P., Fripp, J., Ghose, S., Rose, S., Salvado, O., Connelly, A., Campbell, B., Palmer, S., Sharma, G., Christensen, S., Carey, L.: Lesion segmentation from multimodal MRI using random forest following ischemic stroke. NeuroImage **98**, 324–335 (2014)
8. Pedregosa, F., Varoquaux, G., Gramfort, A., Michel, V., Thirion, B., Grisel, O., Blondel, M., Prettenhofer, P., Weiss, R., Dubourg, V., Vanderplas, J., Passos, A., Cournapeau, D., Brucher, M., Perrot, M., Duchesnay, E.: Scikit-learn: machine learning in python. J. Mach. Learn. Res. **12**, 2825–2830 (2011)
9. Rekik, I., Allassonnière, S., Carpenter, T.K., Wardlaw, J.M.: Medical image analysis methods in MR/CT-imaged acute-subacute ischemic stroke lesion: segmentation, prediction and insights into dynamic evolution simulation models. a critical appraisal. NeuroImage. Clin., 1(1), 164–178 (2012)
10. Tu, Z., Bai, X.: Auto-context and its application to high-level vision tasks and 3D brain image segmentation. IEEE Trans. Pattern Anal. Mach. Intell. **32**(10), 1744–1757 (2010)

# Automatic Ischemic Stroke Lesion Segmentation in Multi-spectral MRI Images Using Random Forests Classifier

Qaiser Mahmood[1,2]($\boxtimes$) and A. Basit[2]

[1] Signals and Systems, Chalmers University of Technology, Gothenburg, Sweden
[2] Pakistan Institute of Nuclear Science and Technology, Islamabad, Pakistan
qaiserm@chalmers.se, abdulbasit1975@gmail.com

**Abstract.** This paper presents an automated segmentation framework for ischemic stroke lesion segmentation in multi-spectral MRI images. The framework is based on a random forests (RF), which is an ensemble learning technique that generates several classifiers and combines their results in order to make decisions. In RF, we employ several meaningful features such as intensities, entropy, gradient etc. to classify the voxels in multi-spectral MRI images. The segmentation framework is validated on both training and testing data, obtained from MICCAI ISLES-2015 SISS challenge dataset. The performance of the framework is evaluated relative to the manual segmentation (ground truth). The experimental results demonstrate the robustness of the segmentation framework, and that it achieves reasonable segmentation accuracy for segmenting the sub-acute ischemic stroke lesion in multi-spectral MRI images.

**Keywords:** Segmentation · Automatic · MRI · Ischemic stroke lesion · Random forests

## 1 Introduction

Worldwide, each year around 15 million people suffer from a stroke and a third of these die [1]. Stroke is a disturbance to the intracerebral blood flow caused by either a clot blocking an artery (ischemic stroke) or bleeding as the result of a burst blood vessel (hemorrhagic stroke) [2]. As a consequence, the oxygen and glucose levels are reduced which in turn rapidly kills the affected brain tissue [3]. Ischemic stroke is the most common type of stroke accounting for about 80 % of cases (the proportion varies between countries) [4].

Multi-spectral magnetic resonance imaging (MRI) [5] can be used for detecting the ischemic stroke lesion and can provide quantitative assessment of lesion area. It can be established as an essential paraclinical tool for diagnosing stroke as well as for monitoring the efficacy of experimental treatments.

For a quantitative analysis of stroke lesion in MRI images, expert manual segmentation is still a common approach and has been employed to compute the size, shape and volume of the stroke lesions. However, it is time-consuming,

© Springer International Publishing Switzerland 2016
A. Crimi et al. (Eds.): BrainLes 2015, LNCS 9556, pp. 266–274, 2016.
DOI: 10.1007/978-3-319-30858-6_23

tedious, and labor-intensive task. Moreover, manual segmentation is prone to intra-and inter-observer variabilities [6].

Therefore, the development of fully automated and accurate stroke lesion segmentation method has become an active research field. In literature [6–8], several automated segmentation methods have been proposed for stroke lesion segmentation over the years. However, the automated stroke lesion segmentation is still a challenging task because of the gradual changes of stroke lesion appearance in multi-spectral MRI images.

Herein, we present a fully automated framework for sub-acute ischemic stroke lesion segmentation in multi-spectral MRI images. The framework is based on an ensemble learning technique called random forests (RF) that is robust against overfitting [9]. The main contribution in the framework is employing a set of meaningful features and the choice of steps for pre-processing the MRI images and post-processing of segmented data.

## 2   Method

The schematic procedure of the segmentation framework is shown in Fig. 1. The framework takes the multi-spectral MRI brain images as input and it includes two-step pre-processing: (1) Correction of bias field using the N3 bias field correction algorithm [10] and (2) normalization of intensity values of each MRI modality to the interval [0 1], done by applying the linear histogram stretching. For each voxel of multi-spectral MRI images, the following set of meaningful features is extracted.

1. MRI scans intensities: These features comprise the intensity in the 4 MRI scans (DWI, T2, T1 and FLAIR) provided by the data and the difference between each two scans. The total number of these features was 16.
2. MRI scans smooth intensities: A Gaussian filter with size $7 \times 7 \times 7$ was employed to each MRI scan in order to extract the smooth intensities. The total number of these features was 4.
3. MRI scans median intensities: A median filter with size $5 \times 5 \times 5$ was applied to each MRI scan to obtain the median intensities. The total number of these features was 4.
4. The gradient and magnitude of the gradient: A gradient in the x, y and z direction and their magnitude was computed in order to get the information about the lines and edges in each MRI scan. The total number of these features was 16.
5. Local entropy: The entropy for each voxel in the MRI scans was computed using the neighborhoods size $9 \times 9 \times 9$. The total number of these features was 4.

All features, mentioned above, were normalized to zero mean and unit deviation. These features are then employed to train the RF [9,11] classifier and classifying the sub-acute ischemic stroke lesion.

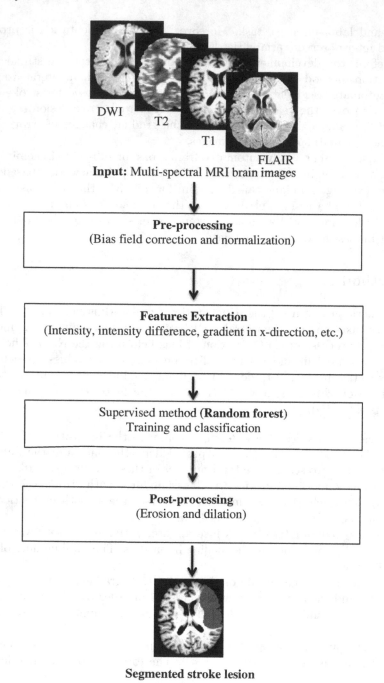

**Fig. 1.** Schematic procedure of the segmentation framework

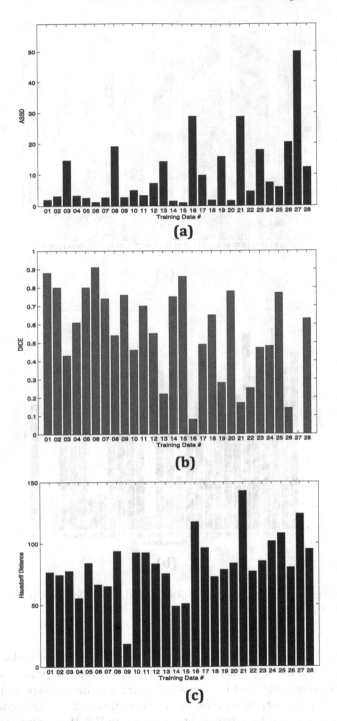

**Fig. 2.** Quantitative results of the segmentation framework for each training data: (a) ASSD (b) Dice and (c) Hausdorff distance.

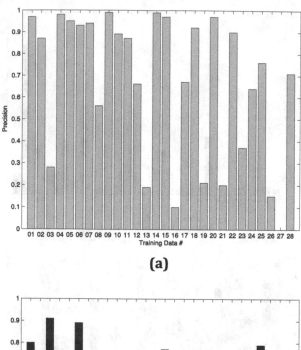

**(a)**

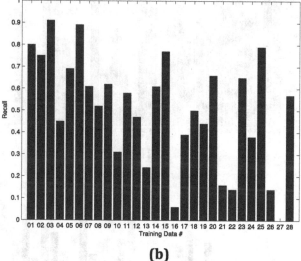

**(b)**

**Fig. 3.** Quantitative results of the segmentation framework for each training data: (a) precision and (b) recall.

In RF the training is performed using labeled data sets provided from the ground truths by building multiple decision trees, wherein every node except the leaves is a decision node that contains a feature and its corresponding threshold. Every leaf node contains a probabilistic class distribution (histogram of class labels for the voxels that have reached that node). In RF, the testing is performed by traversing voxels over the trees starting from the root of each tree to a leaf node.

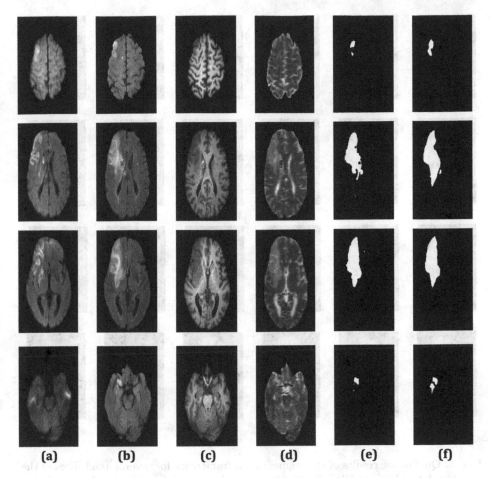

**Fig. 4.** Qualitative results of the segmentation framework for several axial slices of the training data "06": (a) DWI (b) Flair (c) T1 (d) T2 and (e) segmented stroke lesion (f) ground truth.

The voxels are split at a given node based on the learned feature and a threshold value at that node. The average probabilistic decision of the class distribution from all trees is considered the final probabilistic class distribution (voxel label in this scenario).

The two main parameters that can affect the efficiency of RF are the number of trees and depth of each tree. In our work, we set the RF parameters: number of trees = 150 and depth of each tree = 50. The Gini impurity was employed as a splitting criterion. Moreover $\sqrt{44}$ features were considered at each node for splitting. For training, a total of 999,000 data samples (37,000 samples per training data) were used to train the RF classifier. These samples were obtained by down sampling the majority class (non ischemic stroke) data in each training

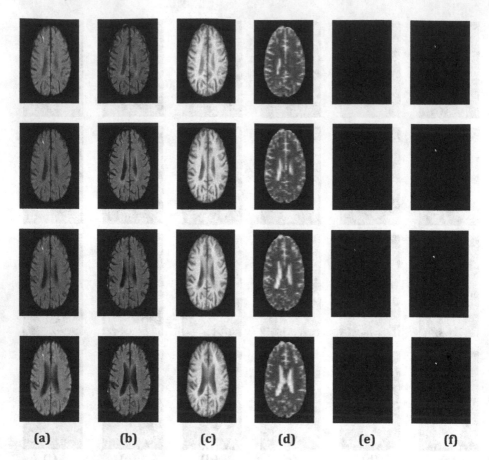

**Fig. 5.** Qualitative results of the segmentation framework for several axial slices of the training data "16": (a) DWI (b) Flair (c) T1 (d) T2 and (e) segmented stroke lesion (f) ground truth.

data set in order to make their frequencies closer to the minority class (ischemic stroke) data. The sampling was done randomly.

Finally, the post-processing is performed using the dilation followed by an erosion operation by employing the 2D $5 \times 5$ square structuring elements in order to remove the small objects classified as stroke lesion.

## 3    Results

The evaluation is performed on training data as well as on testing data, obtained from the MICCAI ISLES-2015 SISS challenge dataset. For the training data, the evaluation is done using leave-one-out cross validation. For the testing data, the classifier, trained from the training data, is applied to segment the stroke lesion. The training data comprise 28 sub-acute ischemic stroke lesion cases whilst the

**Table 1.** Average quantitative results of the segmentation framework over all the training data in terms of ASSD, Dice, Hausdorff distance, precision and recall.

| ASSD (mm) | Dice | Hausdorff distance (mm) | Precision | Recall |
|---|---|---|---|---|
| $10.30 \pm 11.11$ | $0.54 \pm 0.26$ | $82.78 \pm 23.95$ | $0.67 \pm 0.33$ | $0.50 \pm 0.25$ |

**Table 2.** Average quantitative results of the segmentation framework over all the testing data in terms of ASSD, Dice, Hausdorff distance, precision and recall.

| ASSD (mm) | Dice | Hausdorff distance (mm) | Precision | Recall |
|---|---|---|---|---|
| $13.96 \pm 13.77$ | $0.40 \pm 0.27$ | $71.25 \pm 17.02$ | $0.53 \pm 0.35$ | $0.40 \pm 0.28$ |

testing data include 36 sub-acute ischemic stroke lesion cases. The evaluation is done using the online evaluation system provided by the MICCAI ISLES-2015 challenge organizers.

The quantitative results of the segmentation framework for each training data in terms of average symmetric surface distance (ASSD), Dice, Hausdorff distance, and precision and recall are presented in Figs. 2 and 3 respectively. They show that for the training data "01", "02", "05", "06", "07", "09", "14", "15", "18", "20" and "25" the framework has better segmentation performance (lower ASSD, higher Dice and lower Hausdorff distance, higher precision and higher recall) compared to that of other remaining training data. For the training data "16", "21", "26", "27", the proposed framework has poorer segmentation performance (higher ASSD, lower Dice, higher Hausdorff distance, lower precision and lower recall). Moreover for the data "27", there is no overlapping (zero Dice) between the segmented stroke lesion and the ground truth. The reason for poor segmentation for the training data "16", "21", "26", and "27" is that the features used in our segmentation framework are not optimized to detect the small stroke lesion in these data.

Table 1 shows the average quantitative results of the segmentation framework over all the training data.

An example of good qualitative results of our segmentation framework for several axial slices of the training data "06" that contain large stroke lesion is presented in Fig. 4. An example of bad qualitative results of our segmentation framework for several axial slices of the training data "16" that contain small stroke lesion is presented in Fig. 5.

The average quantitative results of the segmentation framework over all the testing data are presented in Table 2.

## 4  Conclusions

In this paper, we present an automated framework based on the RF classifier for segmenting the sub-acute ischemic stroke lesion using multi-spectral MRI images. We employ a set of meaningful features to train the RF and classify the ischemic stroke lesion. The experimental results show the efficacy of the segmentation framework and that it can segment the sub-acute ischemic stroke lesion with reasonable accuracy. For future work, we will explore more robust features in order to improve the accuracy of our segmentation framework. The total execution time of our segmentation framework is about 25 to 30 min for segmenting the stroke lesion for each data using the MATLAB on a MacBook Pro with an Intel processor (i5, 2.5 GHz) and 4 GB RAM.

# References

1. The Atlas of Heart Disease and Stroke. http://www.who.int/cardiovascular_diseases/resources/atlas/en/
2. Fassbender, K., Balucani, C., Walter, S., Levine, S.R., Haass, A., Grotta, J.: Streamlining of prehospital stroke management: the golden hour. Lancet Neurol. **12**, 585–596 (2013)
3. Burns, J.D., Green, D.M., Metivier, K., DeFusco, C.: Intensive care management of acute ischemic stroke. Emerg. Med. Clin. North Am. **30**, 713–744 (2012)
4. Feigin, V.L., Lawes, C.M., Bennett, D.A., Barker-Collo, S.L., Parag, V.: Worldwide stroke incidence and early case fatality reported in 56 population-based studies: a systematic review. Lancet Neurol. **8**, 355–369 (2009)
5. Ball Jr., J.B., Pensak, M.L.: Fundamentals of magnetic resonance imaging. Am. J Otol. **8**, 81–85 (1987)
6. Oskar, M., Matthias, W., von der Janina, G., Ulrike, M.K., Thomas, F.M., Heinz, H.: Extra Tree forests for sub-acute ischemic stroke lesion segmentation in MR sequences. J. Neurosci. Methods **240**, 89–100 (2014)
7. Rekik, I., Allassonniere, S., Carpenter, T.K., Wardlaw, J.M.: Medical image analysis methods in MR/CT-imaged acute-subacute ischemic stroke lesion: segmentation, prediction and insights into dynamic evolution simulation models. a critical appraisal. NeuroImage: Clin. **1**, 164–178 (2012)
8. Mitra, J., Bourgeat, P., Fripp, J., Ghose, S., et al.: Lesion segmentation from multimodal MRI using random forests following ischemic stroke. NeuroImage **98**, 324–335 (2014)
9. Breiman, L.: Random forests. Mach. Learn. **45**(1), 5–32 (2001)
10. Sled, J.G., Zijdenbos, A.P., Evans, A.C.: A nonparametric method for automatic correction of intensity nonuniformity in MRI data. IEEE Trans. Med. Imaging **17**, 87–97 (1998)
11. Criminisi, A., Shotton, J. (eds.): Decision Forests for Computer Vision and Medical Image Analysis. Advances in Computer Vision and Pattern Recognition. Springer, Heidelberg (2013)

# Segmenting the Ischemic Penumbra:
# A Decision Forest Approach
# with Automatic Threshold Finding

Richard McKinley[1]([⊠]), Levin Häni[1], Roland Wiest[1], and Mauricio Reyes[2]

[1] Department of Diagnostic and Interventional Neuroradiology,
Inselspital, Bern University Hospital, Bern, Switzerland
richard.mckinley@gmail.com
[2] Institute for Surgical Technology and Biomechanics,
University of Bern, Bern, Switzerland

**Abstract.** We propose a fully automatic method for segmenting the ischemic penumbra, using image texture and spatial features and a modified Random Forest algorithm, which we call Segmentation Forests, which has been designed to adapt the original Random Forests algorithm of Breiman to the segmentation of medical images. The method was trained and tested on the SPES dataset, part of the ISLES MICCAI Grand Challenge. The method is fast, taking approximately six minutes to segment a new case, and yields convincing results. On the testing portion of the SPES dataset, the method achieved an average Dice coefficient of 0.82, with a standard deviation of 0.08.

## 1 Introduction

In patients presenting with acute stroke, it is important to be able to quickly identify hypoperfused tissue-at-risk, in order to assess the suitability of intra-arterial therapy. Thresholding maps derived from perfusion-weighted imaging provides a usable but crude assessment of this volume of tissue: the technique is prone to artifacts in the processing of the perfusion maps, leading to, for example, identification of tissue as at-risk on the contralateral side of the brain or in the ventricles. Fast, automatic methods for identifying the tissue at risk that improve on thresholding are therefore needed. Previous attempts to automatically segment perfusion lesions in stroke [1] have used manually defined algorithms to exclude cerebrospinal fluid, air, and imaging artifacts and small objects. More recently [2], attempts have been made to identify the perfusion lesion in stroke using Random Forest classifiers [3] trained on image textures.

In this paper we refine this method. The algorithm uses simple features, derived from multimodal imaging, to train a decision forest model which assigns to each volume element a label indicating if it should be considered part of the perfusion lesion. Decision Forest algorithms such as Random Forests are a popular machine learning algorithm in medical imaging applications, but (as we indicate in this paper) standard algorithms for training Decision Forests are not

© Springer International Publishing Switzerland 2016
A. Crimi et al. (Eds.): BrainLes 2015, LNCS 9556, pp. 275–283, 2016.
DOI: 10.1007/978-3-319-30858-6_24

optimal for medical imaging data, which is (a) highly correlated at the patient level, and (b) unbalanced, with the target class often having a prevalence of 1 % or less. We therefore introduce in this paper a new algorithm for training Decision Forests, called Segmentation Forests, which avoids these problems by bootstrapping training data first at the patient level, and by using the resulting out-of-sample patients to empirically discover a threshold at which the Dice coefficient of the segmentation is maximized, avoiding the need for holding out training data to tune the classifier.

We begin the paper by recalling the notion of ischemic penumbra (Sect. 2) and summarizing the details of the ISLES challenge (Sect. 3). The Segmentation Forest Algorithm is introduced in Sect. 4. Results of applying this technique to the ISLES acute stroke dataset are reported in Sect. 5, with Sect. 6 being devoted to a brief examination of the method, looking at the effect of hyperparameter optimization and the differences in performance between Segmentation forests and ordinary Random Forests.

## 2    The Ischemic Penumbra

Stroke is the second most frequent cause of death and a major cause of disability in industrial countries: in patients who survive, stroke is frequently associated with high socioeconomic costs due to persistent disability. In clinical practice, advanced neuroimaging techniques are increasingly employed for a quick, reliable diagnosis and stratification for therapy. Tissue-at-risk estimation is frequently performed by MRI, with the infarct core being identified as an area of restricted diffusion on diffusion-weighted magnetic resonance imaging (DWI-MRI). The surrounding severely hypoperfused and potentially salvageable tissue (i.e. the penumbra) is characterized by its delay in arterial transit time using perfusion-weighted MRI. The clinical image interpretation is routinely performed as a visual analysis done by neuroradiologists and/or neurological stroke experts, since manual volumetric analysis would be too time-consuming to incorporate into a clinical workflow. Recent studies by PET and MRI indicated that a Tmax threshold of >6 s improves the prediction of penumbral salvage volume in acute stroke and correlates well with xenon CT and PET cerebral blood flow measures. Thus, Tmax may be currently regarded as the most valid MR marker to estimate the ischemic penumbra in stroke trials.

## 3    The ISLES Challenge (SPES)

The ISLES challenge (http://www.isles-challenge.org/) was a Grand Challenge held at the International Conference on Medical Image Computing and Computer Assisted Intervention (MICCAI) 2015 (www.miccai2015.org), which consisted of two separate subchallenges: sub-acute ischemic stroke lesion segmentation (SISS) and acute stroke outcome/penumbra estimation (SPES). This paper documents a method used to compete in the SPES portion of the challenge. The SPES dataset consists of multimodal imaging (T1 contrast, T2, ADC, and TMax, TTP, CBV and CBF perfusion maps) from acute stroke cases, together with a semi-manual segmentation of the perfusion lesion based on a TMax threshold of 6 s. The goal is to build a technique which, learning from a training set of thirty cases, is able to best approximate the semi-manual segmentation on a dataset of twenty additional cases. The metrics used to compare segmentations were Dice coefficient and average symmetric surface distance.

## 4   Segmentation Forests

Decision tree classifiers are, in general, low bias, high variance classifiers. A Decision Forest is a simple form of ensemble model, consisting of a set of decision trees whose output is determined by averaging the outputs of the individual trees. The ability of a Decision Forest to outperform a single decision tree relies on *decorrelation* of the trees in the forest to reduce the variance of the model (Fig. 1).

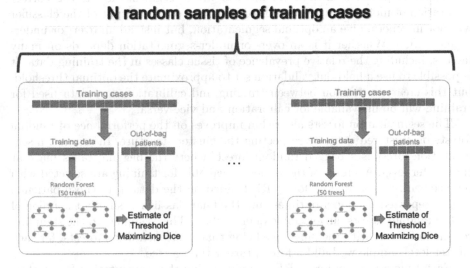

**Fig. 1.** Diagram illustrating the segmentation forest algorithm: N random forest classifiers are trained, each on a random sample (with replacement) at the patient level. The Out-Of-Sample patient cases are then used to find a threshold which optimizes the mean Dice coefficient. The final classifier is obtained by averaging the outputs of the N random forests, and then thresholding with the average of the thresholds obtained during training

The Random Forest algorithm due to Breiman achieves this decorrelation by inserting two sources of randomness into tree construction: bootstrap aggregation and the random subspace method. The random subspace method restricts the feature set available when building each split node of each decision tree, and bootstrap aggregation (or bagging) refers to the practice of building each tree of the ensemble on a bootstrap sample of the data, rather than on all the data available.

The success of the Random Forest algorithm depends on the ability of the algorithm to decorrelate the decision trees it constructs. Medical imaging data presents a particular problem, in that the voxel-wise data contained in a single volume is *clustered*. Given a training set, such as the SPES training set of 30 patients, any bootstrap sample of the voxel-wise data contained in that training set will be very similar to the original dataset: put simply, bagging on clustered data is less effective at reducing variance than bagging on unclustered data. In addition the out-of-bag error of a Random Forest classifier is not reliable if the data it is trained on was clustered, as most out-of-bag datapoints will be correlated to in-sample training datapoints.

An existing solution to this problem of subject-level clustering can be found in the RF++ algorithm of Karpievitch et al. [4], which replacing the bootstrapping algorithm of Random Forests with a two-stage sampling: first at the cluster level, then over data aggregated over the clusters.

A second problem inherent in medical image segmentation is the correct calibration of models: a naive threshold of 0.5 set on the output of the classifier will not in general give an optimal segmentation, but instead an over- or under-segmentation. Whether it is an over- or under-segmentation depends on many factors, including the relative prevalence of tissue classes in the training data. It is possible to use a hold-out validation set to approximate the optimal threshold, but this creates a tension between training and calibration: any data used for training will be unavailable for calibration and vice-versa.

The segmentation forests algorithm improves on the performance of random forests on clustered data, by respecting the cluster structure. In essence, a segmentation forest is a bagged random forest, where the bagging takes place at the cluster level. A subset of the patients available for training are selected with replacement, and a random forest RF trained on the data from those patients. This is repeated a number of times, and the final classifier is simply the union of all the random forests: an ensemble of ensembles. This is similar to the sampling regime in RF++, with the difference being that in segmentation forests, for each cluster-level sample we build a forest, rather than a tree.

Each time a random forest $RF_j$ is built during the segmentation forest algorithm, there is a set $S$ of "out-of-bag" (OOB) patients not used to construct $RF_j$. This set can be used to assess segmentation performance as follows: for each $i \in S$, find the threshold $\theta_i^j$ which maximizes the mean Dice coefficient over $RF_j$ applied to $S \setminus i$. Each $\theta_i^j$ is an estimate of the optimal threshold of $RF_j$ which did not use the data in case $i$, either for training or calibration, and can therefore be used to evaluate the performance of $RF_i$ on case $j$. An estimate $\theta_j$ for the optimal threshold for $RF_i$ is given by the average over $S$ of the $\theta_i^j$, and the average over all random forests of the $\theta_j$ gives an estimate of the optimal threshold for the whole ensemble.

# 5  Segmenting the Ischemic Penumbra Using Segmentation Forests

Our segmentation algorithm uses pre-processing and texture and spatial features inspired by the features used in the BraTumIA brain tumour segmentation tool [5] and a previous pilot study on stroke segmentation [2].

## 5.1  Standardization and Feature Processing

Prior to model construction, features were extracted from the multimodal imaging volumes using the Insight Segmentation and Registration Toolkit, available from http://itk.org.

Before feature extraction, the structural image modalities (T2 and T1 contrast) are smoothed (using the GradientAnisotropicDiffusionImageFilter from ITK version 7.4.2) and a window filter is applied to the TMax map (with minimum value 0 and maximum value 100) to suppress abnormally high values. All feature maps were then rescaled with ITK version 7.4.2 to lie within the range [0, 256].The T1c image is coregistered to an atlas to allow extraction of atlas coordinates and the location of the mid-sagittal plane.

We then extract, for each voxel of the volume, and each image modality, a feature vector, consisting of the following features: - local texture features, extracted over both 3-by-3-by-3 and 5-by-5-by-5 voxel volumes - mean intensity - intensity variance, skewness and kurtosis - signal to noise ratio, entropy and energy - local intensity percentiles - local image gradient features (gradient magnitude computed using GradientMagnitudeRecursiveGaussianImageFilter from ITK version 7.4.2, with a sigma of 1.0) - point intensity of the gradient magnitude - mean of the gradient magnitude over 3-by-3-by-3 and 5-by-5-by-5 volumes - variance of the gradient magnitude over 3-by-3-by-3 and 5-by-5-by-5 volumes - a symmetry feature computed using a corresponding point on the contralateral side of the brain (found using the previously computed atlas coordinates): the difference between the voxel intensity and a smoothed intensity (computed using a SmoothGaussFilterType from ITK version 7.4.2) from the contralateral side.

Additional features were the unscaled image modalities, atlas coordinates, and an indication of whether the voxel is on the ispi- or contralesional (inferred by comparing the means of the scaled TMax on each side of the brain.)

## 5.2  The Segmentation Forest Classifier

The classifier used to compete in the 2015 ISLES challenge was built using the following parameters: the classifier was an ensemble of ten Random forest classifiers, each built on a random sample of 20 cases from the 30 training examples, with a maximum tree depth of 30 and an "mtries" parameter of 60. The segmentation forest classifier was implemented using the SpeedRF Random Forest implementation of the H2O machine learning package (Version 2.8.4.4), and the accompanying R package, both acquired from on CRAN or via http://h2o.ai.

This implementation of Random Forests is faster and more memory-efficient than the standard R implementation, allowing for the use of all data in the training sets, without downsampling of the background class.

An example of the output of the classifier and the resulting segmentation can be seen in Fig. 2.

### 5.3   Results

The out-of-bag analysis of the classifier yielded a mean Dice coefficient of 0.851. On the testing data, supplied by the ISLES challenge, the mean Dice coefficient was 0.82 with a standard deviation over the testing cases of 0.08.

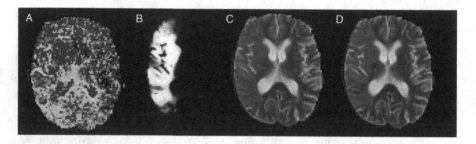

**Fig. 2.** Sample output of the Segmentation forest classifier. (A) The TMax map. (B) The raw output of the classifier, displayed as a heatmap. (C) The segmentation obtained by thresholding on the output. (D) The Ground truth as provided in the SPES dataset.

## 6   Properties of the Classifier

By examining the out-of-bag error of the classifier, we can investigate the extent to which the Segmentation Forest classifier outperforms ordinary random forest classifiers, and the effect of data imbalance on performance.

### 6.1   Methodology

The following results are derived from the out-of-bag analysis of a number of segmentation forest classifier constructions. In each case, the same sed was used to select cases for the construction of the constituent Random Forests, and so OOB data should be comparable between different parameter settings.

### 6.2   Random Forest Parameters

To assess the effect of varying the random forest parameters depth and mtries on performance, we performed a small grid search on alternative parameters. The results are displayed in Table 1.

**Table 1.** Effect of changing random forest parameters on segmentation forest performance: full data

| mtries | Depth | ntree | Mean AUC | Mean Dice |
|--------|-------|-------|----------|-----------|
| 30     | 20    | 50    | 0.991    | 0.847     |
| 30     | 30    | 50    | 0.991    | 0.849     |
| 40     | 20    | 50    | 0.991    | 0.849     |
| 40     | 30    | 50    | 0.992    | 0.850     |
| 60     | 20    | 50    | 0.992    | 0.851     |
| 60     | 30    | 50    | 0.992    | 0.851     |

### 6.3 Benefit of Segmentation Forest over Tuned Random Forest

Each ensemble resulting from the above OOB performance analysis has a different size, ranging from two to seven models. Since each random forest has 50 trees, this means the resulting decision forests have between 100 and 350 trees. To verify that patient-level bootstrapping has the expected effect on the strength of the model, we built ordinary Random Forest models with 400 trees (depth=30, mtries=60), each trained on the data from 20 patients and calibrated using the remaining nine patients. This resulted in a mean Dice coefficient of 0.845, with an mean AUC of 0.992.

### 6.4 Benefit of Using More Trees

We also built a single Segmentation forest with 400 trees in each random forest, to assess the benefit of using more trees. The resulting decision forest (with 4000 trees) took roughly twelve hours to train (versus just over an hour and a half for the model built using 50 trees in each random forest), and had a mean Dice of 0.853.

### 6.5 Effect of Undersampling the Background Class

We reran our original grid search, this time using data which had been balanced by undersampling so that the balance between lesion and background voxels was roughly 50/50. The results are displayed in Table 2, showing a modest boost in the classifier performance over using all available data.

### 6.6 Effect of Using Default Thresholds

To assess the contribution of the optimal threshold estimation, we also calculated the mean Dice coefficient using a default threshold of 0.5. For the classifier trained on all available data (mtries = 60, depth=30) this resulted in a decreased Dice coefficient of 0.844. For the classifier trained on balanced data the result was even more pronounced, with a threshold of 0.5 resulting in a Dice coefficient

**Table 2.** Effect of changing random forest parameters on segmentation forest performance: balanced data

| mtries | Depth | ntree | Mean AUC | Mean Dice |
|--------|-------|-------|----------|-----------|
| 30 | 20 | 50 | 0.992 | 0.850 |
| 30 | 30 | 50 | 0.992 | 0.852 |
| 40 | 20 | 50 | 0.992 | 0.851 |
| 40 | 30 | 50 | 0.992 | 0.852 |
| 60 | 20 | 50 | 0.992 | 0.852 |
| 60 | 30 | 50 | 0.992 | 0.854 |

of 0.824. The mean optimal threshold for the models built on balanced data was 0.70, emphasizing that setting the correct threshold is vital to give a good segmentation, even if data is balanced. We can conclude from this that the Segmentation Forest method of generating segmentations is robust to different levels of data imbalance, at least for the SPES dataset.

## 7    Conclusion

This paper introduces a new algorithm (Segmentation Forests) for training decision forest classifiers, designed to overcome problems inherent in the segmentation of unbalanced datasets with clustering, such as medical imaging data. The algorithm was the best performing entry in the 2015 SPES competition. Our subsequent analysis suggests that the patient-level bagging employed by Segmentation Forests has a much stronger influence on the performance of the classifier than the parameters for construction of trees, or number of trees, or the number of trees used. A follow-up study is in progress to apply the classifier to other datasets and study its properties in a systematic fashion.

In addition, we are applying the same methodology to the *prediction* of final lesion volume in stroke, using a delineation of the three-month follow-up lesion as a ground truth. Our goal is to predict the lesion extent in the case of a successful reperfusion (by, for example, mechanical thrombectomy), and also to predict the lesion extent in case reperfusion is unsuccessful. The difference in these predicted lesion volumes will, we hope provide additional information on which treatment decisions in acute stroke can be based.

**Acknowledgments.** The authors would like to thank the organizers of the ISLES challenge, and the Brainles Workshop, both part of MICCAI 2015. This work was supported by the Schweizerische Herzstiftung.

## References

1. Straka, M., Albers, G., Bammer, R.: Real-time diffusion-perfusion mismatch analysis in acute stroke. J. Magn. Reson. Imaging JMRI **32**(5), 1024–1037 (2010)

2. Bauer, S., Gratz, P.P., Gralla, J., Reyes, M., Wiest, R.: Towards automatic MRI volumetry for treatment selection in acute ischemic stroke patients. In: Conf. Proceedings of the Annual International Conference of the IEEE Engineering in Medicine and Biology Society, vol. 2014, pp. 1521–1524, August 2014

3. Breiman, L.: Random forests. Mach. Learn. **45**(1), 5–32 (2001)

4. Karpievitch, Y., Hill, E.G., Leclerc, A.P., Dabney, A.R., Almeida, J.S.: An introspective comparison of random forest-based classifiers for the analysis of cluster-correlated data by way of RF++. PLoS One **4**(9), e7087 (2009)

5. Porz, N., Bauer, S., Pica, A., Schucht, P., Beck, J., Verma, R.K., Slotboom, J., Reyes, M., Wiest, R.: Multi-modal glioblastoma segmentation: man versus machine. PLoS One **9**(5), e96873 (2014)

# Input Data Adaptive Learning (IDAL) for Sub-acute Ischemic Stroke Lesion Segmentation

Michael Goetz[(✉)], Christian Weber, Christoph Kolb, and Klaus Maier-Hein

Junior Group Medical Image Computing,
German Cancer Research Center (DKFZ), Heidelberg, Germany
m.goetz@dkfz-heidelberg.de

**Abstract.** In machine learning larger databases are usually associated with higher classification accuracy due to better generalization. This generalization may lead to non-optimal classifiers in some medical applications with highly variable expressions of pathologies. This paper presents a method for learning from a large training base by adaptively selecting optimal training samples for given input data. In this way heterogeneous databases are supported two-fold. First, by being able to deal with sparsely annotated data allows a quick inclusion of new data set and second, by training an input-dependent classifier. The proposed approach is evaluated using the SISS challenge. The proposed algorithm leads to a significant improvement of the classification accuracy.

**Keywords:** Adaptive learning · Lesion segmentation · Machine learning · Random forest

## 1 Introduction

Learning from large datasets becomes more and more important in computer vision and specifically in the context of medical image analysis. A special challenge in this context is the high variability of the data – not only because of the variety of imaging modalities and imaging configurations but also because the appearance of pathological changes varies greatly.

An example of such variance is shown in Fig. 1. All four images are taken from the SISS-challenge (see Sect. 3.1 for more details). Each one shows a slice with a visible sub-acute ischemic stroke on a T2-weighted Magnetic Resonance (MR)-image. It is easy to imagine that a classifier that is trained with all three annotated examples is outperformed in the classification of the fourth image by a classifier that is only trained on the left image.

Another source of differences is the inter- and intrascanner variability of MR scanners. The transfer function of MR-scanners depends on multiple factors like the time of acquisition, temperature changes, design differences, material differences etc. [9]. While most differences can be reduced by normalizing the images, there are usually still differences, especially between the images of different devices [7,8]. Due to this, different approaches has been proposed to reduce the variance.

© Springer International Publishing Switzerland 2016
A. Crimi et al. (Eds.): BrainLes 2015, LNCS 9556, pp. 284–295, 2016.
DOI: 10.1007/978-3-319-30858-6_25

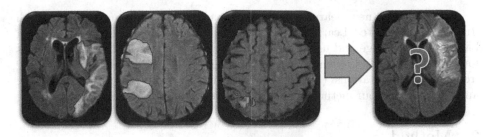

**Fig. 1.** Even though all four images are from patients with sub-acute ischemic strokes, the appearance of the pathology is very different. Only one of the three training patients has a similar appearance to the test patient on the right side.

Van Opbroek et al. [10] proposed to increase the weight of images of scanners with similar transfer functions during training to reduce the effect of different scanners. They estimate the weight by comparing the intensities from multiple images of each scanner. The weights are higher if the intensity distribution of a scanner is similar to the distribution of the target scanner. While this allows to reduce the effect of scanner variability, the different appearances of pathologies are still present in the training data and need to be learned during classifier training.

Based on the observation that all training data are different, Zikic et al. [11] proposed to encode each image within a single classifier. This is done by training each classifier with a single image but allowing over-fitting. The prediction of all training data is then derived from merging the predicted segmentation of all classifiers. This allows for encoding all information within the final classifier, by training multiple sub-classifiers. But the influence of the best matches is reduced by merging all results in the final state. If most of the training images are different from the test image – for example like in Fig. 1 – the influence of the different images might cancel out the positive effect of the similar image.

Another idea from computer vision is clustering of the training data or finding the closest training images based on global image features. After the pre-selection of the best training data, model-based approaches are used to transfer the labels to the previously unlabeled image [12–16]. While these approaches use only a subset of the training data set, the closest neighbors are defined by feature distance. However, this distance does not necessarily reflect the best training images as there might be features, which are irrelevant for the final training but influence the feature based distance.

Ischemic strokes are a disease with highly heterogeneous appearance. This makes the segmentation of ischemic strokes challenging. Reliable segmentations are necessary to locate, segment, and quantify the lesions. Without an automatic segmentation findings like suitable markers for treatment decisions, are subject to observer variability. Due to this reason automatic ischemic stroke segmentation is important to support clinicians and researchers to provide more robust and reproducible data [19,20].

We propose a new, learning-based approach for lesion segmentation. With 'Input Data Adapted Learning' (IDAL) we propose to learn the best training base for every image and use this to predict a subgroup of best training images for every previously unseen image. We incorporate 'Domain-Adapted Learning from Sparse Annotations' (DALSA) to allow the fast adaptation to new dataset and to prove that our method is able to be incorporated in more complex setups.

## 2    Method

Instead of training a single classifier that is used to predict all unseen images we propose to adaptively train a new classifier for every new image. This allows to use only few, but similar images during training. While such an approach makes each classifier less general, we expect that the so-trained classifier is better suited to deal with the afore mentioned heterogeneity.

We realized this approach with a three-staged algorithm (Fig. 2). During the first stage, that is performed offline like traditional classifier training, we train an similarity classifier (SC) which can group images based on some similarity measure.

The offline trained SC is used in the second stage – the online training – to find images that are similar to the new, unlabeled image. Based on this individual, input-dependent subset of training images, a new voxel-based classifier (VC) is trained. For this, we used the approach presented in [5] which allows to train a voxel-based classifier (VC) from sparsely and unambiguously labeled regions (SURs). This VC is then used in the last stage to label each voxel of the new image, leading to the prediction mask.

### 2.1    Preprocessing

A simple preprocessing was applied before the images were used for training or prediction. The brainmask includes all voxels for which neither T1 nor T2 are zero.

The intensities of the MR-images were linearly normalized so that the mode of ares showing CSF and the overall brain tissue were 0 and 1, respectively. We found that using mode instead of mean provides a more robust normalization since the mode is less affected by the size of the lesions. We obtained the CSF-area by training a simple classifier using only pure voxel intensities.

### 2.2    Similarity Classifier (SC)

The main idea of our work is to identify a subset of similar images which are then used to train a voxel classifier. The similarity between two images is defined by the ability to successfully use them to train a classifier. Accordingly, we define the similarity $\rho(I_0, I_1)$ of two images $I_0$ and $I_1$ as the Dice score that a voxel classifier trained with $I_0$ scores if the mask for $I_1$ is predicted.

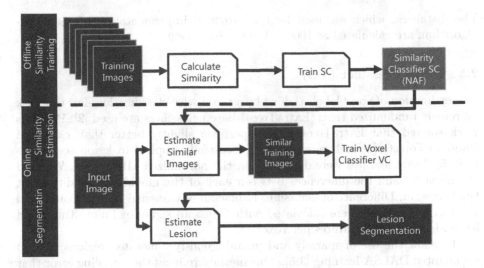

**Fig. 2.** Overview of the workflow of the proposed IDAL-algorithm. A similarity classifier is trained a-priori based on the defined similarity between the training images. Using the so-trained SC, a selection of the training data is made for every new input image. This selection is then used to train an input-dependend voxel classifier and finally estimate the lesion using the individual VC.

While it is possible to directly calculate the Dice-score based similarity of two images with known voxel labels, it needs to be estimated for new images with unknown voxel labels. We chose Neighbourhood Approximating Forests (NAF) for this task [1]. NAFs are trained to find the most similar images based on a high-dimensional representation by training trees that group the training data such that the similarity within each leaf node is maximized. For the prediction, the new images are then passed down each tree and all samples within the leaf node are returned. The more often a specific training image is returned the more similar it is to the test image.

To train the NAF and to use it as SC we first calculated the similarity of all training images according to the previously given definition of $\rho(\cdot, \cdot)$. We then built a feature vector for every patient based on the normalized $T_1$, $T_2$, DWI, and FLAIR images by calculating the first order statistics for the whole brain (Intensity minimum, maximum, range, mean, variance, sum, median, std. deviation, mean absolute deviation, root means square, uniformity, entropy, energy, kurtosis, skewness and the number of voxels). Although these are all image-derived values, the proposed approach also allows the use of additional information like patient age, diagnosis, etc., which are not included in the challenge data.

We trained the NAF with 100 trees, a minimum of two samples at each leaf, 30 random tests for best split at each node during the training and a maximum tree depth of 12. After predicting a new patient (Online Training stage, see Fig. 2) we chose the three highest ranked training images to train the new VC.

The distances, which are used by the provided implementation of the NAF-algorithm, are calculated as $1000 - 1000 * similarity$.

### 2.3  Voxel Classifier (VC)

The estimation of voxel labels is done by a voxel-wise classification. For this task extremely randomized trees (ExtraTrees)-based classifiers are used [2]. Previous work showed that ExtraTrees usually perform slightly better than canonical Random Forests [4] and were already successfully applied in lesion segmentation [6]. Voxel features were derived from the normalized MR-images. We used the intensity and the differences between each of the modalities. Additionally, the Gaussian, Difference of Gaussian, Laplacian of Gaussian (3 directions), and Hessian of Gaussian were calculated with Gaussian sigma of 1 mm, 3 mm, and 5 mm, leading to 82 features per voxel.

To allow the use of sparsely and unambiguously annotated regions (SURs) we adapted DALSA-learning [3,5]. This method reduces the sampling error that is introduced by the sampling scheme by weighting all samples according to the number of labeled samples and the overall number of similar samples within the brain. It therefore improves the classifier quality if SURs are used for the training and was already successfully applied to different scenarios [17,18].

Even though all data are already labeled, we relabeled the training data again using SURs. This was done in less than $2^{1}/_{2}$ h for the complete data set. To incorporate DALSA, every training sample $x$ is weighted with a correction weight $w$ which is set to ensure that the probability for this sample in the training data equals the probability $P$ for this sample in the complete image, i.e.

$$w(x) = \frac{P_{\text{Complete Image}}(x)}{P_{\text{SURs}}(x)} \qquad (1)$$

We estimate the unknown $w(x)$ by training a parameter-less logistic regression that differentiates between voxels that are labeled by SURs and voxels that are within the brain mask. By using the probabilistic output of this method, $w$ can be estimated [5] without performing a division.

Each ExtraTrees classifier was trained with 50 trees and the Gini purity as optimization measurement. The maximum tree depth was not limited. During each training (during similarity calculation and final VC training) the best class weights and minimum samples at leaf nodes were independently estimated using cross validation.

## 3  Experiments

### 3.1  Data

We chose the data of the 2015 SISS challenge, a part of the 2015 MICCAI ISLES challenge [19]. The objective of this challenge is the segmentation of sub-acute ischemic stroke lesions in MR images. The performance of the contributed methods is evaluated using a test set consisting of 36 patients, the provided training set consists of 28 patients.

Four different modalities, namely: $T_1$-, $T_2$-, DWI-, and FLAIR-weighted MR-images, are available for every patient. All images are co-registered to the FLAIR-weighted images and resampled to a common isotropic spacing of $1\,\text{mm}^3$ and the brain is stripped. A manually created ground truth with annotations of sub-acute ischemic stroke lesions is provided for the training data. All training data originated from the same center, while the test data is provided by two different centers.

A more detailed description of the data, the applied preprocessing, and motivation for the challenge can be found at [19, 21].

## 3.2 Evaluation of Similarity Classifier

We calculated the similarity matrix for all training data. This is done in the same way as it is done during the complete training algorithm, i.e. one cell of the matrix corresponds to the dice score that is obtained if an classifier, that is trained on the corresponding training image, is used to segment the corresponding test image. The resulting matrix indicates how similar the patients are to each other. Please note, that our similarity measurement is not symmetric and the corresponding matrix is therefore also not symmetric.

We then trained SC based on this matrix, using a leave-one-out approach. We removed the column and row which corresponds to a single patient, trained the SC and then predicted the removed patient. Based on this routine, the three patients that were closest to the current patient are marked in the diagram.

## 3.3 Evaluation of Complete IDAL Algorithm

We evaluated IDAL using the training data of the SISS challenge. We conducted a leave-one-patient-out experiment using three different types of classifier. The first approach is a traditional approach, using all training data to train a single classifier using the same voxel classifier (same normalization, features and classification algorithm). This classifier is then used to predict the unseen patient. We did no further selection of the training data. The results of this classifier are used as baseline.

The second classifier is the proposed scheme. Based on the prediction of the SC, three patients are used to train a patient-specific classifier. The SC is trained without knowing the left-out patient, i.e. similar to the approach described in Sect. 3.2.

The third classifier is used to further evaluate the influence of the SC used. Instead of predicting the closest neighbors, we determined them from the pre-calculated similarity matrix. This is of course not possible for new data since the real best is not known for data without the ground truth. Nevertheless, we chose to report the results of these experiments to show the impact on the SC for the results. This also shows what the expected best results would be if a perfect SC would be used.

## 4    Results

The results of our experiments for the similarity matrix are displayed in Fig. 3. The true similarity is color-coded with higher values appearing darker. The SC-selected training patients are marked with crosses. For a perfect SC, the crosses would always be at the position of the darkest cells, i.e. the most similar patients.

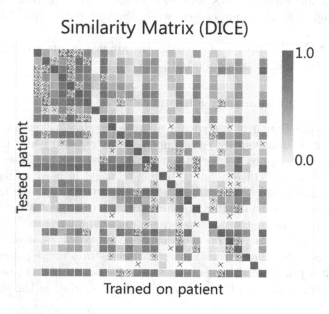

**Fig. 3.** The calculated similarity between different patients from the training data set is color coded. The crosses mark the training patients that have been selected by the similarity classifier during the leave-one-out.

The result of the evaluation of IDAL with the training data is shown in Fig. 4. The proposed method (IDAL) does return better results compared to a naive approach. The same result was observed for the test results where we obtained Dice-Scores of $0.37 \pm 0.30$ and $0.39 \pm 0.33$ with the conventional and proposed method respectively. Using a perfect SC further improves the segmentation quality and gives the best result. Of course, this is a theoretical result, as this method cannot be applied to images with missing segmentation.

### 4.1    Qualitative Results

Example results that are achieved with our proposed method are given in Figs. 5 and 6. There are some example slices given from data of the testing dataset. For every displayed patient, the FLAIR, the segmentation obtained from the conventional approach, as well as the segmentation obtained from IDAL are shown.

Classification Scores (DICE)

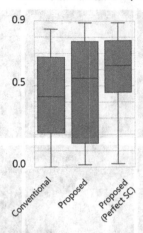

**Fig. 4.** Dice-scores obtained during the leave-one-out experiments. Left: Traditional approach, a single classifier was trained for all images. Middle: IDAL as proposed in this paper. Right: theoretical best result that can be obtained with IDAL if a perfect SC would be used. This approach cannot be used for previous unseen images since it requires the knowledge of the dice scores.

## 5    Discussion

The results of our leave-one-out experiment showed that the use of IDAL leads to a visible boost of segmentation performance. Within the training case, the median dice score is increased by roughly 0.1 if IDAL is used instead of a single classifier (Fig. 4). It is also visible that further improvement is possible if a better similarity classifier is used, based on the fact that using a perfect similarity classifier leads to a 0.1 improvement compared to the proposed method. Therefore, we conclude that there is further potential for improving this technique.

The improvement of the similarity classifier can be done by either changing the used technique or by using a better set of features to describe the images. This could be image-related features, like spatial pyramid [22], gist [23], or the histogram. Another possibility is to use non-image related patient data, for example patient age or time since stroke. These data can be included without changing the algorithm, making the proposed method very flexible. We strongly believe that including these data would further improve the quality of the similarity classifier, but we were not able to show this, since these data are not part of the challenge data set.

We used three images to train the voxel classifiers during our experiments for this paper. This number was chosen only as a starting point without any closer evaluation as to the best number of images – this choice will be evaluated with further experiments. We think that the proposed method will perform even better if the number of used image is adapted to the given data set. We also plan to evalu-

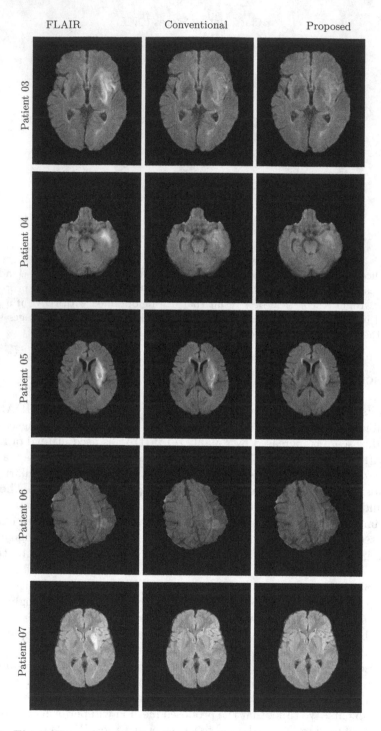

**Fig. 5.** Exemplary results of a single slice for test-patients 03–07.

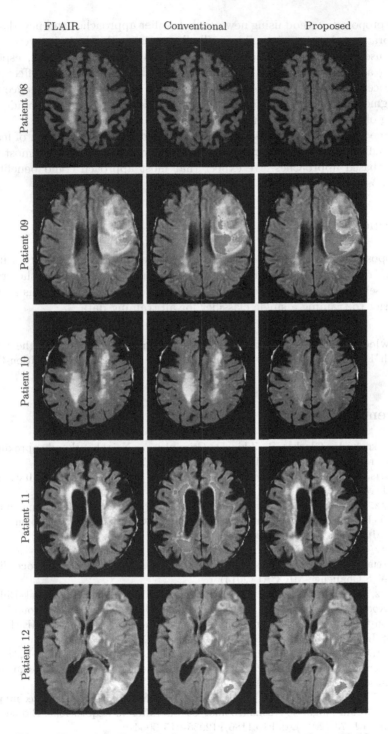

**Fig. 6.** Exemplary Results of a single slice for test-patients 08–12.

ate the proposed method using new voxel classifier approaches and new datasets. Incorporating a larger training base will allow more sophisticated statements.

We used a very basic approach for our challenge contribution, especially avoiding all post-processing. We did this in order to reduce the effect of the post-processing. Since the post-processing seems to have a big influence in the final segmentation quality, a further increase could be achieved by an additional cleaning of the segmentation mask.

As the proposed method does not depend on a given combination of features or a specific voxel classifier, it is possible to incorporate IDAL with most other, learning-based approaches. We expect that most approach could benefit from the proposed method.

## 6    Conclusion

We proposed a new, learning-based approach that allows to learn from heterogeneous training data. The algorithm reduces the variance within the training data by selecting a patient-specific training base. We showed that this approach is superior to training a single classifier for all training data.

**Acknowledgment.** This work was carried out with the support of the German Research Foundation (DFG) within project I04, SFB/TRR 125 Cognition-Guided Surgery.

## References

1. Konukoglu, E., Glocker, B., Zikic, D., Criminisi, A.: Neighbourhood approximation using randomized forests. Med. Image Anal. **17**(7), 790–804 (2013)
2. Geurts, P., Ernst, D., Wehenkel, L.: Extremely randomized trees. Mach. Learn. **63**(1), 3–42 (2006)
3. Goetz, M., Weber, C., Stieltjes, B., Maier-Hein, K.H.: Learning from small amounts of labeled data in a brain tumor classification task. In: NIPS Workshop on Transfer and Multi-task Learning: Theory Meets Practice (2014)
4. Goetz, M., Weber, C., Bloecher, J., Stieltjes, B., Meinzer, H.P., Maier-Hein, K.H.: Extremely randomized trees based brain tumor segmentation. In: Proceedings of BRATS Challenge-MICCAI (2014)
5. Goetz, M., Weber, C., Binczyk, F., Polanska, J., Tarnawski, R., Bobek-Billewicz, B., Koethe, U., Kleesiek, J., Stieltjes, B., Maier-Hein, K.H.: DALSA: domain adaptation for supervised learning from sparsely annotated MR images. IEEE Trans. Med. Imaging **35**(1), 184–196 (2016). doi:10.1109/TMI.2015.2463078
6. Maier, O., Wilms, M., Gablentz, J., Krämer, U.M., Münte, T.F., Handels, H.: Extra tree forests for sub-acute ischemic stroke lesion segmentation in MR sequences. J. Neurosci. Methods **240**, 89–100 (2015)
7. Sun, X., Shi, L., Luo, Y., et al.: Histogram-based normalization technique on human brain magnetic resonance images from different acquisitions. Biomed. Eng. Online **14**, 73 (2015). doi:10.1186/s12938-015-0064-y

8. Shinohara, R.T., Sweeney, E.M., Goldsmith, J., et al.: Statistical normalization techniques for magnetic resonance imaging. Neuroimage Clin. **6**, 9–19 (2014). doi:10.1016/j.nicl.2014.08.008

9. Hashemi, R.H., Bradley, W.G., Lisanti, C.J.: MRI: The Basics. Lippincott Williams & Wilkins, Philadelphia (2012)

10. van Opbroek, A., Vernooij, M.W., Ikram, M.A., de Bruijne, M.: Weighting training images by maximizing distribution similarity for supervised segmentation across scanners. Med. Image Anal. **24**(1), 245–254 (2015). ISSN: 1361-8415, http://dx.doi.org/10.1016/j.media.2015.06.010

11. Zikic, D., Glocker, B., Criminisi, A.: Atlas encoding by randomized forests for efficient label propagation. In: Mori, K., Sakuma, I., Sato, Y., Barillot, C., Navab, N. (eds.) MICCAI 2013, Part III. LNCS, vol. 8151, pp. 66–73. Springer, Heidelberg (2013)

12. Liu, C., Yuen, J., Torralba, A.: Nonparametric scene parsing via label transfer. IEEE Trans. Pattern Anal. Mach. Intell. **33**(12), 2368–2382 (2011). doi:10.1109/TPAMI.2011.131

13. Liu, C., Yuen, J., Torralba, A.: SIFT flow: dense correspondence across scenes and its applications. IEEE Trans. Pattern Anal. Mach. Intell. **33**(5), 978–994 (2011b). http://doi.org/10.1109/TPAMI.2010.147

14. Hays, J., Efros, A., et al.: IM2GPS: estimating geographic information from a single image. In: IEEE Conference on Computer Vision and Pattern Recognition (CVPR 2008), pp. 1–8. IEEE (2008)

15. Russell, B., Torralba, A., Liu, C., Fergus, R., Freeman, W.T.: Object recognition by scene alignment. In: Advances in Neural Information Processing Systems, pp. 1241–1248 (2007)

16. Tighe, J., Lazebnik, S.: Superparsing, scalable nonparametric image parsing with superpixels. Int. J. Comput. Vision **101**(2), 329–349 (2013)

17. Goetz, M., Skornitzke, S., Weber, C., Fritz, F., Mayer, P., Koell, M., Stiller, W., Maier-Hein, K.H.: Machine-learning based comparison of CT-perfusion maps and dual energy CT for pancreatic tumor detection. In: Proceedings of SPIE Medical Imaging (2016) (to appear)

18. Goetz, M., Heim, E., Maerz, K., Norajitra, T., Hafezi, M., Fard, N., Mehrabi, A., Knoll, M., Weber, C., Maier-Hein, L., Maier-Hein, K.: A learning-based, fully automatic liver tumor segmentation pipeline based on sparsely annotated training data. In: Proceedings of SPIE Medical Imaging (2016) (to appear)

19. ISLES: Ischemic Stroke Lesion Segmentation, MICCAI Challenge (2015). http://www.isles-challenge.org/

20. Kabir, Y., Dojat, M., Scherrer, B., Garbay, C., Forbes, F.: Multimodal MRI segmentation of ischemic stroke lesions. In: 29th Annual International Conference of the IEEE Engineering in Medicine and Biology Society (EMBS 2007), 22–26 August 2007, pp. 1595–1598 (2007). doi:10.1109/IEMBS.2007.4352610

21. Proceeding of the Ischemic Stroke Lesion Segmentation (www.isles-challenge.org). http://www.isles-challenge.org/pdf/20150930_ISLES2015_Proceedings.pdf

22. Lazebnik, S., Schmid, C., Ponce, J.: Beyond bags of features: spatial pyramid matching for recognizing natural scene categories. In: 2006 IEEE Computer Society Conference on Computer Vision and Pattern Recognition, vol. 2, pp. 2169–2178. IEEE (2006)

23. Oliva, A., Torralba, A.: Building the gist of a scene: the role of global image features in recognition. Prog. Brain Res. **155**, 23–36 (2006). Chapter 2

# Author Index

Printed in the United States
By Bookmasters